Everyday Ruptures

Everyday Ruptures

Children, Youth, and Migration in Global Perspective

Edited by Cati Coe, Rachel R. Reynolds,
Deborah A. Boehm, Julia Meredith Hess,
and Heather Rae-Espinoza

Vanderbilt University Press

Nashville

© 2011 by Vanderbilt University Press
Nashville, Tennessee 37235
All rights reserved
First printing 2011

This book is printed on acid-free paper
made from 30% post-consumer recycled content.
Manufactured in the United States of America

Library of Congress Cataloging-in-Publication Data

Everyday ruptures : children, youth, and migration
in global perspective / edited by Cati Coe . . . [et al.].
p. cm.
Includes bibliographical references and index.
ISBN 978-0-8265-1747-0 (cloth edition : alk. paper)
ISBN 978-0-8265-1748-7 (pbk. edition : alk. paper)
1. Emigration and immigration—Social aspects.
2. Immigrant children. 3. Transnationalism—Social aspects.
I. Coe, Cati.
JV6225.E94 2010
304.8—dc22
2010028349

Contents

Acknowledgments

This book comes out of a January 2008 workshop held by the Working Group on Childhood and Migration in New York City funded by the Wenner-Gren Foundation for Anthropological Research. We are grateful to all the participants in the workshop for helping us develop the ideas expressed here, the Wenner-Gren Foundation for its support, and Union Theological Seminary for conference space. As the workshop papers developed into an edited volume, the enthusiasm of Michael Ames at Vanderbilt University Press pushed this project along. Two anonymous reviewers developed the chapters further with their generous advice and suggestions. Special thanks to Valerie Roybal for creating the artwork on the book's cover.

As anthropologists, we were each used to working in isolation from our colleagues, and so collaborating on a project of *five people* seemed a bit daunting. And yet it fell into place from the start: at the end of the workshop, some felt moved in one direction and some in another, such that the division of tasks was clear and easy. From that moment on, the process was smooth and harmonious, to our surprise and delight, as we shared drafts of the Introduction back and forth or spent long hours on conference calls; the volume represents the work of us all. So, last but by no means least, we are also deeply grateful to each other—for the respect, cheerfulness, persistence, flexibility, and intellectual seriousness with which we have each engaged in this joint endeavor.

Introduction

Children, Youth, and the Everyday Ruptures of Migration

Deborah A. Boehm, Julia Meredith Hess,
Cati Coe, Heather Rae-Espinoza, and Rachel R. Reynolds

Migration and movement across multiple borders characterize the current global moment. As people move about the globe, continuity and change are intertwined, resulting in what we understand to be "everyday ruptures." Migration is inherently characterized by rupture—a break, change, distance, division—and it necessarily includes the everyday: even in, during, or perhaps because of cases of acute disruption, social life persists. Paradoxically, rupture is often situated within or occurs alongside the mundane; in some circumstances it may even be animating, stimulating the imagination or changing the course of a life (Kerrigan 2008, 2). The theme of "everyday ruptures," then, captures the seemingly contradictory processes shaped by, on the one hand, disjunctures and breaks and, on the other, the consistency that accompanies everyday life. The chapters in this volume pay attention to both these dynamics— rupture and the everyday—and offer the ethnography of lived experience as evidence of the ways disruption and daily life work in tandem.

We consider the persistent and interrupted social fabric of migration through a specific focus on those who are often at this nexus of rupture and the everyday—children and youth. Current research demonstrates how young people are the "makers and breakers" of society who "shake and shape society but are also shaped and shaken by it" (Honwana and De Boeck 2005, 3). Whether "at the crossroads" (Hess and Shandy 2008) or "caught in the crossfire" (Grossberg 2005), young people are at the center of myriad social, cultural, political, and economic processes. Jennifer Cole and Deborah Durham (2007, 2008) argue that generations and age-based relationships are key to understanding processes of social change and social regeneration (see also Montgomery 2009), and Sharon Stephens (1995) posits that what is happening to children is crucial to historic restructurings of capitalist society (see also Katz 2001), locating young people as agents in various social exchanges.

It is not that rapid social change necessarily creates intergenerational conflict (Bucholtz 2002). Rather, children's creative negotiation of the variety of discourses, knowledges, and practices around them is necessary for the continuation and transformation of social life. Furthermore, because their subjectivities and perspectives can differ from those of social actors in other generations, children and youth reveal how the everyday is itself fractured in time and space. Helen B. Schwartzman argues that anthropologists should study "the experiences of children as children" (2001, 3), rather than the processes by which they become adults (see also Bucholtz 2002). The experiences, perspectives, and relationships of young people, then, provide an important window onto the changes and continuities entailed by migration.

The categories of "children," "youth," and "adult" are unstable ones, constructed and understood differently in various historical and cultural contexts that are themselves always changing (e.g., Ariès 1963; Boocock and Scott 2005; Bucholtz 2002; Cole and Durham 2008; James and Prout 1990; Jenkins 1998; Levinson, Foley, and Holland 1996; Moffatt 1989; Scheper-Hughes and Sargent 1998; Stephens 1995; Terrio 2008, 2009; Thorne 2007). At the same time, it is our perspective that children and youth—however they may be emically defined—do represent in most communities a category of person that is distinct from others. In other words, although cultural definitions of who embodies childhood or even personhood vary tremendously (e.g., Scheper-Hughes 1992), there are discourses in diverse cultural settings that commonly construct and describe children as different from adults. Children, possibly everywhere, have discursive and symbolic links to time, because they are seen as people in the process of becoming and because it is through children that a community's reproduction is actualized (Cole and Durham 2008).

Children and youth are expected to grow up in ways that represent the values of their communities. Children are brought up with an eye to the future, and thus are often seen as symbolic carriers of a changing world, embodying futurity and possibility (Cole and Durham 2008). Although most of the chapters in this volume understand "children" to be, at least in part, an age-related category, "child" can also be a relational or status role. For example, in her contribution to this volume, Maarit Forde examines how "ritual children" are marked by their relative lack of knowledge and spiritual development in opposition to ritual specialists positioned as "parents." Even when children and youth are defined by their age, they are perceived as "social shifters," established in relation to other categories of personhood (Durham 2000, 2004). Childhood and adulthood are significant life stages for people of all ages; children of émigrés from Ecuador, for example, use ideas of maturity and immaturity to pattern their own behavior in response to a parent's migration (Rae-Espinoza, this volume; see also DeLoache and Gottlieb 2000). In this way, "children" and "youth" must be understood as constructed categories that continually shift both within and across cultures.

Although diverse ideologies and constructs of childhood and children circulate globally, Western middle-class conceptions of childhood loom large because of their common ideological currency, reflected in the underpinnings of international conventions that address the rights of children, such as the Convention of the Rights of the Child, and international nongovernmental organizations' (NGOs) policies with respect to children (Scheper-Hughes and Sargent 1998; see also Goździak 2008; Horton 2008). Several chapters in this volume show the uneven and partial nature of the adoption of these ideas, whether in family interactions or through state interventions. When we see children as different from adults—as more flexible learners or as inheritors of a future world—we must ask where these ideas originate and question their degree of salience cross-culturally.

As our ethnographic research shows, children are often at the center of migration processes—as motivators for migration or as migrants themselves—and diverse research within migration studies has led to our emphasis on the experiences of children and their family members. Chapters in this volume address how parents frequently migrate on behalf of children, often to create a better future for children and families. Increasingly, those perceived as children or youth—in their home or new communities—are themselves migrants, ranging from infants to young people who move between culturally specific notions of "youth" and "adults." A focus on children and childhood within migration flows provides a view of an imaginary about childhood that parents and children themselves are increasingly engaging in and actively constructing.

All movement and migration is arguably associated with dislocation and social rupture, but what kind of rupture and how is it experienced? The theme "everyday ruptures" provides a way to move beyond the often linear and reductionist character of assimilation theories, on the one hand, and the sometimes overly optimistic social theories of transnational flows and connections, on the other. Historically, research within migration studies focused on migrants' assimilation, a concept that highlights rupture. Rupture has been conceptualized as a migrant's dislocation from the homeland and as discontinuities between the first- and second-generations as the children of migrants adopt the practices, norms, and language of the social order of the receiving country more quickly than do their parents (e.g., Gibson 1988; Knörr 2005; Rumbaut and Portes 2001; Zhou and Bankston 1998; see also discussion in Ong 1999, 8–12). Children and youth have therefore figured prominently in studies that focus on assimilation.

Although assimilation theories have been modified to account for the diversity of second-generation experiences, such as with the concept of "segmented assimilation" (Portes and Zhou 1993) and a focus on the 1.5 generation, an assimilation model assumes bounded and often static cultural contexts and can overemphasize distinctions based on generation. Moreover, assimilationist frameworks tend to focus on destinations in the United States and Europe, rather than on the many communities around the globe impacted by migration. Ultimately, assimilation theories do not adequately account for or elucidate the variation of experiences captured in ethnographic study. For example, the generational categories implied in assimilation do not explicate the experiences of young people affected by a parent's migration who do not migrate themselves, often referred to—from the perspective of migration researchers—as children "left behind." It is also the case that children may migrate alone, without their parents, while their families are "left behind" and among those affected by migration. Additionally, children may move back and forth between nation-states as what Susan Ossman identifies as "serial migrants" (2004; see also 2007). These common migratory trajectories complicate an assimilationist emphasis on the distinctions between generations.

Theories of transnationalism and transnationality have problematized the notion that flows of people occur in unilineal or predictable ways (e.g., Appadurai 1996; Basch, Glick Schiller, and Szanton Blanc 1994; Glick Schiller 2005a, 2005b; Ong 1999; Rouse 1991; Wimmer and Glick Schiller 2003). By focusing on how migrants maintain ties to their homelands—in particular through remittances, political activity across borders, and networks of family and community—this scholarship has emphasized everyday experience and the continuity of social life. Despite the importance of this work in providing a more nuanced understanding of migrants' lives, however, children and youth have been undertheorized as "key players" in globalization and transnational processes (Maira and Soep 2005, xix). For example, research about the political engagement of migrants in their home countries or the economic flows between migrants and their families in the form of remittances have not always focused on the experiences or role of young people, although economic and political transnationalism are often implicitly, if not overtly, for the well-being of children and future generations. Young people may be leaders in diasporic political activism (Hess, this volume); development projects through migrant hometown associations are often geared toward children's needs (Burton and Gammage 2009; Kabki, Mazzucato, and Dietz 2008); and remittances may be guided by children's requests or used to substitute for a parent's presence (Parreñas 2005; Schmalzbauer 2004).

Where children have become significant in the transnational literature has been in the study of transnational families, which has focused on the extended networks that facilitate migration (e.g., Bryceson and Vuorela 2002; Foner 2009; Olwig 2007). Children have also figured prominently in the literature about women's migration, particularly in terms of partner relations and mothering (e.g., Gamburd 2000; Hondagneu-Sotelo 1994; Hondagneu-Sotelo and Avila 1997; Menjívar and Agadjanian 2007; Parreñas 2005; Pessar 1999). Our work builds on such analyses, adding to a burgeoning literature about the effects of transnational migration on children that considers topics ranging from the ways that children participate actively in family migration (Orellana et al. 2000), to the effect of family separation on immigrant children's educational success (Gindling and Poggio 2009) and emotional development (Suárez-Orozco, Todorova, and Louie 2002), to the ways that children "left behind" understand their parents' migration (Coe 2008; Dreby 2010; Olwig 1999; Parreñas 2005; Schmalzbauer 2004). These works have noted how the degree of rupture or continuity in children's experiences is associated with young people's perceptions of movement, meanings that depend on ideologies of family, notions of home and household, and degree of support from caregivers.

Through a focus on daily life, the body of work that employs a transnational framework provides a nuanced understanding of migrant experience and has considerably informed current anthropological and other disciplinary and interdisciplinary research about migration. However, recent critiques of transnational theories, within and outside of the field of anthropology, have pointed out how early transnational scholars were perhaps too quick to celebrate the opportunities and possibilities of rapid globalization, increasing international migration, and social change. Furthermore, transnationalism—a term that highlights the nation-state as the root of disjuncture—may not account for the way that people imagine their communities as they experience relationships across a set of spaces connected by travel and communication (e.g., Friedman 2002; Gardner 2008; Olwig 2007).

When surveying global media and discourse, it is easy to ascertain processes that represent the theme of rupture, from climate change to global financial crisis to persistent Cold War polarities. Recently, scholars have revisited work on transnationalism and problematized earlier understandings of global flows by analyzing the "darker sides of globalization" (Appadurai 2006, x), ranging from "friction" as "the awkward, unequal, unstable, and creative qualities of interconnection across difference" (Tsing 2004, 4) to "violence, exclusion, and growing inequality" (Appadurai 2006, x). In conversation with this recent turn in anthropology, we look at the nuances of global migrations, the breaks and disruptions but also the continuities of daily life, yet we do so through the study of children and youth, persons who have often been in the background of transnational study (see also Cole and Durham 2008; Maira and Soep 2005). Our emphasis on children and "everyday ruptures" allows us to bring into sharp focus the kinds of ruptures that people of all ages face and the social processes that endure.

This volume is organized around four overlapping and intersecting themes: the ways institutions, families, and ideologies construct and constrain children's agency; how families and individuals create and maintain kin ties despite or through disjunctures; how emotion and affect are linked to global divisions and flows; and the ways states create ruptures and continuities that are often competing and contradictory. We use these themes to elucidate and understand the experiences of children who migrate, with or without family members, and children who do not migrate while their parents or other family members do, highlighting the many motivations for movement—including political exile, war, labor, education, lifestyle change, and socioeconomic opportunities and necessities—within diverse cultural and geographic contexts. The chapters explore the experiences of urban-rural migrants in Britain, youth in the Tibetan diaspora, children who have fled war in Côte d'Ivoire and Liberia, members of Caribbean religious associations in New York, the families of Ghanaian internal and international migrants, Ecuadorian children whose parents emigrate, children and youth on both sides of the United States–Mexico border, and unaccompanied Moroccan migrant children in Spain. Putting the experiences and perspectives of children and youth front and center helps us better understand the ways migration can be both a rupture and a continuation of social life.

Part I—Child Agency/Adult Power: Negotiating Movement and New Identities

Our focus on everyday ruptures leads us to ask, who is creating the fissures as well as the consistencies that structure the lived experience of migrants? Over the last decade, scholars of migration have recognized that much of the dominant theorizing has not sufficiently acknowledged the agency of migrants themselves, instead focusing on economic and political push-pull factors (e.g., Castles and Kosack 1973; Piore 1979; Stark 1991). Building on this insight, we suggest that the agency of children has been overlooked or, at the very least, underplayed. Scholars have attended to the role that children play, at least discursively, as motivators for parental migration (e.g., Constable 2004; Parreñas 2005). It is important to assess the role that children make in migratory decision making (Orellana et al. 2000), as well as to look at situations where children themselves are migrants, whether accompanying kin or migrating independently (Bhabha 2008). We distinguish among the different kinds of agency children exercise and the varying degrees this is recognized, institutionalized, or ignored by parents and institutions involved in migration phenomena.

To begin refining our understanding of agency and the way it might be applied to the study of children, it is useful to first consider the domains in which children have or display agency and the level of agency they deploy. Generally defined as the ability to exert one's will and to act in the world, agency includes aspects of independence and autonomy. Yet there is a need to examine the ways agency is made manifest. Although many scholars have focused on agency as resistance to cultural norms and hegemony, or as creativity in generating new semiotic fields (e.g., Grady 2002;

Ogbu 1987), agency may also perpetuate existing power arrangements. Furthermore, there are forms of passive agency, such as when people act on what they understand to be another's desire or interests. Ethnographic study reveals what participants in a particular social context mean by agency, as well as captures different levels of agency that are present. For instance, in this volume, Julia Meredith Hess explores how Tibetans infuse their conceptualization of agency with Buddhist notions of karma and Western ideas about the link between individual and social progress. While all people are agentive—children as well as adults—their agency is both circumscribed and created within different contexts.

Next, in what ways are children perceived as having agency, or presumed to have a type of exaggerated or inflated sense of agency? The concept of agency itself may be too easily denied or ascribed to children. For example, preschools in the United States view children's free expression and decision making as primary goals (Tobin, Wu, and Davidson 1991). However, such "empowerment," when adults determine how agency should be appropriately expressed, is perhaps more accurately understood as tokenism (Tyrrell, this volume; Behera 1998). As Cindy Dell Clark has noted (2008), part of the understanding of childhood in the West is the idealization of children's collective agency, and the hope that children will solve problems inherited from previous generations. These potentially burdensome expectations arise from the construction of children as innocents and from the mythologizing, utopian force of mobilizing their perceived innocence and fresh industry to resolve the sins of their forebears (see Grossberg 2005). These examples illustrate what is perhaps adults' co-optation of child agency or domains in which children are "given" agency, itself a perplexing notion.

While it is often tempting in this theoretical climate to celebrate agency, our focus on international conventions regarding children, on state regimes, and on power imbalances within families leads us to take seriously the limitations of agency, and the violence and disruption that structural forces cause in the lives of children and adults. It is crucial to analyze the ideological dimensions that construct child agency or actively erase or deny it. For example, the guiding philosophies of international organizations that focus on children are often built on the dual premise that children need protection and are simultaneously human beings whose agency should be recognized (e.g., Ensor and Goździak, 2010; Nordstrom 1999; Rosen 2008; Stephens 1995). Paradoxically, young people may also be perceived as both vulnerable and threatening (Terrio

2008, 2009; Uehling 2008). Thus, child agency is recognized ideologically and structurally in different domains, and different definitions of childhood are implicit in such constructions. Both agency and nonagency stem from a series of negotiations and shifts in discourses and power within and between these domains (Foucault 1980).

Ethnographic examples in this collection further problematize the tendency to reduce children's agency to something simply either present or absent. For example, as Naomi Tyrrell describes, middle-class British parents migrate to rural environments "for the sake of the children," inculcating children with a sense of agency, but doing so within limited parameters. Moroccan boys who migrate to Spain as "unaccompanied minors" would seem to have the kind of agency idealized but circumscribed in the British households that Tyrrell studies, but Núria Empez Vidal complicates this perception by showing that family members participate, albeit passively, in the migration process, since family well-being motivates the boys' movement. In another example, Susan Shepler demonstrates how international organizations such as the UN Children's Fund (UNICEF) and the UN refugee agency (UNHCR) assumed that children who arrived in Guinea fleeing war in Côte d'Ivoire and Liberia had little agency in finding new caregiving arrangements, which turned out not to be the case. The notion of "best interests" is key throughout these chapters, as parents, the state, and others in a position to make decisions for and about children fall back on the idea that young people are not sufficiently mature to make decisions for themselves. How are children being socialized as agents in these domains, particularly if they are receiving mixed messages about the appropriateness of their having agency in diverse contexts?

Additionally, are there spheres in which children have more agency than is commonly acknowledged? Children have resiliency and an ability to construct new social meanings that surround their status, regardless of how adults in the community—and adults in the academy—may interpret the experiences of children and youth. For instance, in this volume, Heather Rae-Espinoza examines how children cognitively construct individual responses to the new, potentially stigmatizing social category of "children left behind" in Ecuador. Without sensitivity to cultural nuances and individual perspectives, personally significant forms of agency might hardly be noticed as such. Always embedded in broader structures, child agency, like adult agency, is inevitably partial and conditioned by multiple factors.

Part II—Social Reproduction: Family and Kinship across Borders and Generations

The headline of an article by Jason DeParle in the April 22, 2007, *New York Times Sunday Magazine* about Filipino transnational migration, "A Good Provider Is One Who Leaves," suggests that global capitalism is restructuring social reproduction. While production and the capital associated with it are highly mobile, social reproduction remains largely place bound (Katz 2001), resulting in a global "care drain" (Hochschild 2003, 17) as people in developing countries leave their own families to work in the North and the West, caring for the children and elderly relatives of others. Furthermore, disinvestment by the state, corporations, and civil society in social reproduction has shifted its burdens and costs much more squarely onto the shoulders of the domestic household, which can be stretched to the limits of its resiliency in meeting those demands (Katz 2001; for earlier work in this area see Meillassoux 1975 and Griffith 1985). Living transnationally may be a survival strategy for families coping with the disinvestment of the state in local social reproduction (Schmalzbauer 2004). State immigration regimes can further shift reproduction to other nation-states (Van Hear 1998; Wilson 2000, 2006), such as when the care of children who are U.S. citizens is transferred to Mexico, as Deborah A. Boehm discusses in her chapter.

While movement can result in what may be perceived as a kind of desocialization or a rupture of family and community ties, we again turn our attention to the complexities of and interactions between rupture and the everyday. Bourdieu's concepts of habitus and doxa are central to understanding social reproduction (e.g., 1977): he views individuals as situated in external structures that they internalize and reproduce, consciously and unconsciously. His work can fruitfully be applied to the continuities and ruptures we are discussing with respect to migration and children. An analysis of reproduction in migratory contexts should include attention to the complex interactions of culture, internal motivations, and external structures in both sending and receiving communities. As Cati Coe argues in this volume, for example, family ideologies and discourses that appear "traditional" and disrupted by new practices of transnational migration may themselves have been composed during an earlier period of everyday ruptures, including a history of movement and mobility. Although migration is associated with social disruption, social relations are also—and have always been—reconstituted translocally.

Social reproduction occurs throughout the life course, and children are not solely cultural persons in the midst of becoming, but producers of culture themselves (Gottlieb 2004; Hirschfeld 2002). Researchers have looked at family linkages and divisions in a transnational context (e.g., Bauer and Thompson 2006; Bryceson and Vuorela 2002; Glick Schiller and Fouron 2001; Leinaweaver 2008; Lubkemann 2008), demonstrating how social forms and family ties are maintained or transformed with migration. Although we emphasize how socialization occurs through families, it also takes place within neighborhoods (Brooks-Gunn, Duncan, and Aber 1997), through state agencies such as schools (Brittain 2002), and in other social contexts. Global movement generates a type of resocialization—novel forms of kinship, alternative forms of care, new and multiple locales where family members live, shifting understandings of who constitutes family and community, and even emergent notions of family itself.

It is not only children affected by migration who experience rupture (Levin 2005; Levy 1973). Disjuncture can occur for young people in any context, for example, in contrasts between home and school (Heath 1982; Phillips 1983), between local and hegemonic discourses (Anderson-Fye 2003; Blackwood 2000), or even in the before and after of initiation ceremonies or weaning (Spindler 1997). Furthermore, ruptures may include continuity in unexpected ways. Parents and children reconfigure and reinterpret their roles through migration and still engage in meaningful relationships without daily face-to-face interactions. Migrants may explain the restructuring of their household through existing discourses, such as saying that motherhood means providing materially for children rather than being present in their daily lives (Hondagneu-Sotelo and Avila 1997). Finally, that which appears to be discontinuity may, in fact, generate family collectivity, cohesion, and well-being. In this collection, Empez Vidal explores how the migration of young people to Spain can provide, for example, economic support for the marriage of a sister or health care for a mother in Morocco, illustrating how the migration of family members contributes to familial reproduction.

The authors in this volume challenge narrow constructions of family and household, demonstrating how people maintain, reemphasize, or transform their conceptions of relatedness and locales of residence as they migrate. For example, child care shared among and distributed across several caregivers can be valued as the appropriate way to bring a child into a web of kin, as Rae-Espinoza reports in her contribution. As Shepler's chapter highlights, Ivorian and Liberian children fleeing war were taken in by adults in Guinea, with children and adults creating novel care arrangements; although relief agencies sought family reunification for separated children at the end of a conflict, the children themselves expressed a range of desires, including staying with their foster parents permanently. Similarly, Forde reminds us that modes of relatedness that are not based on notions of biological kinship can connect members of a religious community dispersed across nation-states.

Another prominent theme running through this collection is the construction of the self in new social contexts. Shifting configurations of family usher in novel subjectivities and shifting roles that children choose or are expected to enact. Yet these new configurations often entail significant connections to previous "cultural logics" by "giving old forms new meaning" and "giving new forms old meaning" (Fischer 2001, 13). As individuals and families leave, maintain, or recreate home in multiple locales, children, siblings, parents, and extended kin take on new positionalities—this process is inevitably situated within both sending and receiving communities, and can even be constituted through movement itself. Young people may, precisely because of movement, be required to navigate new subjectivities of race/ethnicity and national membership (e.g., Coutin 2010; Rosas 2007; Smith 2006; Zilberg 2004) or experience significant shifts in class position within families and across generations.

Migration within states has long been recognized as one way individuals and families try to improve their socioeconomic status. The work of Aihwa Ong and Donald M. Nonini (Ong 1999; Ong and Nonini 1997) illustrates how, with increased opportunities for global migration, flows have shifted in scale from national to transnational. Children are often at the center of such economic migrations, as motivators of their parents' desire for class mobility or as agents who make their own decisions related to potential economic opportunities by migrating, staying behind, or not returning (Boehm, this volume; Empez Vidal, this volume). Paradoxically, class identities can impact a family's ability to migrate, and also intersect with nationality and other subjectivities to affect how states in receiving countries deal with child migrants and refugees. For example, Susan Terrio's work on Romanian street children and their treatment by the French judicial system (2008, 2009) and Greta Uehling's study of unaccompanied minors in the United States (2008) underscore how constructions of child migrants are informed by culturally specific and class-specific understandings of childhood within destination communities.

Language use is another way that children express their positionality and take on new roles within families and communities. Migration deeply affects the linguistic practices of children, especially language learning, negotiation, and experimentation in contexts where language is an instantiation of identity. Children who move, or whose family members migrate, are often expected or understood to be "translators"—language interpreters, preservers of cultural practice, and mediators of cultural difference (Orellana et al. 2003; Valdés 2003). Such negotiations of "translation" create an ever-changing assemblage of performances of self, subjectivities that intersect with other aspects of identity (see, for example, Hoffman 1989; McKay and Wong 2000; Mendoza-Denton 2008). Family relations and the broader notion of social reproduction, then, are always situated within hierarchies of class, nationality, and race, among others.

Community members of any age understand cultural change in particular ways. As we have argued, every community places expectations on children for the present and the future, expectations that are altered as children accept, negotiate, and challenge these aspirations in the world around them. Children's participation in cultural and social life helps us understand how cultural change and continuity occurs—these everyday ruptures—whether slowly and imperceptibly over time or in the sudden disruptions that require new articulations or new combinations of older articulations. Often seen as the linchpin of social regeneration, children enhance our understanding of the interconnected web of family relations, cultural life, and social change that inevitably accompany global migration.

Part III—The Circulation of Affect: Emotion, Children, and Global Flows

Every migration, whether inside a nation-state or across national borders, includes some form of fragmentation, as well as the constancy of daily life. Much of this ambiguity is expressed through the multiple, and often ambivalent, expressions of emotion that accompany migrations. Affect is part of the space of the everyday; in fact, the intimacy of emotion and its intertwining with our humanity can make it a difficult topic to analyze. From their infancy, people learn their communities' affective practices, notably researched with attachment theory (e.g., LeVine and Norman 2008, 128). Throughout the life course, cultural shaping mediates how people evaluate a situation, understand their response as indicative of a particular emotion, or articulate an emotion to others (Levy 1984). Thus, an analysis of emotional expressions enhances our understanding of how children experience and comprehend global connections and disconnections. Because people's emotions not only respond to but also shape their migrations—and the migrations of others—we maintain that a focus on children's affective expressions can bridge macroanalyses with the intimate spaces of family life.

Much of the research on transnationality has fruitfully theorized the structural dimensions of the global movement of people and capital (e.g., Kearney 1996; Massey et al. 1987; Piore 1979; Portes and DeWind 2004; Sassen 1998; Stark 1991). Yet, perhaps in the endeavor to understand and explain the structural factors driving global migrations, scholars have often overlooked the decidedly affective dimension of the global movement of people. We suggest that an emphasis on relations of capital, state power, and large-scale global flows can also lead to an understanding of the accompanying circulation of affect. Migrations can be guided, impacted, or undermined by economic need and broad structures of power, as well as by intimate relations and the emotional aspects of everyday life. Indeed, these systems are woven so tightly that theorizing one without the other leaves unexamined a significant dimension of migration.

Affect and emotion have long been topics of study in anthropology and other fields (e.g., Hinton 1999; Kleinman and Good 1985; Levy 1973; Lutz 1988; Obeyesekere 1984; Parish 1996; Rosaldo 1980; Shweder and LeVine 1984, Spiro 1967), often in global perspective (e.g., Ahearn 2001; Besnier 1995; Lutz and Abu-Lughod 1990). A growing literature explores the emotional aspects of migration itself (e.g., Boehm and Swank, forthcoming; Escandell and Tapias 2010; Faier 2007; Svašek and Skrbis 2007; Wise and Chapman 2005). Increasingly, researchers have made children and youth central to such analyses (Coe, forthcoming, "What Is Love?"; Stryker, forthcoming; Suárez-Orozco and Suárez-Orozco 2001; Swank, forthcoming). An emphasis on the emotional expressions of young people elucidates how discourses of emotion are evoked as family members migrate, how affect is expressed and altered for those who migrate and those who do not, and how emotions are experienced differently at diverse stages of the life cycle. Closely paying attention to affect, particularly when studying migration and children, is crucial for a finer-grained analysis of motivations for migration, the process of settlement, and the construction of transnational identities (see also Knörr 2005).

Ruptures such as migration result in multiple and often contradictory emotional expressions. In a global context, movement can be associated with profound pain and suffering; separation, distance, loss, nostalgia, and longing characterize migration ruptures (e.g., Ainslie 1998). Perhaps more difficult to convey is the emotion that expresses the continuity of the everyday and connects family members: expressions of love, caregiving, intimacy, affection, and devotion. Remittances, transnational gifts, and other forms of economic support are linked to affect, again demonstrating that flows of capital and emotional bonds are intertwined (Castellanos 2009; Parreñas 2005; Schmalzbauer 2004). Finally, many of the motivations for migration are bound up with the present and future security and well-being of children. The study of children and migration highlights these contradictory and simultaneous manifestations of emotion in a transnational world: sadness and joy, bonds and disconnections border one another and are not easily disarticulated.

The chapters explore a wide range of emotionality: emotions children express through migration, the affective character of relationships between and among children and adults, and the multiple sentiments children and their caregivers feel. Coe's and Rae-Espinoza's chapters, for example, examine how children "left behind" understand, respond to, and adapt to their parents' transnational migration and relationships with caregivers. International conventions and states can privilege or disregard particular kinds of affective relationships within families and between citizen and nation. For instance, refugee agencies often assume that children would prefer to live with a biological parent in their home nation-state, rather than with foster parents in another country (Shepler, this volume). Conversely, states may deny children's ties to multiple nations (Hamann and Zuñiga, this volume) or make it difficult for migrants to structure family as they wish (Boehm, this volume). The protective and punitive actions of governments and nongovernmental organizations not only have particular emotional content, but also, by shaping people's lives, generate profound emotional responses. For example, Hess's chapter discusses the sadness and anger expressed in the lyrics of young diasporic Tibetan rappers who seek a Tibet free of Chinese rule and Boehm's chapter highlights the emotional struggles within mixed-status families.

It is perhaps because of ideologies that link childhood and emotion in the contemporary United States and Europe that the study of children and migration brings to the fore the affective dimensions of global movement. Yet focusing on emotions also challenges the Western concept that codes children primarily as vulnerable, dependent, and domestic (Panter-Brick 2000); instead, it encourages an awareness of and desire to support the resilience and coping strategies of families and children. Such a focus allows us to analyze the dialectic between structures and affect, bridging the study of global flows with that of emotionality.

Part IV—Status and the State:
State Power, Migrant Responses, and Constructions of Childhood

As mentioned earlier in relation to agency, family life, and emotional experience, any discussion of migration must include an examination of the role of the state and its institutions. The state and its agencies are, of course, not monoliths. The state is constantly being produced through the actions of individuals (Abrams 1988; Alonso 1994; Corrigan and Sayer 1985; Lipsky 1980; Nagengast 1991, 1994). There are many ways to view and analyze state power—through policies, legislative and judicial decision making and implementation, the reach of various institutional arms of the state, and the state's manifestations in everyday life. State policies are often competing, contradictory, and continually acted upon by individuals and groups. In spite of international agreements and the ways that citizenship increasingly transcends or crosses national borders (e.g., Mostov 2008; Nordstrom 2003), we still live in a world system where the rights and exercise of citizenship are largely ordered around state sovereignty. Thus, despite the global circulation of what might be considered Western middle-class or elite understandings of childhood through international agreements, these conventions have uneven purchase globally, as some states sign on to them and others do not, and further, states implement them in strategic ways in light of what they perceive as their own best interests (Rosen 2008).

The legitimacy of the modern nation-state to govern has long been intertwined with the governance of children, in creating policy, programs, and rhetoric around young people (Chatterjee 1999; Coe 2005). As Tyrrell describes in this volume, children are currently one of the most governed groups in Europe, a claim that is probably true in many parts of the world. Children often become sites for anxiety about the welfare of the nation, with their personal development perceived as central to national progress (Boli, Ramirez, and Meyer 1985). For example, the importance of rearing future soldiers for expected, continued wars became a popular topic of U.S. rhetoric in the 1950s, at the height of the Cold War (Fontaine 1998). Because schools organize many hours of most children's daily lives, states can be far more prominent in the lives of children than in the lives of adults. Although national and international forms of governance recognize—even sentimentalize—the importance of family and communal forms of socialization (Coe 1999), they also take children away from "village-based enculturation models" (Lancy 2008, 148) by organizing new kinds of social relationships for children through schools and other programs. Especially in times of rupture, states and international organizations—in the name of the best interests of children—may assume responsibility for children's socialization and well-being.

State policies contribute to the everyday ruptures of child migrants and their families in multiple ways. States' definitions of the categories "child," "youth," and "adult," as well as "migrant" or "refugee," are variously understood and legislated in different contexts. While many categories of persons that affect migrant families and children are included and described in international conventions, they are diversely interpreted by states, or even by institutions within the same state, largely in an attempt to protect state interest or respond to public opinion about the nature of the body politic. For example, as Edmund T. Hamann and Víctor Zúñiga argue in this collection, educational institutions can ignore the transnationalism of their students; in Mexico, students who have lived in the United States are treated as Mexican citizens, while in the United States they are seen as immigrants who will stay, even though many go back and forth between the two countries. As Hess outlines in *Immigrant Ambassadors* (2009a), the way states categorize migrants impacts motivations to migrate or to stay, as well as questions of identity, economics, and politics, as migrants make new homes and develop transnational relationships with people and institutions in their homeland.

Another reason for the contradictory effects of state immigration policy is that while most immigration policy focuses on individual subjects (Sassen 1996), family and community ties structure migration (e.g., Bauer and Thompson 2006; Dreby 2010; Hondagneu-Sotelo 2003, 1994; Hondagneu-Sotelo and Avila 1997; Menjívar and Abrego 2009; Pessar 1999; Pessar and Mahler 2003). For example, although U.S. immigration policy is formally structured around family reunification, many policies actually serve to separate families (Boehm 2008). As a result, as Boehm argues in this volume, Mexican migrant children in the United States are "contingent citizens" who are situated both "here" and "there." Dianna Shandy's work on the African diaspora in Ireland (2008) shows how the Irish state changed its *jus soli* citizenship policy, in part due to public concern over an increase in Nigerian women coming to give birth to children who would be de facto Irish citizens. Immigration policies, working conditions, and lack of social services for migrants can prevent parents from bringing their children with them when they migrate, with implications for their relationships with their children (Coe, this volume; Rae-Espinoza, this volume). Finally, as Empez Vidal's and Shepler's chapters demonstrate, states often fail to take into account child agency, even as their policies repeatedly change in response to the actions and the presence of children (see also Cheney 2007). Thus, a focus on the contradictory and changing aspects of state policies toward children and migrants brings together the interconnected and overlapping themes we explore in this collection.

The Continuities and Discontinuities of Migration

Children and youth, at the nexus of rupture and the everyday, are important for an examination of changing ideologies of social reproduction in the context of global migration. As the impetus for family migration, those at the center of decision-making processes, or migrants themselves, young people have at times been overlooked or understudied, and their agency is often downplayed in social scientists' discussions of migration. Addressing both "the marginal child in adult-centered societies" and what has often been "the missing child in anthropological writing" (Scheper-Hughes and Sargent 1998, 10, 13), we maintain that a child-centered approach is essential for understanding migration processes at this historical moment. Our endeavors should be focused on coming to know how people of any age encode the world in their negotiations of external and internal forces. Furthermore, not only are children at the center of social reproduction, they also have a central role in the production of new, emerging, and necessarily complex subjectivities that arise in the context of global migration.

With his discussion of the expansive and far-reaching impact of the "global imaginary," Arjun Appadurai (1996) provides a tool for analyzing the development of an interpenetrating and connected set of discourses and practices, spread through various economic, media, and technological means, that are shaping the imaginations and future aspirations of new generations of children and youth (see Maira and Soep 2005). Quite simply, young people today have access to more images, aesthetics, ideas, and discourses of being and belonging than ever before. Migrants, including children and youth, engage with these ideas at "home" as they make decisions to migrate, attempt to migrate, succeed or not at migration, resettle in their new home or homes, return to the previous ones, or do not migrate when others do. It seems that, in light of the collective research presented here, child agency is more often today incorporated and recognized in multiple domains. How children and youth engage with these increasingly global imaginaries provides a glimpse of possible worlds in the making.

Nonetheless, structural constraints and frameworks are important in the construction of subjectivity and the experiences of migrant children on local, national, and global scales (Hess and Shandy 2008). As we have discussed, international and nation-state institutions continue to be salient, be they departments of state, schools, or social service organizations (see also Smith and Guarnizo 1998). A focus on children and migration illuminates the ways in which migration decisions, outcomes, international instruments, and state policies define social categories, and the ways people respond to them creatively. The study of children within global flows—these everyday ruptures—thus takes us straight to the core questions of anthropological theory.

This volume encourages scholars from multiple fields—anthropology, sociology, geography, migration studies, and childhood studies, among others—to examine migration and children in tandem. The chapters contribute to several often overlapping academic conversations, including debates about the degree of disjuncture and continuity experienced by migrants; the making of kinship and social reproduction; the affective aspects of global movement; the presence of state power in the lives of young people and their families; and, centrally, expressions of and constraints on children's agency. It is our hope that this volume will stimulate and contribute to ongoing exchange about the possibilities for our scholarship when we put children and youth at the center.

PART I

Child Agency/Adult Power: Negotiating Movement and New Identities

Chapter 1

Children's Agency in Family Migration Decision Making in Britain

Naomi Tyrrell

Traditionally, studies of why families migrate tended to focus on economic motivations for migration (Fielding 1992; Halfacree and Boyle 1993; Halfacree 2004; Smith 2004). A flurry of gender-sensitive research into migration decision making over the past two decades has analyzed women's involvement, in particular if the women "trail" men and make sacrifices for the family (Bielby and Bielby 1992; Bonney and Love 1991; Boyle 2002; Cooke and Bailey 1996; Green 1997). However, despite the potential for this work to open up the "black box" of family migration decision making and recognize the roles of different family members, much research on family migration tends to be "adultist" (see Ackers 2000). This means that analyses of family migration decision making are rarely sensitive to age; researchers focus on adults' experiences of family migration without due consideration to the experiences of children in migrant families (McKendrick 2001). This is surprising given that concepts such as life stage and life course have significantly influenced the development of family migration theory (see Boyle, Halfacree, and Robinson 1998; Empez Vidal, this volume; Rossi 1955). In addition, the lack of attention to children as potential migration decision makers in families is surprising because children's presence within families often is considered to influence *motivations* for family migration, to varying degrees (see Bailey and Boyle 2004; Henderson 2005; Khoo, Hugo, and McDonald 2008; Mazanti 2007; Ní Laoire 2007; Valentine 1997). Despite this, researchers have assumed that children have little involvement in family migration decision making.

There has been a burgeoning of interest in the ways in which children participate in family migration in recent years (e.g., Young and Ansell 2003; Orellana et al. 2000; Orellana 2009; Thomson and Crul 2007; Schmalzbauer 2008; Waters 2005; Parreñas 2005), although discussion of how children specifically contribute to family migration decision making often is minimal. Therefore, exploring children's agency in migratory situations is timely. Children's agency in migration needs to be considered within the context of children's rights within societies, as well as their everyday experiences of decision making within families. In this chapter, I discuss ways in which changing childhoods in a European context require us to rethink family migration decision making; I then go on to discuss children's agency in family migration decision making using examples from a study in Britain.

Changing Childhoods and Family Migration Decision Making: Britain in a European Context

Structural changes within and between families are occurring in European societies, such as family dissolution and reformulation, single-parent and dual-earner households, lower marriage rates, higher divorce rates, increased cohabitation rates, and delayed childbirth. These changes have directly impacted migration and increased the mobility of families (Bailey and Boyle 2004; Flowerdew and Al-Hamad 2004). A related, but often overlooked, aspect of these changes is connected to children's positioning within their families and broader society. Children's rights, roles, and responsibilities as decision makers have been changing at a legislative level in Britain. The ways in which these changes interlink with social, cultural, and economic changes require further research, particularly how they influence and affect migrant children and their families.

Children are one of the most governed groups by both the state and civic society in Europe, and in governing children, the state often dictates what is "good" for them (Hill et al. 2004). Within this context, parents are expected to care for their children and act in their best interests (Lansdown 1995). Simultaneously, adults are encouraged to promote and develop children's agency by including them in decision making (UNCRC; Children Act 2004). There has been increased recognition of children's rights within Europe (for example, individual EU states' children acts) and globally (for example, the UN Convention on the Rights of the Child or UNCRC, ratified by all member states except the United States and Somalia). Evidently, sociocultural changes in contemporary constructions of childhood are also becoming influential in the political sphere. The right of children to be involved in making decisions that affect their lives is now broadly recognized as being in children's best interests in formal decision-making procedures in Britain, such as when children are in government care or when their families fragment. Children's participation was an important tenet of the Labour government's Every Child Matters program, which was initiated by a government green paper in 2003. Participation is usually in line with a developmental perspective on childhood and considers a child's age and perceived level of competence (as outlined in the UNCRC).

The boundaries between childhood and adulthood have become "fuzzy" in recent times, according to Sibley (1995), and children's roles within some families have become more equal to those of parents (Beck 1992; Sibley and Lowe 1992). Recent waves of multidisciplinary studies of children and childhood have explored children's involvement in making decisions within their communities and families (e.g., Hart 1997; Hill et al. 2004; Maxey 2004; Wyness 2003), and to a greater extent, children's involvement in making decisions when their families fragment or re-form (e.g., Butler et al. 2003; Flowerdew and Neale 2003; Forsberg and Pösö 2008; Gollop, Taylor, and Smith 2000). This body of research is helpful when thinking about family migration decision making specifically because the researchers discuss how, and to what extent, children are involved in making both everyday and more complex decisions within families and other contexts. The findings strengthen the suggestion that migration researchers should consider the possibility that children are involved in making family migration decisions because they conclude that children are involved in making decisions in families and that adults do not always retain all of the decision-making power.

The binary categorizations of adult and child perhaps are not helpful when thinking about migration decision making in family contexts because of children's and adults' changing roles and responsibilities. Increasingly, childhood is undergoing "familialization," meaning that family contexts are becoming spaces in which children are allowed to express choice, exercise autonomy, and work at self-realization (Näsman 1994). Sibley and Lowe (1992) highlight the phenomenon of "personalizing" families, in which decision-making processes are less hierarchical than in traditional families, and in which discussions take place between children and parents. In addition, Smith, Taylor, and Tapp (2003) suggest that children's participation in family decision making may help facilitate their growth toward mature and responsible adulthood. Therefore, it could be argued that familialization may be in children's long-term best interests. These theorizations usefully inform our thinking with regard to children's involvement in family migration decision making because it is helpful to consider the context of children's cumulative experience of decision making within families. Clegg (1989), building on Foucault (1979), suggests that power is not inherent within powerful subjects (e.g. adults) but is dispersed throughout complex networks of relationships (e.g. families). Within families, the positioning of parents as powerful over children is not inherent but occurs within the practical and discursive consciousness of parents and children (Giddens 1984). However, current adultist theories of family migration decision making in Europe support the view that power is inherently parental, reifying parents as the only decision makers within families and consigning children to positions of powerlessness. New ways of theorizing family migration decision making need to be developed (see Bushin 2009).

Background to the Study

In this chapter, I explore children's agency in family migration decision making, drawing on the findings of a research project with internal migrant families in Britain. An examination of Special Migration Statistics for England and Wales (devised from the 2001 UK Census, detailing origins and destinations of internal migrants) indicated a high level of counter-urban child migration, that is, of families moving from urban to rural locations. Devon, in southwest England, was chosen as the location for the research because Census data for 2001 and National Health Service data for 2000–2005 (useful as an indicator of migration because it records re-registrations with general practitioners) indicated that Devon was the county that gained the highest number of child migrants from other parts of Britain. Moreover, more rural locations in Devon received the highest numbers of child migrants. I made the assumption that child migration was a good indicator of family migration because the majority of the children would have been migrating to Devon with at least one parent or guardian or to join a parent or guardian.

Much of Devon is classified as rural, with tourist and agricultural industries predominating. All the families interviewed had migrated from urban locations—often in or close to large conurbations such as Birmingham or London—to rural locations in Devon. Three urban areas—Exeter, Plymouth, and Torbay—lie near the families' rural migration destinations, and the larger city of Bristol is within commuting distance for some of the families. Although the population of the urban areas in the region is socially mixed in terms of age and ethnic background, the populations of the rural locations that the families migrated to are predominantly white and aging (Devon County Council 2007). The Devon County Council describes the county as "made up of many small and scattered communities built around larger market and coastal towns and the vibrant city of Exeter" (ibid., 3). Data on ethnicity from the 2001 Census indicate that Devon is 98.9 percent white, compared with 90.9 percent white for England as a whole (Office for National Statistics 2001).

I developed a children-in-families approach to researching family migration decision making during this study, with both children and parents participating in the research (see Bushin 2009). As I argued earlier, theorizations of family migration decision making are incomplete if they do not include the perspectives of children within families. However, it is also erroneous to engage only with children in the context of family migration research, as this would mean partial perspectives on family migration would be revealed. Adults' perspectives were not held to be more valid than children's or vice versa. The approach is designed to better reflect the experiences of all individuals within families, allow for arrays of family contexts, explore the notion of children's best interests within family contexts, and build on the idea that power can be dispersed within family networks.

I contacted the majority of families via primary and secondary schools across Devon, and all the participant families had migrated within the previous two years. Social grading of the families was carried out: twelve of the thirty-seven families were graded as upper middle class, thirteen as middle class, one as lower middle class, six as working class, and five as lower working class. I interviewed children and parents in their homes, separately where possible (see Bushin 2007), using a life-course approach so that the migration process could be placed within the broader context of the interviewees' biographies (Halfacree and Boyle 1993; Ní Laoire 2000). Here, I draw on current theorizations of family and childhood to demonstrate how a children-in-families approach can allow nuanced understandings of family migration decision making and reveal the degrees of agency children have in making migration decisions. I also discuss, in the context of changing childhood and family cultures, the factors that limited children's agency.

Children's Agency in Family Migration Decision Making

The interviews with children and parents revealed that children had varying degrees of agency in making the decision to migrate as a family:

1. Parent(s) decided to migrate and informed child of the decision.
2. Parent(s) consulted child over the decision to migrate.
3. Child participated in making the decision to migrate.

In twenty of the thirty-seven families, parents informed children of the decision to migrate when it was definite that the family would be migrating. Children had no input into the decision. Some families made a visit to the migration destination for the children to see the location and to visit the new residence (or possible residences) and schools prior to moving. In other families, parents made the migration decision very quickly and children were informed a few days before they moved or, as in one case, on the same day. The ages of the children who were informed of the migration decision varied, as did the motivations for the migrations. None of the children who were informed of the migration decision said that they would have preferred to have been consulted or to have participated in the migration decision. Indeed the majority had not expected to be involved in making the migration decision, which may reflect the children's usual experiences of family decision making.

Parents consulted their children over the initial decision to move in ten families. In these families, parents discussed the possibility of moving with the children, talked through the likely process of migration, and asked the children's opinions (similar to Hill et al. 2004). The decision-making power remained with the parents, but they considered the children's views before making the migration decision:

> Jenny: My mum did ask me how I felt about moving. I didn't really know what would happen with the house and things, or what it would be like to move.
> Naomi: Did you feel as though you had a choice?
> Jenny: I s'pose so. They did ask me [what I thought]. It's just that I didn't know what it was going to be like 'til we got here.
> (*Jenny, age fourteen*)

One of the differences between the children who had participated in the migration decision and those who had been consulted was their level of surprise. The children who had been consulted had not usually expected the issue of migration to arise and were rarely prepared when their parents asked their opinions, which may have also limited their agency.

In the families in which children had been consulted, parents made the final decision to migrate after they had talked it through with children. The majority of the children believed that they had been properly consulted, although it became clear that a minority did not feel they had a real say in the decision to move:

> Clare: I didn't want to move down. I always had that thing about if it isn't broke don't fix it and I was quite happy with my life up there, but looking back on it, I don't think I mind too much. I've had quite a lot of fun and I like my life down here.
> Naomi: Were you apprehensive then?
> Clare: My parents asked if it was all right with me, and I just said that I didn't mind because I knew it didn't matter what I say, we'd still be moving.
> *(Clare, age fourteen)*

Clare did not seem convinced that her parents had properly consulted her about the decision to migrate and implied that the consultation process had been tokenistic. Also, she had not been honest with her parents about her feelings concerning the move, because she thought that her opinion would have had no bearing on the final decision. Interestingly, when interviewed, all the parents of the consulted children conceded that the family would have migrated even if the children had rejected the idea:

> Naomi: Did you all sit down and talk about moving?
> Mother: Oh yes, yeah. Whenever we make a decision, we sit down and talk about it as a family. Yeah, we talked about what they wanted and they were so excited, you know, it wasn't a problem really. I mean, had they not been it wouldn't have changed the decision, umm, but fortunately for us they did [want to move]. I mean, we knew [our son] Alan wanted to come anyway, so we knew he wouldn't mind.
> *(Mother of girl, age eight, and boy, age twelve)*

Although these children had been consulted, their agency in making the migration decision had been restricted, something that only some of them had realized at the time. The consultation process can be considered to have been tokenistic in the majority of these families because the ultimate decision to migrate remained firmly with the parents—the children's views had not always influenced the parents' final migration decision.

Children participated in the decision to migrate in seven of the thirty-seven families at the beginning of the migration decision-making process, when the idea of migration first arose:

> Alistair: Well, Mum said about it [the idea to migrate] and then we all sat down and talked about it.
> Naomi: So did you feel that you had a choice?
> Alistair: Yeah, it wasn't like she forced us or anything. We talked about it.
> *(Alistair, age twelve)*

Children who participated in the decision to migrate were more fully involved than children who were consulted or informed, and they were encouraged to discuss with their parents the advantages and disadvantages of moving, often considering the benefits or drawbacks for each family member. Children and parents had more equal decision-making roles in these families, listening to each other's opinions and feelings and then discussing whether or not to migrate:

> Claudia: We talked about it and obviously it was a difficult time for me with college and everything, but then I just kind of thought, "It can't be that bad; it won't be too bad." I don't know why I started thinking that. I don't know why.
> Naomi: What do you think would have happened if you hadn't wanted to move?
> Claudia: Mmm . . . God, I don't know. No, umm, yeah, I do. I think 'cos of our ages . . . they couldn't have made us move. Not that it came down to that anyway. We are close though so I think if we had really said no we all would have stayed up in [name of place]. God, it would have been hard if it had come to that.
> *(Claudia, age seventeen)*

Unlike the children who were informed or consulted, the children who had participated in making the decision to migrate emphasized the process of migration and all the interlinked factors involved in making the decision. Therefore the participant children had a sophisticated understanding of how decision making operated within their families. The children who were informed of parents' migration decisions were less aware of the migration process, the time scale, and all the separate decisions that had been made than the children who had more agency. Some families changed their destination locations, house purchases fell through, or job opportunities changed. The general difficulties that the families attributed to migration were more obvious to the children who had a higher level of involvement in decision making.

Factors Affecting Children's Agency in Family Migration Decision Making

In the majority of the families interviewed, children did not participate in making the migration decision despite government legislation and active encouragement that promotes children's rights to participate in decisions affecting their lives. This is not particularly surprising and perhaps points to disparities between children's rights in their home/family contexts and in wider society. In Britain, the government is often criticized for operating a "nanny state" in which politicians interfere in the private sphere, e.g., family life. However, when family lives do not live up to societal expectations and deviant or criminal practices are exposed, often the blame for letting children down falls on government services and agencies, which are subsequently restructured (as occurred in 2003 with the publication of the green paper "Every Child Matters" following the inquiry into the death of eight-year-old Victoria Climbié). Legislation promoting children's rights, including agency, is put into practice in legal contexts involving family fragmentation and children in the care of state agencies, although not always comprehensively. However, there appears to be a tendency to shy away from discussion of decision-making practices in families and children's agency within family contexts.

Frequently cited factors that prevented children from having a high degree of agency in their families when the decision to migrate was being made were children's age, children's level of understanding, parents' views of children's best interests, and motivations for migration. Children's age was a common barrier, often because parents had a developmental view of childhood (Lansdown 1995). Parents frequently intertwined a child's level of understanding with a child's age in their comments on why they had not encouraged children to be active in participating in the family migration decision. The age range of the children who participated in making the decision to migrate was seven to sixteen years; all the children six years old or less at the time of migration were informed of the decision to migrate. Legislation governing children's involvement in official decision making recommends that children's participation should increase in line with their age and maturity (UNCRC). Children's participation in family migration decision making did increase from the younger ages through the middle ages of childhood but tailed off toward the older ages. It was apparent that younger children were often confused about the migration process, but whether they were confused because they had not had a high level of involvement in making the migration decision or because of their age was not clear.

Older children's agency also was sometimes limited. In eight of the twenty families in which children were informed of the decision to move, at least one child was over thirteen. In three of those families, all the children were over thirteen but had not been allowed to participate in the migration decision, nor had they been consulted. When the older children in two of those families were informed of the decision to migrate, they had been confused over whether their parents were seriously considering moving and they had also thought that their parents would probably change their minds:

> Naomi: And were you both involved in the decision to move too?
> Sam: No.
> Cathy: No.
> Naomi: Did you know that your Mum and Dad were thinking about it or...?
> Cathy: Yeah, because they'd been looking at all sorts like up [name of place] way and then they started talking about Devon and I'd never been here before but then yeah, we came here....
> Naomi: So how did you feel when your Mum and Dad first said that they were thinking about moving?
> Sam: I didn't really take any notice of them.
> Naomi: Right.
> Cathy: You just think that they won't.
> *(Cathy, age seventeen; Sam, age fifteen)*

Parents in two families in which the older children were informed of the decision to migrate but had not been enthusiastic about it suggested that they felt their decision to migrate had been vindicated because their children were now happy and content in their destination locations. The children in both these families agreed that their migration had been beneficial, and in one case the children stated that they were now better off, in social and educational terms, than they had been in their original location. Analysis of the interviews with older children and their parents revealed that the primary reason older children's agency in making the migration decision had been curtailed was because parents thought that the children would soon be leaving home:

> Mother: It didn't stop us [moving] because we felt that it was something we were going to do and they've still got their whole lives ahead of them to make their own decisions about where they settle and they won't want to be in our pockets anyway when they're in their twenties . . . it won't make that much difference.
> *(Mother of two boys, ages fourteen and fifteen)*

Although the parents of the older children often looked ahead to when the children would leave home, there is evidence that young people are living at home for longer periods of time, especially in rural areas (Jentsch and Shucksmith 2004). Hence, young people may live in the migration destination longer than the parents anticipate, and young people themselves may not be thinking ahead to a time when they might leave home.

Parental perception of the best interests of children was another common factor that limited children's agency in contributing to the decision to migrate. The majority of the parents who had limited their children's agency felt that decisions such as whether or not the family should migrate were adult decisions. This may be more understandable for parents of younger children, with these parents thinking that it was in children's best interests to be protected from what they perceived to be the realm of adult decision making:

> Mother: In my experience children need to feel safe and have security in the things around them, so it wouldn't have been good for them to have known about everything too soon, would it?
> *(Mother of two boys, ages five and seven)*

However, parents of the older children who had not had a high level of involvement in making the decision to migrate also pointed to migration decision making being an adult responsibility:

> Dad: They didn't have a choice really. I think umm . . . when they first found out we were moving they were probably a bit upset and would have preferred to stay where they were simply because they felt comfortable. Initially it was a bit of a shock.
> *(Father of two boys, ages fifteen and sixteen)*

The contrast between this protectionist view—and how it is put into practice in families—and children's rights legislation is stark. On the one hand, according to parents, children's best interests are served by limiting their agency in decision making when it involves family migration because of the need to protect their childhood; on the other hand, state, EU, and UN legislation promotes children's agency in making decisions that affect their lives, in line with their age and maturity. Parents' own expressions of what constitutes good parenthood and good childhood may be more at odds with the conceptualizations of the governing powers than has hitherto been recognized, particularly because the contexts in which children's rights legislation is applied do not always cross over the boundary between the private (family) and public spheres.

None of the children who had been informed of their parents' migration decision appeared to have been excluded from the migration decision-making process because their parents feared the consequences of their participation, such as arguments and questions about their authority, although this may occur in other cases. Some of the children who had been prevented from contributing to the family migration decision were sensitive to the factors that denied them agency, such as the motivation for migration. The majority of the children who were informed of their parents' migration decision had been offered the opportunity to discuss the migration process with their parents; however, unlike the experiences of the consulted children, this discussion took place after parents had made the final decision to migrate. In families in which young people were informed of the migration decision, the decision-making power remained firmly with the parents.

Children whose migrations were motivated by parents' employment had usually been informed of the migration decision once it had been made by parents. The majority of these parents stated that because they were migrating for employment reasons, the children's involvement in making the migration decision had been limited. A minority of these parents expressed guilt associated with the low level of involvement of their children in decision making. However, they felt that their children's agency had been limited because of the primary motivation for the migration rather than because they had made the decision not to include the children in making the migration decision. Job relocation was often cited as a barrier to children's participation in migration decision making. Indeed, parents themselves sometimes felt that concerns about income and employment limited their own power as migration decision makers:

> Mum: I don't think any of us were really over the moon about coming down. Yes. Yes. We explained it very carefully to them. It was just sort of one of those things that you had to do.
> *(Mother of boy, age nine, and girl, age thirteen)*

The young people generally accepted their lack of participation in the decision to migrate when it was based on employment factors, such as job relocation. They recognized the need for the family to have an income and understood that parental employment was important for the whole family:

> Naomi: And do you think that you had a say in whether or not you moved?
> David: It was the job. I didn't have a say. But that was all right. I couldn't really.
> *(David, age eighteen)*

In a minority of families the decision to migrate was made quickly, such as when family circumstances suddenly changed. If a parental relationship broke down, as was the case for five families, the migration decision could be made very quickly, even though the relationship may have been failing for some time. Sometimes this prevented children from participating in the decision to migrate, but not always. Children in two out of the five fragmented families expressed a high level of agency and participated in the decision to migrate. In these two families, the style of parenting appeared to differ from that in many of the other families, with negotiations between mothers and children about when and where the family would move. This more equal relationship may be connected to the idea of the child becoming a substitute partner or friend for a parent who is left to raise children alone (Beck and Beck-Gernsheim 2002; Mayall 1994).

In the two fragmented families in which mothers had informed the children of their migration decision, all the children were below the age of nine. In these families, the mothers said that the children had not been told of the reasons for their parents' separation because they wanted to protect the children (another demonstration of the intertwining of parental interpretation of children's best interests with other factors) and because they found the reasons difficult to explain to the children.

If children had not had a high level of agency in making the migration decision, they were sometimes confused about what had motivated the move. There may have been several reasons for this confusion, including the length of time between the migration and our interview. However, it may also have been because the child was not involved when the motivations for the move were discussed or when the advantages and disadvantages of moving had been considered. This lack of involvement sometimes resulted in children blaming parents for the migration, being unsure about the migration process itself, or lacking an understanding of the reasons for the move. This confusion occurred most often in families in which the informed children had migrated primarily because of employment:

Naomi: Can you see why it happened? Why you moved?
Felicity: No.
Naomi: Do you know why you moved to [name of place]?
Felicity: No.
Mum: Oh, you do!
Felicity: No. Why did we move?
Mum: Because Daddy left the army.
    (Felicity, age ten, and mother)

In the majority of the families in which children had been prevented from having a high level of involvement in family migration decision making, parents said that they had tried to weigh the positive and negative consequences of the move for the children specifically; that is, they had considered the children's needs as part of their (parental) decision making. In five of the families, the parents did not consider the impact of the move on the children to be particularly important when they were making the decision to migrate. They considered factors other than children's best interests more important, or they had not thought that migration would have an impact on the children. Research into family migration decision needs to acknowledge that not all families spend a large amount of time considering whether to migrate and what the impact of migration might be on family members. Similarly, research into children's rights and roles in families needs to recognize the multifarious contexts and decision-making situations that children and parents have to negotiate.

Conclusion

Although "the era of the post-family" has been announced (Beck and Beck-Gernsheim 2002), the majority of migrant children in Britain migrate within families (Dobson and Stilwell 2000), and it is important to recognize these contexts for their migrations. An analysis of children's involvement in family migration decision making, using a children-in-families approach, reveals the extent to which children have agency in their families and allows the dynamics of power between family members to be explored (Bushin 2009). Thus, including children in frameworks for researching family migration decision making makes possible more nuanced understandings of these processes. Children-focused researchers have argued that the boundaries between adulthood and childhood have been eroded in recent times, with adults exerting less authority over children than in previous eras (Beck and Beck-Gernsheim 2002; Valentine 2003). Some of the discussion in this chapter has shown that the supposition that children have no involvement in family migration decision making in European contexts is inaccurate, as in almost half the families, children either were consulted or participated in the decision-making process. This finding supports the contention that in some families, child/adult relations are less hierarchical than traditional models of the family would indicate; children's roles have shifted from being seen and not heard to being encouraged to have active agency at times. However, in the majority of families, a traditional style of parenting was practiced and children's agency in family migration decision making was limited because of parents' views of childhood and their perceptions of children's best interests, as well as factors perceived to be less in parents' control.

None of the children interviewed said that they wished that their experiences of decision making had been different. This may suggest that the children were content with their lack of agency and parental decision making on their behalf. However, it may also be the case that children who are not used to having a high level of involvement in decisions that affect their lives are not experienced enough in different practices of parenting and family life to say that they would have liked to have been involved. Children who had experienced higher levels of involvement in making migration decisions, and had been allowed a greater degree of agency, were often more aware of the difficulties of the migration process than children who had been informed of decisions made by parents. However, the children who had participated in making the decision to migrate were not always aware of the full range of factors that motivated parents' initial idea to migrate to rural Devon specifically. Hence, although some children were active in decision making, their agency was not equal to that of their parents.

Contemporary societal trends in Britain and in wider Europe that impact family migration processes—such as increased rates of family fragmentation, family reformulation, debates concerning good schools, and relocation for employment—look set to ensure that migration decision making will remain a complex issue for many families, perhaps necessitating the renegotiation of children's roles and responsibilities. Further research exploring children's agency and involvement in family migration decision making will increase our understanding of the migration experiences of children and adults in Europe and beyond.

Chapter 2

"For Tibet"
Youth, Hip-Hop, and Transforming the Tibetan Global Imaginary

Julia Meredith Hess

On October 30, 2007, I watched Tenzin Norgay, a Tibetan high school student living in Albuquerque, New Mexico, who raps under the name Lazzyboi, perform a song that he had written entitled "Fighting for Tibet" at the Tibetan community center in Santa Fe. Dressed in baggy jeans held up by a belt with a crown-shaped belt buckle, a long orange polo shirt covered by a black jacket, and a backward baseball cap, Tenzin Norgay performed his rhymes in front of a Buddhist altar adorned with a large photograph of the fourteenth Dalai Lama. The audience was composed of his peers and their parents, with a sprinkling of Westerners like myself, seated on the floor of the main gathering space. His performance was recorded by another high school student and subsequently posted on YouTube.

Here are the opening lyrics of the rap by Tenzin Norgay (a.k.a. Lazzyboi):

> yeah yeah yo
> yeah yeah yo
> i have cried and cried
> for all the tibetans that died
> would shout out free tibet
> but never knew what it meant
> so i took a look at his Holiness teachings
> days later i started to repent started to represent

> where im from what i wanted to become
> then people looked at me like i was dumb
> said i knew nothing about freedom
> cant you understand i live in a free land
> so now i stand up proud
> fist in the air
> dont even care if people stare
> u should share the love thats whats its all about
> dont pout if aint going ur route
>   —Tenzin Norgay, a.k.a. Lazzyboi, "Fighting for Tibet"

This chapter considers how Tibetan youth in the diaspora are negotiating the "everyday ruptures" that shape their lives.[1] These youth are often three generations removed from Tibet. Their grandparents are typically of the generation that fled to India soon after the flight of the current Dalai Lama from Tibet to India in 1959. Many of their parents were born, raised, and educated in India and Nepal. These youth—many of whom were born in India—have spent much of their lives in the United States. They make up what I call the "transnational generation." Glick Schiller and Fouron (2001) and Boehm (2008) have used this term in an attempt to move away from the idea that clear-cut distinctions can be made between first-, 1.5-, and second-generation immigrants with attachments to multiple places and experiences in a variety of national contexts. I employ it here for those reasons and also to emphasize the importance of transnational connections and the flow of ideas, technology, and capital that contribute to Tibetan identity as the diaspora has gone global.

The Tibetan youth I profile in this chapter are adept at using an array of influences from the places and institutions that affect their everyday lives and those of their families. These influences include the local communities throughout the United States where they have settled, the Tibetan government-in-exile based in India, the Dalai Lama, and myriad other influences ranging from Hindi film to, as we will see, hip-hop. Remarkably, however, many Tibetan exile youth are driven to channel these influences and ideas into a message and transnational activism to call attention to the struggle over their homeland, Tibet.

Through a focus on agency, especially as it relates to youth, my goal is to highlight the ways in which the ruptures entailed in migration can be continuities in disguise. In other words, while on the face of it, a Tibetan youth who raps in front of an altar dedicated to the Dalai Lama might seem a radical break with Tibetan norms and values, I argue here that we must closely examine the message and the intent of the artist to uncover the cultural continuities in such practices.

Taking Youth Seriously, Putting Agency into Perspective

In her book *Anthropology and Social Theory* (2006), Sherry Ortner has written about the ways in which social theorists expand upon or reject the concept of agency. She writes about the antihumanist bent of some social scientists who ignore agency to give precedence to powerful structures that undergird and constrain individual action and thought in conscious and subconscious ways. Ortner, however, vigorously defends the usefulness of an ethnographic approach to agency, in which we explore the ways individuals transform their social worlds through action. She provides a useful three-part consideration of agency: "The issues involved in defining agency are perhaps best approached by sorting out a series of components: 1) the question of whether or not agency inherently involves 'intentions'; 2) the simultaneous universality and 'cultural constructedness' of agency; and 3) the relationship between agency and power" (2006, 134).

Ortner has important insights about the interrelated nature of two kinds of agency: one that consists of the pursuit of "culturally defined projects," and the other that is about "power," "acting within relations of social inequality, asymmetry, and force" (139), generally associated with resistance. The Tibetan youth I discuss in this chapter are engaging both types of agency. The first is a cultural project related to exile imperatives of preserving one's culture and regaining independence. The second consists of resistance against predominant social forces and institutions within the cultural project and outside of it. The inside power relations that Tibetans resist include the political strategizing of the government-in-exile. The outside power dynamics Tibetans are resisting are related to the structures predominant in U.S. society, China's policies toward Tibet, and Chinese representations of Tibet and Tibetans.

Following Ortner's framework, I first address the intentionality of the Tibetan youth who are producing these cultural performances. Human action always plays out on conscious and unconscious levels. In her discussion of intentionality Ortner writes:

"Intentionality" here is meant to include a wide range of states, both
cognitive and emotional, and at various levels of consciousness,
that are directed forward toward some end. Thus intentionality in
agency might include highly conscious plots and plans and schemes;
somewhat more nebulous aims, goals, and ideals; and finally desires,
wants, and needs that may range from being deeply buried to quite
consciously felt. In short intentionality as a concept is meant to include all the ways in which action is cognitively and emotionally
pointed *toward* some purpose. (2006, 134)

It is clear that the youth I am profiling here do consciously craft a message and choose a particular musical and aesthetic mode in which to
transmit their message. And yet, social scientists since Durkheim have
shown us the ways in which social and structural constraints confine
our actions, discourses, and thoughts in fairly rigid and yet unconscious
ways. For example, Tenzin Norgay may be fairly radical in choosing rap
music, an artistic mode overtly associated with resistance to authority,
to relay his message and perform his Tibetan identity. Or he may just
be using the most appropriate, understandable format to reach his audience. Thus, while to the casual observer it might seem exotic to see a
Tibetan teen rapping in front of an altar dedicated to the Dalai Lama,
when viewed by peers it may seem a logical extension of Tibetan identity being emplaced in new settings in the United States. In addition, to
an anthropologist, it may be a sign of cultural conservatism as Tibetan
youth literally and figuratively rap with the Dalai Lama behind them.
To use the terminology of this volume, while to some it may look like a
rupture, it can be interpreted as a cultural and discursive *continuity dis-
guised as rupture.* When I asked Tenzin Norgay's father what he thought
about his son's chosen means of expression, he replied, "I think it's great,
as long as the message is right," which suggests that as long as the message reiterates specific ideas related to being Tibetan and the issue of Tibet, his father has no problem with his son's using rap as a medium of
expression. As the editors of this volume suggest, migration does entail
rupture, but it is a rupture that at times affords opportunity to express
long-held beliefs and attitudes in new forms that are readily understood
in new contexts. Continuity and rupture are most illuminating when
we consider them not as opposites, but as interlaced with and informing
each other. What I explore in this chapter is how Tibetan youth are using new media and a hip-hop aesthetic to express their identity, whether
they are saying anything new to their parents and grandparents and to

the world at large, and whether their efforts are transforming what I call here the "global Tibetan imaginary."

Second, I address another point Ortner makes: although there is general agreement that agency is universal and "is part of a fundamental humanness," it is also culturally and historically constructed (136). Here I ask how Tibetans culturally and historically construct agency, and how this understanding and practice of agency differs from Western understandings of agency.

Probing Tibetan understandings of karma can help us better understand emic views of agency. While many suppose that Buddhism is synonymous with Tibetan culture and in fact most Tibetans consider themselves Buddhists, the extent to which they practice Buddhism in their everyday lives varies greatly. Yet Buddhism has an undeniable impact on Tibetan values, worldview, and identity in deep yet changeable ways. Among the most important Buddhist concepts that permeate Tibetan outlooks are impermanence (*mi rtag pa*), rebirth (*skye ba blangs*), and karma (*las*). Karma (Sanskrit) is *las* in Tibetan.[2] Directly translated, *las* means "action."

Karma means that "one's actions in this life, or more precisely one's intentional states, have effects in future lives, just as one's fortune in this life results from the karma of one's past actions" (Samuel 1993, 25). As in discussions of agency, the intentionality of the action is important in understanding karma. Unintentional or un- or subconscious action does not carry the same karmic weight as intentional action.

Geoffrey Samuel argues that for Tibetans, unlike Indians, karma is a "foundation for ethics and morality. One should avoid morally bad actions because of their unpleasant consequences in a future life, and cultivate morally good actions that will both help to ensure a good rebirth and provide a sound foundation for eventual escape from the cycle of rebirth" (1993, 378). Similarly, Dorsh Marie DeVoe, who writes about the belief in karma among the Tibetan refugees living in India, emphasizes how karma influences Tibetans' responses to the challenges of everyday life:

> Tibetans say that because they believe in karma, the motivation for hard work, for instance, would not be to change one's material situation, for that hardly has to do with "improving" one's life. Hard work would be a source of contentment in itself, regardless of the material profit it brought. While it may not alter the present stage of being, which [h]as evolved through thousands of reincarnations to

this point, especially if the work is beneficial to others, one can contribute goodness to one's own karma in future lives. The important teaching is that one must accept present circumstances. (1983, 84)

My interviews with Tibetans have confirmed this view of karma and the important teaching "that one must accept present circumstances." The following excerpt is from an interview I conducted with Tsering, a young Tibetan woman raised in India, who was pursuing higher education in Europe:

Sometimes, I used to be very depressed, thinking I have such a hard life. And then I would think, oh my god, it's not a hard life. I would think of my grandparents crossing the Himalayas and I would think that's nothing compared to what I am doing. I think again of what my mom always tells me of the Buddhist idea that you are always better off than so many people that don't have any eyes, or no legs. My mom would always tell me, you know that you are always better off even if you are in the worst state in the world. That has given me a lot of energy and passion for life, because I feel like I am really blessed. There are not many people in Tibetan society who are depressed, because they are happy to have everything and anything that they have.

And they even consider that the Chinese invasion was part of their destiny. They try to get the best of their situation. They are always satisfied. I think that is also one thing unique about Tibetans that I don't find in other cultures—maybe there are in other cultures, but I think it's uniquely Tibetan. Highly satisfied people.

Tsering is expressing an important way that belief in karma orients Tibetan thinking about life: no matter what the circumstances, one should attempt to be happy with what one has. Tsering pairs this idea with overt intentionality and action that in many ways mirror the upwardly mobile migration trajectories of many cosmopolitan youth. In the pursuit of her educational goals, she applied to a range of schools and accepted the one with the best reputation and best financial aid package. In addition, Tsering references the widely shared belief among Tibetans, including the Dalai Lama, that collective Tibetan karma plays a role in the ongoing exile and Chinese occupation of Tibet.

Karma, then, still infuses Tibetan conceptions of agency, but it today must be understood along with other kinds of discourses related to action and intention. Instrumental among these are Western ideas about individualism and progress that have developed in exile schools and an array of other institutions that structure and serve the goals of Tibetan exile life in India and Nepal. In India and Nepal, universal secular education for both boys and girls has become the norm. This educational system combines elements of the British-Indian educational model with a curriculum developed in the Tibetan language. Unlike a traditional Tibetan education, the curriculum does not depend wholly on religious textual sources but incorporates subjects such as science and math. Individual and collective achievement are valued in this system. Scholars of the Tibetan diaspora generally agree that over the last fifty years of exile in South Asia, this educational system, combined with other institutionalized efforts to preserve Tibetan culture, has resulted in a Tibetan identity that links being Tibetan with patriotic feeling and attachment, as well as with an activist commitment to a future democratic Tibet (DeVoe 1983; Nowak 1984; Diehl 2002). For example, in interviews, Tibetan youth in India and the United States voiced professional aspirations and were working assiduously to become doctors, lawyers, and architects—but with an eye to helping make an independent Tibet a reality. Thus, individual achievement is acceptable and laudable if paired with a collectivist commitment to one's people and the imagined future of the polity. In this way, the karma orientation has been infused with Western notions of progress and the estimable potential of individual action, if grounded in honorable intentions of improving life for the collective—which is, of course, a very Buddhist outlook. At least two generations of Tibetan exiles have been taught not only to recognize that individual and collective karma plays a role in their present circumstances of exile, but also to act toward changing these present circumstances, specifically by engaging in political action to regain their lost homeland.

Third, Ortner suggests that we examine the relationship between agency and power. Giddens also emphasizes power as an important aspect of agency: "The connection of 'action' to 'power' can be simply stated. Action intrinsically involves the application of 'means' to achieve outcomes, brought about through the direct intervention of an actor in a course of events"; further "power represents the capacity of the agent to mobilize resources to constitute those 'means.' In this most general sense 'power' refers to the transformative capacity of human action" (Giddens 1993, 108–109). For my purposes here, "transformation" refers to identifiable changes in the way Tibetans talk about themselves and the Tibet issue to themselves and for a range of audiences—to peers, between generations, to outsiders where they live, to the Chinese government and people, and to a global audience through media, particularly the Internet. While it is clear that Tibetans readily adopt new technology, especially in the service of the Tibet movement, I am reluctant to suggest that engagement in what Appadurai (1996) calls the mediascape and the technoscape constitutes agency in and of itself. These youth are adept at using the tools and technology at hand, but to examine agency closely, we must examine to what ends the technologies are put. It is for this reason that I turn to the ways in which Tibetan youth are using new media and technology as a means to transform the ideoscape of Tibet.

Appadurai developed a framework of "scapes" to analyze global processes (1996, 33–36) that is useful for analyzing the various overlapping domains and processes involved in globalization. My goal here is to illuminate the agency behind Tibetans' engagement with the technology, media, economic capital, and ideas that overlap in processes of globalization. They rap and write blogs, use photography, digital recordings, webcams, and the Internet to project themselves onto a global stage. This is not just exposure for its own sake, because these Tibetans have a message and a goal: in these ways they continue to build on the association between identity and political activism that is a crucial aspect of diaspora consciousness.

Although the scapes framework has been critiqued as obscuring agency (Tsing 2000), I agree with Appadurai that engagement with and transformations in these scapes are important in analyses of processes of globalization, yet merely availing oneself of new technology or media does not necessarily reflect agency in the sense that Ortner uses it as a cultural project or a form of resistance to power. In a 2009 interview with MC Rebel, whose work I examine more fully later in the chapter, I asked why he used rap as a medium of expression. He said that not only was rap an essential part of his boyhood exposure to music, but it was a "natural" format for him to use as it is readily understood and appreciated by his peers. Therefore, rather than see the use of rap as innovative, it is important to examine what Tibetans *do* with the technology and media at their disposal. What is the message? Who is the audience? And what are the effects of this work? Looking at another of Appadurai's scapes—the ideoscape—is instructive as we examine the transformative effects of Tibetan agency in diaspora.

Appadurai defines ideoscapes as "concatenations of images, but they are often directly political and frequently have to do with the ideologies of states and the counterideologies of movements explicitly oriented to capturing state power, or a piece of it. These ideoscapes . . . consist of chains of ideas, terms and images including *freedom, welfare, rights, sovereignty, representation, terrorism*, and the master term *democracy*" (1996, 36). Many of these are important elements of the Tibetan ideoscape. The Tibetan ideoscape is global in scope. Because the Dalai Lama has been willing to recognize Chinese sovereignty over Tibet, he and the exile government have represented the Tibet issue as being about freedom of cultural and religious expression, and more generally, human rights. The government-in-exile describes its work as democratizing the Tibetan government and social system in exile. Since 9/11, the government-in-exile has accused the Chinese government of terrorizing Tibetans, while the Chinese government has labeled Tibetan dissidents as terrorists (Hess 2009b). The Tibet movement has represented itself as conscientiously nonviolent in the face of Chinese oppression. Thus, sovereignty, freedom, rights, democracy, terrorism, and nonviolence are all key aspects of the global Tibetan ideoscape. This discursive framework is used extensively throughout the Tibetan diaspora to frame, debate, and expand upon cultural, political, and other developments in more established forms of media, such as newspapers, journals, and radio, and in new media, including blogs, Facebook, YouTube videos, Twitter, and other Internet sources. I propose to explore one particular kind of expression—hip-hop—and the ways in which the message of these young performers utilizes and overlaps with other voices and expressions to reach a global audience.

Local Hip-Hop, Global Hip-Hop

Tibetans are members of an increasingly globalized youth culture, yet their membership is rooted in specifically Tibetan cultural logics as well as local and national understandings and practices. When Tibetans rap, they use a recognized global aesthetic as a platform and a medium to express their ideas (see also Yeh and Lama 2006 on Tibetans and hip-hop). Between 1985 and 1995, hip-hop was well incorporated into mainstream U.S. popular culture (Kitwana 2004).[3] Further, hip-hop has been a global phenomenon since the 1990s. Rap music has long been associated with resistance—in the United States, resistance of African Americans to mainstream white-dominated society, and globally, resistance of marginalized, politically disenfranchised political groups, for example, the Maori in New Zealand, Algerians in France, and Arab-Israelis and Palestinians (see Mitchell 2001). Rap music has joined the mainstream and the ascension of rap stars to celebrity status has led some to assert that rap artists have sold out, largely abandoning their resistant stance for mega-dollars and celebrity. Yet, Kitwana (2004, 2) has written about the underground political elements of hip-hop and the spoken word movement as feeding an emerging political movement.

Thus, it is not surprising that Tibetans are rapping, or that they are creating politicized rap.[4] In 2009, MC Rebel told me that he was drawn to politicized rap and "backpacker rap": "I have more affinity towards politically conscious hip-hop probably because of what is going on in my own country [Tibet], so it becomes more relative to my own comprehension of the world." A closer look at what they are rapping about brings into relief some of the core struggles of Tibetan youth identity politics in diaspora.

Turning once more to the lyrics of Tenzin Norgay, a.k.a. Lazzyboi, we see that "freedom" is an important theme in his music:

> [they] said I knew nothing about freedom
> cant you understand I live in a free land
> so now I stand up proud
> fist in the air

Tenzin Norgay's interest reflects a broader concern with freedom among Tibetan exiles generally. Because Tibetans are stateless, they have been forced outside the margins of discourses that depend on nationalist ideas that link ethnic identity and territory. In their stead, Tibetans have creatively engaged with discourses based on human rights and freedom of cultural and religious expression (see Huber 1997; Iyer 2008; McLagan 1996). The Chinese occupation has forced the Dalai Lama and other exile leaders to express their political vision in new ways. Thus, the Dalai Lama's vision for Tibet does not include independence; rather, he speaks about *interdependence* and making Tibet into a "zone of peace." One could argue that the Dalai Lama's stance is one of political weakness given that the Chinese have repeatedly stated that to begin negotiations on Tibet's status the Dalai Lama must recognize China's sovereignty over Tibet and give up asking for Tibetan independence (see Sperling 2008). This is one view, yet the Dalai Lama has attempted to articulate an alternative vision for Tibet that does not rely on traditional notions of state sovereignty. In this way, the "freedom" and constraints of statelessness have come together in a political vision for the future that is not easily categorized.

In my work with Tibetans in the United States, I have been struck by how often young Tibetans cite individual freedom as an important aspect of their identity. I have noted instances of intergenerational tension between parents who emphasize collective responsibility and children who are internalizing notions of individual freedom of choice. Yet, as Mary Bucholtz has noted, anthropologists have often questioned the easy assumption that "the tension between the tantalizing promises of modernity and the expectations of tradition-minded adults may be thought to create resentment among the young people caught in the middle. . . . Admittedly, youthful challenges to adult authority are widely documented, but the phenomenon is neither so wholeheartedly rebellious nor so intimately connected to modernity" (2002, 531). Her insight is important in the effort to untangle the discursive elements reflected in Tibetan rap and youth expression in general. It is too simple to say this is a generational shift; after all, many of the parents of the transnational generation I am describing here are among the first generations of Tibetans to be educated in exile and many are themselves the beneficiaries and architects of Tibetan identity predicated on deterritorialized identity, modern education, and a cosmopolitan outlook on the world. Although I may be overgeneralizing, the parents are of the generation that established the Tibetan Youth Congress, one of the first Tibetan exile nongovernmental organizations, and one that has been a staunch advocate for Tibetan independence even when the Dalai Lama's position has differed. In this way, they are no strangers to ideas of independence. What is notable in Tenzin Norgay's lyrics, and the ones I will discuss below, are not only the discursive elements that reflect important aspects of the ideoscape, but the surprising way he plays them off each other to give expression to unique meanings. The way I interpret the lyrics of Tenzin Norgay, a.k.a. Lazzyboi, is that the freedom he experiences in the United States underlies his awakening as a Tibetan and his activist leanings; the freedom of a pluralistic democracy obligates him to understand his identity and fight for it on a global stage.

Tenzin Norgay is not alone in using rap as a medium to express his Tibetan identity. As he told me the night I watched him perform, entering the search terms "Tibet" and "rap" into the search engine on YouTube reveals a list of videos made by Tibetan rappers all over the world. There are videos by a young man, Chino, who is part Jamaican, and part Tibetan and lives in London. There are videos of Tibetans rapping at cultural events in New York, and there is ample evidence of a thriving Tibetan hip-hop scene in Germany. For the rest of the chapter I focus on the rap music of a group of three young men in Brooklyn, New York, who call themselves MC Rebel and the Yeti Crew. MC Rebel's lyrics are extensive and rich with meaning. They provide a window into the ways he uses rap to bridge his experience of growing up as a Tibetan in the United States and his consciousness about what this means in terms of action. MC Rebel constructed a rap and video built on will.i.am's song "Yes, We Can!," which gained popularity during President Barack Obama's 2008 election campaign. The expression, in turn, was borrowed from the United Farm Workers' slogan coined by César Chávez and Dolores Huerta in the 1970s, "Sí, se puede!" or "Yes, we can!" MC Rebel adds "Free Tibet!" to the repeated refrain: "Yes, We Can Free Tibet!" In the video, MC Rebel sings: "Three words that will ring coast to coast, and across the globe, followed by two that my people will die for. Tibet will be free." Significantly, the rap begins with a description of daily life in the United States of Amala (Tibetan for "Mother") and Phala (Tibetan for "Father"):

> Amala is going to work, she doesn't have a chance to kiss her
>   babies goodbye
> whenever she leaves her house she's hurt.
> Amala needs to catch the 6 o'clock train, to make it on time
> the train doors close, that's when the toilet seat opens
> she's on her own, cleaning the bathroom while her boss is at a
>   fancy office working
> she left Amala the keys on the table, there's a note and
> "make sure the rooms are spotless, do the laundry."
>
> She got rid of the marks from the time her boss was sweatin'
> she tries her hardest, so that her kids won't see how much
>   their mama's feeling in pain
> it makes you want to quit dreaming, reality is to blame
> she comes back home, her kids are speaking a different
>   language, her reality won't change
> she's trying to manage, but her mentality is getting strange
> feeling like she's babysitting someone else's kid
> her babies almost forgetting how their ancestors used to live
> on the great open plains, the majestic rivers that reveal the
>   future
> the prospective reader will unveil who's the tutor
> life's lessons that we learn

> Amala makes sure her kids know where Tibet *is*, so when they
> grow up they have a place to call their own
> the message that leaves her body whenever the train doors
> close
> she's keeping the struggle alive so her family can survive.

> She found me, remember, when I was losing all hope.

MC Rebel is making sense of the complex migratory trajectory of his familial and social history that reflects his current circumstances and those of thousands of other young Tibetans in the United States. The video skillfully and poignantly pairs images of a monochrome gray New York cityscape and its multicultural pedestrians bundled against the cold with photos of Tibetans living life "on the great open plains, the majestic rivers that reveal the future," representing the way of life his grandparents were forced to leave behind. As the lyrics attest, the experience of Tibetans in the United States is similar to that of other recent immigrants: in their pursuit of the American dream, parents work low-paying jobs, often in the service sector, and struggle to meet the needs and burgeoning material desires of their children.

> Phala turns off the TV
> news reporters don't know the situation in Tibet; they can't
> deceive me
> Phala said I spoke to my relatives, they living in constant
> threat, yet they still tease me
> "Yes, I am a millionaire, my sons and daughter are doing fine,
> growing up here." He hangs up the phone, goes back to his
> taxicab job
> His sons are out drinking, daughter's not listening, he looks at
> the rearview mirror, right now his life is kind of hard

The next passage refers to one of the most distinctive markers of Tibetan exile identity, the longing to return to Tibet:

> Another customer enters his cab, they never ask Phala where
> he wants to go
> the land that's always in his dreams, his eyes become his
> camera, images brought back when he's feeling sad, Tibet
> is the place he wants his children to grow

> Phala! Your kids are asking why they are being teased at
> school and this building feels like prison. "Do you really
> want to live here when you get old?" Phala smiles as if he's
> hiding something, and said, "They tease because they are
> jealous of who you are, and when imprisoned, your mind
> is free, reminding you, you should never forget who you
> are." As the taxi door close
> Phala drives off, nope Phala hasn't lost hope!

At this point in the video we see brutal images of the unrest that
unfolded in Tibetan areas of China in March 2008. Images of burning
cars, fleeing Tibetans, ranks of police dressed in riot gear, and bloody
Tibetan corpses are graphic reminders of the grim conditions in Tibet
under Chinese rule. MC Rebel's lyrics reflect a number of ideas discussed
earlier in the section on karma and agency. Although MC Rebel is talking about the complicated and often paradoxical realities of life in the
diaspora in conjunction with a bleak picture of contemporary Tibet, he
sings: "Phala hasn't lost hope." The song continues with the refrain, "Yes,
We Can Free Tibet! Yes, We Can Free Tibet!"

Next, MC Rebel raps specifically about what it's like being a Tibetan
in the United States:

> I'm making the proper adjustments
> my family is back home, submitted my college applications
> now admitted as a freshman
> Atlas Shrugged when the weight was too heavy. Now the
>   burden is placed on my backbone
> I guess, I stopped, today I am not ready to do this all alone
> Madness. I dropped, fell in the bathroom stall, going crazy,
>   looked in the mirror, who do I call my own? My parents
>   tell me I'm Tibetan, everyone else tells me I'm Chinese
> Embarrassed to tell people I am Tibetan. You should be proud
>   of your nationality, Amala, you don't have to remind me
> but sometimes the pressure, is too great, I feel everybody
>   about to swarm me
> I ran out the stall, my older brother should have warned me
> They tear you down and try to hurt your pride
> When you have nothing else, that's exactly when your Tibetan
>   side seems to shine.

In the following stanza we see the explicit linking of Tibetan identity with activism. MC Rebel describes the burgeoning motivation and strength that transforms a young Tibetan into an activist willing to take a stand for Tibet:

> Took a taxi going nowhere. Phala, I have the opportunity to
>   get an education.
> Gather the Family
> Tibet will go there
> the community, in front of the Chinese embassy.
> The protests have stopped
> I emerge with a fist in the air
> everyone follow me.
> Three words that will give us hope, followed by two that will
>   become a reality
> Three words that will ring coast to coast, and all across the
>   globe, followed by two that my people have died for.
> Tibet will be free. Let's make this a reality. Let's make this a
>   reality.

Sovereignty and Violence in the Tibetan Global Imaginary

MC Rebel's music does more than reference the current local, lived experience of Tibetans in the United States; in another video published on YouTube entitled "Yeti Mixed Tape," he and the Yeti Crew are also addressing a global audience:

> Check it out, check it out.
> This here goes out to all the people who really don't know
>   what Tibetans are going through in their own country.
> Thinking Tibetans are enjoying foreign rule.
> Yall are so wrong. So wrong.

Here, the global incorporates the other who might not know about Tibet, or who might have a pro-Chinese view, but importantly, the global now includes others like themselves: fellow diasporic Tibetans who may reside in Santa Fe, London, Berlin, Dharamsala, or Kathmandu. The rappers are talking to themselves: sometimes repeating the messages of their parents and the Dalai Lama (don't lose faith in humanity, don't hate the Chinese, remain Tibetan) and sometimes jettisoning them:

> My mama tells me to try to keep my faith in human beings.
> Situation has gotten worse in Tibet it seems.
> Living free in Tibet could be more than just dreams.
> Present our state of beings to governments abroad and go the
>   hardest, regardless if China is the largest.
> If they use guns, and all we have is words, we'll still be the
>   strongest.
> Take it to the next level, in my raps. Be like Pun the rawest
>   hardcore artist
> Flawless poetry, words aligned in perfect symmetry.

In his book *The Open Road* (2008), Pico Iyer writes that the Dalai Lama is an architect of new and innovative political discourse who brings a distinctly Buddhist perspective to his articulation of the Tibet issue. Tibetans in general are exceeding the bounds of traditional nationalist discourse by virtue of the limitations of their statelessness. Thus, when the Dalai Lama speaks of the interdependence of China and Tibet, he is using a Buddhist term to articulate a political and cultural reality. Looking closely at these rap lyrics, however, I have been struck by how these young Tibetans are articulating very traditional notions of state sovereignty in their desire to make a case for Tibetan independence, and at the same time are rejecting violence as a means to achieve their political ends.

The lyric "Present our state of beings to governments abroad" reflects recognition of the importance of sovereignty, in this instance not for Tibet itself, but with respect to Tibet's appeal to the international community. MC Rebel is playing an ambassadorial role, saying that Tibetans should continue to press their case in the international community, that they have right on their side, and that in the end truth will triumph over might. One of the responsibilities for Tibetans in exile is to speak and act for Tibetans in Tibet whose voices are muted. In this performance he expresses some ambivalence about his role in this regard, but the performance itself functions as this kind of act. Further, it seems that there is an imperative, implicit in many kinds of rap music, to "take it to the next level," to push the limits of creative, lyrical, and poetic expression and, ultimately, create change in the world.

One of the central debates and fissures among Tibetan exiles is the political utility of the Dalai Lama's Middle Way, which is characterized by appeasement and the desire to negotiate with the Chinese. In his 1988 Strasbourg Proposal, the Dalai Lama effectively gave up his call for Tibetan independence, declaring that he would accept "genuine autonomy" for Tibet under a sovereign Chinese state. Many young Tibetans who have grown up in secular democratic states have come to separate the Dalai Lama's role as a spiritual leader from his role as a temporal leader of the Tibetan people, thus finding it easier to disagree with him in terms of strategy for regaining their homeland. For example, they refuse to give up the dream of independence, yet they still revere him as the Bodhisattva of Compassion.

In Tibet, writers and bloggers have been removed from their jobs, had their writings censored, and been subjected to house arrest and imprisonment. The most prominent is Woeser, a Tibetan-Chinese writer based in Beijing. Her book *Notes on Tibet* thrust her into prominence as an intellectual who dared to criticize the Chinese government's treatment of Tibetans. She writes a blog, frequently switching servers to evade a government shutdown of her vehicle of expression. One important result of globalization and the confluence of both the Internet and the expansion of the Tibetan diaspora is that there are more possibilities for Tibetans in China and those in diaspora to be in conversation with one another through various media and actions on the ground. At no time was this more evident than during the 2008 protests that began in Lhasa and quickly spread all over the world against the backdrop of the buildup to the Beijing Olympics.

There has been increasing restlessness among Tibetan youth, some of whom are questioning the Dalai Lama's Middle Way and nonviolence as the most effective strategy for gaining the world's attention for the situation in Tibet (see Iyer 2008 and Mishra 2005 for journalistic accounts of this phenomenon and Norbu 2008 for an example of Tibetan writings on the subject). Protests erupted in March 2008 after police cracked down on monks who were protesting nonviolently in the Tibet Autonomous Region of China. The uprising quickly spread to other ethnically Tibetan regions of China. Some Tibetans turned to violence—principally looting and burning Chinese shops and goods. According to an Amnesty International briefing to the United Nations Committee on the Elimination of Racial Discrimination regarding China: "There are huge discrepancies between the official accounts on the unrest and external observers. For the number of deaths, the Chinese authorities reported that one Tibetan 'insurgent' was killed and another 20 people were killed by violent protestors, the Tibetan Centre for Human Rights and Democracy documented more than 120 Tibetans dead from unnecessary or excessive use of force by the police and military, and the Tibetan Government in Exile put the estimate at 220" (Amnesty International 2009). The Chinese media made much of the violent nature of Tibetan actions, while many in the Western media characterized the Tibetan response as a natural reaction after almost fifty years of pent-up anger and frustration over Chinese domination and subsequent human rights abuses in Tibet. The Dalai Lama unequivocally denounced the violence and exhorted Tibetans to stick to peaceful means in their struggle. Tibetans recognize the role a romanticized portrayal of them as highly realized spiritual and inherently nonviolent beings plays in their movement. Further, they understand the moral weight of nonviolence in relation to the rightness of their cause. Yet there are some Tibetan intellectuals as well as youth willing to put the violence option on the table. The most prominent of these voices is that of Jamyang Norbu, an influential Tibetan writer and intellectual now living in the United States. Norbu, whose age qualifies him as an elder, was one of the first exiles to articulate a stance that differs from that of the Dalai Lama and the government-in-exile in substantive ways. In a 2008 essay posted on his blog, he reflected on the question of violence in the Tibetan struggle:

> Tibetan[s] need to ask why the Palestinian issue and the conflict in Afghanistan, with their fanatics, suicide bombers, terrorists, warlords, mullahs, jihadists, and just plain murdering lunatics, receive far more attention and support than the Tibetan issue ever has? Is it possible that violence or even the threat of violence is what actually motivates the world and organizations as the United Nations to take an issue seriously? Could it be that if your struggle is a declaredly non-violent one then it can be quite safely put on the back burner, or even completely forgotten, without any problem?
>
> Don't get me wrong. I am not advocating terrorism. I am all for people being peace-loving and compassionate. But if we want to be like that we should be so out of genuine moral conviction, not as a roundabout way to ingratiate ourselves with the Chinese Communist dictators (who are anyway much too cynical to fall for anything as feeble as that) or to entice sponsors in the West, where, more often than not, it has worked—up to now. (Norbu 2008)

Many young Tibetans in both India and the United States are sympathetic with Norbu's ideas. They are frustrated with China's iron-fisted rule in Tibet. They are dismayed that although the international community professes alarm at Chinese actions in Tibet, neither the United Nations nor any state is willing to take substantive action. Thus, some wonder if violence would at least gain the world's attention and underline the seriousness of their endeavor. However, many fear that violence would jeopardize their moral high ground. Rap is often seen as a mode of expression that glorifies violence, yet all the raps I have listened to by young Tibetans articulate a view that violence is both untenable in the face of Chinese might and a morally indefensible position. At the same time, Tibetan rappers are adamantly rejecting the romanticized view of Tibetans as passive victims. In this way, the definition and portrayal of violence in the Tibetan global imaginary continues to be an issue, and one that, according to MC Rebel, "we must discuss openly. Before we can even talk about independence versus autonomy, we need to talk about violence." As MC Rebel said when I asked him about Tibetans addressing the issue of violence in their cause:

> I am trying to remember what I said in one of my YouTube rap videos, something to the effect that if we use violence then we'd be far worse than them. I mentioned how we need to follow in the footsteps of Gandhi and MLK. I referred to them as this god in human form. Both successfully addressed the recurrent problems in their community through nonviolence; we can do just as much! What's the point of going back? There have been many talks on fighting for independence or [relying] on a notion of limited self-autonomy. However, before we begin talking of our desired goals we must look at the methodologies of how we plan to get there and for that to occur, it is pivotal for us to address violence first. Violence doesn't solve anything; like His Holiness the Dalai Lama always says, we can't battle hatred with guns, we must ultimately battle it with love.

Bucholtz reminds us in her review essay on the anthropological literature on youth and violence that it is essential to examine youth not just as victims of violence (who often in turn become perpetrators), but as intimately involved in the cultural politics of violence (2002, 534). In the rap songs I have analyzed, violent tactics are considered but ultimately rejected as antithetical and ultimately harmful to the Tibetan cause. Here's MC Rebel:

Stardom? Sort of came from the bottom, yall could feel my pain.
We're thinking alike, you and I, we probably share the same
brain. My mind's insane. Cuz I want to put all the Chinese
officials in the guillotine, their heads I want to decapitate.
But I need to rise above this way of thinking. Become David Blaine
and try to levitate, find an escape, alternate mode of living.
But my mind has been jerked back and forth, so my thoughts are
raped.

It is notable that MC Rebel voices the graphic description of imagined violence against the Chinese only to jettison it. He then likens the violent struggle with these ideas in his own mind to "rape." In this way, he seems to be wrestling with portrayals of Tibetans as victims, but also presenting himself as a (potentially) strong actor. In this way, MC Rebel's rap expresses a range of contradictions with respect to violence: he is playing with ideas, using strong language to convey the strength of his ideas and feelings, then deliberately choosing a nonviolent approach reflecting the philosophical approach to nonviolence of Mahatma Gandhi and Martin Luther King built on the premise that only through peaceful means can a movement produce the desired ends.

Another audience for Tibetan hip-hop is the Chinese leadership and people themselves. The 2008 protests and subsequent media coverage resulted in a fiery nationalistic response by Chinese people both in China and abroad who staged counterprotests on many university campuses and who are also using the Internet—comments on journalists' pieces and blogs—to oppose Tibetan claims to cultural distinction and former political independence (Osnos 2008). MC Rebel told me that he had received a large number of comments on his YouTube videos from Chinese people condemning his view of Chinese rule in Tibet. I speculate that Tibetan rappers and other artists in the diaspora will begin to address the Chinese government and Chinese people more directly in their work. One example from MC Rebel comes at the very end of the rap: "Hard-hearted brothers better fear that we don't turn into them."

Conclusion

It was one of the express intentions of the exile government to increase the political power of the diaspora when its members agreed to seek out and support Tibetan migration to the West (Hess 2009a). Giddens's and

Ortner's insistence that we look at agency as it relates to power and its intentional effects leads me to ask in what ways the discourse of young Tibetans I have described has transformed the global Tibetan imaginary. The responses of the Tibetan diaspora to the March 2008 uprising and the continued protests around the Beijing Olympics are a testament to the increased political capital Tibetans in the United States and elsewhere in the West have developed over the last decades. Tibetans who rap are using a new aesthetic to frame ideas that are already circulating among the transnational generation. Rap is readily associated with resistance, and for this reason it is especially appealing to Tibetan youth. Rather than resisting primarily dominant white society in the United States, however, Tibetans are resisting romanticized notions of themselves, Chinese claims, and what they see as a weak political stance of the Dalai Lama and the government-in-exile. This kind of agency can be misunderstood or misrepresented by those who fail to look closely at the historical, sociocultural, and political contexts and the messages these youth are sending. We must further ask to what extent this agency exhibits Giddens's requirement of "transformative capacity." Are these ideas penetrating elite Tibetan discourse?

In the midst of the recent protests and the media discussion of the restlessness of Tibetan youth, which included comments on the possible usefulness of violent tactics, the Dalai Lama addressed these concerns: "Yes, it is true now a . . . sort of feeling of frustration growing among Tibetan[s] is understandable. So, the criticism toward my stand also increasing. Sometimes they won't listen to my suggestions or my advice. But, of course, I respect—you see, they are utilizing freedom of speech, freedom of heart. I'm always telling them I have no authority to say, 'Shut up.' It is up to you" (Australian Broadcasting Corporation 2008). The Dalai Lama's speech contains references to what I suggest are increasingly important features of the Tibetan ideoscape as the diaspora expands in the United States—freedom of speech, as well as respect for independent individual action. The most important indication of the power of youth responses and interventions in Tibetan discourse was the Special Meeting in Dharamsala in November 2008. The Dalai Lama called this meeting, which was attended by more than five hundred delegates from all over the Tibetan diaspora to debate the utility of continuing with the decades-old Middle Way strategy, as it had not advanced the Tibetan cause with the Chinese. Tenzin Tsundue, a self-described "youth" and vocal political activist, reported on the outcome of the meeting:

The Meeting resolved to follow the Middle Path as a public mandate but decided to suspend with immediate effect, sending delegations to China, as Beijing did not reciprocate appropriately to the dialogue process. If, in the short period they continued their policy of not responding to our efforts to find a negotiated solution, we would reinstate Independence as the goal of the Tibetan struggle and demand the right of Self Determination. And it would be us who would [decide] what "short period" would be.

The eight-point resolution received five standing ovations and brought tears in the eyes of many delegates as we rose to sing the Tibetan National Anthem, we felt once again reunited for one common cause under one leadership. Whatever we spoke for was all for the freedom of Tibet and our main concern was for our brethren inside Tibet who are living under Chinese occupation. The exile government and the people will now be more active in our non-violent struggle and stop being conciliatory. We will now be more confrontational and aggressive, but we are unanimous in our resolve in maintaining our struggle non-violent. (Tsundue 2008)

The Dalai Lama, the first generations of Tibetan exiles, and the transnational generation are together producing an ever-evolving Tibetan ideoscape that incorporates more and more ways to be Tibetan as the diaspora expands, and at the same time reflects complex cosmopolitan or global forms of being Tibetan. Yet more than just reflecting identity processes, ideoscapes are, as Appadurai reminds us, explicitly political and strategic. In this way, we can see that identity production is inextricably linked to collective imaginings of a world with a place in it for Tibet.

PART II

Social Reproduction: Family and Kinship across Borders and Generations

Chapter 3

Transnational Fosterage

The Novel Care Arrangements between Guinean Caregivers and Ivorian and Liberian Children Fleeing War

Susan Shepler

> Globally, there is growing evidence that many separated refugee children are not embraced within programmes providing care and protection or family tracing. In many contexts, there are large numbers of boys and girls who have become separated from their families and have never come into contact with agencies or interventions to assist them. These children may be living within their extended family network, or with others who fall outside their traditional system of care, such as unrelated families, groups of peers or siblings, or on their own. Some may be living, for example, as street children within their own countries or in the cities of neighbouring states. Others may provide domestic service for strangers, in exchange for food or shelter, or work as farm labourers in areas bordering refugee camps.
>
> —Gillian Mann, "Not Seen or Heard: The Lives of Separated Refugee Children in Dar es Salaam"

Starting in 1989, conflict has affected the nations of Liberia, Sierra Leone, Guinea, and Côte d'Ivoire. The effects of these interrelated conflicts have overrun national boundaries; flows of resources, armed combatants, and refugees have made this a subregional issue. Hundreds of thousands of people in West Africa have fled across borders to escape war. A large fraction of these refugees are children. Many unaccompanied children, rather than seeking shelter in camps, seek support wherever they find it, perhaps from international extended family or ethnic networks, perhaps from strangers. Especially in the early stages of a migration crisis, during periods of self-resettlement, fleeing children turn to such solutions out of necessity and are frequently absorbed into communities.

This chapter focuses on a set of children who fled war in their own country (either Côte d'Ivoire or Liberia) and ended up separated from their families and spontaneously settling with Guinean families.[1] In the sample studied, Liberians were in the minority, trickling into this part of Guinea over a decade of conflict. The majority, from Côte d'Ivoire, had fled during a spike in the conflict that lasted several weeks in 2002. At the time of my interviews, more than three years had passed since they left their homes.

A handful of personal stories from children and their foster care-givers about how they met and arranged their fostering relationships introduce the population and foreshadow some of the themes I discuss later.

> I was in school when we heard gun sounds. The teachers released us to go home. I ran to the house, but I couldn't find anyone. I saw some people running, so I joined the group. We took the Guizé road, that is, we passed through the bush. In the bush we came upon a small village. The people I came with joined a vehicle and left me there. I started crying. Someone in the village called me over and said I could spend the night. I explained my story to him and said, "I will live with you and work so you can feed me." After a few months, the man asked if I had been attending school before. The man brought me to Nzoo to register me for school. The whole time the man was afraid that my parents would come and accuse him of stealing their child.
>
> *(A sixteen-year-old boy from Côte d'Ivoire)*

> When the war came, I was at home, but my father and mother were out. My neighbor said, "Let's find somewhere to go," and we came together all the way to Nzoo. My neighbor was from Kaolenta near Nzoo. The woman continued on, and left me in Kaolenta. I was sitting in the market in Kaolenta, wondering what to do. I went and sat next to a woman who was selling and explained my problem. The woman said, "OK, you can come and stay with me."
>
> *(A fifteen-year-old girl from Côte d'Ivoire)*

Three years ago, I went to the waterside to wash dishes and I found four boys there crying. I had some extra rice in one of my pans so I gave it to them to eat and asked what was wrong. They explained that they had fled from Côte d'Ivoire with a group of people but had been left behind and now they didn't know where their parents were. I said, "OK, you can come and live with me until we can find your parents." That was three years ago and they are still with me.

(A thirty-year-old woman with two children of her own, born and raised in Guinea)

We were going to the football field to play. I saw a boy; his feet were swollen. The boy explained his situation. I took him home and fed him and decided to keep him.

(A thirty-year-old man from Guinea)

In a crisis situation, unaccompanied children may have no other option but to join existing households. Throughout war-affected West Africa, legions of children separated from their families or rejected by their communities have found new homes with foster parents. The ability of people within communities to absorb unaccompanied children and the relative ease of these transactions is remarkable, especially for people who are themselves struggling with poverty and the disruptive effects of subregional warfare. It is clear that child fosterage has been vital to knitting together the West African postwar social fabric.

The editors of this volume state that "every migration . . . includes some form of rupture, as well as the constancy of daily life." The questions we address in this book are: How do rupture and "the everyday" coexist? How can we understand each through the lens of the other? What can a rich understanding of the domestic realities of wartime teach us about war, and what can the everyday strategies of survival in the face of rupture teach us about culture? This task is part of a recent movement in anthropology toward extending ethnography into realms of conflict. Carolyn Nordstrom (2004, 2006), in particular, has been a pioneer in both documenting lived war experiences from the ground up and analyzing them through the lens of anthropological theory and political economy (see also Greenhouse, Mertz, and Warren 2002). As the introduction to this volume states, we are interested in cultural production in the midst of cultural change.

While anthropologists have turned toward the study of war, there have also been movements toward a fresh anthropology of childhood

(Best 2007; Hirschfeld 2002; James and James 2004; James, Jenks, and Prout 1998) and even an anthropology of children and war (Boyden 2004; Das and Reynolds 2003; Korbin 2003). In this framework, childhood is seen as a social construction (albeit one with some basis in biology) and children are understood as agents rather than objects. These anthropological approaches to childhood are in response to the more standard discourses on the children who are the topic of this study.

Two Hegemonic Frameworks

The primary, and most powerful, framework for understanding the children in this study is the international human rights framework.[2] This framework underlies actions by UN agencies such as the UN High Commissioner for Refugees (UNHCR), charged with care of refugees, and the UN Children's Fund (UNICEF), charged with care of children, and the child protection nongovernmental organizations (NGOs) working with them.

National boundaries in Africa, though vitally important in many ways, are often arbitrary and easily traversed by those living near them. In particular, national boundaries often cut through ethnic boundaries. Studies of African culture point to a complex structuring of identity, at times strategically referencing nation, at other times referencing ethnicity, clan, gender, or other forms of social membership. Moreover, there are long-standing cross-border ties and kinship relations throughout this region, and indeed throughout much of Africa. However, international aid agencies often make policy as if nationality were the primary element of identity. In her analysis of the Liberian influx into Sierra Leone in 1990 and 1991, Melissa Leach concluded: "Whilst agencies focused on nationality, host-refugee relations were structured according to differential geographical, kinship and ethno-linguistic boundaries of local and sub-regional importance" (1992, iii). For local people, historical and recent cross-border ties, kinship relations, and prevailing attitudes toward strangers make informal refugee settlement an obvious approach.

Although the field of refugee studies has been turning toward self-settlement and refugee-host relations in informal settlement (Andrews 2003; Gale 2006; Jacobsen 2001; Leach 1992), the camp setting is still the primary site for the study of refugees. Within this framework, children are primarily understood as victims, and the role of agencies is child protection. The framework is also built on national sovereignty, and therefore national borders. As a result, after the care and feeding of separated children, the next most important task is to return them to their families and countries of origin.

Within the human rights framework, the Convention on the Rights of the Child (CRC) is the universal standard, and it is rare in practice to try to understand child protection needs from a local perspective. Rather, too often a normalizing notion of the "best interests of the child" silences local people and fails to acknowledge alternate solutions. As Mann concludes: "Understanding a particular culture or community's definition and goals for child development has not yet been the focus of research with separated children" (2004, 15).

That said, fosterage is of increasing interest to child protection policy makers. In addition to its importance in postwar settings, the system of child fosterage is also of increasing interest in parts of Africa where AIDS is devastating adult populations and children are forced into novel living arrangements. In particular, there is growing agreement that separated children are best cared for in a community setting rather than in institutions (Tolfree 2003).

However, even when the effectiveness of community care is acknowledged, there is still often a call for external monitoring and a fundamental mistrust of the social institution of fostering, as the following quote aptly illustrates: "In the light of anthropological knowledge about traditional patterns of fostering, . . . some traditional forms of substitute family care are not based on the best interest of the child and may both have negative impact on child development and infringe on children's rights . . . ; fostering programs need to be firmly embedded in the local community and supported by an agency with a solid knowledge of child development and child rights" (Tolfree 2003, 5).

Agencies' primary concern is that fostered children are treated differently from biological children, particularly in the areas of forced labor, differential access to health care and other family resources, and educational inequity between fostered and nonfostered children. Based on a study of education of orphans in Africa, Kobiané, Calvès, and Marcoux (2005, 472, 474), cite conflicting results on schooling of nonrelative children in West Africa. They cite Pilon 1995 and Kobiané 2003 to claim: "Studies in the West African cities of Lomé in Togo and Ouagadougou in Burkina Faso show that school attendance rates are lower among children of other relatives, as compared with the children of the household head. Those who are worst off, in terms of school attendance, are children living with nonrelatives . . . ; children residing in households headed by nonparental relatives or nonrelatives are less likely to attend school, and this is particularly true for girls" (472). On the other hand, they cite Nyangara, who reports that "paternal orphans in Namibia and maternal orphans in Mozambique and Nigeria were more significantly likely to enroll in school than non-orphans" (2004, 33). They further cite Foster et al., who state that "the majority of orphaned children were being cared for satisfactorily within extended families, often under difficult circumstances. . . . There was little evidence of discrimination or exploitation of orphaned children by the extended family caregivers" (1995, 474). Clearly, there is no consensus from the research on the effects of fosterage on child rights outcomes, but there is continuing concern about the potential for abuse.

In summary, the international human rights framework is based on a system of national sovereignty, takes international standards of care as a starting point for child protection, and is ambivalent at best regarding local solutions to crisis.

The second major framework for understanding the children in this study is the academic study of fosterage. Here, the emphasis is not on prescribing solutions for war-affected children but on describing cultural forms of child exchange. "Fosterage" is an umbrella term for a number of different types of relationships, generally involving the exchange of children within an extended family or outside the extended family, in the case of craft apprenticeship. Kobiané, Calvès, and Marcoux describe several types of fostering: "kinship fostering, crisis fostering, alliance and apprentice fostering, domestic fostering, and educational fostering" (2005, 473). The practice of fostering is quite common in West Africa and has been written about extensively in the anthropological literature on family structure in West Africa (Bledsoe 1990a, 1990b, 1993; Goody 1982; Schildkrout 1973) and elsewhere (Fonseca 2003). Most recent studies of child fosterage in West Africa have been based in demography (Ainsworth 1996; Isiugo-Abanihe 1985), public health (Oni 1995), or economics (Eloundou-Enyegue and Stokes 2002), often addressing the pressures to the system of child fosterage that grow out of economic breakdown. Notermans supports my reading of the field: "In the 1990s demographers picked up the anthropological interest in fosterage, but instead of focusing on kinship structures they looked at three other domains of social life in Africa: the relationship between fosterage and high fertility . . . , the relationship between fosterage and high infant mortality . . . , and the relationship between fosterage and schooling. . . . An economic approach

based on analyses of costs-and-benefits characterises these three domains of interest" (2004, 49). From the demographic literature, it is clear
that the practice of child fosterage is widespread throughout West Africa (from 25 percent to 40 percent of children are fostered, as reported
in various studies).[3] From the economic literature, some of the reasons
for fostering are to increase family unity, to spread the burden and the
benefits of child rearing throughout an extended family, and for access to
education or training. These studies have mainly investigated fostering
as an exchange between adults, with the desires of the children involved
as an afterthought, if at all.

The type of fostering discussed in these studies is generally kinship
fostering, and therefore national boundaries are unimportant. Children are easily sent back and forth across borders to members of their
extended family. This presumption about fosterage colored the assumptions of those making policy around the separated children at the heart
of this study. The assumption was, especially on the part of UNHCR,
that any children fostered in Guinea must already be settled with members of their extended families or at least with members of ethnic networks. However, the circumstances of fosterage in this case are quite different than the two frameworks I have outlined would lead one to expect.
I refer here to *emergency* fosterage, involving an agreement between an
adult and a child rather than the usual agreement between two adults.
This is a completely new phenomenon for academic study, and it speaks
to the central concern of this volume: social reproduction in times of crisis, everyday ruptures.

Methods

This research project started due to a disagreement between UNHCR
and UNICEF. As I have noted, UNHCR was reluctant to admit that a
large group of refugees were living unregistered along the border region.
Their legal definition of refugee indeed made this impossible (a refugee
must present him or herself and be registered within a set period of time
after crossing a national border). UNICEF, on the other hand, had been
hearing reports of large numbers of separated children and wanted to
document their presence. They saw the issue as one of child protection.
Guinean government ministry officials and Guinean nationals working
in local NGOs agreed that there was a large population of children who

had fled from conflict in villages along the border, but admitted that they had no resources to register them or address their needs and left the definitional squabbles to the bigger players.

This research was originally carried out at the behest of UNICEF, which accordingly influenced the research questions and methods. In general, it meant starting from a rights-based approach, and thinking about policy-relevant results.[4] In particular, it meant focusing on issues of child labor, access to education, and other rights outcomes. What I present here is a distillation of the results several years later, with different questions in mind.

The flows of refugees from Sierra Leone, Liberia, and Côte d'Ivoire made the southeast region of Guinea (Guinée Forestière) an ideal area in which to carry out this research. Rather than survey the whole area, the research plan was to pick one village close to the border and try to identify as many cases of "transnational stranger fosterage" as possible, and in the process gain insight into questions for possible future research. After conversations with child protection NGOs in the area, I selected the village of Nzoo primarily because I was told that it would be easy to tell the Ivorians from the Guineans there, and that most had never registered with any agency because they had passed through the bush and settled in the village close to the border. Nzoo is just east of Nzérékoré, near the border with Côte d'Ivoire (see Figure 1). Of course, one weakness of the method is that I do not know what happened to children who were unhappy with their living arrangements and left town, or to those who may have already returned to Côte d'Ivoire.

I hired two research assistants, one to translate from French to English (he also spoke Mano, Malinké, and Peul) and one a local community activist with strong ties to the community (he spoke Kono—the primary language in Nzoo—as well as Yakouba and Mano.) In Nzoo and environs, our three-person research team conducted 120 interviews, of which approximately half were with children and half with caregivers. We conducted many of the child interviews with the eldest sibling of a set of siblings, giving a population of about a hundred children. After discarding outliers, there were 150 data points—fifty-six caregivers and ninety-four children.

Cognizant of the latest theories of how to ethically conduct research with war-affected youth (Boyden 2004; Das and Reynolds 2003; Mann and Tolfree 2003), in each case I interviewed the child and the foster parent about their arrangement. We separated the child and the parent for

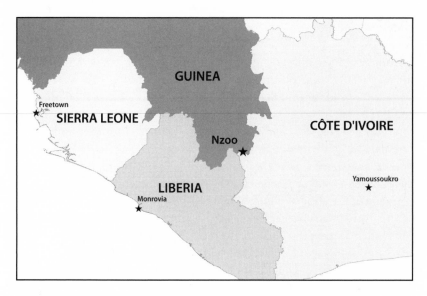

Figure 1. Map of Guinea and bordering countries. (Map courtesy of BBC News.)

interviews. We explained that I was not registering them for benefits but merely conducting research and wanted to hear their stories. I did not record the names of participants.

Questions for caregivers:
Why did you take in this child?
Have you been satisfied with the child's behavior?
Would you be more likely to take in a child: From your own ethnic group or nationality? A boy or a girl? Of what age? Who is attending school?
What sort of assistance would make it more likely for people like you to foster unaccompanied children?

Questions for fostered children:
How did you find your foster caregivers?
Did you search for someone of your own ethnicity? Nationality?
What are your plans for the future? Do you hope to return to your community or do you want to stay where you are? Why?

Findings

The shape of the children's age distribution was bimodal, with one hump for very young children and one for adolescent children. The first hump represents children who fled war three years ago, essentially before they could talk. Their consequent lack of knowledge of their homes has meant that they have had no choice but to stay in Guinea. The other hump represents children who are in Guinea to complete their schooling. Some of these may have a place they could return to in Côte d'Ivoire, but they have chosen to stay in Guinea for the functioning schools.[5]

Most of the children interviewed were Ivorian and had fled from the conflict three years earlier. Some gave "Guinean" as their nationality because their father was born in Guinea, although perhaps their mother was Ivorian or Liberian and they had most likely never visited Guinea before the conflict. A handful of children had fled Liberia as much as eight years earlier. The caregivers were mostly Guinean, with a few Ivorians who had fled with previously unknown children they met on the way.

The hypothesis was that people would be more likely to foster a child from the same (or related) ethnicity. I grouped similar ethnic groups by language, across borders. (By similar, I mean that the language is often mutually intelligible, or that people said in interviews, "I am Guerzé . . . or Kono—it's the same thing.") Most of the population of both children and caregivers were of the primary ethnic group in the area (Kono-Guerzé-Yakouba). Due to the ethnic makeup in the sending and receiving areas, there are more Dioula children (the primary name of the related ethnic groups in Côte d'Ivoire) and more Kono and Mano caregivers (the primary names of the related ethnic groups in Guinea).

Most members of the sample were strangers before they met in a crisis situation.[6] To the question, "How did you meet the child?" caregivers responded:

60%   Met them here in Guinea.
23%   We knew each other before.
16%   I saw them in Côte d'Ivoire when I was running.

Simply due to the prevalence of one ethnicity in the cross-border area, we would assume a certain percentage of pairings to be between caregivers and children of the most populous group. Indeed, even a random pairing with the same population of caregivers and children would yield

40 percent same-ethnicity pairings. If we look at the actual data on ethnicity of child-caregiver pairs, we see that 62 percent of the time, the child and caregiver were of the same ethnicity (if ethnicity is grouped as outlined earlier).[7] This figure shows a slight preference for same ethnicity fostering, but not a hard rule. Indeed, some of this preference can be explained by the relative ease of communication between children and caregivers who speak the same language. However, at least one refugee child expressly sought out a caregiver of his own ethnicity—Peul. Perhaps for minority ethnicities it is even more important to find someone of one's own language and culture with whom to connect. The Peul boy from Côte d'Ivoire said:

> We were at the Protestant School. We heard firing. The teacher let
> us go. I came to the house and found it locked. I saw people running
> up and down. Since I knew Guinea, I went straight to the lorry park
> to take a car to the border. We started walking in the bush after
> we crossed the border. We got to a small village and they gave us
> food and water. After that, I looked for my parents in the village
> but couldn't see them. I saw a car coming this way [toward Nzoo].
> I joined the car with my small brother. When we reached Nzoo, we
> went straight to the mosque. I saw one Peul man there. I explained
> our situation to him and the man took us home. The man checked
> around for our parents and said we should live with him until
> he found our parents. The principal later came to ask if we were
> refugees and said we should register for school.

Most of the fostering pairs occurred between children and caregivers of the main ethnic group in the area affected (that is, the sending and receiving areas). Among pairs with different ethnic backgrounds, there was no discernible pattern of ethnic preference. Caregivers were only slightly more likely to care for children of their own ethnicity. Most frequently, they took in strange children out of "human feeling" or because they would like to think that someone would do the same for their children in similar circumstances.

Overwhelmingly, neither caregivers nor children knew the location of foster children's parents or family. When asked, "Do you know the location of the child's parents or other family?" almost all caregivers said no. Even some of those who had known the child before the conflict had lost track of the parents—only 2 percent said something other than no. Of course, according to my criteria of people to interview, I excluded from the sample anyone who was living with family. One boy met some extended family for the first time when he arrived in Nzoo.

Furthermore, almost everyone said yes to "Would you like help finding the child's family?" (Though it is frankly hard to imagine anyone saying no to an offer of help.) Future researchers should find a better way to ask the question in order to get at how important it is to the caregiver that the child's family be found. The interesting results came when I asked, "If the family is found, would you prefer the child stay here or go to the family?" The caregivers gave four types of responses, though often an answer would contain several of the responses. I categorized based on who seemed to have the final decision.

33%   Stay here (either because it's too dangerous there, or because I've grown used to the child, or because I want the child to continue schooling)

27%   The family will come and we'll discuss it. It's up to the family.

24%   It's up to the child

16%   Go to the family

The children answered more simply, based on their own desires, such as to continue schooling, or fears, such as of war in their country. Twenty-two percent said they would like to return to their parents, and 78 percent said they would like to stay where they were.[8] A sampling of children's responses to the question "If your family were located, would you stay here or go there?" gives a sense of what they would prefer:

I'd like to go back to my family.

I'd like to stay here. I'm afraid of the war.

If they find my parents, my parents will come and tell my tuteur thank you. ["Tuteur" and "tutrice" are the terms used in the area for foster carers.]

I'd be doing the same work with my brother that I'm doing here, so I'd rather stay here.

I'd like to stay here but occasionally go see other members of the family.

If they find my brothers, I'd prefer to stay here if there is any training for me.

I'd like to stay here. I don't know my parents that well.

My sister might come and help me.

Since I'm in school here, I'd like to tell my parents where I am.

Since I'm doing well in school, I'd like to stay here. If I find my
family, I'll tell them I'm attending school here.
Now I'm going to school and playing football. I don't want to go
back to war, so I'd tell my people to come visit me.
I'd rather stay with my tutrice to continue my schooling.
I'd rather stay here. Liberia is not yet safe.
I'd like to go back to my parents.
If there's still war in Côte d'Ivoire, I'll stay here for schooling.

These answers call into question relief agencies' belief that the best
outcome for refugee children is to reunify them with parents or other
family. In some cases that may be best, but it may also be the case that
it is in children's best interest to support them in functioning fosterage
arrangements.

If ethnicity is not an explanation, how do caregivers themselves explain their decision to foster a strange child? To the question "Why did
you agree to take on this child?" caregivers answered:[9]

76%   I felt sorry for the child
15%   I knew the child before
5%   Ethnicity (spoke same language)
3%   I've traveled, I know more

Far and away the most popular answer depended on simple human feeling. When people spoke of ethnicity as a reason, it was usually in terms
of making communication easier. No one expressed the sense that there
was a greater obligation to foster children of one's own ethnicity. Indeed, the emotion (wanting to take care of these children) is partly what
surprised UN agencies when the reports on my research came to them.
The children all got foster placements faster than any agency could have
placed them. We might say the power of human feeling was greater than
the power of human rights—the technocratic and bureaucratic domain
of Western agencies. Of course, there is a danger here of essentializing
the African other by claiming that "they" are more emotional and "we"
are more intellectual. Yet, what I am arguing is more subtle than that,
and it gets back to childhood studies. In the Western construction of
childhood, children are the site of emotion because they represent the
nuclear family. To be more precise, when adults are making decisions
about children, there are strong emotions in part because of the conceptual unity of children, emotion, nuclear family, and the private sphere.

It's as if there are emotions only appropriate to the private sphere/child/ nuclear family nexus. And this nexus produces an "appropriate" emotional reaction to a child separated from his or her parents: the assumption of the naturalness of the emotional horror of a child's separation from his or her biological parents, not necessarily located in the child or the adult, but for the whole situation. So the set of social practices like the one I describe shocks because it throws into question the assumed naturalness of that nexus: some children do not want to go home to their biological parents. It requires us to understand a different affective geography, where emotion (around children, between children and adults, of adults about children) is not necessarily linked to the nuclear biological family. A culture in which flexibility of domestic arrangements is the norm, where ad hoc family relationships can flourish, means that *feeling* for children is enough reason for adults to act.

Several people spoke of their experiences as a "stranger" in another country as making them more sympathetic to the refugee children. An unexpected piece of data that arose from the results may be an important question for further research: among caregivers, 43 percent had lived for some period of time in Côte d'Ivoire, and 12.5 percent had lived for some period of time in Liberia. I am not certain, but my sample has probably been more mobile across international borders than the Guinean population generally. In some ways these findings fly in the face of expectations. The literature points to a conservative extended family and ethnicity system to explain high rates of child fosterage, yet it may be that international travel and relative cosmopolitanism are a better explanation.

These are the results I gave to UNICEF (and therefore they lie within the human rights frame): There is an impressive child protection capacity in the area. Every child I interviewed found someone to care for him or her within a few days. A child protection agency could not have done better at matching up children and foster parents in the same period of time. Furthermore, the children and the caregivers I interviewed are generally content with their living arrangements.[10] Refugee children are well integrated into the community. I saw very little differentiation between refugee children and local children in daily interaction. However, these children, technically unregistered refugees and separated children, are receiving none of the benefits that other separated children and unaccompanied minors are receiving. They are an invisible refugee population. Without assistance, they will be absorbed into the population and most likely never find their families again.

For the long term, it will be necessary to document the longitudinal effects of child fosterage. The current study cannot address the question of different outcomes for children who fled with people from Côte d'Ivoire versus those who met people in Guinea. Young people may realize what they have lost only when the time comes to marry and they find they do not have all the same lineage rights as others.[11] Obviously, long-term research will be needed on this issue. As Tolfree notes: "There have been no studies into the long-term impact of fostering in situations of armed conflict and forced migration . . . : in particular, we need to know more about how fostered children, disaggregated by gender, fare during their adolescence and how they, and their caregivers, cope with their entry into adulthood, raising questions of marriage, economic self-sufficiency and inheritance. It is also important to know the extent to which community-based support structures continue to provide effective monitoring and support to young people and their caregivers" (2003, 16). Despite these concerns, there is some promising evidence that points toward sustainability of these unique family relationships into the second generation. Helen Charnley's work, based on long-term follow-up with children in Mozambique who were separated from their families by war, points to some hopeful news for the children in this study. She presents the findings from an empirical study exploring the sustainability of the substitute family in supporting children separated from their families during Mozambique's sixteen-year civil conflict: "children and substitute families have achieved lasting relationships through new forms of mutual support that typify indigenous coping mechanisms in times of stress" (2006, 223).[12] Mozambique is very far from Guinée Forestière, but the similarities in findings are surprising. Perhaps it is not too much to hope that the positive long-term outcomes Charnley reports for children fostered by stranger families in Mozambique may also be the case for the children in this study.

There is certainly an impressive child protection capacity in border communities. One of the principles of a local solution is the fact that most foster caregivers (76 percent) took in a child simply because they felt sorry for a child in crisis and felt it was the right thing to do. What could be a stronger basis for programming? In Nzoo, with no external help, a very effective child protection system emerged spontaneously. It is clear that in efforts by UNHCR and UNICEF to design programs for the benefit of these children, it would be foolish to ignore the communities' existing heartfelt and generous care for the young strangers in their midst. These findings were what I shared with UNICEF.

The rights framework starts with the presumption of abuse, what Pupavac (2001) has called "the misanthropy of the child rights regime." It is better, I think, to acknowledge the incredible care capacity of these communities—struggling themselves with the effects of war—and figure out how to support them rather than to monitor them for abuses.

Conclusions

The anthropology of war and the anthropology of children are both underdeveloped. Neither war nor childhood has been of much interest to anthropologists because they are abnormal. Anthropologists have waited to study a culture until the disruption of war was over. And children have been understood as not yet people, and therefore not interesting in their own right. As anthropologists, we have tended to be interested in the calm reproduction of culture. It is vital that we understand that children are not just about reproduction and the future. They are participants in social worlds now. I hope this work can be seen as a contribution to a child-centered scholarship that breaks free from both the human rights framework that sees children as victims to be protected and the economistic framework that understands child fosterage solely as the result of calculations carried out among adults.

I have purposely avoided making any claims about what sort of policies would make sense for these children, mostly because the data do not support any sweeping claims about the success of child fosterage as an alternative policy. Perhaps it is enough to hear the stories of the children and caregivers, to be transported into their affective worlds, to force us to reconsider what makes an effective program.

Chapter 4

Modes of Transnational Relatedness

Caribbean Migrants' Networks
of Child Care and Ritual Kinship

Maarit Forde

Regional and oceanic migrations have been part of Caribbean strategies of making a living for several generations. Because of this tradition of mobility and the positive values attached to it, the notion of rupture that recurs in the essays of this volume cannot connote anomalous disruption of normally sedentary social groups or families in analyses of Caribbean migrations. And yet, members of working-class families seldom all migrate at the same time, and more often than not kinship networks stretch across islands, national borders, or continents. Although not co-residential, families can remain emotionally and materially close-knit. Looking into Anglo-Caribbean migrants' family networks, I explore cultural practices of motherhood and reciprocal obligations between parents and children. The kinship networks I evoke include relatedness produced through child-caring arrangements as well as through ritually constituted, religious relationships. I am drawing on ethnographic material gathered during two and half years of fieldwork in the Anglophone Caribbean, mostly in Tobago, and in the Caribbean neighborhoods of Brooklyn and Toronto between 1996 and 2004. The people I have been working with in New York come from various countries in the Anglophone Caribbean, for example, Trinidad and Tobago, Jamaica, Grenada, and St. Vincent, and they practice religions developed in the region, such as Orisha, Revival Zion, and Spiritual Baptist.

Migration and transnational families are nothing new in the Caribbean. Contributing to the formation of global capitalism since the sixteenth century, Caribbean plantation societies were linked to Europe, Asia, Africa, and the Americas by the routes of colonizers, slaves, and indentured workers (Drayton 2002; Mintz 1989; Trouillot 2003). Regional labor migrations peaked in the late nineteenth and early twentieth centuries. Hundreds of thousands of men and, to a lesser extent, women migrated in this period, often in a process of serial migration. A major destination was Central America, where the massive construction projects of the Costa Rican railway and the Panama Canal as well as U.S. agribusiness demanded labor. Also, the development of oil industries in Trinidad and Venezuela, along with increasing U.S. investment in banana and sugar plantations in Cuba, Dominican Republic, and Jamaica pulled workers from less industrialized parts of the region (McLeod 1998; Newton 1984; Putnam 2002). Migration to the United States increased in this period as well, only to be curbed by the introduction of national quotas to U.S. immigration policy in 1924. From the late 1960s onward, steady flows of Caribbean migrants have moved to the United States. The United Kingdom also received migrants from its Caribbean colonies in the late nineteenth and early twentieth centuries, but the major influx of workers to "the mother country" began after the Second World War, continuing until the early 1970s, as Anglo-Caribbean men, women, and eventually families immigrated in response to demand for labor in postwar England (Chamberlain 2005; Foner 2001).

In consequence of this complex migratory history, regional as well as hemispheric family networks of communication, remittances, and mobility have characterized Caribbean kinship and contributed to local economies since the early 1900s. Household structure and child-raising arrangements within extended families have enabled both men and women to migrate (Chamberlain 2001), and migration to the United States has become increasingly feminized. Along with economic and political circumstances, cultural values and ideals developed within the migratory history have motivated and shaped Caribbean migrations (Chamberlain 2006; Olwig 2002). Migration is normal rather than exceptional, and generally quite positively valued. And yet, in spite of the longevity of mobility in Caribbean societies and the migratory ethos, movement across state borders is not free or uncomplicated. On the one hand, passports, visas, and airline tickets are costly, and frustrations with processing times and embassies' seemingly random decisions over visa allocations continue to fuel local debates. On the other hand, migrants can get stuck in their country of destination if they lack necessary documents. Undocumented migrants' isolation from their family as well as the marginalization they experience in their new home societies can cause severe emotional and economic distress.

In the past decades, the U.S. Northeast and particularly New York City have become the main destination for Caribbean migrants, with considerable numbers also heading to Miami or Atlanta, or in Canada to Toronto and Montreal. West Indians are among the largest migrant groups in New York. While students, academics, and professionals contribute to these northbound flows to an extent that concerns about brain drain are commonly voiced in Caribbean societies, most migrants find entry-level employment in less esteemed occupational niches.[1] Their labor is irreplaceable in the low-paid, insecure, and largely nonunionized private service sector, particularly in health and child care, in which most Anglo-Caribbean women find employment (De Genova 2002; Kasinitz 1992; Model 2001). Caring for children and the elderly, Caribbean women—like women from the Philippines, Sri Lanka, and various other parts of the global South as well as Eastern Europe—move to the North to "do women's work" (Ehrenreich and Hochschild 2002; Yeates 2009). As the neoliberal economic order would have it, public day-care services in New York are quite insufficient in relation to the number of families in which both parents work outside the home (e.g., Cheever 2002, 32). Although the pay and the terms of employment in the semi-informal sector of care work leave much to be desired, working as a nanny or as a carer for an elderly person still appears an economically viable solution to a large number of Caribbean women, whose employment opportunities back home may be scarce and pay scales even less lucrative.

Vulnerable and exploited as a migrant with this mode of livelihood may be, working abroad is often rationalized as instrumental and, above all, temporary. Many Caribbean migrations are circular processes rather than one-way transitions, and the objective of ultimately returning home to the Caribbean is very common (Horst 2006; Plaza and Henry 2006). Ideally, migrants travel between old and new homelands, and nonmigrants visit their family members in northern metropolises (Duval 2004; Foner 2001; Forde 2007; Levitt 2001).

Children and Transnational Relatedness in the Caribbean

In the past few years we have witnessed increasing social scientific interest in Caribbean migrants' kinship systems and practices (Bauer and Thompson 2006; Chamberlain 2001, 2006; Goulbourne 2001; Olwig 1999,

2002, 2007; Sutton 2004). These studies have identified continuities of Caribbean family culture in spite of migrations and changing economic and social environments (e.g., Chamberlain 2006, 179; see also Yanagisako 1985, 20.) One of the features of Caribbean kinship that remains significant throughout migration processes is its extensiveness and inclusiveness as compared to Euro-American notions and practices. The white middle-class family, nuclear and patriarchal, was the ideal family type that for Alexis de Tocqueville (1994[1831]) was a basic tenet of U.S. democracy. In David Schneider's landmark study of U.S. kinship as a cultural system (1968), the middle class Anglo-American family follows the nuclear, coresidential pattern, and kinship is defined according to two basic principles—blood and love. Blood here refers to shared biological or genetic substance. The prevalence of ideals of the coresidential nuclear family and kinship based on blood ties has various practical ramifications in social policies and immigration legislation: for example, the U.S. Citizenship and Immigration Services allows migrants to sponsor only their husband's or wife's and unmarried son's or daughter's visa petitions. Some recent studies suggest that migration and migrants' transnational activities have become oriented toward the nuclear, rather than the extended, family—for example, Ghanaian Pentecostal migrants in the Netherlands prefer to send remittances to their immediate nuclear families and ignore traditional exchange obligations within larger matrilineal units (van Dijk 2002; see also Gamburd 2004 on Sri Lankan women's remittances, and Richman 2008 on Haitian Protestants in Mayami).

These patterns are not alien to Caribbean notions and practices of kinship: the nuclear family has been an ideal form in middle- and upperclass kinship in the Caribbean, and Caribbean people do recognise the idea of kinship based on shared blood or biogenetic substance—or procreation. The nuclear family was an important element of the value complex of "respectability" in Peter Wilson's influential, although repeatedly critiqued, analysis of Anglo-Caribbean culture (1972). Holy matrimony, a nuclear family, and a male-headed household were central among the Victorian moral norms that colonial administrations and missionaries sought to instill into postemancipation Caribbean societies (Hall 2002), and they remain significant as indicators of upward social mobility. Moreover, the middle-class family structure and economy—the ideal of "respectable livelihood," ideally earned by the male head of household in the professions or business—are major objectives for migrants aspiring to "better" their own and their families' lives (Olwig 2002, 86). However, a large number of mostly working-class Caribbean people live in extended family households that do not necessarily consist of biological relatives. This is evident among Caribbean migrants in the United States as well: many are engaged in networks of social relations based on the idiom of family and kinship that exceed the nuclear group of parents and children and do not rely on biological connection. There are class differences in values attached to motherhood and practices of mothering: whereas the ideal of having children only within marital unions is strong among middle classes, also in the context of migration (Olwig 2002, 99), laboring people in the Caribbean and in migrant destinations are less likely to be shunned or excluded from their families if they have children out of wedlock. As I am going to show later on in this essay, working-class migrant mothers' material contributions to their children's well-being are valued as a legitimate element of mothering, in contrast to the model of a patriarchal nuclear family economy upheld in middle-class practices.

Researchers of Caribbean kinship have accounted for its cultural specificity by discussing, for example, "neighborhood families," "fictive aunts and uncles" (Chamberlain 2006, 179); by "stylizing" distant or non-kin people into one's kinsmen (Baumann 1995, 732); and by drawing attention to the "flexibility" and "pragmatic selectivity" of transnational kinship (Bauer and Thompson 2006, 4). "Substitute parents" and "substitute families" are concepts that come up in many of these recent studies. Patterns of child care are an important area of Caribbean kinship production that create relatedness across the boundaries of the nuclear unit. Child shifting, as it is sometimes called, is an old institution in the region. Children are sent to live in a household other than those in which their biological parents live. Grandmothers, aunts, friends, and neighbors foster children, often until their adulthood and beyond. The trend is that children move from younger households to older ones and to older caretakers (Gordon 1996[1987]), as younger adults are often economically more vulnerable and also more prone to migrate. But Gordon notes (ibid., 113)—and this is supported by my own data as well—that child shifting cannot be explained by economic rationales alone. Children may ask to live with a grandmother or aunt they are attached to, or a neighbor can ask for a child whose well-being she cares about to come and live in her household. When a Tobagonian man with eleven siblings told me about the child-shifting arrangements in his childhood, with a brother and a sister sent to live with their maternal grandmother in another village, he made the point that the grandmother had asked for the children because "she enjoyed having them around," not (only) because they would have been a burden in their original home or because the grandmother would have needed help in household chores. The receiving households are not necessarily economically better off than the sending ones.

It has been noted in the literature that Caribbean parents often prefer the environment, day-care, and education options available for their children in their home countries to those in the inner cities to which they have migrated. Lisa, a Tobagonian flight attendant in her early thirties, joined her husband, Thomas, in Brooklyn in 2000. Their daughter, Nerissa, was born there, and Lisa and Thomas worked in shifts until she was two years old to be able to take care of her at home. After that, they decided to send Nerissa to live with Thomas's sister in Tobago. "We don't want her to grow up here because the children here have no brought-upsy. They rude, they carry on just like their mothers, just wild. I don't want Nerissa to grow up in that," explained Lisa. Employed by an airline, she is fortunate to be able to travel to Tobago several times a year to see her daughter. Although separation can be painful to parents and children, child shifting produces enduring, often life-long, affectionate and reciprocal relationships between children and their carers (Bauer and Thompson 2006; Gordon 1996[1987]; Smith 1978).

As the institutionalized practice of child shifting partly suggests, mothers' migrations or the families and households of migrant mothers are seldom socially condemned in the Caribbean, in contrast to some societies where migration is also female dominated, like the contemporary Philippines (Parreñas 2003, 2006). Instead of a hindrance to a woman's plans to migrate, having a child, or preferably children, is actually thought to facilitate the migration process. Most Caribbean migrants come to the United States with a tourist visa, and as it is quite difficult to secure a green card, at least within a reasonable period of time, many overstay their visas and become undocumented. A belief that often surfaces in Trinidadian and Tobagonian discussions on U.S. immigration policy is that the local embassy is more likely to give tourist visas to applicants perceived as attached to people and institutions in their country of origin. Thus, applicants who are married, have children, or are employed in the public sector or by established companies would be more successful than those without similar ties.

Extending Kinship: Modes of Relatedness

When researchers analyze relationships and networks of relationships like those involved in child shifting, it is not always clear whether the terminology used, and the kinship system implied, reflect emic notions and classifications, or whether they are analytical concepts formulated by the researcher. For example, the distinction between biological and fictive kin as proposed in the literature on Caribbean kinship remains largely unproblematized. Anthropologists have used categories such as fictive kinship or artificial kinship to distinguish between biological and imagined or pretended kin relations (e.g., Bloch 1971). However, since Schneider's study on U.S. kinship in 1968, it has been largely accepted that kinship is not based on a single, universal set of biological facts upon which cultural variants would grow; rather, the notion of biological kinship itself has been examined as culturally constructed. The opposition of biological and social kinship has been challenged in new kinship studies (e.g., Carsten 2000, 2004; Franklin and McKinnon 2001; Strathern 1992). As the enduring ties formed between children and their carers in child-shifting arrangements are beginning to receive attention in studies of transnational kinship, I suggest that we expand our perspective even more and look into relatedness in the realm of religion.

Practitioners of Caribbean religions at home and abroad form ritually constituted families based on dreams, visions, divination, initiations, distribution of knowledge, and reciprocal exchange, rather than shared biological substance. Tropes of ritual descent are central to contemporary Vodou (Richman 2005) and Regla Ocha (Brown 2003; Palmié 2006), and to Spiritual Baptist and Orisha religions, although the ritual lineages in the latter seldom exceed four generations. These ritual relations, conceptualized in the idiom of kinship, are enduring and mutually recognized. In Anglophone practice, terms like "Mommy" or "Mother," "Father," "Daddy," "Granny," "Sister" and "Brother," and more recently in the context of Orisha religion in Trinidad, "Iya" (mother) and "Baba" (father) are used to refer to one's ritual relatives. Religious kinship entails rights and responsibilities underpinned by the notion of reciprocity, and generates notable transnational practices, including material exchange.

Although the modes of relatedness presented here are not necessarily equal or interchangeable with other modes, they are nevertheless significant, enduring, socially recognized forms of kinship, and quite tangible as well—ritual families entail much more than mere kin terminology. These often lifelong relations can engage migrants in quite fundamental ways, and analytically differentiating between them and other kin relations may not reflect actual lived practices.

Much of Caribbean worship is conducted within families. In many Spiritual Baptist churches and Orisha compounds in New York, as well as in the Caribbean, the leaders, ritual specialists, and core group of ritual participants are members of an extended family. As in Caribbean families more generally, descent rather than affinity is the defining metaphor of these ritual groups, and many such families are matrifocal.[2] Religious leaders in many churches and compounds are assisted by their siblings, children, and grandchildren, although marital couples in the roles of the male and female leaders are not rare. Many of these families are transnational, as is that of King Shepherd, a respected Spiritual Baptist leader in Queens.

King Shepherd's grandparents, parents, aunts, and uncles have been notable Spiritual Baptist elders in Tobago, and he continued his parents' work in leading a prominent church on the island before moving to New York in the early 1990s. He has stayed in contact with his family and also his Spiritual family, the congregation of his church back home. When he organized a rite of passage at his New York church in which certain members' advancement in the elaborate church hierarchy received public sanction, King Shepherd decided to invite his maternal aunt, who is a reverend mother, and his brother-in-law, a bishop in Tobago, to conduct the lengthy and important ritual. He also advises members of his congregation back in Tobago to consult these senior relatives of his when they call him for advice on spiritual matters. Families have been the main units of worship in domestic Vodou as well: the *lwa*, spirits or deities, are inherited and worshipped within landholding descent groups. Migrants are still connected to their land and family in Haiti, and Karen Richman (2005) has vividly described how healing rites performed on the "inheritance" land by their home family can help migrants who have fallen victim to vengeful spirits in Florida, Virginia, or New York.

In Orisha, Spiritual Baptist, Regla Ocha, and urban Vodou congregations, the idiom of kinship extends beyond these coworshiping core families. Entire congregations based on voluntary membership are perceived and reproduced as families, with a male leader as the father and a female leader as the mother. Spiritual Baptists refer to their congregations as "spiritual families," and each member has a spiritual mother and father, the ritual specialists who initiated her. One's relationship to Mommy or Daddy is often intimate, affectionate or, at times, rebellious and difficult, and always unquestionably hierarchical. Again, these ritually constituted families are almost always transnational, so that members of Caribbean congregations reside or travel abroad regularly, and sisters and brothers living in the United States attend their home churches whenever they visit their countries of origin. While motherhood and the mother-child relationship are central motives in Afro-Caribbean religions, ritually constituted fathers, as well as ideas of male spirits or God as father(s), are also very important.

Another noteworthy area in Caribbean understandings of kinship is relatedness between humans and spirits. In most Caribbean religions, people communicate and reciprocate with anthropomorphic spirits. These spirits or deities can relate to people as highly revered kinsmen or kinswomen. In Haitian domestic Vodou, the lwa are unique to each lineage. Yet they are also distinct from the ancestors, who are worshipped in their own right and whose primary role is to mediate relations between kin groups and their inherited lwa (Richman 2005; see Boddy 1989 about matrilineal inheritance of *zar* spirits, and Brown 2001 about matrilines and lwa). In urban Vodou temples, for example in New York, voluntary congregations replace descent groups, and marriage produces kinship to the spirits, although some of the spirits are inherited as well (Brown 2001). Initiation to one's *mèt tèt*, protective spirit, is conducted as a marital ceremony.[3] Such unions with people and spirits are by no means unique to Caribbean religions: for example, in Arabic cultures people can engage in marital and sexual, even procreative, relations with djinns, anthropomorphic spirits.[4] In addition to marrying spirits, voduisants relate to them consanguineously as their children and regard—and call—particular lwa as their mother or father. Further, Vodou spirits, as well as many Orisha deities, are related to one another by marriage and descent. These divine families reflect patterns familiar in Caribbean kinship, such as multiple partners, "outside" children, child shifting, and matrifocality (e.g., Brown 2001).

Relatedness to spirits is often understood as a shared substance, not altogether unlike biological kinship. It entails a profound, lifelong tie, and has tangible manifestations. In the Caribbean religions addressed here, initiated practitioners usually have a personal, protective spirit or saint. The tie between human and spiritual counterparts can be foreseen by diviners and experienced ritual specialists, or one can encounter the protective spirit during ritual meditation or a manifestation. In Vodou, the *mèt tèt* does not reflect one's most obvious characteristics, writes Brown (2001), but rather more fundamental, latent features of the devotee. Many devotees experience illness, sometimes for a prolonged period of time, prior to their initiation to a particular patron saint or spirit. It is understood that neglecting one's relatedness and obligations to the spirit causes physical symptoms.

Relatedness and Reciprocity between Parents and Children

I continue by exploring how Caribbean families, ritual and profane, reproduce relatedness between parents and children through reciprocal exchange. Gifts and remittances, especially those channeled toward nurturing, are important constituents in the emotional and social production of relatedness in transnational families.

In recent anthropological theorizing, the center of attention has shifted from kinship systems to the processes of kinship production and creation. In the context of fostering, Janet Carsten (1997) has shown how everyday acts of feeding and living together in the same house create kinship in Malaysia. Among Caribbeanists who have described the importance of emotional and practical reciprocity in the production of Caribbean kinship ties, Olwig writes of "sharing and caring" as constitutive of Nevisian kinship (2007, 167), Sutton (2004) draws attention to family reunion rituals that reaffirm and create kin connections among widely dispersed people, and Chamberlain stresses emotional and material links between family members (2006, 96). Along these lines, I suggest that reciprocity is a central value in the creation and reproduction of kinship ties within the child-shifting and religious networks described here.

Studies linking migration and remittances to the reproduction of Caribbean peasantry analyze remittances and gifts as ensuing from children's obligation to support their parents and their families more generally (Griffith 1985; Richman 2005). In Griffith's sample, the vast majority of Jamaican remittance recipients were mothers, who channeled much of the money toward the health care, well-being, and education of their children. Migrants sending remittances, on the other hand, were usually men: sons, boyfriends, and husbands (1985, 679). The rationale underpinning the distribution of "migradollars" in Griffith's analysis follows the often-quoted function of children as a future resource of social security. In Richman's work, Haitian migrants' obligation to send money to their families enables the recipients to remain peasants within an economy reduced to producing little else than alienable migrant labor.

Another take on remittances, however, explains them as generalized reciprocity (e.g., Faist 2007, 6), giving and sharing for which no particular returns except satisfaction, social cohesion, and status enhancement are expected (see Sahlins 1972).

In Anglo-Caribbean migrant family networks, children's role as recipients of gifts is no less important than their obligation to send remittances when they have grown up. Remittances directed to children are a constituent part of transnational parenthood, but they also align with Anglo-Caribbean traditions of feeding and giving gifts to children in a mode of generalized reciprocity.[5] While children may not always be direct recipients of remittances and gifts sent from overseas, money and goods remitted to their carers back home are usually partly channeled toward their upkeep, clothing, education, and hobbies.

The flow of material gifts from northern metropolises to the Caribbean reproduces and solidifies relatedness between parents and children across geographical distances and state borders. Dozens of shipping companies in New York specialize in delivering barrels, large cylinder-shaped cardboard containers, to various Caribbean destinations. Also, other containers, appliances, household items, and even cars can be shipped back home with the help of such companies. Brown barrels are a familiar sight in Caribbean kitchens, verandas, or bedrooms, where they serve as storage space, but also in New York and Toronto, where half-full barrels stand in bedrooms amidst piles of clothes, shoes, school stationery, appliances, and other gifts. Sometimes these barrels contain merchandise, like underwear, t-shirts, or trainers to be sold by family or friends. Some migrants send their parcels as airline cargo, if they get good prices. Giselle, a twenty-three-year-old Tobagonian woman, has five aunts in New York. Laughing, she recalled how one of her aunts had "just gone mad" when Giselle's daughter was born. The aunt sent a package with ten baby bottles and sets of clothes for the newborn. For the christening, the aunt came to Tobago with bulging suitcases full of baby clothes and items, including five hundred diapers (all the same size), baby formula, fifty baby bottles, bottle brushes, toys, mobiles, and teddy bears. Instead of condemning gifts like these as attempts to substitute for the absence of a migrated family member with mere material things, Giselle and many others consider nurturing from a distance an acceptable and valuable expression of relatedness.

Gifts between Ritual Kin

Whereas gifts to children (in the sense of minors) adhere to the norms of generalized reciprocity, exchanges between ritually constituted kin display balanced reciprocity. (While the ritual families I discuss here consist of initiated adults, children in the sense of minors are by no means absent from Caribbean migrants' religious networks; young children often accompany their parents to religious rituals—most often their mother, as Caribbean congregations are largely female.)[6]

Uninitiated minor children have no status in the intricate hierarchy of positions that characterizes the structure of Spiritual Baptist churches and also partly motors their ritual cycle, so that expectations of reciprocity do not apply to them. But as far as initiated adults—children in relation to their ritual parents—are concerned, gifts, assistance, loyalty, and support are no less important in ritually constituted kinship than in mundane kinship. Migrant members of ritual families are obliged to send remittances to their ritual parents to fund ritual work at their home church; many also send ritual paraphernalia, clothes, and other objects needed at the church. Ritual specialists from the Caribbean are paid to travel to the United States to conduct rituals or to visit their spiritual children, and as they leave, they often receive elaborate gifts (Forde 2009).

Lorna's networks and objectives of distribution attest to the many sides of Caribbean kinship, and help clarify the logics of exchange in religious or ritual contexts. A Tobagonian Spiritual Baptist woman in her sixties, Lorna has worked as a live-in home aide for the elderly, in New Jersey since the 1980s. She has a green card and travels to Tobago every other year. She usually stays in Tobago for a year, sometimes for six months, and returns to the United States to work for a period of six months or a year. When in Tobago, she keeps a thanksgiving, a large sacrificial ritual culminating in the sharing of a festive meal. (Many of the thanksgivings I have attended in Tobago, Trinidad, and Grenada have been organized and paid for by migrants working in the United States, who wanted to give thanks for their success, ask for further blessings, consolidate their relationship to God, and reaffirm their relations to their spiritual family.) In summer 2004, when we both were in New York, Lorna told me that she had "made it well" there and that "God had truly blessed" her. She wanted to give gifts to the people in our church in Tobago, because she had "been so blessed here [in the United States]." She was in the process of shopping for baby clothes and other gifts to her Spiritual sisters' and brothers' families back home. In addition to sending money to members of her profane family in Tobago, she also remits money regularly to her spiritual mother, who is only a couple of years her senior. As far as her own plans were concerned, she had by then saved enough money to build her own house in Tobago—the inalienable possession, if you will—and was looking for a suitable location. Lorna's earnings in care work have helped her to maintain relatedness not only with her children's families, but also with her spiritual family, and particularly her ritually constituted mother. Moreover, her investment in rituals of sacrifice implies a reciprocal relationship between the sacrificer and God; by giving thanks through ritualized distribution of food, Lorna reciprocates for God's blessings, and hopes to receive further blessings in return.

There is a steep hierarchy between ritually related children and parents. It is reproduced through spatial divisions in churches and other ritual spaces, through titles and modes of address, dress and insignia, ways of greeting, division of labor at the church, the order in which meals are shared out, and so forth. Although Lorna and her spiritual mother are good friends and spend a lot of time together in sacred as well as quite mundane settings, she always addresses her as Mommy and shows her respect, for example, by giving her the best seat or serving her food or drink before other women. Lorna's spiritual mother, on the other hand, may ask Lorna for favors and may expect her to partake in sometimes very laborious preparations for rituals or to give her gifts; should she have a reason, she would be morally entitled to give her daughter a public scolding at the church.

Lorna's spiritual mother arranges several major rituals of sacrifice every year. In these rituals, the paraphernalia can be elaborate and large amounts of food are served to sometimes more than a hundred participants. This would be impossible without remittances from her migrant spiritual children, like Lorna, as well as gifts of money and food from those living in Tobago. In return for their gifts of money, labor, and time, the children are mothered: it is the mother who is responsible for distributing food in a generally acceptable way, who listens, counsels, and heals; it is the mother who makes sure that the clothing and appearance of her children conform to the standards of the church. Moreover, a gifting relationship between a spiritual daughter and mother certainly cannot harm the former's chances of advancing her status in the church, and spiritual sons and daughters can depend on their mother's skills as a ritual specialist and healer. Similar hierarchical relatedness, under-

pinned by principles of balanced reciprocity, can characterize relationships between ritual children and fathers. Whereas children in the sense
of minors benefit from giving and sharing without expectations of re-
ciprocating—at least not immediately or directly—ritual children are
obliged to engage in quite concrete gifting, and ritual parents, perhaps
more implicitly, to reciprocate.

Listening to loyal daughters like Lorna, the rationale behind continued reciprocal exchange does not come down to self-serving instrumentalism, buying one's way up on the church hierarchy. Gifts to ritual parents, like sacrifices in the ritual cycle of their religion, are (or at least,
should be) made for the ultimate purpose of a lasting communion with
God. Open-handed ritual children benefit from the fruits of their sacrifices in smooth relations to the spirit world and blessings they receive
from God. And yet, hidden mechanisms of accumulation underneath religious reciprocity do sometimes arouse antagonism between ritual parents and children, or between ritual specialists.[7] Gifts received by a ritual
specialist signify not only popularity, but also ritual authority. "Mother
Gertrude must be the best mother in Tobago," stated an elderly Spiritual Baptist leader somewhat wryly during one of our evening chats on
the veranda of his house. "If she want to go to London, her children go
buy she a ticket!" In this leader's view, the mother in question was not
a particularly noteworthy ritual specialist, and he questioned the moral
basis of such accumulation of wealth through gifts from spiritual children. Direct breaches between ritual kin are not unheard of. Sister Katie, a successful businesswoman, owner of a restaurant and guesthouse,
was engaged in a quite open-handed gifting relationship with the mother
of her church. She donated ritual paraphernalia to the church, cloth to
make church dresses for the girls in her mother's household, and a lot
of foodstuffs to be distributed in rituals of sacrifice at the church; she
also presented her mother with personal gifts, including plane tickets.
Although a senior member of the congregation in terms of her age—she
was in her sixties at the time—Sister Katie always remained a sister. The
elders of the church felt that more rites of passage as well as dedication
to ritual practice more generally were needed before she could reach the
rank of a mother. Eventually the sister left the church, not satisfied with
merely transcendental rewards for her sacrifices, and she and her spiritual mother have not had much to say to each other since. The child in
this relationship, as in a few similar cases, failed to locate herself in a
satisfactory position within the ritual family. Instead of adhering to the
norms and expectations of the spiritual dimension of the family, she pri-

oritized (or confused) her obligations to her ritual parents with her obligations to God.[8]

Like rituals of sacrifice such as thanksgivings indicate, reciprocal obligations and material transactions mark relationships between people and spirits. In rural Haiti, feeding is "the essential means to creating, or realizing, relationships" to people as well as to lwa. Dead kinsmen, as ancestors, need to be given food and drink, and serving the spirits means feeding them (Richman 2005, 41). In the Orisha religion, an initiate's relatedness to her protective orisha is sanctified in an elaborate ritual of sacrifice. Initiated members of the religion entertain their protective orisha through manifestations and repeated sacrifices, offerings of food, drink, or perfumes and scented waters, which the orisha reciprocates by protecting, guiding, helping, and healing the sacrificer. Many Spiritual Baptists entertain and feed the saints, or the Spirit, like orishas, except that most Spiritual Baptists condemn animal sacrifice. Saints, like orishas and lwa, have their personal tastes in food and other ritual paraphernalia; the animals, dry foods, and drinks offered to these spirits are carefully prescribed. Spiritual Baptist migrants use considerable resources and time on rituals of sacrifice, and the return gifts from God are often interpreted in terms of success in the migration process, although the ultimate aim of these rituals is the maintenance of a lasting relationship to God by "giving thanks." Failure to serve God, or spirits, can be thought to cause failure in migration—for example, sickness, unemployment, or inability to receive rights of residence (Forde 2007; Richman 2005; van Dijk 2002).

Conclusion

The modes of relatedness I have introduced in this chapter in connection to child-care arrangements and religious practices are integral to the lives of many Caribbean migrants. They involve people (and spirits) who are not biologically related, but whose relatedness is enduring, socially recognized, and formulated in the idiom of kinship. Investigations into such kin networks can help us discover ideals, norms, and practices of kinship and parent-child relations that could be ignored if we define kinship according to Euro-American norms of family structure or notions of biology. Motherhood and childhood, then, take on much wider meanings than those confined to a coresidential, biological relationship between a woman and her offspring. Roles attached to motherhood can be shared between two or more women who cooperate in caring for minor children, so that from a child's point of view, a grandmother, aunt, or neighbor becomes a surrogate mother who complements, if not replaces, the biological mother. Later on in life, a ritual mother may for her part contribute to such plural mothering, her responsibilities and obligations toward the child further expanding the scope of motherhood. Particularly heightened in families of laboring people in the Caribbean and beyond, reciprocal giving and sharing is a major element of motherhood. Whereas underage children are not expected to reciprocate directly for the gifts they receive from their migrant and nonmigrant family members, in ritually constituted mother-child relations the obligation to give is mutual.

Within the transnational paradigm in migration studies, recent research has elucidated ways in which migrants deal with the everyday ruptures caused by migration. These can be bridged by communication and exchange along networks of social relations, like the reciprocal exchanges between mothers and children described in this essay. Extending the scope of analysis beyond the biological when investigating migrants' kinship networks uncovers a wide range of transnational as well as local—not to mention divine—ties, obligations, and exchanges—connections largely ignored in the existing literature on migration and remittances, hometown associations, or development. Although many writers have now abandoned the model of the autonomous *homo economicus* whose migration is determined solely by economic or political push-and-pull factors and have recognized the importance of family networks at all stages of migrations, economic goals and rationales still underpin much of this literature. But there must be more to the transnational exchange of gifts between parents and children, and not least in the case of ritual families, than aspirations toward material affluence or status enhancement. Whereas Caribbean norms of generalized reciprocity guide migrants' endeavors to support children left behind, exchange between ritual parents and children is underpinned by expectations of more specific returns. At the same time, exchange between ritual kin complements larger patterns of rituals of sacrifice in Caribbean creole religions, which aim at transcendental communion with spirits and God.

PART III

The Circulation of Affect: Emotion, Children, and Global Flows

Chapter 5

How Children Feel about Their Parents' Migration

A History of the Reciprocity of Care in Ghana

Cati Coe

Many studies of transnational family life have argued that transnational migration challenges norms and ideals of family life. Most of these studies have focused on the marital bond in which gender roles and household labor are redefined and contested in migrant households, but a few also examine how children of migrant mothers experience the loss of maternal affection and feel shortchanged when a mother migrates (Hondagneu and Avila 1997; Parreñas 2005; Suarez-Orozco, Todorova, and Louie 2002; Wolf 1997; more nuanced in this regard are Gamburd 2000; Glenn 1983; Olwig 1999; and Rae-Espinoza in this volume). These studies highlight how the mismatch between ideologies of family life and a new labor environment results in a renegotiation of those ideologies.

Lacking in this line of research is an appreciation of how family life is composed from a history of everyday ruptures. That is, family traditions, ideals, and norms have been negotiated over time, in contexts of continued instability and change induced by migration. Studies of globalization and transnational migration rarely reference earlier research on internal migration from the 1960s and 1970s, although many transnational migrants first migrated to a city or factory in their home country before going overseas (Sassen 1998; Trager 2005). Without this knowledge, we cannot fully understand ruptures that emerge under conditions of transnational migration. Family ideologies challenged by transnational migration may themselves be a product of a particular historical moment or particular economic conditions. They may have been forged during an earlier period of internal or regional migration or an encounter with an earlier phase of global capitalism.

Families are crucial to the development of labor necessary for capitalism. Yet, fundamentally, "the family—with its unpaid labors, its allocation of work and resources by solidary social relations, its flows of values from the haves to the have-nots, in brief, its kinship economy, not to mention the emotions associated with all this—the family is structurally an anticapitalist system" (Sahlins 2004, 147). One anticapitalist dynamic within families concerns "the reciprocities of care" and entrustments that come from the performance of parenting (Goody 1982; Shipton 2007). Although there are expectations that care of children and elderly will be reciprocated, equivalencies between resources and energy flows are not measured by the same standards as sales in the market. Instead, it is through reciprocities of care that the haves in a family—particularly its working members in the prime of their lives—ensure the continued care of the have-nots, such as those who cannot work because of age, frailty, or sickness. Reciprocities of care are maintained by emotion, for emotions guide people in their actions and responses based on their understandings of what is right and their sense of personhood (Reddy 2002). This chapter examines the frictions and fault lines in the reciprocities of care between children and parents in Ghanaian transnational families to highlight the demands global capitalism places on families to ensure social and labor reproduction in particular historical periods.[1]

A Short History of Migration in Ghana

Legends recount how kingdoms and towns in West Africa were founded by wandering hunters and groups of people moving from one area to another (Johnson 2003; Kwamena-Poh 1973). Historically, people have also migrated as part of their individual paths to success, going far afield for new knowledge, skills, relationships, and trade and bringing these resources back to their home communities to achieve wealth and status (Guyer 1993). Refugees and migrants have long been welcomed and incorporated into settled communities in West Africa, because powerful men required followers to indicate as well as generate their wealth and status (Guyer and Eno Belinga 1995). Transnational migration simply extends these migrations farther afield—as Paul Stoller (2002) puts it, New York City and Paris are the newest points on long-distance Hausa trade networks in West Africa.

International migration helped form an elite political and economic class in colonial and postcolonial Ghana, which became independent from Britain in 1957 and was previously known as the Gold Coast. During the 1950s and 1960s, some Ghanaians studied abroad in Europe or the United States for a few years and usually returned to take up high positions in the government bureaucracy, churches, schools, or hospitals. During the economically difficult and politically unstable 1970s and 1980s, international and regional migration increased as Ghanaians traveled to Nigeria and Libya (Twum-Baah, Nabila, and Aryee 1995), but now every country in the world that is economically better off than Ghana is a potential destination—from the United Kingdom and Europe to Australia, South Africa, Israel, Japan, the Caribbean nations, and the United States. Statistician K. A. Twum-Baah (2005) estimates a population of 21 million Ghanaians resident in Ghana and another 1.5 million outside the country, although the European Union estimates between 2 and 4 million Ghanaians abroad, or 10 to 20 percent of the population (Eurostat/NIDI 2001).

Currently, more Ghanaians would leave Ghana if they could, because they find it increasingly difficult to make a living and raise a family there, but it is generally members of the urban middle class who are able to migrate. Many migrants hope to return to Ghana once they have earned enough money to build a house, start a business, or pay for their children's education, although some are planning to remain abroad until retirement, finding it too difficult to earn enough in Ghana to sustain a middle-class life.

Ghanaian migrants, both men and women, primarily go abroad to work. Many migrate in the prime of their lives, between the ages of twenty and forty, when they also wish to marry and have children. Although women in Ghana manage to combine motherhood with income-generating activities quite easily, they do so in a context where other women and children over the age of eight are willing and available to assist with child care, whether for short periods of time or in more long-term arrangements known as child fosterage, a common practice in West Africa (Ardayfio-Schandorf and Amissah 1996; Clark 1994; Goody 1982). However, many Ghanaian parents find that raising children abroad is difficult, given their work hours, the lack of affordable child care, and the lack of relatives to assist with child care. As a result, many find that sending their children to Ghana or having them stay there when they migrate makes better social and economic sense. Rather than spending six hundred dollars a month on child care abroad, they can send home two hundred dollars and support both the child and the caregiver, generally another family member such as a parent's sister or mother who would also expect remittances from the migrant. A child can go to a well-regarded private school in Ghana rather than to schools in the lower-middle-class neighborhoods where parents tend to live in the United States. Instead of spending afternoons and evenings without parental supervision while the parent works long hours, children and adolescents will be better supervised in Ghana, where there are more adults in the household, and more income generation is integrated into household work. Although they may raise their children in Ghana, many transnational migrants expect that their children will become migrants as well, particularly by the time they have completed secondary school (see Reynolds 2002 for a similar situation among Nigerian Igbo migrants to the United States). This is partly because of the competitive admissions policies of state universities in Ghana, but also because as young adults, they can begin to work and contribute to the household income.

Thus, many Ghanaian transnational families live in a situation that one child of Ghanaian migrant parents termed "scattered"—parents and children live apart from one another. It is striking that through these arrangements, transnational families may be distributing the costs of the care of children—and the training of the next generation of labor—to their countries of origin (Meillassoux 1975). This chapter explores the feelings of children and parents about the situation of the scattered family, placing those feelings in the longer historical context of family life and migration in Ghana, in order to understand the discontinuities and continuities in Ghanaian family life. Social change may create new benefits for some, costs for others. While social change can lead to emotional pain, emotional pain does not in itself signal social change; that is, one may experience emotional pain in a situation that is relatively stable.[2]

Understanding Family Life Today and in the Past

My contemporary data come from interviews and participant observation with people from all over southern Ghana—from the coastal areas of Cape Coast, Sekondi/Takoradi, and Accra; the hilly Eastern Region, and the inland Ashanti Region. I have been conducting participant observation in a Ghanaian church in a major East Coast city in the United States since 2004, and through contacts through the church, I interviewed parents and young people who came to the United States as teenagers. Another set of interviews came through a visit to Ghana in the summer of 2005, when I visited the children and families of four parents I had interviewed in the United States. I also conducted focus-group interviews with a total of forty-two students in three secondary schools and one private school in a town of approximately nine thousand people (Akropong in the Akuapem area of the Eastern Region) and a city of just over a million (Kumasi in the Ashanti Region). I also visited twenty-nine of those students' guardians, with whom I had informal, untaped conversations for about half an hour. I then interviewed those children's parents who were living in North America (one was in Canada, the rest in the United States) in late 2005. Thus overall, this chapter is based on thirty-five interviews with parents (either singly or as a couple) and focus-group discussions or private interviews with fifty-two children.

The migrant parents interviewed in this chapter reflect the dimensions of migration in Ghana. The period of parents' residence in the United States ranged from one to thirty-five years, with an average stay of ten years. Fourteen (or 40 percent) were raising their children in Ghana; another fourteen were raising their children in the United States; and the remainder had children in both places. The most common occupations of parents in Ghana were teaching, government work, and trading; in the United States, they tended to work in health-care or retail establishments. The majority (63 percent) had resided in a major city prior to migration. A minority (20 percent) had received a university degree in Ghana.

Similar data on families from earlier historical periods has been difficult to come by. One productive source has been records from family disputes heard in courts run by chiefs and elders in Akuapem, a cocoa-growing area in the Eastern Region, and courts run by colonial officials in Accra, the capital, where Akuapem people sometimes had their cases heard, because of its relative proximity. The court records reveal relationships that were troublesome and conflictual at a particular historical moment, illuminating social fractures (Fallers 1969; Roberts 2005). Although the court records differ in form from interview data, both can be mined for information about idealizations of family life as well as about areas of conflict between family members regarding the reciprocities of care. The court case data is supplemented by accounts of local African Christians, catechists, and ministers in a Twi-language newspaper produced by the Basel Mission that was located in Akuapem and other parts of southern Ghana, as well as by oral history interviews conducted with cocoa farmers between 1955 and 1960 in Akuapem by geographer

Polly Hill, whose papers reside in the Herkovits Library of African Studies at Northwestern University. Although the geographical locations of
the court case data do not correspond to those of the interview data, my
argument based on the court cases supports the research of other scholars using historical data from the Ashanti region (Allman and Tashjian
2000; Austin 2004; Clark 1994), and thus one could argue that it broadly
reflects social patterns in southern Ghana.

Children's Pain about the Scattered Family

As a group, children expressed more pain about the migration of a parent or both parents, with or without their siblings, than did their parents.
They complained about two aspects of this migration: the scattering of a
nuclear family—of two spouses and their children—by transnational migration, and the quality of care that they received from their caregivers
in the parents' absence.

Children of migrant parents were more likely than migrant parents
to openly express sadness, lamenting a family now scattered. Beatrice,
age thirteen, said in Twi that she would like it if "our family would be
one and live together. . . . We are all one family and we could live together."[3] Her father went to the United States eleven years ago, her
mother followed him six years later, and they now have a new baby.
Beatrice is being taken care of by her mother's younger sister, whom
her mother helped raise. A secondary school student, a boy of fifteen,
whose parents and another sibling are in Italy while he and a sister are in
Ghana, said, "The family is, is like scattered, because I hardly see them."
Emma, age fourteen, complained that migration "brings about separation of the family." Her father had migrated some years ago to the United
States with her mother, leaving behind her elder sister and brothers in
Ghana. When the mother died tragically and suddenly in the United
States shortly after managing to bring over their children, the father de-
cided to move back to Ghana, taking Emma with him, and leaving his
oldest three children—now young adults—to attend college in the United
States.

Many of the children seemed to hold up as an ideal a nuclear family
ideology in which parents and siblings lived together. It is significant
that in Beatrice's quote in Twi, she used the English word "family," for
which there is no equivalent in Twi (the word *abusua*, sometimes used
as a translation of "family," refers to lineage; the term *fie* refers to house-

hold). The presence of siblings is as important as that of parents for these children, which is not surprising given that in their parents' generation, older siblings sometimes played a major role in bringing up their younger siblings, paying their school fees or fostering their younger siblings.

Children also talked about missing migrant parents, using the term "love" with the modifier of "maternal," "paternal," or "parental," to indicate that this kind of love was special and unique, something only such a person—mother, father, parent—could give. It is significant that this phrase was also in English, and it seemed tied to a romantic version of a family promoted by Christianity as well as by Western, West African, and Asian videos shown on local television stations and available for sale. Children also mentioned love much more than their parents did. However, they did not distinguish between parental gender in these statements, missing fathers as much as mothers, unlike the findings of some studies from Latin America and Asia (Aranda 2003; Moon 2003; Parreñas 2001; Schmalzbauer 2004). At a focus group discussion at one secondary school, two girls talked about missing the migrant parent intensely, even though one parent stayed behind. Bertha, age sixteen, said that she stayed with her father but missed her mother who was abroad. Even though she talked regularly to her mother on the phone, "still I even cry. I wish she was here. I miss her." Mercy, also age sixteen, said: "When my dad was here, I was very close to my dad. I was always with my dad. Now since he's left, I've lost that kind of paternal love. So whenever my dad calls, when I call him and I talk to my dad on the phone, I fall sick—I don't know—because, like, I miss him." A year later in a private interview, she told me again that she felt sick after her father left. He used a certain cologne and if she happened to smell it, she would feel sick again. But gradually she became used to his absence.

Children sometimes linked the absence of the migrant parent to a lack of resources, even though the migration of a parent theoretically is associated with greater material resources. The key indicators of material care were food, clothing, and money, and the Ghanaian English term they tended to use was "cater," meaning "to provide for." Dinah's parents had lived in London since she was two, and she lived with her grandmother. Now sixteen years old, she said: "As for me, I don't have any problem with them [her parents] staying there, but most people complain, because as for their parents, they don't cater them. They go there and that's all. They never hear from them again." Some explained this lack of material care by complaining that their caregivers were diverting the parent's remittances for purposes other than their care. Grace, age fifteen, who was sent back to Ghana because she was not doing well in her Canadian school, said: "One of my friends, her mom went and her dad went; they left her with the mom's sister, and [she] always maltreats the girl. When they bring her clothes or money, instead of using it to cater for her, they use it for their [own] children. Oh—it was bad." Beatrice said that she wanted to live with her father and mother, both of whom were in the United States. When I asked her why, she replied in Twi: "Maybe if I live with my mother, I will be more comfortable than living with someone else. Because if I live with my mother, my mother will do what I like for me." Many of the students in the focus group at Beatrice's private school complained about not getting all the money that their parents sent back and said that they felt sad and materially deprived. The idiom of material deprivation was a culturally resonant complaint that they could wield about the relationship.

As the children described it, the lack of emotional connection was related to material care: they were shy about telling their caregiver of their material needs, as they would not be in telling a parent. Grace said that one of the negatives of her situation was "being without my parents. My siblings are out there. Sometimes I feel lonely; I won't lie. At times, you can't get what you want, because my parents are not here and it's just my grandmother. I can't always be worrying her." Daniel, age sixteen, said that the difficulties of staying with relatives "make you miss your parents too much." When I asked about the nature of those difficulties, he responded that while parents will provide for you, you do not get even "petty, petty things" (such as pocket money for snacks at school) from your relatives. Others in the focus group at his prestigious government secondary school agreed with his assessment.

Many migrant parents likewise took seriously their financial obligations to provide for their children, sending both cash and gifts. While it is more expensive to mail or ship material objects than to wire money, children consider gifts more valuable than cash, because they are signs of the parent's attention and commodities from a prestigious world. One mother ships a big crate of food to her three children in Accra. While her friends tell her they can get imported food in stores in Ghana, she says she would rather send them food than give them money to buy it themselves, so that they know she is thinking of them. A father says that when his children were in Ghana, he called them every week faithfully and sent them clothes, toys, and shoes. Everyone knows how much he's given his children, he told me, saying that he hasn't "played" with them, meaning he takes caring for his children as a serious matter. Of course, there are parents who are no longer in contact with their families, usually fathers who did not have a formal relationship with the mother of the child, and have children with other women to whom they are more committed.

In return for this material care, parents expect children to reciprocate in the parents' old age. Just as the parent cared for the child as the child's teeth were coming in, so should the grown child care for the parent as the parent's teeth are falling out, goes a well-known Twi proverb.[4] One father advised me to have children: "When you are old, you want to have children who can look after you." A minister in a Ghanaian church in an East Coast city blessed a middle-aged couple and their children, saying that the children are "an investment." He continued: "When the parents are old, their children will take care of them. Hopefully, their children will become 'somebody' "—important people who are respected and materially wealthy. For Ghanaians, like other West Africans, the reward of parenting is the lifelong ties of obligation among those one has raised (Bledsoe 2002; LeVine 2003). The accomplishment of this goal requires that at least one child be able to materially provide for a parent and want to do so, through his or her good character and sense of obligation.

Thus, while there is a desire to provide one's children with the material resources that will set in motion reciprocal relations, parents also do not wish to "pamper" their children, something which would "spoil" their characters, as they put it. Parents were also ambivalent about the effect of material goods on the behavior of the child's caregiver back in Ghana: they worried that a caregiver would do anything to keep a child from complaining and thus jeopardizing the flow of the parent's remittances. A mother thought that only 20 percent of her friends would raise her child properly: "Because they [her friends] will want the money, they will spoil and pamper the child." She felt that only her mother or sister cared enough about her to discipline her child. One father said that there are "problems when people raise" your children. They might "pamper the child because of remittances." Ghanaians, like Sierra Leonean parents (Bledsoe 1990), value hardship and struggle as important components of training a child to be disciplined, respectful, and hardworking, the attributes necessary for success. Some parents resort to sending a child who has been misbehaving in the United States back to Ghana. But the father just quoted believed that, if one sent children back, one should "send them to places where conditions are hard," such as a village near Tamale in northern Ghana, associated in the minds of southern Ghanaians with a lack of development and amenities. Parents thus felt some ambivalence about providing material care to the extent that it might interfere with the child's later ability or desire to respond reciprocally.

One might expect that state forms of social support in the United States would encourage Ghanaian immigrants to be less reliant on their children for eldercare and thus to change some of their goals of child socialization. To some extent, this occurs, but many Ghanaian immigrants in the United States work in the health-care field, and many women in particular work as home-health aides or in nursing homes. As a result, they have firsthand knowledge of how the elderly are cared for in the United States, and it dismays them. Their work experiences serve as a sharp encouragement to return to Ghana by the time they are old. For instance, one woman who works as a home-health aide in the United States told me about a friend, a male migrant whose mother and sister had deceitfully taken away the house he had built back in Ghana—their betrayal caused him to decide never to return to Ghana. My informant reported that she had told her friend that in his old age, he would regret his decision because she sees what the elderly in the United States go through. In her opinion, only if one is upper middle class could one afford quality care; nursing homes, she commented, are not nice.

Those migrants whose adolescent or young adult children are in the United States do not expect their children to accompany them back to Ghana upon the parent's retirement, but rather to continue with their education and work in the United States, sending remittances back home to help support the parents. Having followed his father and stepmother to the United States, one young man, age twenty-two, was attending community college and sending back some of his meager pay from a retail job to his mother in Ghana. Children's ties of obligation to their birth parents continue to be important, albeit through remittances rather than bodily service.

While parents miss their children, what is paramount in their minds is anxiety about raising their children to be model persons—successful and responsible. They, like their children, also desire a household composed of the nuclear family, but somewhat paradoxically they see migration as a way to accomplish this goal. One father told me that he was building his own house in Ghana because "I would not like to go back and live in someone else's house." Living on his own in the United States while his wife and children were in Ghana, he said: "I only want to live with my wife and kids, so I spend a lot on rent in Ghana too because I want my privacy." Another girl, age sixteen, explained that her father's migration allowed her mother and siblings to live together; previously, they had been living in a compound house with "other people." Employment as civil servants, medical personnel, or teachers encourages this ideal of the nuclear family household, because employees in such jobs are more likely to receive housing through their employment that accommodates only a nuclear family. Christianity has also played a role in encouraging obligations to the nuclear family and in cutting ties to the extended one (Meyer 1999). Migration may result in a family's ultimately being able to live together but causes tension in the short term when family members live apart.

Studies of transnational families have argued that migration facilitates the commodification of love, that material goods from an absent parent replace the emotional intimacy of a present parent. Furthermore, transnational migration—with its split families living in multiple households—is seen as disrupting nuclear family households in which women fulfill domestic duties (Parreñas 2005; Schmalzbauer 2004). Neither representation applies to Ghanaian transnational families. The reciprocal responsibilities that migrant parents and their children expect of one another show how material and emotional bonds are intertwined, allowing an exchange of resources between generations. As such, they are critical to how families manage their own survival and reproduction within existing and changing economic conditions. Furthermore, the significance of both material ties and nuclear family households arises from the history of family life in Ghana, forged during an earlier period of internal migration and global capitalism. What may seem to be a rupture that causes pain among the children of migrant parents is the result of ideals formed from earlier ruptures at an earlier stage of global capitalism. To illustrate this point, I turn to an examination of the reciprocities of care among families from the area of Akuapem in southern Ghana who migrated to participate in the cocoa boom that began in this area in 1892 and ended around 1917, when the world price of cocoa fell.

Reciprocities of Care among Akuapem Cocoa Migrants, 1905–1930

In the early twentieth century, the towns of Akuapem tended to be deserted as a result of migration (Ofori 1907). Akuapem was a traditional kingdom, comprising seventeen towns along a ridge and farm villages in the valleys below, located in what is now the Eastern Region. Because of its history, Akuapem was made up of two ethnic groups who defined themselves as Guan and Akan, differentiating themselves on the basis of language and kinship practices. The primary reason for migration during this period was cocoa, a newly introduced cash crop grown for export: to grow their cocoa trees, Akuapem peasant-farmers, on their own initiative, gained access to land to the west, traveling farther and farther afield for prime forestlands. Men also traveled to the inland city of Kumasi for trade or the coastal city of Sekondi to work on the railway, and men and women migrated to nearby cities and towns for trade, as part of the growing informal urban sector, itself fueled by the cocoa boom and the railway.

During the changes and ruptures caused by the move from subsistence and regional market-based economies to export cash-crop farming, the need for capital and the need for labor prompted many transformations within the family. Significant here are some of the transformations that contributed to the nuclearization of the family. As has been observed in other parts of southern Ghana, migration tended to spur nuclear family residence, at least during the period of migration. Decades later, for example, when Asante men established cocoa farms far from their hometowns in the 1930s and 1940s, they took their wives and children with them as laborers (Allman and Tashjian 2000); and when Kwahu people migrated to the cities in the 1970s, husbands, wives, and children tended to live together and share their resources and expenses with one another far more than they did when the families returned to their hometown, where a husband and wife might each go back to stay with their respective kin (Bartle 1980). Akuapem cocoa migrations did result in nuclear family households, but split family households were also common. A man might well stay with his wife and children near his farm plot, but some men with several wives and cocoa farms in multiple locations might leave a wife and her children at each farm to care for it, while he rotated between these locations.[5] Sons and nephews who followed men to work for them were likely to receive a share of the land, but "if a son did not serve his father, he would get nothing," reported a chief to Polly Hill.[6] As school became more popular, children might be sent to live with relatives or a teacher in a town on the ridge while they attended school, while the parents stayed at the farm village, where there were no schools or only primary schools (Brokensha 1966; Opoku 1893).[7] A man might migrate alone, for the purposes of trade, leaving his wife and children behind. Both nuclear family and split family households might include fostered children and apprentices, migrant laborers from other areas, tenants, and other family members.

The Basel Mission, which came to Akuapem in 1835, promoted nuclear families, and although Christians were more likely to live in nuclear family arrangements than were non-Christians, it is doubtful that this arrangement was prevalent even among ministers and teachers. Reflecting on marriage and migration in the Twi-language Basel Mission newspaper, one African Christian commented that Christian men who traveled to seek work often left their wives and family behind. He advised them not to stay away more than a month or two in their travels; if a man was going to stay longer, then his wife and family should come with him to help in the work (Oben 1895). Ministers and teachers were themselves likely to be peripatetic, moving from one mission station or school to another in the course of their careers, and would not always take along their wives and children (Kwamena-Poh 2005). As adults migrated, children tended to circulate between households, helping relatives during the cocoa harvest, becoming apprentices to skilled workers, and becoming domestic and commercial servants for urban dwellers and more wealthy households.

Relations with children were crucial to the changing social and economic conditions of the Gold Coast. Children's labor contributed to the growing and harvesting of cocoa, a labor-intensive endeavor. Furthermore, their service generated capital for families in times of illness or hardship, or to gain access to cocoa lands. Men were able to raise capital through their rights to children through a practice known as pawning or pledging: when a person received a loan from another, the debtor transferred a relative—a pawn or pledge—into the hands of the creditor as security for the loan; this pawn or pledge would stay with and work for the creditor until the loan or the loan and interest were repaid. In the absence of bank loans, pawning was crucial to the emerging capitalist economy of the Gold Coast, allowing men to raise capital for economic ventures. Polly Hill's interviews with elderly Akuapem cocoa farmers in the late 1950s show that many of them raised the capital to buy land in the early twentieth century through the pawning of relatives, although others used profits from oil palm and rubber or their earnings from trade or crafts work.[8] "Pawning is common," said a witness in a court case in 1907.[9] Children over the age of eight were often used as pawns, because they could be hidden from colonial officials as birth children and members of the household (Haenger 2000). However, as the colonial courts began to prosecute pawning in the early twentieth century, men lost access to the labor of slaves and pawns just as new cocoa farms required inputs of labor. To ease the rupture of the loss of labor and capital, they turned to wives and children as a labor and capital source, control that was facilitated by the payment of bride-price.

Fathers' rights to their children were dependent on debt relationships with their wives (or wives' families) and, to a lesser extent, with their children. Marriage payments increased sharply in the late nineteenth and early twentieth centuries, fueled in part by the cocoa boom (Amoa 1907; Asare 1917).[10] As a result, the meaning of the marriage payment changed: it was now taken to be the equivalent of a loan from the husband to the wife's family. As occurred in Asante (Allman 1997; Allman and Tashjian 2000; Grier 1992), through marriage payments, a husband gained creditor rights over his wife and children, who essentially became his pawns. For instance, in one case, the court ruled firmly in favor of the father's custody of his children, stating: "In the native laws, if a man has married under the rules of the natives and has paid any dowry in so doing after the death of the woman, the husband has to claim all children."[11] Because of the importance of children as a form of wealth in this social and economic context, fathers and other male kin tussled over who had rights in children, and if they had paid bride-price, fathers usually won.

Fathers also had various obligations to their children's continuing care: they paid for children's debts and helped them in court cases, paid for their maintenance or provided food, paid their medical expenses when they were sick, and helped male children get land and marry. In return, fathers had rights to their children's labor (including farmwork) and to their daughters' marriage payments (an increasingly important source of capital). Court cases from chiefly tribunals from four of the ridge towns for which records were available show what happened when parties broke this kind of social contract. Fathers who did not pay their children's debts or give them land were not entitled to their service.[12] Increasingly, the legal system appeared to reinforce fatherly rights to children's labor and make more tenuous the rights of other kin.

As fathers gained rights over children, potential guardians who were kin were losing rights over children, which they sought to maintain through debt relationships. From 1906 onward, family members who had customarily had kin rights in children but were not birth parents—generally paternal uncles in patrilineal Guan towns and maternal uncles in matrilineal Akan towns in Akuapem—sought to control the residence and service of their dependents by paying their debts. It is not always clear from the records how these young people got into debt, but there is one case involving a boy in which school fees were judged a form of debt.[13] In a case heard in March 1910, a man testified that when his uncle did not pay his debt, he stayed with another man who did (it is not clear whether this uncle was on the maternal or paternal side).[14] The uncle then reported to the colonial officials in Accra that the nephew had been pawned, and because this practice was illegal, the creditor had to set the nephew free. The nephew then brought the uncle to court for severing his relationship with the creditor. The uncle was annoyed that the nephew had not stayed with him after he paid a pound of the nephew's five-pound debt, which the nephew had contracted in his travels. This uncle thus sought to control his nephew's labor when he had paid only a little of his debt, even to the point of preventing him from pawning himself to another man. In a sense, the uncle expected his nephew to be in debt (and thus pawned) to him, not to another.

Likewise, in patrilineal towns, paternal uncles, also called fathers, expected young men to take them as their fathers in exchange for paying off their debts. A paternal uncle said about his nephews who were minors and whom he had inherited from their father—his older brother—who had died: "If the children would take me as fa [father] then I would pay all the debts, take the children, and let the land remain unsold [whose sale would otherwise pay for the nephews' schooling]."[15] In another custody case, when a father pawned his eldest child, a girl who had been fostered by his sister, the girl's maternal uncle redeemed her from the pledge. The uncle argued in court: "I have paid all necessary fees to ransome [sic] the child, therefore I have the power of using them [the girl and her younger sibling]." The uncle seemed to mean pawning in his phrase "using them," as the father claimed that the uncle had pawned the girl and her sibling for twenty pounds at the cocoa village of Adawso.[16] In essence, those who were nonfatherly kin to dependents and children sought to gain the rights that fathers increasingly had, namely, to access children's residence and service or to use them to raise further capital, through paying debts associated with them. In the meantime, children sought to keep open the array of adults around them who might support them and would run away from one location, provided they could find another relative to take them in. Thus, at this earlier period of time, fathers sought to control the nuclear family unit, while children tended to seek the protection and support of more extensive relations.

The reciprocal responsibilities that young people and adults owed one another were being negotiated to enable the emergence of new relations of production around cash crops. In relation to the contemporary data on transnational migration, we see the importance of material exchanges of resources as crucial to the definition of relationships between fathers and children. Rather than signaling the growing commodification of intimate relationships with the physical absence of parents, family relations in Ghana have long had an economic aspect, perhaps even to the extent of always being somewhat commodified, such that marriage became modeled on a creditor-pawn relationship. Thus it makes sense that children's idioms of complaint about separated families in contemporary transnational families tend to focus on the lack of material support, and that parents focused on producing respectful, hard-working, and obedient children. Furthermore, unlike the focus on material exchanges, we see that the history of nuclear families in Ghana is relatively short. With the increase in marriage payments, families became more oriented around the nuclear unit, as fathers monopolized the reciprocities of care with children to the detriment of other male relations and sought children's service as labor on cocoa farms or to raise the capital to buy land for such a farm.

Where Is the Rupture in Transnational Migration?

Early capitalist modes of production, such as cash-crop agriculture dependent on smallholder farmers, generated more nuclear-family arrangements. Other kin who had previously had rights to children gradually lost those rights to fathers, in both matrilineal and patrilineal towns. In this situation, living together as a nuclear family was important because children's labor was a significant resource for their fathers as they developed their cocoa farms. The chiefly tribunals provided the legal support for reciprocal obligations between fathers and children during an era in which men sought access to labor and capital from their wives and children, when other sources of labor and capital through slavery and pawning were declining and cash-crop agriculture was generating new demands for labor and capital. The length of time in which children met their reciprocal obligations was considerably shorter then than it is today. After about the age of six or seven, children began contributing to the domestic household, whose labor was closely tied to other economic ventures, whether agriculture or trading, with the value of their labor increasing with their adolescence and young adulthood (see Table 5.1).

In the conventional narrative of modernization, capitalism and wage labor is associated with the nuclearization of households and families, and this model seems supported by the evidence presented here, as fathers sought to control the residence and labor of their wives and children to support the development of cash-crop agriculture. However,

Table 5.1. Comparison of the Two Key Periods

	Early twentieth century in Akuapem, Eastern Region	Late twentieth century in southern Ghana
Kind of migration	To rural areas for cocoa farms and to urban areas for employment	To rural and urban areas; to overseas and throughout the subregion
Time scale of exchange	More immediate: children could contribute their labor to domestic household	More delayed: reciprocal contributions to the child's success in life and to the parent's old age
Kind of obligation	Material exchanges	Material exchanges and emotional connection
Family residence	Split household with nuclear becoming more popular	Nuclear as ideal but split household common

advanced capitalism, characterized by an even greater mobility of capital and labor, generates conditions in which there are good reasons for members of a nuclear family to live apart and rely on extended family members to support the care of children. In fact, evidence seems to be building that extended family structures are well suited to the increased mobility of labor in a global economy, helping sustain the low wages paid to immigrant workers by lowering the costs of maintaining nonworking family members (Jones 1992; Ong 1999; Schmalzbauer 2008).

One might expect Ghanaian families to cope with the conditions of global capitalism quite easily, given the importance of extended family and of material exchanges for maintaining relationships between children and parents. Material exchanges do not require the physical presence of parents taking care of children, or grown children taking care of elderly parents. Instead, migrants can maintain their reciprocal obligations in the relationship by sending home remittances, and they can better meet those reciprocal obligations *through* migration, to the extent that the migration is moderately successful. At the same time, such a system requires the involvement of underemployed extended family members, and about this, both parents and children are ambivalent, albeit in different ways. Although both are suspicious that the caregiver does not have the children's best interests at heart, parents are concerned that the caregiver—perhaps even a member of the parent's nuclear family such as a grandmother or aunt—will spoil or pamper the child due either to a desire to continue to receive remittances or to a lack of strength to physically punish the child; children emphasize the lack of emotional intimacy with caregivers that they see as necessary for proper care.

Has transnational migration created ruptures in Ghanaian family life? Yes. Have Ghanaian parents and children had to adjust their ideals of family life, sometimes painfully? Certainly. But one can also see how their assessments of their obligations are built out of older conceptual models, now reworked, and that ideals like "tradition" and "the traditional family" were built out of similar ruptures and negotiations between family members in a previous era and in different economic conditions. Transnational migration also seems more disruptive to newer ideologies of family life—like love—than to those of material care, which provide some flexibility in living arrangements. Following Sahlins (2004), we can see in both the flexibility and resiliency of conceptual models and discourses in the midst of economic change that discontinuity, looked at from another vantage point, can look like continuity.

Chapter 6

The Children of Émigrés in Ecuador

Narratives of Cultural Reproduction and
Emotion in Transnational Social Fields

Heather Rae-Espinoza

In the study of migration journeys, we must look not only to the experiences of the migrants themselves but also at how the effects of these journeys weave through the cultural values and experiences of the people who stay. In the literature, much of the concern for those who stay has focused on the children, whom researchers perceive as "left behind." Images of children without adult figures raising younger siblings without social, economic, or psychological support shape perspectives on parental emigration. However, generalizing from worst-case scenarios and across cultural boundaries is not warranted. Even when émigrés' macroeconomic and sociopolitical motivations for migration are similar, the experiences of those who stay may not be. Culturally shaped concepts of the child and parenting practices greatly affect how children adapt and adjust to parental emigration. For this reason, the children who stay do not necessarily experience psychological difficulties or aberrant developmental pathways.

An established base of research on alternative or non-normative families—with acknowledged difficulties over the referential framework to a norm—details the role culture plays in emic ideas of children's needs, natural abilities, and desires. In these families, siblings (Weisner and Gallimore 1977), fathers (Hewlett 2001), or larger kin networks (Stack 1997) fill the role of child caretaker. These alternative family structures can be strategic and adaptive in the face of both economic limitations (Coontz 1992) and technological innovations (Shanley 2001).

However, the alternatives are often merely variations with a similar set of internal processes for meeting children's needs, based on a Western notion of a dependent, vulnerable child.[1] Across cultures, families are thought to universally fulfill procreation, orientation, status-giving, and economic functions (Queen, Habenstein, and Adams 1961). In other words, the kinds of care that children receive are not altered in these so-called alternative families; instead, the sources of care differ from those in an idealized nuclear family. With transnational families, we can see not just changes in the *sources* of care, but drastic alterations in the *forms* of care. Children may or may not come to accept new methods of receiving affection, responding to discipline, and expecting rewards with globalized, transnational ties. Yet, migrants demonstrate that family ties can cross borders. Roles can be sustained without physical contact, testing accepted concepts of family not only in how the family unit is constituted to provide care, but also in regard to what being a member of a family entails. As children learn, innovate, or reject cultural norms in the process of cultural reproduction, the children of émigrés experience not just novel sources of care, but also novel forms of care.

The concern over traumatized children's emotional experience arises from insistence on a natural human reaction to ruptures that are implicit in migration trajectories. However, this focus overlooks children's individual perspectives on the everyday. Because of cultural variation in the concept of the child, we cannot infer any inevitable emotional experiences for the children of migrants, especially without employing a more nuanced theory of affect. With transnational families, the pervasive nature of developmental research's equation of physical affection with love can spur assumptions in regard to children's emotional state without the necessary, contextualized, in-depth observations of children's feelings. The omission of taxonomic, ecological, semantic, and regulative values surrounding an emotional expression indicates an omission of understanding emotion in context (Shweder 1985, 182). For instance, we should not assume that the children of émigrés will experience anxious attachment based on a single emotional manifestation, or, even worse, on the reports of parents at distant locations with their own projections as fodder for interpreting children's internal emotional states. Even attachment theorists who brought to light this emotional state as the result of parental separation warned against ignoring the covert deprivations and resiliencies that are apparent only in accord with the child's internal working model of a parent (Ehrenreich and English 2005). More general contentions of "emotional trouble," as if a ubiquitous set of unproblematic emotions exists for others throughout development, are even more dubious. Looking merely at the eliciting situation and the succeeding expression of a particular emotion does not tell us a child's emotional experience. A holistic approach to emotional development over time in the context of social relations and internal processes, or an ontogeny of emotion, can further migration research on affect.[2]

Transnational family structures challenge canonical ideas on the processes of cultural reproduction and the ontogeny of emotion, and thereby expand our concepts of agency as well. Through the use of case study data on the construction of narratives, we can see the unique, internal negotiations as the children of émigrés psychologically adapt and socially adjust to parental emigration. External factors and internal processes continuously shape narratives—a process true for all children, not just those who stay. To understand the contextualized process of constructing narratives, it is necessary to realize that enculturation requires not just cultural transmission, but cultural internalization as well (Spiro 1997). Learning about a cultural value through social interactions is not sufficient; the individual must also find the cultural value personally significant to take it in through psychological operations. Theory on cultural reproduction should not automatically equate the values that are out there to the values that a person will follow. Moreover, the process of internalization is not random. In constructing narratives, children discussed here select beliefs from a wide array of values that interpret their émigré parents based on the factors involved in their parents' emigration, the characteristics of substitute care, social interactions in the settings they move through daily, and other dynamics. The children who stay after parental emigration in Ecuador construct narratives in a particular cultural context while in social relationships with people in Ecuador and transnationally.

The use of case studies for understanding the experiential level of culture has a long-standing place in anthropological investigation (Crapanzano 1980; Mintz 1974; Obeyesekere 1984; Shostak 1983). Through qualitative research focused on the experiential level of children over the course of three years of fieldwork in Ecuador in 1998, 1999 to 2000, and 2003 to 2004, I present children's representations of themselves through narratives within their families and their communities.[3] Between 2003 and 2004, my primary location for recruiting research participants was a middle-class private school in Guayaquil, Ecuador. Fifty-four children from ages six to twelve and their families participated in this study, which combines anthropological fieldwork methods with psychological techniques. Over the course of research, the use of projective techniques involved several different stimuli as a focus of discussion, including the children's own drawings and a multicultural adaptation (Gardner 1989) of the Thematic Apperception Test (TAT), the Storytelling Card Game. The Storytelling Card Game directs children to tell stories with paper-doll cutouts of different ethnicities with a wide selection of line drawings as settings. Like the TAT, the Storytelling Card Game asks the respondent to tell a story about some pictures, "necessarily expressing his or her motives, interests, and anxieties" (Adams, Milner, and Schrepf 1984, 290). During these interviews, behavioral observation also provided significant data, both for analytic and ethical purposes.[4] In addition to the twenty-five to forty hours I spent per child in interview sessions and interviews with children's teachers and caregivers, participant observation of class time, structured and unstructured play, and home life were integral to assessing children's experiences of parental emigration. For expository reasons, the following analyses of case study data include only emblematic statements of children's narratives in these interviews. The goal is to demonstrate how these children's statements in representing themselves elucidate both processes of cultural reproduction and emotional development in their particular setting.[5]

This chapter examines the narratives of four children. The majority of the children I studied in Guayaquil were able to psychologically adapt to parental emigration by minimizing losses from emigration, downplaying the uniqueness of maternal care, describing distinctions in age-graded care, and emphasizing connections to transnational parents. These children could normalize parental emigration and understand the loss as legitimate. However, the four children described here experienced unique challenges with parental emigration in comparison to their peers, and for this reason their narratives are more informative for revealing the individual processes of internal agency. Questioning the stability of their current family structure, Ana and Michelle represented themselves within cultural norms that distorted their ages. Negotiating the confusing emotional expressions of their caregivers, Wilson and Sebastian developed distinctive manners of emotional expression for discussing their experiences. The four children's narratives reveal the unique nature of their reactions to parental emigration and the role of their own internal agency. Their cases uncover processes of cultural reproduction and emotional ontogeny that demonstrate the need to analyze the experiences of children of émigrés beyond simplistic group risk labels.

Ecuadorian Migration

When the financially unstable middle class became borderline destitute after an economic crisis and a period of political instability in the late 1990s, many Ecuadorians, incapable of meeting their families' accustomed standards of living, emigrated. In addition to a continuing flow of male migrants, the number of female Ecuadorian émigrés increased substantially, especially to Spain and Italy. This trend has been widely documented for other countries as well (e.g., Ehrenreich and Hochschild 2002), as "occupational niches" in receiving societies have led to a feminization of migration (Maher 2004, 180). In 2003, the Italian consul Joyce Ginetta told me that "Ecuadorian" is now synonymous with "nanny" in Italy. According to Spain's Instituto Nacional de Estadísticas (2009), the number of Ecuadorian female migrants (193,264) in 2007 was just short of the number of Moroccans (195,483), the largest foreign community in Spain.

Many émigrés are parents who normally have their children stay in Ecuador because of the availability of affordable care and because they do not plan extended migration journeys. The émigrés remit portions of their income to Ecuador, principally to their mothers and sisters. These remittances primarily care for the émigrés' children who stay. In most cases, as with the cases of Ana, Wilson, and Sebastian presented here, these remittances, along with the joining of nuclear family households into multigenerational households, can signify an increase in class status. In rare cases, as with the case of Michelle, emigration can mean a decrease in class status when there are debts incurred from migration journeys, limited remittances (especially early in migration journeys), or the need for hired help to compensate for the émigrés' previous household contributions. Often, in these instances, there is a nuanced interplay of noneconomic migration motivators.

This research contrasts with much existing work on Ecuadorian migration, which tends to focus on the historical migration of indigenous groups emigrating from the Andes (Colloredo-Mansfeld 2003; Hidalgo 2004; King 2008; Pribilsky 2008).[6] In contrast, the four case studies presented here, and my migration research after 2000, comes primarily from the urban, coastal, middle-class Mestizo population of Guayaquil, where international migration was not as established before the economic crisis of the late 1990s.[7] Guayaquil is a unique and understudied area of the country. Guayaquil is Ecuador's largest city, the country's most important port, and capital of the province of Guayas. With the exportation of bananas, shrimp, petroleum, and roses central to the national economy, Guayaquil is a powerful source of political opposition to the capital city, Quito, and President Correa divided the province to weaken its political and economic power in 2007. Individual entrepreneurship and pressures from external influences characterize the residents' lifeways in this port city (Townsend 2000). National identity and local economic practices impact decisions to migrate, which affect the cultural context of children's development of cultural understanding and emotion.

Cultural Reproduction

The cultural reproduction of family ties can entail surprising continuities despite ruptures for the children of émigrés. Geographically distant transnational parents can feel emotionally present to children; children can equate alterations in custody arrangements with substitute caregivers with previous nurturing relationships; children can minimize new distinctions from the lifestyles of peers in interpersonal interactions; and children can obscure resulting mismatches with institutional ideologies of families, such as those that schools and governmental programs espouse, through pairing certain family characteristics with mainstream values. To establish continuity with ruptures in these social relationships, children selectively internalize propositions from the existing patterns of culture in a unique way in order to cope with their own set of psychodynamic pressures. The acceptance of cultural values entails both psychological adjustments to address internal processes and social adaptation in accordance with surrounding contexts. Children dynamically negotiate cultural values to construct a narrative that represents their family as an internal certainty with predictable experiences, indicating a foundation of trust (Erikson 1963, 247).

The two case studies I present here highlight the culturally meaningful distinction between the kinds of care that a small child needs and the kinds of care that an older child needs. This age-grade in care was meaningful to émigrés' children in Ecuador. Benedict (1938) claimed that cognized distinctions between the kinds of care children receive at different ages, or age-grades, can alleviate the psychic threat from discontinuities. In this case, not only was the age-grade helpful for children's understandings of developmental discontinuities, but also it helped them normalize parental emigration; they recreated the everyday across a rupture. Distant parents were conceptualized as present. Age-graded care was a unifying theme among children who seamlessly accepted parental emigration; by distinguishing between the kinds of care a small child needed in comparison with an older child, some families saw parental emigration as appropriate parenting in the best interests of the child. In the Ecuadorian concept of the child, small children need proximate, physical attention, whereas the needs of older children focus on increasing economic demands of private school tuition. Also, older children are thought to be able to understand the purpose and sacrifices of the migrant's journey. Instead of describing case studies that demonstrate the systematic and direct internalization of transmitted cultural values, I have selected two cases that show how cultural values are reproduced even in unique narratives. Cultural reproduction is not programming but involves the acquisition of cultural values on different levels of personal significance (Spiro 1997, 8).

In constructing their narratives, Michelle and Ana, two daughters of émigrés, both reproduce cultural values that demonstrate continuities with their families through transnational ties to meet individual psychic needs. Both nine-year-olds had one parent abroad. Because of the characteristics of their particular situations, neither could accept the care they received as normal, since caregivers told them that it was a temporary phase based on their particular age. Reflecting the cultural ideals of age-graded care, they represented their maturity levels to rearrange external reality. In other words, they depicted themselves in ways that countered what others might consider actuality to suit their own psychological needs. In what follows, Ana and Michelle seek to distort their ages in order to represent familial ties as fitting cultural norms.

Ana's Manipulation of Cultural Values

Ana's father had migrated to the United States four years earlier, just after Ana's fifth birthday. She lived with her mother, but maintained extensive contact with her father. He often called and returned frequently with gifts. His departures surprised Ana a number of times after his visits; he left surreptitiously to avoid having to refuse his daughter's request that he stay. Although some children could normalize similar experiences of parental emigration, Ana could not. She did not see her situation of care as normal: she was told it was a transitory, temporary state. I understand Ana's difficulty in normalizing parental emigration as stemming from the way that her mother comforted her about her father's migration. To comfort Ana that her family was still a unit, her mother told Ana that when Ana was older, her mother would go abroad to join her father. Following cultural values on age-grades, her mother told Ana that she would not leave before Ana was a big girl. At a school soccer game, Ana's mother discussed this with me to indicate why she saw her family as unique in comparison to other families of émigrés where the marital unit dissolves.[8] Despite the intent, her mother's statements failed to comfort Ana. To Ana, these statements meant her mother could leave in the middle of the night like her father. I see evidence of this interpretation in her difficulty understanding her father's emigration, in her linking the father's migration journey to her description of a mother, and in her behavior representing herself as younger. Even though this narrative did not lead to the most successful social integration, it mitigated her concern over her family arrangement.

While some children three years younger than Ana told me that their parents' emigration was best now that they were a "big kid," Ana did not see her situation as such. Ana could not see her father's departure as a way to address her more urgent economic needs now that she was older; if she viewed herself as older to accept her father's emigration, it would mean that her mother should leave too so that her parents could be together. Ana expressed difficulty understanding her father's emigration. She said she asks her father whenever he visits for Christmas or her birthday why he has to leave. When I asked her what he says, Ana replied, "He says he leaves because he has a lot of responsibility and loves his children lots and wants to take care of them." This explanation was not sufficient for Ana. Although most émigrés' children could explain the educational advantages from remittances, Ana told me that whenever her father calls, she still asks him why he left. Ana could repeat her father's reasons for emigrating, but she insisted that she did not know "why Daddy had to go away," seemingly lacking cognitive skills like cause-and-effect explanations or taking on other's perspectives normally achieved at her age (Piaget 1968). Rather than interpreting Ana as having a cognitive defect that limited these skills, I argue that she did not want to understand her father's explanation for psychodynamic reasons.[9] Understanding his explanation would increase her fear that her mother might join him.

Based on interview discussions, I believe that Ana transferred an understanding of her father's emigration to the likelihood that her mother would emigrate. In an interview about what a "good mother" does, she echoed her father's reasons for emigrating: "A good mother loves her children and has many responsibilities to take care of her children." She said that her mother was a good mother. Even though these interviews were more than two weeks apart, and many other children viewed the duties of a mother as distinct from the duties of a father (regardless of which parent was an émigré), Ana expressed a solid link between the two parental roles in her narrative of cultural values. In addition to a connection between the motivations for emigration, Ana saw a connection in the possible mode of departure for emigration. Ana feared her mother emigrating in the night like her father; in an interview defining emotions, Ana stated, "Sad is when you can't sleep because your mother goes with your father." Fearing her mother's emigration, rather than representing herself as older to justify her émigré father's distance, Ana represented herself as younger to solidify her mother's closeness.

Ana was more dependent on her mother than other children her age to prevent her mother's departure. Ana refused to accept more mature expectations. As homework requirements increase, parents are more likely to send children to "homework controls," where hired tutors supervise the children's homework. When Ana's mother had the maid help with homework, Ana refused to do the work and began failing her classes. After a parent-teacher meeting, Ana's mother resumed helping Ana, who diligently completed her homework for hugs and kisses. By being more immature on culturally significant indicators of entering a new age-grade, Ana avoided indicating to her mother that she was old enough for her mother to emigrate.

The view of herself as younger was not only at home. She seemed much younger than her same-age peers at school as well. Ana was the only girl over six who wore pigtails. She sat on my lap during recess and announced without qualms how much she cries because her father left.[10] Other children her age danced about with career aspirations of being singers, or talked about how much they liked animals and wanted to be veterinarians. Ana did not speak of growing up. She did not prepare for a real or imagined distant future, or bargain for more independence in accord with her growth.

Ana's manner of communication seemed younger than that of her peers as well. The stories Ana told in doll play lacked the strict narrative structure of a beginning, middle, and end typical of other children's stories. In Ana's stories, no crisis developed, nor did learning occur. In the longest story, over ten minutes, for all research participants, Ana told how a little girl was awoken, fed, bathed, dressed, taught at school, then came home and went to bed to repeat the series again.[11] Passive voice made it clear that the protagonist received care. Ana represented the actions of the narrative's protagonist in the passive voice, going against common usage: "The little girl was talked to for two hours, was brought home, and then other children came to visit." However, she used the active voice to describe the actions of the other characters in her stories. The story had a never-ending cycle without any development. Her protagonist neither grew nor completed tasks on her own.

Acting younger than the other children did limit some of Ana's friendships, but children were not mean to Ana, just as they would not be mean to a younger sibling. Older siblings do not adopt a competitive nature but pride themselves on their role as a positive example and a mother's helper. Kindness to younger siblings is an indication of appropriate social behavior and worthy of merit (Rae-Espinoza 2010). Even though Ana's self-representation prevented some social integration with her peers, it did reflect the use of cultural values to create a narrative that prevented cognizance of undesirable perceived consequences at home for growing up. Ana psychologically adapted to a fear of her mother's departure with "intrapsychic controls against the fully conscious eruption of such thoughts" (Levy 2005, 455). She sacrificed some social adjustment for a psychological adaptation (Vaillant 1977, 360).

Michelle's Manipulation of Cultural Values

Michelle's mother had migrated to New York two years earlier when her marriage did not work out. After living with a maternal aunt for a little over a year, Michelle now lived with her father. Although Michelle's father agreed that his ex-wife's emigration was a good idea, he thought she should have taken their daughter and was upset that no one had explained her plans to Michelle. Michelle was told only that her mother was going to New York to drop off a relative. Like Ana, Michelle could not normalize her situation of parental emigration. With the move from her aunt's house to her father's house, Michelle could see that her care was not stable and permanent. Although her father told Michelle that the move was because of religious differences, Michelle discussed how her misbehavior at the time brought about her move. Her aunt did not have enough time to go to school for parent-teacher meetings. Michelle said, "My aunt got mad and sent me to my dad's house." Since her father did not think that it was appropriate for a girl to be separated from a female caregiver, he told Michelle that as soon as she was old enough, she would join her mother in New York. In a discussion over a game of pool, Michelle's father pointed out how rare it was for a father to take over the care of children when the mother emigrates, which accords with government claims (Asamblea Nacional 2003, 19). By announcing his desire to resolve the distance between mother and daughter because fathers do not take care of children, he emphasized that distance between mother and daughter. I understand Michelle's difficulty in normalizing parental emigration as resulting from a fear that she could be sent away for needing care. For this reason, Michelle wanted to be grown-up already. If she were older, she would both join her mother and not need the care that made people send her away. I see evidence of this interpretation in her surprising ability to understand adult perspectives and her avoidance of rules associated with children. Like Ana, Michelle did not find a great amount of social integration, but she could mitigate concern over her family situation.

Although some children normalized transitions through several households as the way their émigré parent had decided to take care of them, Michelle did not. She did not see living with her father as the way that her family provided care because she feared that her need for care could lead to another move. Michelle actively refused care. She circumvented her one rule that meant she was a child: she could not prepare her own food by cooking. When told to eat what was prepared for her, she shirked the child role and pointed out how her paternal aunt, an international model, did not eat. This would cause an argument between her father and his sister about women's bodies—was she a "bone" lacking meat, or was he a rube who didn't get fashion? Michelle told me, "When they argue, they're funny and I can do whatever I want." She looked at their relationship as siblings from their perspective, rather than as parental figures to her, their role from her perspective.

Her ability to take on adult perspectives meant that she would often see through explanations given to children. When a group of children I was studying advanced from fourth to fifth grade, the new teacher had approved less time for me to take the children out of class for interviews. When children complained about the decrease in time, I informed them that since they were older, class was harder and they needed to spend more time in instruction. Michelle laughed and said, "She scares you just like she scares me. She's big and loud!" In my opinion, the teacher was scary—her direct, unexpected feedback, lack of warnings on impending discipline to children, and monotone declarative phrases were quite intimidating and different from other teachers. Michelle had read my behavior just as I had read hers. While Ana lacked an understanding of cause and effect, Michelle grasped others' perspectives (Piaget, Inhelder, and Mayer 1956).

Michelle's self-representation as older seemed to be successful at home. She was given more independence than other children her age. Michelle's father did not realize that his daughter behaved uncharacteristically for her age. With the bottle of Johnny Walker Red on the pool table in the living room, he often treated his daughter like a roommate, and she spent a lot of time at home on her own. When her father reprimanded her for opening the door to me the first time I visited, she rolled her eyes and told me the reprimand was for my benefit. Again referring to adult perspectives, she told me he wanted to look like a good father to me. Since he had said, "How could you know it was safe? You can't see through the peephole" (rather than "Children aren't allowed to open doors"), Michelle had placed a box next to the door to stand on for the next time I visited. In indicating that she did not need assistance in receiving a guest, Michelle cued that she was not a child whom someone might want to send away because the burden of care was too much.

Michelle was not only manipulative of adults based on her awareness of adult relationships with her paternal aunt and father. While Ana could not understand her father's motivations to emigrate, Michelle could understand adult motivations very well. For instance, she did not like the system that an adult had to approve my visits to her family home. She said that if we could find her father to ask, he would certainly say yes. Otherwise, she would be home alone. She knew both that her father liked having me around and that I did not like her being alone. In her emotion interview, she calmly told me, "Worried is when your dad doesn't return even when he says he would . . . that happened yesterday." Michelle smiled and said, "So you should come over tonight to watch *telenovelas*." Michelle could subtly play others' preferences to get her way. She did not throw tantrums or cry as Ana did, but joked and cajoled. She sent me text messages when she was bored to see what I was up to. I often felt that she needed more attention than the other children, but her desires for contact were similar to adult informants wanting to spend social time together rather than like the children who wished I would bring my markers to their house. Michelle had progressed beyond her years.[12] I believe Michelle's narratives fulfilled a psychodynamic function similar to Ana's narratives. Both precluded some psychic distress resulting from characteristics of their home life through age distortion while allowing some social integration with peers. Our own cultural emphasis that prioritizes increasing independence over the development of true interdependence should not obviate the similar manipulations of self-representations in the two girls' narratives.

Michelle established herself as an adult in interviews. She specified all her mother's care as occurring "before, when I was little." She sometimes made fun of the games I had designed for collecting data, calling them childish. To gather information on the roles that different people fulfilled in families and society, I designed a set of playing cards as prompts in a modified game of Go Fish. Michelle laughed at the playing cards and said, "Why is 'child' in here? Children don't do anything." However, she had no trouble describing what she did. She was not a child. She would quickly finish stories with requisite pieces of beginning, middle, and end so that we could chat about the previous night's *telenovela* episode, a frequent topic of conversation in my interviews with adults.

In regard to social integration, Michelle acted as if the other children were too young for her, but the boys had crushes on her and the other girls admired her. She could have made friends. Michelle was the only child who carried a purse full of makeup to apply during recess, rather than to show off to friends; having makeup to show off and share was a way to gain friends for girls in her grade.[13] One boy begged me to rearrange the group activities so that he could come at the same time as Michelle. She did not seem to find comfort in her popularity, and when asked who her best friend was, she named her paternal aunt. For her social adjustment, Michelle chose not to have many friends her age in her constructed self-representation to successfully adapt psychologically to her new home as a stable arrangement. Like Ana, she sacrificed some social adjustment for a successful psychological adaptation. By being an adult who did not need care, she would not be sent to the care of someone else while waiting to join her mother.

The two girls altered their self-representations to create innovative narratives that still reflected existing cultural values on age-grades. Ruptures from parental emigration do not necessarily create new cultural values for socialization but generate distinct motivations that direct how children internalize cultural values in creating their own narratives. All children have unique social, cultural, and psychological motivations that direct their construction of self-representative narratives. In her ethnography of dying children, Bluebond-Langner wrote that children's self-expressions "arise out of situations which in turn affect the view that the child has of himself and the world around him." These children and their caretakers avoided "mutual acknowledgement of the prognosis" so they could fulfill "their social roles and responsibilities" (1978, 49, 229). Ana and Michelle constructed narratives using agreed-upon cultural values to find some social confirmation for their own models of familial structure to meet their psychic needs. In their individual innovations, they perpetuate cultural values of family, specifically in regard to age-graded care. These two girls thus define themselves through narratives that find social approval, allowing them to grow together with their society and within themselves (Erikson 1963). Even though each of these cases represents a unique response to parental emigration in comparison to their peers, their narratives still follow a cultural logic. Fischer wrote: "Continuity is maintained by giving old forms new meanings and giving new forms old meanings" (2001, 13). We should not underestimate the role of underlying cultural logics in children's unique narratives, as culture is reproduced in novel ways. Every child adapts and adjusts to perceived ruptures while simultaneously maintaining aspects of the everyday.

Ontogeny of Emotion

Similar to the argument that cultural reproduction continues across ruptures for the children of émigrés as they draw on cultural notions, including age-graded care, to respond to parental emigration, emotional ontogeny continues across ruptures as well. A holistic analysis of emotional development in context reveals stability in how children acquire cultural understandings of emotions with transnational families. The emotional ontogeny of the children of émigrés is not irrevocably harmed, limiting them only to the expression of sadness and distress; in fact, analytic frameworks that focus only on negative emotions miss not just the expressions of positive affects but also the way several kinds of emotions are expressed, managed, and understood systematically in concordance with each other and a particular setting. An understanding of emotional functioning delves deeply into cultural, social, and psychological processes (Shweder 1985). To understand the emotional experience of the children of émigrés, we must look to the dynamic factors that shape emotions in context at home and in relationships with their émigré family members.

As with all children, the case studies here show how understanding the ontogeny of emotion involves both the observation of children's affective expressions in response to culturally meaningful elicitors and the social regulation of sentiments with significant figures. The differentiated emotional experience of children develops in the course of sociocultural interactions (Shweder 1985, 207). The children of émigrés came to understand their emotional expressions as those abroad and at home purposely modified and unknowingly displayed their own emotions. Other children in my field site who adapted and adjusted well to parental emigration displayed a full range of emotional expression in regard to both their émigré parents and their substitute care. Growing children have moments of time when their caregivers are heroes or impediments to desired activities. I selected two case studies that show how children systematically reveal a conflict in their development of emotion. Rather than being passive recipients of frameworks for emotional experiences, these children developed an affective system that dynamically influenced their self-representations. As with all children, we can see "the derivatives of the unconscious in material observations" (Freud 1965, 14). I present evidence of hidden internal negotiations as they created self-representations to meet psychic needs under the pressure of a particular cultural and social context.

Both Wilson and Sebastian constructed narratives while engaged in social relationships in a particular cultural context. They internalized psychologically meaningful experiences to shape their affect. Both were in their maternal grandmothers' care while their mothers were abroad. These children altered affective experiences to prevent problematic realizations about familial expectations in their particular situations as they dynamically constructed narratives. They developed their understandings of emotion in a context where both grandmothers cried when they believed the children did not hear them but instructed the children to feel positively about emigration. Amidst these confusing emotional directives, Wilson and Sebastian constructed narratives that hid problematic affects and represented acceptable ties to their émigré mothers and to their grandmothers who provided substitute care.

Wilson's Manipulation of Emotional Expression

Seven-year-old Wilson had been living with his maternal grandmother and four-year-old cousin for two years. Wilson's maternal grandfather and paternal family were not involved in his life. Without sufficient male support, his mother migrated to Italy. Her remittances were the only source of income for his grandmother, him, and his cousin. Unlike many other émigrés' children I studied, Wilson experienced his mother's emigration as a loss because, I believe, his grandmother limited the development of an alternative representation of his family life. I believe that her constant reminders of her own representation of his family life inhibited his ability to see his situation of substitute care as something normal through a recodification of family roles. Wilson could not view his grandmother as fulfilling the role of a redefined grandmother and his mother as a readjusted mother as other émigrés' children did because his grandmother declared incessantly that he was not missing anything—she provided him with everything he would need from a mother. To Wilson, these declarations indicated that his mother did not provide for him. I base this interpretation on his grandmother's emotional difficulty with her daughter's emigration, Wilson's confusion of kin roles, and his avoidance of emotional expression. Wilson's evasion of family discussion and turning inward did not lead to successful social integration, but it allowed him to avoid difficult topics.

Having developed an extremely close bond with Wilson, his grandmother emphasized her substitution as Wilson's mother to solidify his attachment to her and prevent Wilson from forgetting her in case he reunited with his mother. In a tearful discussion at school, Wilson's grandmother told me how difficult her daughter's emigration was for her. She said that émigrés want too much. She had agreed to take care of Wilson and has therefore "given him all her love," yet her daughter can still decide to take him and all that love away. She told me this would break her heart. She expressed the idea that she was emotionally his mother, but without the legal rights that went with this expenditure of her soul. Whether her daughter brought Wilson abroad or returned to Ecuador, Wilson's grandmother viewed the mother-child reunification as her losing a child. Instead of her daughter's return being a reunification of herself as mother and her daughter, Wilson's grandmother viewed it as the separation of herself as mother and her son.

Wilson's grandmother's concerns triggered kin confusion for Wilson. He had trouble answering questions in a discussion of roles, although children younger than he could complete this activity. He could not explain his opinion about the positive characteristics of a mother in general. Children usually echoed statements they had heard that fit their family well, or explained experiences that they enjoyed. Sometimes children gave answers that did not reflect reality; one girl said her mother was not a good mother. However, children always gave answers. Wilson shrugged. I believe that since Wilson's options—to state his experiences with his mother or to state his grandmother's views—countered each other, he could not respond. Responding would obligate him either to recognize that his mother does not fulfill the physical, proximate tasks his grandmother claimed were what made her his mother, or to indicate a continuing tie to his mother, which would upset his grandmother.

Wilson could describe his grandmother as a mother when the overlap was not problematic to a continuing connection with his mother. Eventually, avoiding the general category, he said that a good mother is his grandmother but at first could not explain why she is. He said he forgot. Then, he said, "She is good because my dad goes to the country-side a lot." She "gives him food and maintains him." Although both grandmothers and mothers provide food in local ideologies of distribu-tive care, "maintain" usually refers to economic child support, which is a fatherly task in Ecuadorian culture. He had no trouble with his grand-mother supplanting his father, who was not an émigré. His father also served to explain his mother's motivation for emigration and thereby confirm her as a responsible mother. These negotiations were difficult for Wilson.[14]

Along with his grandmother's insistences, the cousin who lived with Wilson complicated his kinship. His cousin had adapted to her substi-tute care by referring to their grandmother as her mother. If he referred to his grandmother as "grandmother," not only would he disappoint his grandmother, but also his four-year-old cousin would be his aunt, which would contradict cultural definitions of kinship roles. Yet if he referred to his grandmother as "mother," he would be denying his strong emo-tional connection to his mother. To partially resolve this, he called the little girl his cousin, but when the grandmother was included in a story, he referred to the girl as his sister. Wilson always contextualized his grandmother as like a mother, but his grandmother. Although Wilson's teacher told me that he sees his grandmother as if she were his mother, other children who had made this transition did not need to explain the shift every time. In fact, some teachers did not know about émigrés' chil-dren in their classroom because the children had referred to their grand-parents as their parents since preschool.

With the grandmother wanting neither her daughter to return nor Wilson to go abroad, Wilson could not depict his current family as nor-mal or in progress toward a specific ideal family arrangement in the fu-ture. Under pressure to see his mother as not a mother, Wilson learned to hide the emotional indicators of his deep connection to his mother. Wilson said that he did not tell his grandmother that he missed his mother because, "When I tell my grandmother, sometimes she starts to cry." However, Wilson did not want to sever ties to his mother. He said he just wanted his mother to return. If his mother returned, Wil-son imagined that he would not be separated from his grandmother. Al-though many children imagined all their caregivers living together, Wil-son did not suggest this as a possibility; his grandmother did not view it as a possibility, but I do not know if she had communicated this to him. Still, he found his mother's returning preferable to his emigrating to join his mother without his grandmother. For Wilson, repairing one rupture could mean another rupture in the everyday.

What instigated Wilson's emotional swings was observable only in negative relief: what he *did not say* was what was bothering him. His silence at such moments was obvious because he was so hyperactive and upbeat at other times. Wilson would knock on classroom doors for me and try to demonstrate to me how to fence with the color guard's flagpoles. On the way to my office, he greeted the other teachers. He lit up and became animated when given another piece of paper to draw on. However, when asked about his family, his speech went from rampant, jubilant, loud explanations to slow, quiet, and depressing comments. Wilson would give one-word answers when the questions related to his mother or he would avoid the topic altogether. Even at the first interview, when I asked about his drawing of his family, he hung his head low and I could not hear him. He mumbled, gazed at the floor, and fidgeted. He pouted, frowned, and shrugged. While not words, these behaviors spoke to his emotional experience of parental emigration.

Wilson's attempts at psychological adaptation limited some social adjustment in his peer group at school because he became verbally stalled with troublesome emotions. It might seem that a discussion of family does not occur frequently in the school context, but his emotional troubles were clear to others because of how linked families and schools are in Ecuador. For instance, one assignment to practice adjectives required students to write a paragraph describing their fathers. Many children had siblings at the school and parents came to pick students up. The teacher remembered Mother's Day as a time when Wilson was sad, even though it was months earlier. Following Vaillant (1977, 366), if mental health is success at living (not necessarily a complete cognizance of reality), Wilson was having trouble because he had to shut down in common situations to avoid emotional conflict.

Sebastian's Manipulation of Emotional Expression

Nine-year-old Sebastian had been in his maternal grandmother's care since his mother emigrated four years ago. He lived with his maternal grandparents, a great-grandmother, and a cousin, and from time to time with an aunt, uncle, and their children who came to stay. His mother emigrated for personal safety from his father, rather than for economic security. When Sebastian's mother restocked her clothing boutique through a bank loan, Sebastian's father believed she had received money from another man. Although they had been separated for three years, he burned down the store and ran over Sebastian's mother with a car in a jealous rage. Sebastian's grandmother agreed that her daughter should join the wife of a cousin abroad for her own safety. Sebastian did not view himself as having a continued, solidified bond to his mother as other émigré children did. Some children would talk about phone discussions or items sent from abroad as evidence of their bond. I believe that Sebastian did not because his grandmother emphasized his mother's distance. Like Wilson, Sebastian could not recodify family roles to represent his émigré mother as emotionally present. His grandmother's emotional difficulty with her daughter's emigration led to his emphasis of his mother's absence and subsequent avoidance of emotional expression. Sebastian's unique approach to discussions of his family inhibited some social integration even as it helped him to avoid difficult topics.

I believe that Sebastian's grandmother inhibited his acceptance of his mother's absence with her own incapacity to do so, which forced Sebastian to notice the empirical reality that he was not in a typical family, as many other children of émigrés saw themselves. In contrast to Wilson's grandmother, Sebastian's grandmother insisted that she was not Sebastian's mother, but his mother still was. His grandmother told Sebastian that his mother was still devoted and sacrificed for him through her emigration. Sebastian's grandmother told me the details of her daughter's emigration through tears. As we talked on her second-floor patio, she explained that her daughter was not like other émigrés in that she did not want to leave her family. Sebastian's grandmother saw her inability to have her daughter safe and nearby as especially cruel; she loves her daughter so much that her heart needs her daughter to be far away to know that she is safe. Even though she did not think highly of Sebastian's father, she followed her daughter's example of shielding Sebastian from negative views on his father. Her daughter had encouraged Sebastian to continue to love his father, following Ecuadorian parental ethnotheories that loving a bad father is better than having no father to love at all. Sebastian's grandmother viewed her daughter as an excellent mother. When she sensed a detachment between Sebastian and his mother, she further extolled her daughter's virtues because, she said, "Children have trouble seeing the dedication providing for your family requires." The grandmother's discussions of reunification to encourage Sebastian to stay connected to his mother were at the root of Sebastian's fear that he might lose his grandmother.

Sebastian's grandmother tied her concern about Sebastian lacking his mother to her concern about herself lacking her daughter. When I asked his grandmother if Sebastian misses his mother, she said, "Yes. No mother wants to have a child at a distance, so no one should migrate." Sebastian's grandmother expressed her anxiety at the loss of her daughter in her relationship with Sebastian—she was afraid someone would kidnap him for ransom since he was the child of an émigré, and then she would "have nothing left from her daughter." She feared losing the enduring, personified link to her émigré daughter. Sebastian was not allowed to go to the store like other children his age and was told to be careful when walking in the parking lot from the school building to the school bus. Her fears of his being kidnapped in the parking lot compounded his fears of traffic in the parking lot.[15]

Sebastian displayed his perceptions of his mother's physical absence as emotional distance, rather than as a necessary part of motherhood as other children did. When telling a story with paper cutouts of people in a modified method of doll play and the Thematic Apperception Test (Gardner 1989), Sebastian told a narrative about a mother and grandmother bringing a child with a stomachache to the doctor. Sebastian divided the cutouts on the scene page: the mother was on one side; the grandmother, child, and doctor were on the other. As the grandmother consulted the doctor, he moved the cutouts like puppets, and the child, grandmother, and doctor all had physical contact. He moved cutouts as the grandmother said, "Thank your mother" and as the child cutout said, "Thank you for paying for my treatment." The mother cutout did not leave the far side of the scene. With other children of émigrés, real-world distances did not limit make-believe in which transnational care extended across physical boundaries. In contrast, Sebastian focused on the literal, physical distance rather than on an alternative interpretation that allowed emotional maintenance across distance.

Although Sebastian perceived his mother's distance, his grandmother's representation of him joining his mother as a complete restoration of previous arrangements was not easy to accept either. He was strongly connected to his grandmother. In another narrative, Sebastian pointed out that those who are not present do not know what happened while they were gone. Separating the cutouts once again, a mother waited at home for her children and the grandmother to arrive. The grandmother and children parked the car, and the grandmother told them to be careful of traffic. It took a long time to cross all the children safely, but the grandmother continued with her mission. Sebastian said:

"The grandmother carefully crossed the street with each grandchild one at a time. She said, 'Wait here for a moment' and went back to walk across the street with the next grandchild. Then she went back to get the next one and then the last one. The children watched as their grandmother crossed each of them. Then the grandmother sent them inside the house and their mom said, 'Be careful crossing the street because a car can run you over and then you have to go to the hospital,' and they all said nothing." Here the story ends. When the children entered the house, still physically separated from the mother, they do not inform the mother of the care they received or greet her with a kiss on the cheek. The grandmother took care of the children and the mother did not know of her devotion. Sebastian's representation of traffic as requiring extreme caution was a telling reference to the event that led to his mother's emigration. In projective measures like this, the child tells a story that "inadvertently reveals . . . unconscious tensions; attitudes toward death, violence, sex, and parents; and latent or repressed material" (Adams, Milner, and Schrepf 1984, 290). Although from his lack of emotion one could infer that nothing was bothering Sebastian, the symbolism in his projective tests indicated internal concerns.

Both positive and negative emotions can accompany separation, but I believe that the grandmother's dependence on Sebastian's emotional state denied him either one. On the one hand, Sebastian could not express his sadness at his mother's departure because his grandmother's words contradicted this interpretation. He would disappoint his grandmother if he did not see his mother as fulfilling all maternal expectations. On the other hand, he could not express happiness at his mother's emigration because his grandmother's emotions contradicted this interpretation. Sebastian's grandmother tells him that everything is great, but he hears her sobbing at night. Sebastian's living arrangements reminded him every day of the vacancy that his mother's emigration caused. The extended family was crammed into the second floor of their house rather than using the first floor where he had once lived with his mother.

This dynamic motivated Sebastian to separate the emotion from his thoughts about his mother, a process called intellectualization (Vaillant 1977). The psychological defense of intellectualization can be difficult to explain because, according to Lutz (1988), our cultural models prioritize rationality over emotion. Therefore, the use of intellectualization may not be noticeable. Sebastian was efficient, even-handed, and rhythmic in his answers to interview prompts. He told me: "My mom is in Spain. She left when I was four years old. I live with my grandmother, cousins, and aunts and uncles." The clear, calm discussion of his mother's departure and his living arrangements was notable considering the violent event that led to her emigration. His lack of emotion when discussing his mother's departure may appear to indicate a positive response to parental emigration. However, an absence of emotional expression can indicate a deficiency in an individual's ability to adequately adjust to new social situations and to concordantly adapt psychologically. For children, growing pains may be a necessary part of bemoaning limitations and rejoicing in freedoms as they assimilate new information and accommodate it with previous experiences.

To aid intellectualization, Sebastian projected his emotions onto his nine-year-old male cousin with whom he lived, whose parents were émigrés together abroad. The cousin was not expected to reunite with his parents, and he was placed in the grandmother's care when he was very little. The cousin was the only equal relationship Sebastian had: their grandmother, rather than their mothers, cared for them; they were the same age; neither had siblings; and they were cousins to each other and to all the other cousins. Sebastian's cousin was the perfect person on whom to displace his problematic emotions. In an interview on emotion, he defined happy as "being with all of your family, behaving, and helping your cousins," and for an example sentence said, "My cousin was happy when he went to the circus." He continued to focus on his cousin in defining sad and worried. Sebastian said, "Sad is when you are alone in the house and worried is when Grandma leaves and returns at midnight." Both his example sentences related to his cousin: his cousin was sad and worried when his grandmother was not in the house. He said his cousin feared being alone. Sebastian said this happens when his grandmother has to go out at night.[16] I asked Sebastian what should be done if someone feels this way, and he said there is nothing one can do to deal with an emotion. Sebastian had no responses for the safe management, expression, or dissipation of an emotion, given the grandmother's responses to him and the father's behavior.

Expressing emotions was unsurprisingly confusing and scary to Sebastian. Missing his mother meant he did not understand her need to leave; not missing his mother meant he did not understand her continued dedication. Hatred for his father who harmed his mother was both maternal devotion and maternal treason, since his mother wanted him to love his father. Emotional denial to reassure a beloved caregiver parallels the dynamic that Wilson's grandmother created. Sebastian's affect was not entirely flat, but he lacked the typical variation with excitement for gym, anger at stingy friends, shame at being the center of attention, frustration at homework, or sadness when others ignored their play rules. Sebastian's avoidance of emotion left him lacking the behavior expected in peer groups for social adjustment, but the avoidance helped his psychological adaptation.

Sebastian and Wilson both hid emotions in order to reflect the affective framework of their caregivers for relating to their transnational parents. Completely detaching from a mother to attach to a grandmother or remaining completely attached to a distant mother both challenged cultural ideas of motherhood. The boys had difficulty integrating the values their substitute caregivers offered with their own feelings about parental emigration. Children develop emotional understandings within a framework of stated and observed experiences of others. Among the Inuit, Briggs observed how children learn to control their temper once they gain reason, or *ihuma*, through both "internal" and "autonomous" growth and as their temper is "informed" and "instructed" (1970, 112). In a transition to older childhood, children learn to control their hostility and anger at the loss of maternal closeness (162). As with the children Briggs studies, the emotional experiences of émigré children develop betwixt and between social relations that transmit cultural values and through dynamic cognitive assimilations and accommodations of cultural values. The children demonstrate persistent emotional ties to their transnational family members. Seeing how the embodied experience of emotion reshapes cultural propositions is central to understanding cultural reproduction and reinvention.

Internal Agency

These four cases demonstrate the role of individual factors in shaping children's reactions to parental emigration. Children reproduce cultural values and develop emotional understandings while engaging in their unique situations, particularly with significant others, so we should not assume that all children experience parental emigration in the same way. These cases reveal the individual's role in adapting and adjusting to parental emigration. That the everyday continues during ruptures in cultural reproduction and in the ontogeny of emotion indicates that children are active in their socialization. They seek equilibrium in cultural models to avoid cognitive dissonance and insecurity in an unpredictable world (Festinger 1957). Equilibrium refers to the fact that for efficacious functioning, these models taken together ought to make sense (D'Andrade 1992). Establishing equilibrium among models may not be easy for any child; considering situational variation, others' perspectives, hidden rules, ramifications for different gradations of deviations, and the discrepancy between stated beliefs and actual behaviors, it is surprising that children who cannot adapt are the noted exceptions. Individuals navigate a sea of cultural values to integrate their personality and to belong in society (Obeyesekere 1984). Children of émigrés, like all children, reproduce cultural norms and comprehend the appropriate projective systems for emotion. In effect, these cases expand notions of agency to include internal feats that have great personal meaning but that one would hardly notice without a focus on an individual's perspective. Our ideas of culture cannot ignore individual variation without limiting culture to superficial descriptions. In-depth investigations of individual perspectives can reveal the sources of both continuities and innovations of culture.

As children of émigrés daily form their own ideas of who they are through external factors and internal processes, we can come to understand the construction of these transnational narratives of self and thereby uncover how children psychologically adapt and socially adjust to parental emigration within their own particular cultural context, to meet their own developmental needs, and to attain social acceptance. These processes do not indicate aberrant development and most certainly do not indicate inevitable psychological trauma. The children of émigrés are not stunted, confused, or emotionally numb. Like all children, they are agentive innovators of culture in constructing narratives for the reproduction of culture and for the experience of affect. Children of émigrés, however, are uniquely positioned to exhibit this activity by challenging simplified developmental pathways that interpret geographically separated transnational families as emotionally separated.

PART IV

Status and the State: State Power, Migrant Responses, and Constructions of Childhood

Chapter 7

Schooling and the Everyday Ruptures Transnational Children Encounter in the United States and Mexico

Edmund T. Hamann and Víctor Zúñiga

The system isn't working when 12 million people live in hiding, and hundreds of thousands cross our borders illegally each year; when companies hire undocumented immigrants instead of legal citizens to avoid paying overtime or to avoid a union; when communities are terrorized by ICE immigration raids—when nursing mothers are torn from their babies, when children come home from school to find their parents missing, when people are detained without access to legal counsel.
—Barack Obama, July 13, 2008

The core consideration of this volume is the everyday ruptures that characterize the experiences of transnational children and youth. As the term "everyday" implies, the focus is on the quotidian, the unremarkable, the ordinary or common, in pointed contrast with the term "rupture," which implies violent separation, shock, and break. Per this understanding, the dynamics of ICE raids that separate parents and children, mentioned by then-candidate Obama in the epigraph, qualify as ruptures, but not as everyday ruptures.[1] Important as the obvious traumas of a raid would be for schoolchildren not knowing to whom they will come home, the part of candidate Obama's quote that most interests us here is his location of children involved in migration—that is, at school. It is our contention that the regular practice of schools can be a source of routine rupture for transnationally mobile children and thus that schools need to be accounted for in a thorough depiction of the everyday ruptures encountered by transnationally mobile children.

As is noted in this volume's introduction, definitions of childhood—who is a child, what it means to be a child, and how children should be treated—vary historically and across cultures (Orellana 2009). Yet this diversity of perspectives gets dramatically reduced or ignored in an important way through the processes of schooling. In the United States, both the terms "third grader" and "third-grade reading" level have descriptive coherence, in the first instance describing an eight- or nine-year-old in the fourth year of school and in the second providing a rationale, as well as a norm, for what a reading curriculum should look like for most third graders. In other words, eight-year-olds may vary a lot, but at school much of that variation is ignored while norms about expected competencies are reified.

In Mexico, school is also a vehicle for defining age-related norms, as well as for marking deviancy when children do not meet those norms. In our study of students in Mexico with previous school experience in the United States, a study that informs much of this chapter, we found that such students were three times more likely to have repeated a year of school than those whose experience had been entirely in Mexico (30 percent to 9 percent). In other words, when children came to school with different experiences than were expected, it was often determined that such deviation meant a deficit and students were assigned as if they were behind.

Practically every country in the world mandates that children attend school and then spells out much of what should happen to students once they are at school. Children are thereby subject to state definitions that, as Margaret Mead (1961, 89) once reminded us about the United States, may well be arbitrary, but are no less consequential for that fact:

> Our thought is hidebound by a thousand outworn conventions; real
> school begins only at five or six. Before that, even if the children
> are in groups, it isn't real; it's nursery school or kindergarten. . . .
> What possible grounds are there for believing that education should
> begin at six or four or three, while before that something different,
> called child rearing or socialization, takes place? Why is it of value
> to society to gather children together under outside tutelage that will
> supplement the home when they are five but not earlier?

Mead went on to recommend that U.S. society should consider why its schools are arranged the way they are, why children in those schools are viewed the way they are, and whether these arrangements are optimal. She did not claim they were necessarily faulty, only that their ways merited explicit consideration rather than unquestioning acquiescence.

In that spirit, given the focus on everyday ruptures, it is worthwhile to consider how a typical, unremarkable quotidian activity—the act of attending school—can become the means for subjecting children who have moved transnationally to quotidian moments of shock, disconnection, and reiterated dislocation. Considering the fates and trajectories of transnational newcomers, Carola Suárez-Orozco (2004) refers to an "ethos of reception," in which schools are centrally implicated. It is our contention that, as part of the larger ethos of reception negotiated by transnational students, schools can create everyday ruptures. Schools do so by acting in unfamiliar ways or in ways that ignore or reject the biography and sense of identity that some students bring to school.

As feminist poet and theorist Adrienne Rich (cited in Rosaldo 1989, ix) once memorably wrote: "When someone with the authority of a teacher, say, describes the world and you are not in it, there is a moment of psychic disequilibrium, as if you looked in the mirror and saw nothing." This chapter argues that there are many transnational children—children with experience in two or more school systems—who do not see large portions of their biographies and identities reflected in the everyday practice of school. This is because everyday school practice is associated with the construction of national identity (e.g., Benei 2008; Booth 1941; Levinson 2005; Luykx 1999; Rippberger and Staudt 2003). However, some students do not share the identity being promoted. Some others do embrace it, but only as a portion of their hybrid selves. Those in a third group seek to embrace the national identity espoused by their new country's schools but find that the system denies their bid to assume that identity (Becker 1990), perhaps because their relative incompetence with the behaviors and epistemologies—that is, the "cultural models" (Quinn and Holland 1987)—associated with that identity undercut their efforts to be included.

Schooling's incomplete responsiveness to biography is consequential in at least two ways. First, per a constructivist understanding of learning (Vygotsky 1978), learners make sense of new information by referencing what they already know. Thus a curriculum that is responsive to student biography and a teacher who knows how to help students reference their background knowledge related to a given topic can facilitate or expedite a student's constructivist learning. Put a different way, as Valenzuela (1999) has noted, schooling that does not value the heritage and knowledge students bring with them to school is intrinsically "subtractive," with the real consequence of heightened school failure. Second, as Erickson has noted (1987), learning in the zone of proximal development—that is, learning that a student can do with the help of a teacher, but that is beyond their independent capacity—requires trust. Per this understanding, students will push themselves harder if (a) they do not want to disappoint a teacher (which requires caring about that teacher) and (b) they know they do not risk embarrassment or criticism for wrong or incomplete answers. One way for teachers to build trust is to show an interest in learning about a student's background and a willingness to have that background be respected in the classroom.

The remainder of this chapter uses two datasets to illuminate how schools can be sites of everyday rupture for transnationally mobile children. One dataset comes from a study of students in Mexico who have attended schools in the United States. The second study references older work among Mexican newcomers in a demographically fast-changing small city in the U.S. South. Both authors participated in both studies. The conclusion includes a meditation on the roles of schools in cultural challenge and erasure, as well as in creating national identity and membership.

We start with a case study of a student and her teacher whom we encountered in Mexico. They were interviewed separately. We also include an account from another Mexican teacher (not at the case study school) that offers a complementary illustration of how limitations in teachers' knowledge of transnational students positions teachers to be agents of rupture (wittingly or not). Our goal in this segment is to provide a vivid illustration of everyday ruptures at the scale of a particular individual in a particular place at a particular time.

Everyday Ruptures at the Level of a Single Student and Teacher

The case of Gaby, a Mexico-born student who had lived most of her life in Chicago before returning to Mexico, illustrates the disconnect, reinforced by everyday ruptures, that transnationally mobile students can feel. Later in this essay we further situate Gaby, describing the study through which we met her and considering quantitative data regarding the sense of national identity that complicates transnationally mobile students' experiences with Mexican schools. For now, however, the point to concentrate on is Gaby's invisibility—the portion of Gaby's identity that is unknown or deemed irrelevant in her encounters with Mexican secondary school.[2]

Gaby was in her final year of *secundaria* (ninth grade) when we met her. She had been born in Monterrey and brought to Chicago when she was four years old. She went to Chicago schools from kindergarten through grade eight but had recently returned with her parents and one sibling to Nuevo León. Older siblings remained in Chicago working. She was fourteen when we interviewed her and unusually clear in articulating her thoughts and feelings. She considered English to be her first language, although she spoke Spanish comfortably (as illustrated through our interview of her in Spanish). She did, however, sometimes pause when speaking Spanish as a term in English occurred to her and she had to think about ways to convey the same idea in Spanish.

Gaby described her experience in Chicago schools as rich and said she wanted to return there because the schools "are wonderful, and everybody is good and helps you a lot." ("*[Las escuelas] están muy padres y todos son muy buenos contigo y te ayudan mucho.*") She especially valued the professionalism and the kindness of her teachers. She could recall only one bad teacher, who punished those who spoke Spanish, but the majority of her U.S. teachers she liked and appreciated. She remembered a Filipina teacher who spoke Spanish and an Anglo teacher who wanted to learn Spanish and who asked her Spanish-speaking students to help her. She described in detail Illinois's standardized exams, their frequency, and their importance for advancing. She also described other rites and rhythms of schooling in Chicago, relating clearly how teachers asked questions and what kinds of answers they expected, how they prepared students for exams, how many minutes one usually had to respond to a question, and even when it was time for a snack.

In contrast—and not questioning how well U.S. schools had prepared her for her current Mexican context—Gaby depicted a bleak image of teachers and schooling in Mexico. She said Mexican teachers scolded and punished students, offering little support. According to Gaby, the only thing Mexican teachers did well was yell at students. She said the teachers seemed desperate when students did not quiet down and do their schoolwork. Gaby said she felt isolated in Mexico and wanted to return to Chicago. She had not made friends during her five months back in Mexico. All her friends were still in Chicago, and she stayed in contact with them through the Internet and occasionally through a telephone call. Yet Gaby conceded that her younger brother (who was born in Chicago and thus legally a U.S. citizen) was having a more favorable experience in Mexico and had no interest in leaving.

It seems fair to say that Gaby was not integrated well into her new school. Locating some of the explanation for this circumstance with her or seeing it as epiphenomenal and something that might change with time does not make it any less true. An interview with one of Gaby's teachers, la maestra P., a *secundaria* teacher who taught Gaby's math and chemistry classes, suggested that at least some of Gaby's discomfort came from what she encountered at school in Mexico. La maestra told us that Gaby spoke Spanish well and that her mastery of that language was high, so she guessed that Gaby had been in a school in the *sur* (south) of the United States (presumably Texas, which has many links to Nuevo León). In other words, la maestra did not know that Gaby's U.S. experience had been in Chicago. Although la maestra did not speak English, she alleged that Gaby's level of English was poor. La maestra had never visited a U.S. school, but she was sure that the pace of math learning there was slow and argued that was why Gaby was having trouble with Mexican math. She also said Gaby was struggling even more with history: "Regarding [Mexican] history, she knows nothing. I talked to her history teacher and he said what [Gaby] needs. . . . History is hard. Now the teacher we have is very strict; he demands a lot." ("*De historia no sabía nada, ya hablé con el maestro de historia y le dije lo que necesita. . . . En historia se las ve duras y luego el maestro que tenemos aquí de historia es muy estricto, él le exige mucho.*") This comment also reveals that Gaby was a student whose teachers talked about her, with one teacher reinforcing the negative judgments of another.

La maestra P. did not think there should be a special program for transnational students. Instead she suggested that they should be treated just like any other student—any differences in experiences and perhaps cosmology could be ignored. She also did not think it was necessary to talk with Gaby's parents. In fact, she did not even think it was necessary to talk individually with Gaby, except as she would individualize a comment, like "Please sit down," with any student on rare occasions. La maestra claimed the only important thing was that transnational students integrate with their classmates. For them to succeed, one needed to leave them alone, having them integrate little by little. "We can't shelter them . . . this [integration] is better for them." ("*Porque no los podemos sobreproteger . . . y eso, incluso, es más benéfico para ellos.*") For la maestra,

Gaby's background was incidental. Gaby was just like any other student, although the talk about her with other teachers suggested that la maestra did not actually act as if this were so. Her teacher's proof that Gaby was not different from the others was that she spoke Spanish like the other students, at least in the teacher's informal estimation; Gaby had not been given a Spanish-language proficiency test. La maestra could not envision the school and community realities that Gaby had described to us, but she saw no flaws in her limited perspective.

Gaby's case illustrates how the invisibility of the phenomenon of student transnationalism in Mexican schools can become a source of misunderstandings, subtle forms of rejection, and feeling unwelcome. The dogma of a homogenous national identity in Mexico (Zúñiga 1998) has a clear manifestation in school practices and relations. Gaby's teachers do not know how many years Gaby attended school in Chicago. They do not know much about what she has studied, or how well she did. If la maestra P. is typical, then Gaby's Mexican teachers appear to know practically nothing about her personal or educational history, but they do not find this lack problematic. From her teachers' perspective, Gaby is Mexican; she has no alternative. To be sure, part of Gaby's identity *is* Mexican. But Gaby is not only Mexican, and treating her as if that is all she is leaves out much that she knows and much that would engage her. School is a site where the richness of Gaby's transnational biography is ignored. School is a site of rupture for Gaby; it tells her that only part of how she sees herself is welcome.

Ruptures can be a product of teachers' understandings, something that we can further illustrate summarizing the representations of U.S. schools and education expressed by another teacher—la maestra Y., a junior high teacher at a private school in Zacatecas. La maestra has never been in the United States. However, she trusted what her brother (who spent three years in the United States with his family) told her: "My brother was there [in the United States] with his kids. When his older daughter was going to start *la secundaria* [seventh grade], he decided to come back because everybody told him that the schools were really dangerous there, a lot of drugs. He was afraid his daughter would become a bad person, so he preferred to return to Mexico." La maestra not only described U.S. schools as risky institutions, but also claimed they represented in some sense the opposite of Mexican ones: "There, they have another lifestyle, different ideas. Everything is different."

Next, la maestra Y. admitted she did not know any transnational students matriculated in her own school. (In a very limited sample of the school, our research team found three such students; if that sample was representative then the school may have had a dozen such students. It is our guess that she did know some of these students, but did not know their transnational histories.) Her vision on the transnational schooling experience arises from the stories of her nephew and niece: "Oh yeah, I remember my nephew. He was in sixth grade [when he came to Zacatecas]. He did not know much about our history—he was smart in mathematics, but did not know much about Mexican history, nothing about the Revolution or Independence. He was ignorant of a lot of things. He used to say: 'I feel bad, Mom, but I really do not know all those things.' I think that is why he repeated sixth grade; it was so hard for him." With an overgeneralized sense of what transnational school experience might mean (drawn from her nephew's experience) and a lack of awareness regarding which of her current students might be transnational, it is not hard to imagine la maestra Y. as an unwitting agent of everyday rupture.

Still, Gaby's case or the descriptions of maestra P. and maestra Y. are only interesting and perhaps sad oddities if we cannot place them within a larger context. But we can establish such a context by considering data from the rest of the study that Gaby's story comes from and from another study—an examination of a U.S. school district's response to rapid growth in its Latino newcomer enrollment. In our estimation, both studies illustrate that schools are not settings predisposed to affirm transnational students' full biographies. Nor, because of this, are they complete in readying students for possible transnational adulthoods. If schools presume a task of welcome and affirmation, they see that task, at its broadest, to be a welcome or affirmation of affiliation to the nation-state.

The study described next, which was carried out in Georgia in the late 1990s, led us to engage in the second study, the study of transnational students in Mexico that helped us find Gaby. This next study provides a version of the same dilemmas from the U.S. side: How willing are U.S. districts to honor their transnational students' full biographies and, looking forward, how many are willing and able to have their schooling be preparatory for persistently transnational adulthoods? To be sure, these may seem to be unfamiliar school tasks, but their absence and related partial denial of transnational student ontologies constitute and precipitate the everyday ruptures negotiated by transnational youth.

Here, but Perhaps Not Staying

Throughout the 1990s, Dalton, Georgia (in the U.S. South), the self-described "Carpet Capital of the World," provided an attractive job list for a growing number of Latino workers and thus also became the place of residence for their families, including school-age children. In the mid-1990s, when we first started work in this community, the majority of Latino children enrolled in Dalton schools were foreign born, mainly from Mexico (Hamann 2003). The school district's response was uneven but substantive, and it assumed that the newcomer population needed the skill sets that mattered locally and nationally (e.g., English skills), but not necessarily transnationally.

Dalton's emergence as a key site for "education in the new Latino diaspora" (Wortham, Murillo, and Hamann 2002) was the reason the two authors of this paper met and ultimately found Gaby. Zúñiga went to Dalton in 1996 when a NAFTA-related business connection between Dalton executives and industrialists based in Monterrey, Mexico, led to an invitation for Zúñiga's university, the Universidad de Monterrey (UdeM), to serve as a consultant for Dalton's schools as they negotiated an unprecedented demographic transformation. Zúñiga headed UdeM's participation in what became known as the Georgia Project. Hamann, a doctoral student looking for a site in Georgia to study the schooling of Latinos, was invited at the same time to help Dalton Public Schools draft a federal Title VII—Systemwide Bilingual Education grant that was to provide key resources for the Georgia Project.

We were both invited there because local leaders, including school district leaders, wanted help serving the rapidly growing Latino enrollment, which climbed from 4 percent in 1989 to a majority in 2001. Just what those local leaders were seeking varied (as described at length in Hamann 2003) and was sometimes both ambiguous and contradictory. Yet two ideas that they did seem to agree upon were that (a) the rapidly growing Latino population was a permanent population—that is, it intended to stay—and (b) it was the schools' task to teach the children of the newcomers how to succeed academically and otherwise in Dalton, Georgia. In other words, the inclusive, but perhaps not fully biographically responsive, charge for schooling—to prepare students for the community, region, and nation where they were—was to be extended to the newcomers.

Based on this agreement, the four-component, binational Georgia Project was created, formalizing a role for UdeM to help the Dalton community, particularly the schools. The initial plan for the Georgia Project was not necessarily only assimilation oriented. It included plans to invite teachers from Mexico to work in Dalton schools, plans to engage Georgia teachers in summer professional development travel study in Mexico, a proposed bilingual overhaul of the whole K-12 curriculum, and a community study intended to identify local Latino leaders, discover Latino newcomers' views on educational opportunities for both K-12 and adult education, and initiate political leadership training. Yet, understanding assimilation as a change process in which one group becomes more like another (Gordon 1964), our claim that assimilation was the goal of local school and community leaders was borne out by the varying fates of each component.

The least successful initiative was the bilingual curriculum overhaul, which was officially agreed to, talked about in the abstract for eighteen months, and then unilaterally rejected by Dalton educational leaders. Despite successfully bidding for a Systemwide Bilingual Education grant in 1997, school district leaders ultimately saw no enduring need for the district to have the capacity to offer all its instruction in its two most represented languages. They were modestly amenable to elementary-level transitional bilingual education (TBE), but the point of that kind of a program was to offer instruction in Spanish only as long as necessary to assist a student's academic progress before that student was ready for a classroom environment of only English. Spanish was not opposed in Dalton, but nor was it seen as having enduring value.

The summer travel study for Georgia teachers in Mexico was originally more successful, as seventeen teachers (of more than three hundred in the district) spent an intense month in Monterrey in 1997 learning Spanish, Mexican history, and Mexican curriculum and instruction. Yet despite their rave reviews of the experience (and the decision by several 1997 participants to repeat the experience in 1998), the 1998 summer program was decidedly smaller than the first year's. In 1999, a program change to have only two weeks in Mexico and two at Dalton State College briefly revived the program, but by 2002, after a change in superintendents, Dalton was no longer willing to support teachers for even the modified two-week/two-week experience. The travel-study program faded away because the Dalton leaders who initially hazily embraced it ultimately offered little conceptual support for it. Program participants were not encouraged to share their learning with colleagues. A different curricular intervention—a highly scripted initiative called Direct Instruction (which among many things reduced teachers' professional autonomy and discretion and thus limited their application of professional knowledge)—undercut the rationale for having Dalton teachers better understand the context from which a growing number of students and parents were coming. Returning to the idea of everyday ruptures, a professional development strategy that helped teachers adapt curriculum and instruction to be more familiar to newcomers (that is, to diminish the rupture experienced by newcomer students) was allowed to wither away because the idea that such expertise was needed was not found sufficiently salient.

The most successful and visible Georgia Project initiative brought UdeM-trained teachers to serve as visiting instructors in Dalton schools. The first cohort, which arrived in October 1997, consisted of single, bilingual, young women who, perhaps not unrelated to their publicly acknowledged attractiveness, were welcomed seemingly everywhere they went. Yet if their presence was welcome, their competence was not, at least not fully. As an accommodation to Georgia's teaching certification requirements (which did not recognize credentials from a U.S.-accredited Mexican university as sufficient for full professional status), the visiting instructors were welcomed as paraprofessionals and, as such, always had to obtain formal approval for their activities from a Georgia-certified teacher. As paraprofessionals, it was their task to respond to the lesson plans of the lead instructor. Of course, this design ignored the certified instructors' lack of expertise with Mexican newcomer students as the reason the visiting instructors had been sought in the first place (and it ignored the Mexican instructors' being brought in under H1-B visas, a category that allows jobs to be offered to those with high skills for which there is an inadequate domestic supply).

Not long after their arrival, as the bilingual curriculum they had been told they would help implement was rejected and the scripted, phonics-intensive Direct Instruction model was introduced across the district, the visiting instructors found themselves working with small groups of students teaching English phonetic pronunciations. Per this curricular adjustment, newcomer students from Mexico were taught by teachers from Mexico who, per script, were not supposed to reference their shared cultural background and orientation as a pedagogical resource.

Almost immediately, program coordinators at UdeM questioned the use of the visiting instructors for Direct Instruction. Still, assisting with its implementation remained one of their tasks for as long as the Georgia Project persisted in Dalton. Ultimately, UdeM suspended the visiting instructor part of the Georgia Project in 2000 when a new superintendent in Dalton eliminated an extra compensation—free use of a van—that had been extended to the visiting instructors. While UdeM's response may seem dramatic for loss of a relatively modest perk, it is important to see the van's cancellation through a symbolic lens. As long as the UdeM partners felt that there was recognition in Dalton of the expertise and knowledge that the visiting instructors brought to Georgia—and the van was tangible evidence of such a perspective—the UdeM partners could tolerate the idea of a state-level government bureaucracy (that is, Georgia's education laws) blocking their teachers' full recognition. Even in the face of Direct Instruction, the van was proof of local recognition of the visiting instructors' expertise. When that was taken away, it meant the fully trained, UdeM-originating visiting instructors were no longer distinguished from any of the district's other paraprofessionals.

Put another way, the UdeM visiting instructors originally brought in because they could communicate better with newcomer students quickly found support for that communication constrained by a curricular change that rejected curricular adaptations that attended to the knowledge and background that newcomer students brought with them to school. Then the program ultimately ended when the local modification that had acknowledged that the visiting instructors were better trained and brought relevant information from and about Mexico and Mexican schooling was terminated. It was still acknowledged that the visiting instructors brought skills that were relevant to the educational tasks of Dalton schools, but in the end, it was decided that trained professionals with Spanish skills and familiarity with Mexican ways were not worth any more than untrained paraprofessionals. So an attempt to reduce everyday ruptures for students with migration experiences ended.

Each of the Georgia Project examples considered so far references how portions of Mexican newcomer students' biographies were not valued in the Dalton context, but the final piece of the Georgia Project also raises a different point. It highlights that, at least for a few, the assimilative assumption governing Dalton's participation in the Georgia Project was characterized not only by paternalism or dismissiveness, but also by its mismatch with many students' future trajectories.

The fourth part of the Georgia Project agreement supported UdeM sociologists conducting a multifaceted community needs assessment, as well as some adult leadership-training activities. It is the needs assessment that pertains here, although not because it was locally consequential. It mostly was not. The ten findings of the assessment were politely received and then, except to the extent it confirmed any existing efforts, it was largely ignored.

The fourth of the ten findings did, however, appear to confirm one of the operating assumptions that helped support the Dalton partners' participation. That finding, summarized at the beginning of the needs assessment report, noted: "Dalton's Hispanic community is an established community that believes in building its future in Dalton and [surrounding] Whitfield [County]. This contradicts the idea that the Hispanic community is a temporary migrant community with no roots planted in community life" (Hernández-León et al. 1997, 2). In other words, the finding confirmed that the Georgia Project needed to happen because the Mexican newcomers were there to stay. This claim of general permanence was well grounded. In an article published in *Social Science Quarterly*, Hernández-León and Zúñiga (2000) presented the data that had led to their fourth conclusion. They noted that in a survey of more than a hundred Latino parents in Dalton, they found that only 22 percent of fathers and 24 percent of mothers did not expect to still be in the studied community three years in the future.

Yet, as accurate as it was, the finding left intact two hazards: (1) its attendance to the need for Dalton schools to be responsive to newcomer students' biographies was only partial; and (2) it left unconsidered the issue of what should happen to those who were not permanent. Let us attend to these in turn. Because the Mexican newcomers formed a permanent, if new, segment of the community, one available civic understanding was that the newcomers needed to be integrated. But this posture did not necessarily mean that newcomers were welcome to help shape a new definition of community, only that they needed to be taught what it meant to be *of* Dalton. For the majority of newcomer children then, schooling that was devoted to developing skills, identities, and relationships needed for this new place (that is, for Georgia or the United States) was supported. However, this schooling could sometimes be jarring, confusing, or unexpected because what the newcomers brought to the classroom linguistically, culturally, or just in terms of previous school experience was not necessarily known, valued, or built upon. Everyday ruptures were not foreclosed.

Yet we can also ask about those whose futures might not have been in Dalton, Georgia, or even the United States. First, again referencing the parent survey, intending to stay is not the same as actually being able to stay. So some who intended to stay may not have. Second, nearly a fourth of the interviewed parents thought they would likely move on. Where they would move on to or when was not clear, but national reporting related to the recession following September 11, 2001, identified Dalton as one of the harder impacted communities and reported that many families were returning to Mexico (e.g., Recio 2002, Robertson 2002). In other words, some students who had been in Dalton continued their schooling somewhere else. Indeed, we found two such former Dalton students in rural Zacatecas, Mexico, in the study briefly further described in the next section.

More recently, with ICE raids happening all over the country and U.S.- and foreign-born Latinos telling Pew Hispanic Center pollsters that the reception for Latinos in the United States had become chillier (Lopez and Minushkin 2008), it seems plausible that even more newcomer students who used to be in Dalton schools might have moved on. Our concern is whether the schooling in Dalton was responsive to such a possibility. Did Dalton schooling cultivate the skills needed to live someplace else? Particularly if that someplace else was Mexico? The fates of the various Georgia Project components suggest not. The daily messages Latinos encountered in Dalton schools varied in their degree of welcome (Gitlin et al. 2003), but they were not oriented toward the prospect that some of the students needed to maintain or continue to develop skills that were consistent with a Mexican self-identity or the orientation and substance of schooling in Mexico. As with Gaby, who went from Chicago to Mexico, students with experience in Dalton were set up to encounter everyday ruptures if they relocated to Mexico. For some this would be a second experience of everyday ruptures, as what they had encountered in Dalton may also have been incompletely biographically responsive.

Transnational Students in Nuevo León and Zacatecas

Nonetheless, our sense of students' day-to-day realities in Dalton was limited. Our research designs there considered children only indirectly (focusing instead on administrative maneuvering or the design of the summer teacher institutes, for example). As our projects in Dalton had largely wound down by 2001, we could only consider conjecturally what happened to children who left Dalton, or to Latino newcomers in other U.S. locales who left where they were. To answer this question more directly, we hypothesized that some former Latino-newcomer students might be in Mexico (where they or their parents were born) and we secured funding from Mexico's Consejo Nacional de Ciencia y Tecnologia

Table 7.1

States	Mexican	American	Mexican American	Total
Nuevo León	56.6%	6.3%	37.1%	100%
Zacatecas	60.9%	6.0%	33.1%	100%

Source: survey UDEM-CONACYT Nuevo León 2004; Zacatecas 2005. Subsample of students from fourth grade of *primaria* though third (ninth) grade of *secundaria* (Nuevo León, *n*=203; Zacatecas, *n*=165).

(CONACYT) to see if we could find them and learn about both their U.S. school experiences and their Mexican ones. Beginning in 2004, our CONACYT funding allowed us to visit 1,673 randomly selected classrooms in a stratified random sample of 387 schools in the states of Nuevo León and Zacatecas. At these schools we surveyed 25,702 students—8,021 as part of brief whole-class oral interviews with those in the first three grades of *primaria* and 17,638 using written questionnaires. Those methods helped us locate 512 students with U.S. school experience, of whom 413 were in older grades and gave us written responses. Additionally, we interviewed 121 students with U.S. school experiences and twenty-five teachers about students with such experience. The vignette about Gaby, shared earlier, comes from these interviews. The data in Table 7.1, which highlights how a number of these children did not identify as Mexican or as only Mexican, come from the written survey. The data were generated from a forced-choice question asking (in Spanish) whether students identified as Mexican, American, Mexican American, or other.[3] After "other" there was a space for students to fill in a different label, but as Table 7.1 shows, none did.

As in Dalton, where the majority of Latino newcomer parents felt that they would stay, the majority of transnational students that we found in Mexican schools identified singularly as Mexican, although their understanding of "Mexican" may or may not have matched that of their mononational peers and these students too may have had to negotiate everyday ruptures related to identity. Nevertheless, we draw attention to the smaller portion of students (more than 40 percent combined) who indicated that they self-identified as Mexican American or American. For this smaller but substantial portion of students, we can be more certain that the everyday curriculum would promote an identity and a belonging that did not (fully) fit. In other words, just as the Adrienne Rich quote earlier in the chapter suggested, for these students the curriculum would be a source of partial invisibility and thus rupture.

Raising the prospect that the curriculum was not the only quotidian source of rupture, when we asked the large number of students in our sample who lacked transnational experience whether peers with such experience were or were not like everyone else, many answered that transnational students were different. Among our 7,576 fourth- through ninth-grade student sample of Zacatecas, 5,028 answered the question "Are transnational children the same as or different from us?" Forty percent (n=2,511) of mononational students considered "different" those who had studied in the United States (regardless of those students' country of birth). Their responses allow us to describe with some details their representations. On the one hand, they frequently pointed out the dissimilarities in language they observed: "they do not speak like us"; "they speak more English than Spanish"; "they do not understand us"; "they cannot read"; "it is strange the way they speak." Others described other types of dissimilarity. First, attitudes: "they are showy boys"; "I said they are not like us because they are arrogant, they feel they are richer than us"; "they are so serious"; "they are silent"; "I say they are shy"; "they hate us." Second, cultural traits: "they have other customs"; "they learned other traditions"; "they are more laissez-faire than us"; "they act like gang members"; "they are not able to live in small towns." Third, apparent defects and faults: "they are fat"; "they are not like us because they ugly"; "they are not Mexican, they are gringos"; "they are disrespectful of our norms." Finally, ethnic characteristics: "they are whites"; "they are blond." However, unexpectedly, an important proportion of responses acknowledged positive differences: "they [are] smarter than us"; "they are bilingual"; "they are more school oriented than us"; "they are more respectful of school norms than us"; "they learn better"; "they [are] hardworking students." As we have described elsewhere, this bifurcated perspective among mononational students in Zacatecas about their transnational peers drove us to this conclusion: "the construction of otherness for transnational students in the microsociety of Mexican schools appeared less than solidified or unanimous; different viewpoints coexisted, creating a paradoxical mix of welcome and unwelcome" (Zúñiga and Hamann 2009, 344–45).

From the standpoint of everyday ruptures, this marking of difference could also translate into different treatment. We have written previously of Rosa (Hamann, Zúñiga, and Sánchez García 2006), a seventh-grade student we encountered in Nuevo León who had spent all her life in U.S. schools excepting the two months prior to our visit to her school. She was clearly viewed as different, as everyone in her class pointed at her when we asked if there was anyone in her class that had gone to school in the United States. Later, in an interview, she complained that her class-mates had stolen all her markers for art and that she suspected that the crayons she owned would likely be pilfered next. In turn, Serrano (1998) has written vividly of Nuyoricans, who, having vividly identified them-selves with Puerto Rico, move to the island and find that island-native student peers are resistant to fully including them and mock their lan-guage, their accents, and other of their ways. In other words, school is a forum where peers, as well as the curriculum and perspectives of teach-ers, can be a source of rupture.

The Underexamined Assumptions of Schooling and National Membership

There is a long literature on schools as agents of enculturation (learning one's own culture), acculturation (learning a new culture), and decul-turation (finding one's existing cultural identity challenged or ignored). Because these ideas are so deeply embedded in anthropology—see, for example, the various well-known efforts at creating terminological tax-onomies of cultural acquisition like those in Redfield, Linton, and Her-skovits 1967[1936] and Barnett et al. 1954—they do not need a lot of fur-ther explanation here, with two exceptions. First, we accept Teske and Nelson's (1974) point that different authors use these three terms in dif-ferent ways, hence our delineation of how we understand them. Second, we see the idea of acculturation as a large umbrella that includes the idea of assimilation, although the two terms are not synonymous.

Assimilation, like acculturation, refers to the acquisition of a new body of cultural knowledge and deportments (Gordon 1964; Park and Burgess 1970[1921]). But unlike some kinds of acculturation, assimila-tion assumes a change in the assimilated person's orientation to a new cultural identity and the new society's acceptance of that person's new identity. Grey (1991, 80) summarizes an important component of assimi-lation: "Assimilation . . . is a one-way process in which the outsider is expected to change in order to become part of the dominant culture." By emphasizing the processual nature of assimilation, its unilateral orienta-tion, and the unequal power differential between outsider and insider,

Grey's definition echoes Teske and Nelson's (1974) and that of the Social Science Research Council's Seminar on Acculturation of 1953, which declared: "Assimilation implies an essentially unilateral approximation of one culture in the direction of the other, albeit a changing or ongoing other" (Barnett et al. 1954, 988). In other words, while acculturation is definitionally agnostic in regard to whether the learner of new cultural forms uses that knowledge to attempt to embrace a new identity, assimilation presumes that such a change should be promoted or expected. Thus, when schools face an acculturative rather than enculturative task— that is, when the cultural identity valued at schools differs from the student's sense of self—it is the assimilationist presumption of school that makes schools inadequately responsive to their students' biographies. Similarly, it is the assimilationist presumption, which presumes the irrelevance of large swaths of students' identities and experiences, that is a source of everyday ruptures for students who know and feel attachment to more than one place.

It is a premise of this chapter that schools almost always see their task as enculturative (learning the dominant culture that one is born into) or assimilative (learning the dominant culture that one was not born into and neglecting or rejecting the culture of origin). This is hardly surprising, as around the world the advent of state-supported, broad public schooling has routinely and purposefully been identified with the task of building the nation and shaping society (Brickman 1964; Dewey 1902; Luykx 1999). Texts about or arguing for the founding of public education in Mexico, like Gamio's (1916) *Forjando Patria* (Forging a Nation) and Booth's (1941) *Mexican School-Made Society*, illustrate this principle for that country. So too, for the United States, do myriad texts of long vintage. Both Earl Warren's opinion for the unanimous *Brown v. Board of Education* (1954) decision and Harvard president James Conant's lectures at Teachers College in November 1945 (Conant 1945a, 1945b, 1945c), which were each titled "Public Education and the Structure of American Society," offer American visions for school as a core instrument for fashioning a coherent and unified, if socioeconomically heterogeneous, society. A contemporary of Dewey and Conant, the progressive educator George Counts, identified as U.S. school tasks the challenges of assuring material well-being, including among immigrant and racial minorities; cultivating global leadership and human flowering; and securing democracy. Then he promised: "That such tasks cannot be accomplished by education alone is of course readily granted. Yet it is equally evident that they will never be accomplished without the assistance that organized education can provide" (1952, 21).

Offering a more contemporary version of the same sentiment, Marcelo Suárez-Orozco and Carolyn Sattin recently argued that "schools are failing to properly educate and ease the transition and integration of large and growing numbers of immigrant youth arriving in Europe and North America; many quickly become marginalized as racially, ethnically, religiously, and linguistically marked minority groups" (2007, 3). Here again the task of school is understood as promoting opportunity in the newcomer student's new host society. Left out is any emphasis on continuing to develop the capacity to succeed in the environments from which a newcomer came and might return.

So it should be clear that a long-term task of schools, one that has been formally advocated even by progressive educators, is to tie students to the nation-state that is providing schooling. There are reasons to be dubious of the deculturative presumption of assimilationist schooling for newcomers. There are also reasons to question, for the majority, whether the enculturative intent of their schooling suffices for the social goal of creating equal opportunity, but those are not the core arguments here. Rather we want to emphasize the mismatch, and resulting daily ruptures at school, for those students whose national attachments are plural or to a nation different from where they are attending school. As the unequal penetration of globalization continues to dislocate families and thus children (as the other chapters here so eloquently describe), increasing numbers of children negotiate schools that do not describe them completely and that are not organized for their success—neither academic success nor a sense of affirmed group identity. Carola Suárez-Orozco recently noted: "Individuals who adopt a self-referential label that includes their parents' country of origin seem to do better in school than their counterparts who select a pan-ethnicity (such as Hispanic or Latino) or who refer to only their country of residence (such as American)" (2004, 180). In other words, Mexican newcomer students in places like Dalton should fare better if they identify as Mexican. Following the same logic, transnational students we found in Mexico who identify as American (and who in many instances were born in the United States) should fare better if they preserve their sense of American identity. Yet in both these instances, schools try to make a dissuading case.

The students we studied did not make the relocation decision, whether they were in Georgia or Mexico. They nonetheless did have perspectives on their relocation and schooling. Thus, a student in Zacatecas (Mexico) chafed at the gender and comportment expectations of her current school, though she had thrived previously in a gifted and talented program in Pennsylvania (United States). Another student was adamant she never wanted to return to the United States because she did not want to have to live ever again with her father; she had not fared well in school in either country. A third student claimed a desire to become a teacher of English, perhaps in the United States but perhaps in Mexico. In her case, her professional goal related to skills that she had developed in both the United States and Mexico and that were valued in both places (albeit more narrowly in Mexico).

For transnational students whose "life worlds are neither 'here' nor 'there', but at once *both* 'here' and 'there'" (Smith 1994, 17, emphasis in the original), school can be a source of slights, of challenges to identity, and of ruptures. Looking at the gloomy graduation rate of Latinos in Dalton, Georgia (Hamann 2003) or at the difficult cases we sometimes encountered in Mexico, we see that some children do not overcome these ruptures, and they are marked as not successful or capable by the formal institutions of the state (that is, the school); many do not have much of a favorable sense of self. Yet we would be incompletely relating the findings of our two studies if we focused only on this negative side. Some students are resilient. Some overcome or transcend the ruptures or do their own successful reconciliations of what school teaches and what they need. Still, it seems unfair to make this reconciliation the work of the children. Would it not be better, if difficult initially to imagine, if schools were not sites of everyday rupture?

Chapter 8

Here/Not Here

Contingent Citizenship and Transnational Mexican Children

Deborah A. Boehm

He is here, and he is not here. It is within this condition of existence that they exist.
—Nadine Gordimer, *The Pickup*

There are multiple nonexistences and gradations of existence. It might be most accurate to say that, like characters who experience a temporal rift in a *Star Trek* episode, [unauthorized migrants] come in and out of existence and exist simultaneously in multiple ways.
—Susan Bibler Coutin, *Legalizing Moves*

When I was recently in Mexico, I spent an afternoon with a friend, Liliana, as she cared for a chaotic house full of children. They ran back and forth between a dusty courtyard filled with goats and chickens and the living room where we were talking. "Come, *niños*," she called to the two smallest of the group, "I have someone for you to meet." Liliana then introduced me to her grandsons, Victor and Claudio, ages two and five. "They have been here for nearly a year," Liliana explained. "My son and daughter-in-law—they are *mojados* [unauthorized migrants, literally, "wetbacks"], as you know—and so it is safer for the boys to be here with me. Their parents work all the time, so really it is better this way." Liliana went on to describe the difficulties her daughter-in-law was having, being so far from her young children. "But the boys are U.S. citizens," Liliana proclaimed proudly. "They are the Americans in the family, aren't you, *mis cariños*?" She teased her grandsons, as they ran out of the room laughing. Victor and Claudio are in many ways *here* and yet *not here*, U.S. citizens with what I understand to be a form of contingent citizenship—they are citizens of the United States living in Mexico explicitly because of the undocumented status of their parents.

The situation of these young boys—specifically their parents' placement of them in Mexico despite their U.S. citizenship—underscores the spatial and symbolic shifts across territory, and in understandings of national belonging and exclusion, among individuals within undocumented migrant families or families of mixed U.S. legal status. Among Mexican migrant families, the legal status of individual family members vis-à-vis the U.S. state has concrete implications for the well-being and places of residence of both documented and undocumented children. Describing themselves as "from neither here nor there," transnational Mexicans live both within and on the margins of two countries. I consider this liminality in relation to children and youth against the backdrop of the labor migrations of parents and other caregivers, developing the concept of contingent citizenship.[1] In what ways is the experience of being *here/not here* mediated by age? How do the youngest members of families move in and out of different forms of citizenship or national membership? What do the physical movement and locations of children reveal about the contradictions of citizenship within a transnational frame?

Contingent citizenship is national membership that is partial, conditional, or relational. Contingent citizens include U.S. citizens who are culturally, socially, politically, or physically excluded from the nation, as well as unauthorized residents of the United States who are de facto members by virtue of their employment, education, residence, political participation, and civic engagement. Constructed as simultaneously *here* and *not here*, transnational Mexican children move through layers of belonging and exclusion, "en route" (Coutin 2005) to distinct physical places and the embodiment of particular state categories. Here, the "flexible"—and inflexible—elements of citizenship come into relief (Ong 1999). Six-month-old Julia, who crossed with her mother and a *coyota* last month; Tomás, an unauthorized migrant about to graduate from a U.S. university with a degree in biochemistry; and José and Daniela, U.S. citizens living in Mexico while their mother works cleaning hotel rooms in Los Angeles—all are arguably contingent U.S. citizens; their lives must be understood in relation to U.S. immigration laws and the many U.S. state actions that permeate family life.

My arguments build on the work of scholars of "illegality" (Coutin 2000; De Genova 2002), drawing on research that explores the contradictory ways state regimes construct "legal/illegal" subjects (e.g., Coutin 2000, 2007; De Genova 2002, 2005; De Genova and Peutz, 2010). Much of this research employs metaphors of space and place to analyze migrants' relationship to nation-states: "The social condition of transnational migrants . . . must be understood as a preeminently spatialized one, in which the spatial difference produced and sustained by nation-state boundaries is reproduced in . . . specific sociopolitical statuses" (De Genova 2005, 95). Nicholas De Genova (2005) focuses on the character of boundaries—geographic, but also racial, economic, political, and cultural, among others. For Susan Bibler Coutin, the locations of unauthorized Salvadorans, "legal nonsubjects," are characterized as "spaces of nonexistence" (2000, 27), and in Nathalie Peutz's work, Somali nationals deported from the United States are "out-laws," physically removed deportees who are also "cast outside of the law" (2007, 189). My focus, too, involves how spatial understandings of inclusion and exclusion impact migrants in particular ways, though I turn my attention to an understudied population, children and youth, to consider how they are conceptually—legally and in popular discourse—*here* and *not here*.

Locating Children, Situating Families

My discussion is based on ongoing binational research that studies the intersection of gender, family, and the state among Mexican migrants with ties to San Marcos, a small, rural community or *rancho* in the state of San Luis Potosí, Mexico, and several locations in the U.S. West and Southwest.[2] The project focuses on a network of people that is rooted in the United States and Mexico, and characterized by the movement of members between the two countries and within the United States. Incorporating ethnographic, qualitative methods—including participant observation, visual methodologies, interviews with migrants, and collaborative methods with adults, youth, and children—my research has included extensive fieldwork in multiple sites throughout the United States and Mexico.

My project has been a "multi-sited ethnography . . . in/of the world system" (Marcus 1995, 95), focused particularly on San Marcos, San Luis Potosí, Mexico, and Albuquerque, New Mexico, U.S.A., with stays in other locations where community members live in both Mexico (several small towns surrounding San Marcos and the capital cities of San Luis Potosí and Zacatecas) and the United States (Las Vegas and Reno, Nevada; San Diego, California; and Portland, Oregon). Through a focus that privileges "relations, rather than . . . locations" (Hastrup and Olwig 1997, 9), I have "follow[ed] the people" (Marcus 1995, 106) to create an ethnography of translocal family networks. Although I have been based in particular sites in Mexico and the United States, whenever possible I have traveled with migrants—moving transnationally as they do— between Mexico and the United States for visits, special events, and family celebrations. Such movement has been an important methodological approach: transnational research has raised multiple theoretical questions and enabled me to gather a range of data from people living on both sides of the border.

San Marcos was established as an *ejido* shortly after the Mexican Revolution of 1910. Although bean farming is the primary source of livelihood in the area currently, the terrain is not very hospitable to agriculture, and so today there is a different source of income for most of the families in San Marcos: remittances from migrants. Migration north began with the Bracero program (1942–1964) through which the U.S. government contracted with Mexican laborers; the fathers, grandfathers, and great-grandfathers of today's transmigrants were braceros in the 1940s and 1950s, traveling back and forth between the United States and Mexico as their children and grandchildren do today. The Bracero program, and later migrations to particular destinations in the United States—in this case, Albuquerque, New Mexico and Dallas, Texas—established important routes or "circuits" (Rouse 1991) that remain strong today and that increasingly include the movement of young people.

Within this community, the distinctions between "migrant" and "immigrant" are frequently blurred. Individuals who intend to migrate—stay brief periods in the United States and then return to their nation of origin—may extend their stays because of the dangers and high costs associated with crossing the border. Similarly, individuals who build lives in the United States and perceive themselves as "immigrants" or are defined as "immigrants" by the U.S. state may return or even be forced to return, as recent cases in which U.S. permanent residents have been deported during the naturalization process demonstrate (Preston 2008). Furthermore, the term "immigrant"—"posited always from the standpoint of the migrant-receiving nation-state, in terms of outsiders coming in" (De Genova 2002, 421)—does not capture the complexities of migration flows between Mexico and the United States. Recognizing the difficulties distinguishing between "migrant" and "immigrant," I use the terms interchangeably throughout this discussion.

As my research has shown, children are both on the move and staying put. Children from San Marcos may migrate alone or with their parents; live in Mexico with grandparents and other family while their parents go to the United States to work; stay in the United States with relatives when their parents are deported; or travel north or south for extended stays. Because of these diverse experiences, I understand transnational children to include young people living on both sides of the U.S.-Mexico border. This "transnational generation," then, is made up of those who move and also those who do not (Boehm 2008; see also Glick Schiller and Fouron 2001; Hess 2009a), and is the product of nearly a century of migration. Indeed, children and youth are often "between two worlds" (Dreby 2010, 179), whether or not they themselves migrate.

Children from San Marcos are increasingly migrating to the United States with or without documents. Their transnational movement is part of broader authorized and unauthorized migration flows to and from the United States; according to the Pew Hispanic Center, approximately one-sixth of the U.S. undocumented population, some 1.7 million people, is under eighteen years of age (Passel 2005). As the number of unauthorized migrants living in the United States increases, the number of U.S. citizen children with parents who are undocumented is also growing. My research focuses on both these groups—children living in the United States without papers and U.S. citizen children with family members who are unauthorized.

Central to my analysis are state-migrant relationships and how U.S. policies and actions focus on individual (Sassen 1996), typically adult, migrants. Paradoxically, U.S. policies have repeatedly facilitated the entry of Mexican nationals while simultaneously controlling south-north migration: "illegal immigration has long been officially prohibited but unofficially tolerated" (Coutin 2000, 40). Extensive scholarship has highlighted the ways in which Mexican migration is driven by a demand for laborers (see De Genova 2002, 422, for a review of the literature). Formal U.S. government support of labor migration has primarily taken the form of programs that provide temporary work visas to Mexican migrants, through, for example, the Bracero program and guest-worker programs that are currently active in different regions in Mexico. At the same time, migration is regulated or not permitted through a range of state actions: U.S. Immigration and Customs Enforcement (ICE) raids at worksites, targeted deportations of individual migrants, denial of tourist and other visa applications at U.S. consulates within Mexico, and the heavily militarized U.S.-Mexico border aim to reduce the number of Mexican migrants living in the United States.

In public discourse, a migrant is often represented as a solitary, typically male, adult subject or part of a threatening, dangerous mass of humans moving across the border (Chávez 2001, 2008; Santa Ana 2002). This contradictory representation is perpetuated by laws and state practices aimed at addressing the perceived wave of transmigrants specifically by disciplining individual subjects, through, for example, highly publicized ICE raids, detentions, and deportations. But where are children located in these interactions, and what are the lived experiences of migrant families? The production of "illegality"—by definition focused on the individual—has significant implications for children and youth as they migrate, and do not migrate, specifically as members of family networks. State categorization of individual migrants as "legal" or "illegal" impacts the youngest migrants in particular ways.

I propose extending an analysis of illegality to demonstrate how its construction plays out specifically among families and communities. State action and exclusion are not focused only on the individual "illegal alien." Instead, it is a family affair: the state's production of illegality among particular family members creates a form of contingent citizenship for all members of undocumented and mixed-status families, including those who are U.S. nationals. Building on a rich literature that expands definitions—and explores the often problematic character— of citizenship (e.g., Flores 1997; Rosaldo 1997; Rosaldo and Flores 1997; Flores and Benmayor 1997; Stephen 2003), my conceptualization of contingent citizenship stems directly from the experiences of transnational children. I argue that, as members of families, migrant children often embody this conditional and unstable relationship to the nation-state.

The notions of a solitary migrant or a flood of laborers constructed through legal categories and media representations obscure the reality of everyday lives: migrants are embedded in families (Boehm 2008). Although migrants are categorized according to individual state-ascribed statuses, mixed-status families—made up of members who are U.S. citizens, U.S. permanent residents, and unauthorized migrants—are the norm. Women, men, and children of all ages are moving and staying in a transnational context precisely—and paradoxically—in an effort to provide for children, to sustain families, and to create a sense of wellbeing within migrant communities. Indeed, the increasingly translocal experiences of children highlight the ways that migration itself is driven by, and cannot be separated from, social and familial reproduction. This reality is absent when migrants are characterized as solitary figures or as part of a dangerous wave. Such representations obscure children and youth as actors at the center of migration flows, which they indisputably are, and ultimately have concrete implications in the lives of transnational families. Despite state categories that interpret migrants as individual subjects, they are always embedded in familial and other social relationships.

This chapter explores how this contradictory context, in which U.S. policies both encourage and deter Mexican migration, creates unstable, contingent membership in the nation, particularly among children and youth. In the next section, I turn to the fluidity of state categories, in particular those of "alien" and "citizen," to explicate the inevitable blurring of these supposedly distinct and oppositional statuses. As the lived experiences of children illustrate, these categories are always subject to leakage, despite a focus on, or even a faith in, the integrity of boundaries on the part of the state and its members. Through the construction of "aliens" and "citizens," the U.S. state creates a type of shifting citizenship, a contingent citizenship for children within transnational mixed-status families and networks of unauthorized migrants.

Children as Contingent Citizens

The contingency of one's citizenship or membership in the nation is made transparent through family relations and family affiliations with individuals who may be documented or undocumented. How the state does (or does not) define individual migrant children in relation to the nation depends on the status of parents, siblings, and other family members. Here I focus on two forms of contingent citizenship among children and youth, a tenuous form of national membership that creates what Mae Ngai defines as "alien citizens" (2004, 2), as well as what I understand to be "citizen aliens."

Alien Citizens: Here/Not Here

As I spoke with his mother, three-year-old Emilio peered at me from a doorway, disappearing for a few minutes and then peeking his head out again. "Since we arrived last month, he has been very tentative with people," explained his mother, Mayra. "Even his *tias* [aunts] seem to scare him!" Mayra and Emilio had recently come to the rancho following the deportation of Mayra's husband. Emilio, like Victor and Claudio, is among a growing group of U.S. citizen children who are currently living in San Marcos. These U.S. citizens living in Mexico are what Ngai has termed "alien citizens." In the daily lives of transnational families, the state produces such alien citizens, U.S. citizens who, according to Ngai, "are presumed to be foreign by the mainstream of American culture and, at times, by the state" (2004, 2). Among transnational children, alien citizens are often U.S. citizens who are dependents of undocumented parents or caregivers. Here, the construction of a citizen as "alien" happens precisely because of one's family relations, resulting in a kind of "alienation" (Coutin 2000) through kin ties. The experiences of alien citizens—those categorized as "alien" by association—are varied, ranging from de facto expulsion from the nation when a parent is deported to situations in which parents choose to raise U.S. citizen children in Mexico because of the stress of living without documents in the United States and the increasing threat of their own deportation.

U.S. citizen children are often taken into state custody or forced to "return" with deported parents to the parents' country of origin. A case in the news—that of Saída Umanzor, a Honduran national, and her nine-month-old U.S. citizen daughter, Brittney Bejarano—demonstrates the contingent citizenship of transnational children. As Julia Preston reported in a November 17, 2007, *New York Times* article, "Immigration Quandary: A Mother Torn from Her Baby," when ICE agents took Saída into custody during a search in her home, Brittney was placed under the care of social workers. Saída had been breastfeeding Brittney at the time of her arrest. When she was taken from her mother, Brittney refused to eat for three days and was later weaned to a bottle. Mother and baby were separated for eleven days before Saída was released to await her trial. If Saída is deported, Brittney will go with her mother to Honduras.

Among families from San Marcos, this notion of return for U.S. citizen children is indeed problematic. Because of their parents' undocumented status in the United States and the resulting difficulties crossing the border, the majority of these children have never been to Mexico before. The experience of being what is essentially a deported U.S. citizen—itself a curious concept—brings significant challenges. Frequently, because they are minors, U.S. citizen children whose parents are deported are also forced to return. Although these children are not legally deported, their experience of return is not notably different from that of unauthorized migrant children. For example, one teenager, Beatríz, had been in Mexico for several months when we met at the weekly market near San Marcos. When Beatríz spotted me, the only gringa in the crowd, she immediately approached me and introduced herself in English. She told me that she had been born in the United States and was eager to return to her home in Arizona, where her studies and social life were continuing without her. She described how youth in the rancho treated her. "I don't think they understand me," she explained. "And, honestly, I don't understand them either. It is so boring here! I can't wait to go back."

A report by the Urban Institute and the National Council of La Raza estimates that two-thirds of children with deported parents are U.S. citizens (Capps et al. 2007)—if deported, parents typically have few options but to take their children with them, resulting in both the symbolic and actual "alienation" (Coutin 2000) that underscores contingent citizenship. In some cases, teenagers may remain in the United States when their parents are deported, but parents are hesitant to leave unmarried— especially female—children in the United States for extended periods. Children of apprehended or deported parents are, I argue, understood to be "alien" in the United States explicitly through their family relations. In fact, in Preston's *New York Times* article, spokespersons from both a government agency, ICE, and an anti-immigrant group, FAIR (Federation for American Immigration Reform), said that U.S. citizen children must pay the price for their parents' "criminal acts," reflecting how easily the status of illegality can be transferred from parent to child.

Many U.S. citizen children go to Mexico, often for the first time, if their parents are deported. In addition, the families I work with are increasingly sending their U.S. citizen children to Mexico to live for extended periods. Like Victor and Claudio, whom I described at the beginning of this chapter, Lalo and Mari, ages five and three, are migrants who have recently returned to San Marcos, for their protection and to ease their mother's anxiety. Both children are U.S. citizens, born in Albuquerque while their parents were working there without documents. After their parents separated, their mother, Tina, was struggling to support the children on her own and she desperately feared for their safety. She told me that she had to make the difficult decision to take her children to San Marcos, where they currently live with Tina's mother and sister. Tina said that she is pleased that the children are able to study in Mexico and experience life in the rancho, but she misses her children immensely, and wonders each day if the children should be reunited with her in the United States.

Preemptive relocations of children by undocumented parents highlight the state's presence in family life. By extending illegality to all family members, including U.S. citizens, the state affects each member of mixed-status families. This has profound implications for the nation and how the nation defines membership and belonging. As I have discussed, the forced relocation of U.S. citizen children essentially converts U.S. citizens with unauthorized family members into de facto partial members or even nonmembers of the nation. As contingent citizens, these U.S. citizen children are indeed what Ngai (2004) calls "impossible subjects." Through the state's production of "illegal aliens," the fragility of the U.S. citizenship of these children, these alien citizens, comes into view.

Citizen Aliens: Not Here/Here

"What can I do to protect my children?" Alma asked in a hushed voice. We were attending a community meeting to address immigrant issues, and when Alma learned that I was a scholar working with transnational Mexicans, she approached me for advice. "My family, we are undocumented, and there are so many risks." Alma moved closer, and asked again, "What can be done? Anything?" Alma's questions—How can children be protected? What can be done?—carry an urgency to act. And yet, amid ongoing debates about immigration reform, discussion of a return to an extensive guest-worker program, and ongoing challenges to passing the DREAM (Development, Relief and Education for Alien Minors) Act, which would enable undocumented college students to change their immigrant status and continue their studies, legislative action and substantive change seem unlikely, or at least a long way off. Meanwhile, the government's presence is seemingly everywhere, surrounding, or in the words of one father, "suffocating," migrant families.

Informed by and building on Ngai's analysis, I propose the notion of "citizen aliens"—that is, undocumented migrant children who, in particular circumstances, are de facto members of the nation. Clearly, they are not state-recognized citizens, and they are arguably excluded more often than included, but the reality is that transnational children and youth live in neighborhoods, attend school, work, shop, eat out, go to parks and public spaces, and interact with community members each day (see also Coutin 2000, 40). Alma's children, twenty-year-old Miguel and nineteen-year-old Lila, for example, are both unauthorized immigrants, having lived in the United States without papers for nearly ten years. Both young people, however, are attending college on scholarships—majoring in physics and international relations—and working in the community: Miguel is cleaning offices and Lila is a nanny for a suburban family with three young children. They are active in several groups on campus and spend their weekends socializing with friends from the community, relationships established over the past decade. And yet, their futures are defined by profound uncertainty. Alma is encouraging her children to return to Mexico after they graduate, or to seek employment with an international company. "What else should they do?" asks Alma. "Stay here and work cleaning houses?"

Within families of unauthorized and mixed-status migrants, the U.S. state's construction of illegality permeates daily life: workplace raids, threat of deportation, inability to move freely, and lack of access to health care and education affect children in particular ways. Consider the experiences of Javier, an eighteen-year-old who was deported during ICE raids that took place in Nevada in 2007. According to friends who attended high school with him, after Javier was apprehended, he was sent to a detention center in Arizona and then sent "back" to Mexico. Javier came to the United States from Mexico as an infant and has no recollection of his hometown. His day-to-day life in Reno was no different than that of his U.S. citizen siblings or cousins, and his return to Mexico is comparable in many ways to the forced relocation of U.S. citizen children when their parents are deported. As Roberto G. Gonzales argues, when undocumented children transition to adolescence and adulthood, "they move through shifting zones of legality, creating developmental and legal disjunctures" (Gonzales 2009, 6–7). Javier's experiences demonstrate this passage to "illegality." However, although the U.S. state understands him to be "alien," his de facto membership in the nation is undeniable. Here, the U.S. "cultural citizenship" (Flores and Benmayor 1997) of undocumented children is significant, including young people's contributions and potential contributions to community and nation, their place in the U.S. economy, and their ongoing participation in educational and social communities.

Even as individual rights are threatened, the state's maneuvers that define legality play out among families, impacting the well-being of children regardless of their legal status. The categorization of individual migrants as "aliens" who are "legal" or "illegal," and the many state actions intertwined with the production of illegality, arguably impact all members of transnational migrant families. The Melina family further demonstrates this point. After living in Albuquerque for nearly twelve years, the Melina family faced the deportation of their husband and father, Cristo. Cristo's wife, Lety, returned to the rancho with two of their children, ages thirteen and three. Their thirteen-year-old son was born in Mexico and does not have papers, but their youngest child is a U.S. citizen. Four of the Melina children—seventeen, twenty, twenty-two, and twenty-four years old—however, chose to stay in New Mexico because their lives were firmly rooted there. For example, Bella, seventeen years old, wants to graduate from high school, and Nicolas, twenty-four years old, recently married and had a baby boy, a U.S. citizen. The lives of Bella, Nicolas, and their siblings, are simultaneously *here* and *not here*, not legally recognized by the U.S. state, and yet concretely and undeniably situated in the United States.

Here and *Not Here*: Transnational Children

When a previous neighbor, an elderly woman, learned that I conduct research with transnational Mexicans, she, like Alma, pulled me close and whispered in my ear with a sense of urgency, though her message was quite distinct from Alma's concerns about how best to protect her children. Instead, my neighbor wanted to know, "How can we protect our nation from all these migrants and their many children?" She described the United States as under siege by Mexican migrants. "This used to be the Mexicans' land . . . but they want it back," she warned as her eyes widened. "By having so many children, they plan to repopulate the Southwest. That is what you should study." Her fears reflect the broader contradiction that informs state policies and practices, a tension between production and reproduction that is intertwined with U.S. immigration policy (Chávez 2008; Wilson 2000, 2006). The nation depends on and supports migrant labor, yet U.S. state policies push family life outside the borders of the nation-state. Kinship ties both threaten and are co-opted by the state. It is from this nexus of state-family-individual that contradictory discourses and experiences emerge: this is the space in which transnational children are situated, "from neither here nor there."

The current legal milieu in the United States indeed perpetuates "spaces of nonexistence" (Coutin 2000, 27). The state impossibly expects migrants to be simultaneously *here* and *not here*. Certainly, the state formally and informally solicits migrants to be *here*. As scholars have repeatedly shown, "undocumented migrations are, indeed, preeminently labor migrations" (De Genova 2002, 422). Yet, the state also excludes migrants, constructing them as *not here*, especially, I argue, through its interactions with migrant families. The state brings migrants, as individual laborers, into the nation even as it expels families and communities. Both history and current debates show that the nation desires detached individuals or, curiously, even parts of individuals—"bracero," for example, derives from the Spanish word *brazos*, or arms—to fulfill labor needs.

However, as I have discussed, no individual exists without attachments to others, and in fact, while transnational Mexicans agree that their migrations are labor migrations, they also understand labor migrations to be inextricably tied to family life. Simply stated, Mexicans migrate and work to provide for their families (Boehm 2008). A focus on migrations as solely labor migrations obscures the reality that unauthorized migration takes place to support families and can conceal the everyday experiences of transnational children. My research aims to uncover the experiences of migrant families within spaces that are often understood as domestic, intimate, or private. Public policies penetrate family life in multiple ways; this discussion underscores the intertwined character of public and private life, and the ways that state-defined citizenship and exclusion cannot be understood outside of family relations.

In excluding families, the state creates a bind for itself, for families, and ultimately for children. By constructing unauthorized migrants— children and adults—as paradoxically *not here/here*, the nation-state supports an expendable workforce; and by situating migrant children— especially U.S. citizens—as *here/not here*, the state aims to ensure that reproduction and family life take place outside the boundaries of the nation. Of course, the vision of maintaining migrant children and families outside national borders is only partially realized. Although they are excluded, legally and through state practices, migrant children and their families are undeniably *here*. And still, U.S. policies and practices are likely to further state presence in transnational family life, often locating migrant children and youth, including U.S. nationals, *there*. The state's production of illegality disrupts, separates, and at times dismantles families, perpetuating the impossible expectation that transnational children are to exist *here* and *not here*.

Chapter 9

The Transnationally Affected

Spanish State Policies and the Life-Course
Events of Families in North Africa

Núria Empez Vidal

Changes in Spanish law produce changes in migration strategies in North Africa. These state policies contribute to the everyday ruptures child migrants and their families experience, as I show in this chapter. Spanish legislation on unaccompanied minors is contradictory: on the one hand, they are immigrants in an irregular administrative situation, that is, "illegal immigrants" who should be deported; but on the other hand, as minors, they should be safeguarded by the child protection system or be fostered with families in Spain and thus are treated very differently from other unauthorized immigrants. Spain's policies on migrant children are contradictory in their image of childhood. Children are seen as vulnerable and in need of protection, and simultaneously, the decision to migrate causes children to be seen as adults breaking the Foreigners Law (or La Ley de Extranjería, the popular name for often revised immigration laws associated with a constitutional act originally passed in 2000, about the rights and freedoms of foreigners in Spain).

Using the case of unaccompanied minors—boys who attempt to migrate from Morocco to Spain without the company of a responsible adult—I explore the transnational dimension of life-course events, actions that start in one country which produce vital event outcomes among people in another. This case, which I situate in the wake of national (Spanish and Moroccan) and European Union (EU) policy changes over the last twenty years, shows that regulations and laws governing migration control have a lifelong impact on the boys who come to Spain.

Besides the impact on the individual, this migratory process affects vital events of family members. Such vital events of direct concern to Moroccan families may overlap with the categorical concerns of an anthropologist—marriage, birth, and death, among others—but they are not necessarily the same. Others include experiencing a ritual transition, coping with a serious malady, or entering school. Moreover, vital event changes in individual lives in Spain or changes in the place of origin can, in turn, affect future events in either country. Having a brother in Spain, even if he is still in a minors' protection center, increases the possibility of a young Moroccan woman obtaining a higher-status husband, because having a brother in Europe raises her status. The migration of unaccompanied minors not only produces changes in vital events, but also produces ruptures and breaks that children will have to deal with in their integration into a new social order and in their ties to the family. As a result, I pay special attention here to the concept of linked lives.

Research on unaccompanied minors raises important issues of agency. Some researchers—including Massey (1990), Wood (1981), and Taylor (1986)—argue that families or households are the principal agents of migration decision making. I have found that some families encourage their children to migrate as unaccompanied minors, some even paying to send the boys abroad. Furthermore, most of the minors keep in contact with their families. But there are also many cases in which the minor makes the decision to migrate without consulting his family members. The decision could be taken alone or with peers. The rich effects of such decisions over multiple locations and over much of childhood and early adulthood are illustrated here through empirical findings from fieldwork in Spain and Morocco.

Transnationalism and Life-Course Theories

Transnationalism

Transnational studies have arisen to address the complexity of the globalization process in which movements of people, goods, and capital occur beyond the boundaries of a nation-state. Globalization, which has drawn considerable attention in the last few decades, is usually seen as the increasing connectivity of economies and ways of life across the world. During the 1990s, scholars such as Basch, Glick Schiller, and Szanton Blanc (1994), Portes (2000), Portes, Guarnizo, and Landolt (1999), and Smith and Guarnizo (1998) intensified discussions about the need to create a new concept to designate both contemporary migration that involves all countries in the world and the cross-border relations between migrants in their destination and their compatriots in their countries of origin. Some scholars proposed the word "transnationalism" to describe this phenomenon, a term that attempts to capture the relationships between and among individuals and other entities regardless of nation-state boundaries. "Transmigrants" refers to persons who reside in one country but whose emotional, social or political lives are enmeshed with those living in other countries (Glick Schiller, Basch, and Szanton Blanc 1994, 448). The reconfiguration of global capital obliges migrants to gain new and deeper connections across borders. For example, some studies discuss the transnational process in relation to the sending of remittances by immigrants (Constant and Massey 2002; Guarnizo 2003; Sana 2005; Stark and Lucas 1988). Glick Schiller (2004) argues that transnational studies should also include nonmigrants, individuals who never crossed national borders but are linked to people located in another nation.

I would argue that transnational studies should also include the effects of policies of one nation-state on the patterns of migration in another. The term "transnationally affected," as I use it here, refers to individuals and families who are affected by another country's policies, especially in their migration. As an example, I show how changes in immigration laws and the child protection system in Spain can affect family patterns and migratory dynamics in Morocco.

Life-Course Framework and the Linked Lives Concept
Mayer (2005), among others, has criticized the life-course approach, saying that this approach is unclear about the precise mechanisms and specific forms of institutional support that generate distinct outcomes in people's lives. Thus, he argues, it is true that cohorts or historical periods look different, but the causes of these differences remain indeterminate. In my view, it is difficult to predict the impact of certain policies on individuals, but the life-course approach allows us to look at the past to establish certain patterns of influence, even if it is not clear exactly which influences are most salient in decision making. In this chapter, I analyze patterns of linked lives as the independent mechanism that generates so-

cial change in specific historical contexts. In particular, it is the mechanism through which EU immigration law and policy affects Moroccan families.

The concept of linked lives is one of the principles of life-course theory described by Elder, Johnson, and Crosnoe (2003). This concept addresses the fact that there are interdependent and sociohistorical influences on a person's life and that the events experienced by one member of a family can affect the lives of other family members. Elder and Caspi's (1990) approach to linked lives includes the principle of interdependent life systems, in which the family is a social group, functioning as a whole and differently from the sum of its parts. Changes within the life of any individual may affect all other persons and relationships in a family. A number of scholars have used this approach to analyze the effects of relationships among parents and their children (Elder 1994; Furstenberg, Brooks-Gunn, and Morgan 1987; Macmillan, McMorris, and Kruttschnitt 2004; Minuchin 1985; Smock, Manning, and Gupta 1999). Macmillan, McMorris, and Kruttschnitt have argued that "through the interconnectedness of human lives, particularly among parents and children, the life-course fortunes of one person have important effects on the developmental trajectories of those who are linked to them" (2004, 217). Some scholars in this field of social psychology argue that individuals form part of a family system, and they cannot be truly independent; we must understand individuals in their context (Minuchin 1985).

Most studies, like those cited, focus on the effect of parents on their children and not the other way around. In developed countries, parents are seen as more influential on their children than vice-versa. It is usually the parents who take care of their children, giving them education and health care and ensuring their proper socialization. Moreover, a central parental ideal for raising good children means that although parents do not expect money from their children, they expect them to fulfill their parents' expectations in their professions. But in some countries, like Morocco, depending on the financial situation of the family, children are seen as a source of manual labor, with the capacity and the duty to help families economically. Most Moroccans therefore understand that children can affect their parents' well-being. In other contexts, parents may make decisions for "the best interests of the child," as Tyrell's chapter shows, showing another way that children can influence, even passively, family dynamics.

My study focuses on the impact of a child's migration on his family.

Unaccompanied minors, despite the name, do not migrate unaccompanied. Rather, they travel accompanied by their memories of the past, their goals for the future, and the social networks that they create along the journey (Bargach 2006). As one informant cited by Bargach put it, there was nothing for him to do but "leave to work to move his [family] ahead."[1] In my fieldwork, I have found several motivations for migrating among these youths, but family ties are present in almost all cases. In most cases, young people are assuming roles of responsibility that most people—in Spain and Morocco alike—would agree they should not take on. These children may be physically unaccompanied, but they retain strong ties to their family members.

Transnationally Affected

In a transnational context, what happens in one country may affect people in another country. In particular, the policies of one country, such as its immigration policies, affect the behavior and patterns of migration of people in another country. For example, we can make a direct connection between the implementation of SIVE (Sistema Integral de Vigilancia del Estrecho/ Integral System of Monitoring the Straits), a border patrol system that has been highly effective in locating unauthorized vessels carrying immigrants across the Straits of Gibraltar (the *patera* boats), and concomitant changes of migrants' routes to reach EU shores. As a result of SIVE, people now try to migrate to the EU through more risky routes from Senegal or Mauritania to the Canary Islands, and not directly across the Straits to Andalusia as before.

Some families and some individuals plan their future with migration (regular or irregular) in mind. It is this anticipation that attunes them to the migratory policies of a particular country, which affect their patterns of social reproduction, geographical movement, lifestyles, and value orientations. I refer to those who are directly impacted, whether they can afford to migrate or not, as the "transnationally affected," in contrast to those who do not appear to feel the effect of foreign migration law.

There are many persons affected by transnationalism who have never traveled from their countries, such as those who receive remittances from family members abroad to ensure their survival or to increase their income level, or those who benefit from presents such as televisions and washing machines bought by migrants. But to reiterate, by "transnationally affected," I refer specifically to those who orient their lives and their migratory intentions to another country's policies.

However, I want to emphasize here that not everybody feels the impact of state policy and practice in the same way. The category of the transnationally affected in Morocco can take many surprising forms. There are those who will never reach Spain but who are trying to migrate, such as those living in the port areas of Tangier, whose lives are shaped around the migration industry. There are sub-Saharan African people living in Benyounes and Gurugu forests, on the Moroccan side of the Ceuta and Melillaenclaves, respectively, awaiting the opportunity to jump the fence that separates them from the EU, where they can apply for asylum. There are people looking for a wife or husband with citizenship or residency permits in an EU country. There are those who risk their lives in the *patera* boats. Such people may not have any social networks in Spain, but they are among the transnationally affected. At points in their lives, they are nearly or entirely concerned with what happens in the EU, following policy changes and searching for windows of opportunity for migration.

Changes in Spanish Law and Changes in Moroccan Patterns of Migration

Separated by a mere fourteen kilometers, Spain and Morocco have influenced each other since antiquity, and extensive movement between the two areas has usually been the norm. However, in the last century, migration between the two countries has increasingly been regulated. As a condition for entering the EU in 1986, Spain created its first Foreigner's Law in 1985 (La Ley de Extranjería, Ley orgánica 7/1985, de 1 de Julio, sobre los derechos y libertades de los extranjeros en España), requiring Moroccans and some other nationalities to have a visa to enter the country. Later modifications made the law stricter; for example, Foreigner's Law RD 2393/2004 put the means of legal entry for Moroccans coming to Spain within the reach of only a few. With their options for legal migration to Spain disappearing, some Moroccans started to migrate in an unauthorized way. For those who reach Spain, there are few ways to gain legal residency. But the Foreigner's Law offers legal status to "unaccompanied minors," children who arrive without a responsible adult. When such children arrive in Spain, humanitarian laws governing child protection are supposed to take precedence over the migration laws, treating them as "neglected" children who require the protection of the state as well as that of the international community and offering them the possibility of obtaining legal status.

It is difficult to make an exhaustive evaluation of the direct impact of Spanish immigration laws on those in Morocco and their relation to the unaccompanied minors' phenomenon. It is also difficult to know the exact number of boys crossing from Morocco to Spain, although data from the autonomous region of Catalonia where I conducted fieldwork are similar to those of communities like Madrid and Andalusia, the other two areas in Spain where unaccompanied minors are likely to go. This is because in Spain, the responsibility for child protection lies with the regions or *autonomas*, while the enforcement of migration law belongs to the central government. I must emphasize that not all Moroccan children are trying to migrate, nor do all families want their children to migrate. Nonetheless, there appears to have been an increase in the number of unaccompanied children in Spain, starting in the 1990s. The timing coincides with the visa law of 1985 and the entry of Spain into the EU. As other routes for legal migration were closed off, the migration of "unaccompanied minors" became more attractive, along with "family reunification." Thus, it is possible to correlate patterns of unaccompanied child migration to changes in Spain's Foreigner's Law.

"To Help My Family": Unaccompanied Minors and Their Families' Vital Events

To demonstrate the effects of transnational migration on the life course and of linked lives on the vital events of unaccompanied minors' families, I draw examples from my fieldwork in Morocco from March to October 2006, which included recorded interviews, informal interviews, and participant observation. The cases focus on the motivations of migrating boys ages thirteen to eighteen and their families. Some were boys who succeeded in migrating; others were those who had so far failed. In both cases, there are clear impacts in these life events (or nonevents) on families (Empez Vidal 2005).

The efforts of migrants to send remittances and help their families has been studied by several scholars (Constant and Massey 2002; Guarnizo 2003; Sana 2005; Stark and Lucas 1988); what is new in the cases I discuss here is that, rather than a parent, children are the ones who migrate alone. It is the unaccompanied minor's migration or attempted migration that affects all members of the family, altering familial roles in child rearing and in the household economy.

Studies of unaccompanied minors often indicate that their main motivation to migrate is the need to work and help the family (Capdevila and Ferrer 2003; Jiménez Álvarez 2003; Konrad and Santoja 2005;

Quiroga 2003), which does not mean that families want their minor child to migrate. As Jiménez Álvarez points out:

> After four years of living in Morocco I can say that the irregular migration of a son is lived as a tragedy, with suffering and resignation. If we are talking of minors, this is a double tragedy. It is true that in Morocco, minors have assumed the responsibility of collaborating in the family that makes them work and leave their studies. But the responsibility of supporting the family is not within the capabilities of a boy sixteen years old, and no "normal" family will ask that of their son. In the case of broken families with economic problems, the pressure to leave prompts the minor to go "searching for his life." It is not often that families suggest to the son to risk his life [riding] under a truck. (2003, 41)[2]

All the migrating boys I questioned, whether successful at border crossing or not, answered that their main motivation to migrate was to help the family.[3] They also said that they wished to obtain higher status within their families by helping financially, because success in migration converts young people into breadwinners. Some of the most common answers to my questions were:

I will work to help my parents.
(Boy from a rural area who wants to migrate)

He [cousin in Spain] wants me to go to look for my life and help my family.
(Boy from Tangier who wants to migrate)

My brother has his job here. I am more worried about my other [younger?] siblings. If one day I cross, they will not lack anything.
(Boy from Tangier who wants to migrate)

To help my family and everybody. My mother, imagine my mother. She's sick. No, I don't want that. I want to take her there in Spain; here [in Morocco] there are no doctors, nothing. If you have an eye hanging out, nobody will help you. In Spain, it is awesome.
(Boy from Tangier who had already migrated to Spain as unaccompanied minor)

Now my family doesn't believe I can do it [migrate], but when I reach Spain, I will buy a house for my mother, and then they will believe me.

(Boy from Tangier who wants to migrate)

I want to help my sister to divorce; she's got a bad husband, but I need the money to pay for returning her [return the marriage payment, so she can return to her family]. If I go to Spain, I can save the money and help her. Then I will take care of the house [pay for fixing it up] for my mother, and I will help my older brother to come; I don't want him to risk riding under a truck.

(Boy from a rural area who wants to migrate)

Similarly, most of the families express the conviction that their sons will have better futures in Spain and will help the other family members:

In Spain, they treat children well. They all come [referring to the ones who come back for holidays] and bring things [referring to the presents they bring to their relatives].

(Grandmother of an unaccompanied boy in Spain)

In my view, if God wants, he [referring to his son] will do very well, and as he tells me, he wants to have a nice future relying on himself. Now he left in order to help us; that is what he thinks.

(Father of a boy in Spain)

My sons told me that they are better in jail in Spain than free in Morocco. They don't want to return. Spain good; Morocco zero.

(Mother of two former unaccompanied minors now in jail in Barcelona)

They live better in Spain; there is work, rights, and social security. If I was younger, I would go myself. We paid for our daughter's wedding with the money coming from Spain.

(Father of an unaccompanied minor in Tangier)

Despite the children's desire to help their families and the families' support of their child's migration, it is ironic that children must put themselves in a neglected situation in order to be legally recognized as an unaccompanied minor. Although the idea of neglect is not familiar to the families and children I interviewed, the migration process itself is psychologically and physically hard on the children. In the majority of cases, parents do not give children permission to migrate. Talking with families, I came to realize that much of the process of leaving is tacit, characterized by silence on the part of most children and their families. Most migrating children live temporarily on the streets of Tangier first, waiting to find passage and seeking out jobs and connections among migrant networks in Tangier. Children in Tangier are lonely, they say, while waiting to migrate, as well as in Spain; however, the continued strength of family ties is also very apparent. These migrating minors are not street children, even if they are living on the streets. I understand street children to be those who are socially excluded, who lack the networks, the information, and the ability to migrate. I noted that most of the time the potential migrants interchange periods of living on the streets with periods spent living with their families. They are called and call themselves *harraga*, an Arabic word that describes a person who wants to migrate in an irregular way.

There is no typical migrating minor. Some come from rural areas; some come from really poor families and others from more wealthy ones. The relations of the boys with their families differ. Among boys from rural areas, like Beni Mellal, where I did part of my fieldwork, parents usually know of their son's intention to migrate, because he must move to Tangier first. In my interviews with some of the boys, nevertheless, it became clear that many keep silent on this issue, perhaps because of the danger and the conditions of their migratory journey. Regarding the dangers of migration, boys told me:

> We don't explain our living conditions in Tangier port; we don't want to worry them [referring to his parents].
> *(Boy from a rural area who wants to migrate)*

> We [my parents and I] never talk about that [the situation at Tangier port], but I guess that they can imagine our conditions, but is easy not to talk about that.
> *(Boy from a rural area)*

> If I arrive [home] in the morning with dirty clothes, they can guess that I was in the port, but they never ask.
> *(Tangier minor who wants to migrate)*

Most of the families see the children's activities around migration, on the one hand, as an investment for the child himself and, on the other, as an investment for the remaining family members. For example, they argue that in Spain their sons can have both a better education and better possibilities of work. That one of the motivations for people's movement is to help their families is not new; what makes the case special is that the children initiate or at least inaugurate the chain of migration and its hoped-for benefits.

Not all migrating children succeed in migrating; in fact, most of them never reach Spain. Some even die trying to migrate. Fourteen such deaths were reported during my fieldwork in the Tangier port between May and October 2006. Many of those who manage to reach Spain end up squatting in houses without the protection of the childhood welfare system. Others are sent back as a part of a supposed family reunification. My observations in the field and interviews with reunified boys, some of their parents, and professionals persuaded me that these so-called family reunifications do not fulfill the requirements of the law of family reunification. This law, which was made to guarantee the right of children to live with their family, does not unite all children with their families; some reunifications look more like simple deportation (see also Jiménez Álvarez 2003, 2006; Jiménez Álvarez and Lorente 2004). Moreover, I observed that a child sent back to Morocco will try to migrate again. There also is not a clear pattern of which boys will be reunified. The families of returned boys argue that they do not know the reason they were sent back, reasoning that the reunification must be the result of something wrong that the child did in Spain. But as often occurs with irregular migration, I observed that the experiences of boys who have succeeded are held up in communities as stories of inspiration that create typical expectations for migration, whereas those who did not reach the goal were seen as individual failures. The following case provides an extended example.

In the summer of 2006, I was invited to a wedding in Morocco. The groom was a twenty-year-old boy who had migrated as an unaccompanied minor when he was sixteen. After passing through the Catalan welfare system, he had obtained a residence permit and, later on, a work permit to train as a carpenter. His parents were illiterate, as was he. They came from a rural area (the Rif Mountains), and they had moved to one of the outermost settlements of Tangier several years earlier, where they still live. The now young man had met his bride in Barcelona, and she was also from the Rif area but from a wealthier family. She had migrated to Spain as a part of a familial reunification several years before her groom. The new status of the boy, with a profession and all his permits in order, allowed him to be accepted by the bride's parents.

The wedding took place through ceremonies and celebrations, first in the bride's village and then in the groom's home, as is traditional. One comment I heard during the wedding ceremony in this poor neighborhood directly indicated the intersection of immigration, life event, and altered social status: "Look at him; he migrated as an unaccompanied minor and now is celebrating the fanciest wedding in the neighborhood." Individual weddings like this are among the small example of success that make a more powerful impression in transnational communities than do the much larger number of failures. In such cases, as illustrated by the wedding, extended families gain higher status conferred by the success of a single man who had migrated as an unaccompanied minor.

Although the motivation of helping family is in most cases present for migrants, the migration of a minor can also have an impact on the family's vital events, as in the wedding example. The phenomenon of unaccompanied minors is still recent. We cannot tell if entire cohorts of these now maturing boys are going to invest in their families, because at this moment most of them are still under the guardianship of the Spanish protection system. Others are in precarious and low-paid jobs, still hoping to stabilize their situation, for instance, by getting a home or residence and a work permit. But by thinking of this process as one that creates a group of people who are transnationally affected, we can find some examples of the impact of children's migration among their families.

A single child moving abroad can lead to status and life-event changes for a family. The moment an underage youth or older child reaches Spanish shores, his family gets a new and higher status, no matter the situation of the child. Status increases from then on if the boy obtains a residency permit, a work permit, or a job. This was the case for a boy I met in Tangier who obtained a job contract in Spain, which meant that he could apply for a visa to cross the border to take up the new job, where the permit to work was temporary and connected directly to the employer. Once he obtained the visa that allowed him to go to Spain, he went to the bank in Tangier and asked for a loan to buy a small house in Morocco for his mother. The bank workers used the fact that he had a visa and a job contract in Spain as a guarantee for giving him the loan, even though the bank would have denied him the loan if he was working the same sort of job in Morocco.

Siblings' life events are also affected by a brother's migration. Having a brother in Spain makes one more suitable for marriage, because one has contacts in Spain who may send money home or may help a sibling cross the border in a legal way, such as through a tourist visa or job contract. In some cases, the real situation of the person in Spain does not matter—whether he has a legal status in Spain or even if he is incarcerated. What is significant is the presence of the brother in Spain, which gives the sibling social capital in Morocco. For example, after the migration of her brother as an unaccompanied minor to Spain, a young woman in Morocco had more proposals of marriage than before. The proposals increased in the summertime, when many Moroccans with residence permits living in the EU came to visit, spending money and driving expensive cars. When the mothers of the candidates visited the girl's mother, the fact that she had a brother in Spain was always mentioned as part of the marriage proposal and negotiations.

Though demographers often concentrate on events such as marriage, birth, and divorce as significant in family life, of equal socioeconomic significance can be, for example, the celebration of religious festivities like Ramadan, Ashora, and Tahara (circumcision) or help in paying for funerals. One of the most important issues can be a health crisis. Morocco does not have public health care, so individuals must pay for medical visits, medications, and treatments. Family members must take care of their elders, and frequently diseases do not get treated for lack of money. A family member in Europe can help in times of medical difficulties by sending money or medicine. Sometimes families will try to obtain a visa to get the sick person treated in Spain or another European country. It was thus no surprise, in my interviews with eight social educators working with unaccompanied minors in both Barcelona and Tangier in October 2006 that all referred to the preoccupation of the migrant boys with health problems of their family members. I observed the same preoccupation in my own interviews with the family members and boys. For example, I met a family in Tangier in which the mother was diabetic. One of the main reasons her son wanted to migrate was to pay the costs of the treatment for her illness, which required constant care. When I visited the family, the mother herself referred to the disease, hoping that with her son's remittances and the possibility of obtaining medicines from Spain, she would receive better treatment.

All the social workers I interviewed in Barcelona told me that the boys keep in contact with their families. They call home frequently. These children are worried about the situation of their families back across the Mediterranean; their ties are very strong.

Conclusions

Life-course frameworks follow individuals through time. With transnational migration, the life course adds a new dimension, not just of time, but also of space. People's lives in one country can be transformed by the historical events in another country or by the policies of other governments to become what I call transnationally affected. In migratory processes, space becomes an especially important dimension, because vital events can happen in different nation-states. Movement can also add complexity to the cohort experience. With migration, individuals may share some cohort experience with their peers in the country of origin and some cohort experience within the country of destination. All these movements have to be taken into consideration.

In transnational contexts, by examining linked lives in life-course theories, we can understand the importance of considering the country of origin. Studies therefore should analyze people's lives in the transnational context and not divide people's lives between origin and destination. In the case of unaccompanied minors migrating from Morocco to Spain, we can observe that changes in Spanish immigration law produce changes in the patterns of migration and social relationships back in Morocco. Some boys feel that they are the ones most likely to succeed in the migratory process, but even if they travel unaccompanied, they bring with them a mindset of duties and obligations to their families. Their move will affect not only their own vital events, but also the life events of the rest of the family. By combining transnational studies and life-course approaches, we can obtain more information about how people organize their vital events across time and space. By examining vital events, we can see that state policies affect the migrating strategies of individuals and their relatives.

Notes

Chapter 2

1. I am grateful for the comments of the editors from the Working Group on Children and Migration, as well as for the comments of the anonymous reviewers. Their suggestions and insights have considerably strengthened the chapter. I continue to be grateful to the Tibetan communities in Albuquerque and Santa Fe for their support of my research. Many thanks to Tenzin Norgay, a.k.a. Lazzyboi, and MC Rebel for permission to use their lyrics here. Their music, performances, and ideas contributed so much to this chapter.

2. Tibetan spellings are provided using the Wylie transliteration format (see Wylie 1959).

3. Rap itself is an immigrant phenomenon, developed by Jamaican artists who had long employed dubbing and other technological innovations to create danceable street music in Jamaica using disco music. In response to the decline of disco in the 1970s, Jamaican émigré artists in Brooklyn used these techniques to create a new sound that eventually became known as rap music, part of a larger repertoire of hip-hop style that includes graffiti and break dancing.

4. See Keila Diehl's (2002) ethnography that explores the musical crossroads of Dharamsala, India, where traditional Tibetan music, Hindi film music, reggae, and rock meet and are being melded by Tibetan musicians.

Chapter 3

1. Thanks to Andy Brooks at the West and Central Africa Regional Office of UNICEF for supporting this research. Thanks also to all the people in Dakar, Conakry, and Nzérékoré who granted me interviews and gave me their rich insight. Most importantly, thanks to the people of Nzoo who welcomed me and shared their stories with me. Thanks also to the members of the Working Group on Childhood and Migration, especially Cati Coe and Rachel Reynolds, and to the Wenner Gren Foundation for Anthropological Research for sponsoring our workshop in New York in January 2008.

2. The International Human Rights "regime" (in Foucault's sense of the word) works in part by naming, and indeed, it is hard to talk about these children without using terms like "refugee" and "separated child."

3. The 1974 census of Sierra Leone reveals that 29 percent of Sierra Leonean children whose mothers were 15–19 years old were not living with their mothers; 36 percent of children born to mothers 20–24 years of age were also living away from home. For women ages 25–29 and 30–34 years, the proportions of children away increase to 40 percent and 46 percent respectively. These figures indicate high rates of outmigration of children at relatively young ages (Isiugo-Abanihe

1985, 61). The figures varied greatly by region and ethnic group, with the South and East of the country reporting almost double the rates of outfosterage to the North. Ainsworth (1996, 25) reports that in Côte d'Ivoire in 1985 one-fifth of nonorphaned children ages 7–14 were living away from both natural parents.

4. See the report to UNICEF online at *www.crin.org/resources/infoDetail.asp?ID= 9115&flag=report.*

5. Furthermore, the sample of children may be slightly biased toward older, school-going children since I worked closely with the local secondary school administrators to identify children to interview.

6. I excluded cases of what I considered family fostering, but I included one case of schooling fostering in which the child fled with his foster caregiver.

7. Not every pair was complete (that is, sometimes I interviewed the child and not the caregiver and sometimes a caregiver but not a child.) This calculation is based on the fifty-two complete pairs.

8. Charnley reports similar responses in Mozambique: "These mothers gained a sense of pride in caring for children but were clear they had no 'right' to them in any sense. Asked what would happen if a child's family was identified, one respondent said, 'We'd always accept that he should go with his family' " (2000, 117).

9. Some people gave more than one answer, so I counted some caregivers twice.

10. From a sampling perspective, there is obviously a big selection issue. I am not claiming that all children found successful foster arrangements, only that it was possible to find a large sample of successful foster arrangements.

11. This excellent point was made by an audience member when I presented this data at the American Anthropological Association annual meeting in San Jose, California, in 2006.

12. Charnley cites a study by Maússe and Sitoi (1994) that reveals two sets of complex and inter-related motives for substitute family care in two isolated rural areas: "One set was associated with childlessness, the result of infertility, widowhood, or the departure of adult children. Caring for unrelated children for these reasons was linked to concepts of exchange and mutual support. . . . The second set was expressed in terms of 'taking pity' on child victims of circumstances, and was associated with notions of good citizenship and fulfillment of spiritual obligations believed to bring rewards after death. This study also demonstrated the inviolability of the rights of birth families and the willingness of substitute families to return children to them. Some foster families did expect a return on their 'investment,' but this translated as sufficient resources to perform traditional ceremonies associated with the arrival or departure of family members, or to maintain links so that foster parents could follow children's progress or support them to complete periods of schooling before returning to their birth families" (Charnley 2006, 225).

Chapter 4

1. See Olwig 2002 on middle-class migration from the Caribbean.

2. In the research tradition on Caribbean kinship, phenomena such as matrifocality, male marginality, and the significance of consanguinity rather

than affinity have received much attention (Barrow 1996; Clarke 1957; Rodman 1971; Gonzales 1970; Smith 1988, 1996). Goulbourne and Chamberlain (2001) suggest that consanguineal relations remain more important than affinal relations in transnational Caribbean families. Bauer and Thompson's study of transnational Jamaican families indicates that women, rather than men, are "dynamic activating figures around whom the whole kin system revolves," and that women are often responsible for their families' migration strategies. Young men, as well as older men, seem marginal in transnational kin networks (2006, 213–14).

3. Karen McCarthy Brown (2001) recounts her own wedding in a Vodou temple in a Brooklyn basement, in which the *prètsavann*, a lay Catholic priest, read the ritual formula to the couple—the warrior spirit Ogou, who had mounted the female head of the temple, and Brown, the initiate, all dressed in red wedding clothes (Ogou's color is red). After the vows, the bride got a marriage certificate; blank certificates are sold in Port-au-Prince for this purpose. Ritually purified rings were exchanged, and after the ceremony, champagne and wedding cake were served to all participants. After the ceremony, the newly wedded wife had to show sexual fidelity to her spirit husband by reserving one night each week to Ogou, who can visit her in dreams and visions.

4. On djinns or gins, see, for example, Drieskens 2008; Westermarck 1899. From African studies of relations between humans and spirits (Bastian 1997; Boddy 1989, 1994; Lambek 1993), we have learned of close and intimate, even affinal relationships, but more research is needed on such relatedness in the context of Caribbean religions.

5. The distribution of food to children is an important moral underpinning and culmination of many communal rituals, secular as well as religious, in countries like Trinidad and Tobago.

6. Children can become Spiritual Baptists only through the voluntary initiation of baptism, seldom performed before adolescence. While many people dedicated (i.e., christened) as babies in a Spiritual Baptist church turn to other denominations later on in their lives, adult candidates from various religious backgrounds seek initiation to the Spiritual Baptist religion.

7. I borrow the expression "religious reciprocity" from a comment made by Stephan Palmié at the conference "Obeah and Other Powers: The Politics of Caribbean Religion," Newcastle University, July 16–18, 2008.

8. I compare the logics of ritual exchange with capitalist exchange in the context of Caribbean religious practice elsewhere (Forde, forthcoming).

Chapter 5

1. Funding for this research was provided by the National Science Foundation, the Wenner-Gren Foundation for Anthropological Research, and the Research Council and the Childhood Studies Center, both at Rutgers University. My thanks to Deborah Augsburger, Emmanuel Koku, Rachel Reynolds, and Diane Sicotte for providing suggestions on earlier drafts of this chapter.

2. I am grateful to Deborah Augsburger for this insight.

3. All names are pseudonyms.

4. In the nineteenth century, slaves provided eldercare for their Akuapem masters (Haenger 2000).

5. "The Acquisition of Land by Larteh Cocoa Farmers," Cocoa Research Series No. 14, Economics Research Division, University College of Ghana, November 1958, Box 6, Folder 4, Polly Hill Papers, Northwestern University Africana Library, Evanston, Illinois (hereafter Hill Papers).

6. "Interview Forms: Berekuso" and "Interview in Berekuso with the chiefs and others, February 19, 1959," Box 2, Folder 5, Hill Papers; see also "Interview Notes from 1960," Box 3, Folder 4, Hill Papers.

7. See also "Information given by E. O. Walker, October 7, 1958," Box 4, Folder 7, Hill Papers.

8. "The Acquisition of Land by Larteh Cocoa Farmers," Box 6, Folder 4, Hill Papers.

9. Rex vs. Osaku, January 15, 1907, Supreme Court, Accra, Criminal Record Book, April 6, 1905–July 20, 1907, SCT 2/5/16, Ghana National Archives, Accra, Ghana.

10. See also "Notes, 1958," Box 3, Folder 2, Hill Papers.

11. Ado Kwaku vs. Essei Kwabla and Adjoa Kumah, December 6, 1913, Civil Record Book, Native Tribunal of Adukrom, August 27, 1913–January 2, 1914, ECRG 16/1/16, Eastern Regional Archives, Koforidua, Ghana (hereafter ERA).

12. Ofei Kwasi vs. Gabriel Ayisi, January 19, 1914, Civil Record Book, Native Tribunal at Akropong, October 8, 1913–March 3, 1914, ECRG 16/1/17, ERA.

13. Charles Amponsa for Ya Odi vs. Adu Kumi, April 29, 1919, Civil Record Book, Native Tribunal at Abiriw, February 19, 1913–May 31, 1920, ECRG 16/1/15, ERA.

14. Kwaku Adai vs. Kwadwo Yeboa, March 23, 1910, Civil Record Book, Native Tribunal of Akropong, 7 April 1914-27 November 1915, ECRG 16/1/5, ERA. It is not clear whether this uncle was on the maternal or paternal side, which is important given that families in Akuapem were organized matrilineally, in the case of the Akan, and patrilineally, in the case of the Guan.

15. Mrs. Amaney vs. Yao Dode, September 19, 1912, Civil Record Book, Akropong, Akuapem, Native Tribunal of Omanhene, July 16, 1912–December 30, 1912, ECRG 16/1/14, ERA.

16. Ado Kwaku vs. Essei Kwabla and Adjoa Kumah, ECRG 16/1/16, ERA.

Chapter 6

1. Weisner and Gallimore (1977) challenge this notion of all children being dependent by pointing out instances where one child is the dependent child in need of care yet another child is considered capable of offering that care.

2. An ontogeny of emotion delves deeper than the development of isolated reactions to a particular event.

3. This research was conducted with generous funding from the National Science Foundation, the Fulbright Commission, the Bristol Fellowship, the Center for Iberian and Latin American Studies, and the Fred G. Bailey Fellowship. University of California San Diego, Human Research Protection Program Approval Project #030031. All names are pseudonyms.

4. Keen attention to children's behaviors assesses continued consent to both specific activities and long-term research participation.

5. For a fuller discussion of case data that represents the children's experiences with additional raw data, see Rae-Espinoza 2006.

6. In the comprehensive edited volume on Ecuadorian migration, *Migraciones: Un Juego con Cartas Marcadas* [Migrations: A Game with Marked Cards] (Hidalgo 2004), the four case study chapters focus on migration from the Andes (Sánchez 2004; López and Villamar C. 2004; Patiño and Bushi 2004; Hidalgo and Jiménez 2004). No chapter in the volume focuses on or explicitly discusses coastal migration.

7. For a comparison of the effect of these differences on children's ability to adapt to parental emigration, see Rae-Espinoza 2006.

8. The accuracy of the mother's perception is unclear. I had heard from a number of informants that an émigré must cheat on his or her significant other because it is too expensive to sleep alone. One Ecuadorian abroad in Spain wrote in his testimonial that 90 to 95 percent of émigrés have changed partners while abroad (Oviedo Campaña 2000, 43).

9. Ana performed approximately at age level on the Wisconsin Card Sorting Task (WCST) (cf. Berg 1948) for perseveration and abstract thinking, and had no trouble with perspective taking in other arenas, such as the Kinetic Family Drawing Task (Buros and Kaufman 1970) or with cause-and-effect reasoning on moral dilemmas (Kohlberg 1968). For this reason, I suggest that the particular psychodynamic processes surrounding her father's emigration prevented her understanding this matter, rather than a cognitive deficit.

10. Ana could be considered to have a Childhood Disintegrative Disorder (American Psychiatric Association 1994, 79) or to be using the defense of distortion to regress (Vaillant 1977, 383) to avoid a difficult emotional realization.

11. I eventually encouraged Ana to end the story, but she might have continued much longer.

12. While there is no defense of "progression" where developmental milestones are reached early to contrast with Ana's regression, nor a *Diagnostic and Statistical Manual* diagnosis of an "integrative disorder" to oppose Ana's disintegrative disorder, our cultural focus that prioritizes independence and precocity should not obscure age distortions for similar psychodynamic purposes.

13. In fact, several girls convinced me that in addition to toys, they should be able to cash in the tokens they earned for participating in games and activities for makeup as well. I asked some parents for approval and they thought it was odd that I questioned whether young girls should have makeup.

14. Wilson's behaviors also shaped ethical considerations in regard to his continued research participation. I did not press questions and selectively included him in group activities when the tasks would not be difficult for him but the social integration would be beneficial. Denying him all continued participation could have seemed like a punishment, and he enjoyed spending time gathering the crickets from my office, playing games, and participating in activities that weren't related to family roles.

15. While deeply ingrained in U.S. parenting, fear of strangers is less common in Ecuador, where social interactions take precedence as appropriate social behavior (Rae-Espinoza 2010).

16. On these nights, the boys were in the care of the grandfather and great-grandmother.

Chapter 7

1. Presidential candidate Obama was speaking to the National Council of La Raza's annual meeting, San Diego, California. National Council of La Raza, *www.nclr.org/content/viewpoints/detail/52978/*. Accessed online November 22, 2008.
2. We have told portions of Gaby's story in Hamann, Zúñiga, and Sánchez Garcia 2008.
3. ¿Cómo te consideras que eres? a) Mexicano b) Norteamericano c) México-americano d) Otro, ¿cuál?_____

Chapter 8

1. Thank you to those who commented on drafts of this chapter, including attendees of the Wenner-Gren workshop, the co-editors of this collection, and two anonymous reviewers. Special thanks to Cati Coe and Rachel Reynolds for all their contributions to *Everyday Ruptures* and to the Working Group on Childhood and Migration. I am grateful to the institutions that have supported different stages of this research: Academy for Educational Development; Mexico-North Research Network; Center for U.S. Mexican Studies and Center for Comparative Immigration Studies at the University of California–San Diego; University of New Mexico, University of Nevada–Las Vegas; and University of Nevada–Reno. Above all, many thanks to the migrants—of all ages—who have participated in my research over the years.
2. San Marcos is a pseudonym, as are all names of individuals.

Chapter 9

1. My free translation of: "El menor 'emprenda el viaje,' pero nunca 'viajará' solo, va acompañado con su red social flotante, llega con su historia, sus recuerdos y su proyecto migratorio, que no es otro que 'salir a trabajar para sacar a los suyos adelante.' "
2. My translation.
3. Interviews in Morocco were conducted in Arabic with the help of a fieldwork assistant who then helped translate the interviews into Spanish. I conducted the interviews with educators and minors in Spain in Spanish.

Bibliography

Abrams, Philip. 1988. "Notes on the Difficulty of Studying the State (1977)." *Journal of Historical Sociology* 1 (1): 58–89.

Ackers, Helen Louise. 2000. "From 'Best Interests' to Participatory Rights: Children's Involvement in Family Migration Decisions." Working Paper No. 18. Leeds: Centre for Research in Family, Kinship and Childhood.

Adams, Paul L., Judith R. Milner, and Nancy A. Schrepf. 1984. *Fatherless Children*. New York: Wiley.

Agence France Press (AFP). 2008. "Dalai Lama Condemns Chinese Terror in Tibet." World Tibet Network News, March 16. Issue ID: 2008/03/16.

Ager, Alastair. 2006. "What is Family? The Nature and Functions of Families in Times of Conflict." In *A World Turned Upside Down: Social Ecological Approaches to Children in War Zones*, ed. Neil Boothby, Alison Strang, and Michael Wessells, 39–62. Bloomfield, CT: Kumarian Press.

Ahearn, Laura. 2001. *Invitations to Love: Literacy, Love Letters, and Social Change in Nepal*. Ann Arbor: University of Michigan Press.

Ainslie, Ricardo C. 1998. "Cultural Mourning, Immigration, and Engagement: Vignettes from the Mexican Experience." In *Crossings: Mexican Immigration in Interdisciplinary Perspectives*, ed. Marcelo M. Suárez-Orozco, 283–300. Cambridge, MA: Harvard University Press.

Ainsworth, Martha. 1996. "Economic Aspects of Child Fostering in Côte d'Ivoire." *Research in Population Economics* 8: 25–62.

Akresh, Richard. 2005. "Risk, Network Quality, and Family Structure: Child Fostering Decisions in Burkina Faso." IZA Discussion Paper Series. Bonn, Germany: IZA (Institute for the Study of Labor).

Alber, Erdmute. 2003. "Denying Biological Parenthood: Fosterage in Northern Benin." *Ethnos* 68 (4): 487–506.

————. 2004. " 'The Real Parents Are the Foster Parents': Social Parenthood among the Baatombu in Northern Benin." In *Cross Cultural Approaches to Adoption* (European Association of Social Anthropologists Series), ed. Fiona Bowie, 33–47. London: Routledge.

Allman, Jean. 1997. "Fathering, Mothering, and Making Sense of *Ntamoba*: Reflections on the Economy of Child-Rearing in Colonial Asante." *Africa* 67 (2): 296–321.

Allman, Jean, and Victoria Tashjian. 2000. *"I Will Not Eat Stone": A Women's History of Colonial Asante*. Portsmouth, NH: Heinemann.

Alonso, Ana María. 1994. "The Politics of Space, Time, and Substance: State Formation, Nationalism, and Ethnicity." *Annual Review of Anthropology* 23:379–405.

American Psychiatric Association. 1994. *Diagnostic and Statistical Manual of Mental Disorder*. Washington, DC: American Psychiatric Association.

Amnesty International. 2009. "China: Briefing for the UN Committee on the Elimination of Racial Discrimination: 75th Session, August 2009." Amnesty International *www.amnestyusa.org/document.php?id=ENGUSA20090727001&lang=e*. Accessed online February 20, 2010.

Amoa, Samuel. 1907. "Ayeforohyia ho asɛm [About Weddings]." *Kristofo Sɛnkekafo* 2 (12): 145–46.

Anderson-Fye, Eileen. 2003. "Never Leave Yourself: Ethnopsychology as Mediator of Psychological Globalization among Belizean Schoolgirls." *Ethos* 31 (1): 59–94.

Andrews, B. Lacey. 2003. "When Is a Refugee Not a Refugee? Flexible Social Categories and Host/Refugee Relations in Guinea." *New Issues in Refugee Research*. Geneva: UNHCR, Evaluation and Policy Analysis Unit.

Appadurai, Arjun. 1996. *Modernity at Large: Cultural Dimensions of Globalization*. Minneapolis: University of Minnesota Press.

———. 2006. *Fear of Small Numbers: An Essay on the Geography of Anger*. Durham, NC: Duke University Press.

Aranda, Elizabeth M. 2003. "Global Care Work and Gendered Constraints: The Case of Puerto Rican Transmigrants." *Gender and Society* 17 (4): 609–26.

Ardayfio-Schandorf, Elizabeth, and Margaret Amissah. 1996. "Incidence of Child Fostering among School Children in Ghana." In *The Changing Family in Ghana*, ed. Elizabeth Ardayfio-Schandorf, 179–200. Accra: Ghana Universities Press.

Ariès, Philippe. 1963. *Centuries of Childhood: A Social History of Family Life*. Translated by Robert Baldick. New York: Vintage.

Asamblea Nacional. 2003. *Migración: Implicaciones Económicas, Jurídico-Políticas, Sociales, y Comunicacionales*. Guayaquil, Ecuador: American Assembly.

Asare, N. V. 1917. "Amanne bɔne a ɛsɛ sɛ wogu [Evil Customs We Should Leave Behind]." *Kristofo Sɛnkekafo* 12 (10): 115–16.

Austin, Gareth. 2004. *Labour, Land, and Capital in Ghana: From Slavery to Free Labour in Asante, 1807–1956*. Rochester, NY: University of Rochester Press.

Australian Broadcasting Corporation. 2008. "Exclusive Interview with the Dalai Lama," December 6, *www.abc.net.au/7.30/content/2007/s2273196.htm*. Accessed online February 6, 2009.

Bailey, Adrian, and Paul Boyle. 2004. "Untying and Retying Family Migration in the New Europe." *Journal of Ethnic and Migration Studies* 30: 229–241.

Bargach, Amina. 2006. "Los Contextos de Riesgo: Menores Migrantes 'no' Acompañados." In *Menores Tras La Frontera. Otra Inmigración que Aguarda*, ed. F. Checa y Olmos, A. Argona, and J. C. Checa y Olmos, 51–63. Barcelona: Icaria Antrazyt.

Barnett, H. G., Leonard Broom, Bernard J. Siegal, Evon S. Vogt, and James B. Watson. 1954. "Acculturation: An Exploratory Formulation." *American Anthropologist* 56:973–1002.

Barrow, Christine. 1996. *Family in the Caribbean: Themes and Perspectives*. Kingston: IRP.

Bartle, Philip F. W. 1980. "Who Looks After the Rural Children of West African Urban Migrants? Some Notes on Households and the Non-Family in a Dispersed Matrilineal Society." Working paper. Leiden: Afrika-Studiecentrum.

Basch, Linda, Nina Glick Schiller, and Cristina Szanton Blanc. 1994. *Nations Unbound: Transnational Projects, Post-colonial Predicaments, and Deterritorialized Nation-States*. New York: Routledge.

Bastian, Misty L. 1997. "Married in the Water: Spirit Kin and Other Afflictions of Modernity in Southeastern Nigeria." *Journal of Religion in Africa* 27 (2): 116–34.

Bauer, Elaine, and Paul Thompson. 2006. *Jamaican Hands across the Atlantic*. Kingston: Ian Randle.

Baumann, Gerd. 1995. "Managing a Polyethnic Milieu: Kinship and Interaction in a London Suburb." *Journal of the Royal Anthropological Institute* 1 (4): 725–41.

Beck, Ulrich. 1992. *Risk Society: Towards a New Modernity.* London: Sage.

Beck, Ulrich, and Elisabeth Beck-Gernsheim. 2002. *Individualization.* London: Sage.

Beck-Gernsheim, Elisabeth. 2002. *Reinventing the Family: In Search of New Lifestyles.* Cambridge: Polity Press.

Becker, Adeline. 1990. "The Role of School in the Maintenance and Change of Ethnic Group Affiliation." *Human Organization* 49 (1): 48–55.

Behera, Deepak, ed. 1998. *Children and Childhood in Our Contemporary Societies.* New Delhi: Vedams.

Benedict, Ruth. 1938. "Continuities and Discontinuities in Cultural Conditioning." In *Personality in Nature, Society, and Culture*, ed. Clyde Kluckhohn and Henry A. Murray, 414–23. New York: Knopf.

Benei, Véronique. 2008. *Schooling Passions: Nation, History, and Language in Contemporary Western India.* Stanford, CA: Stanford University Press.

Berg, Esta A. 1948. "A Simple Objective Technique for Measuring Flexibility in Thinking." *Journal of General Psychology* 39: 15–22.

Besnier, Niko. 1995. *Literacy, Emotion, and Authority: Reading and Writing on a Polynesian Atoll.* Cambridge: Cambridge University Press.

Best, Amy L., ed. 2007. *Representing Youth: Methodological Issues in Critical Youth Studies.* New York: New York University Press.

Bhabha, Jacqueline. 2008. "Independent Children, Inconsistent Adults: International Child Migration and the Legal Framework." UNICEF Discussion Papers, IDP No. 2008–02.

Bielby, Denise, and William Bielby. 1992. " 'I Will Follow Him': Family Ties, Gender-Role Beliefs, and Reluctance to Relocate for a Better Job." *American Journal of Sociology* 97: 1241–67.

Blackwood, Evelyn. 2000. *Webs of Power: Women, Kin, and Community in a Sumatran Village.* New York: Rowman and Littlefield.

Bledsoe, Caroline. 1980. *Women and Men in Kpelle Society.* Stanford, CA: Stanford University Press.

———. 1990a. " 'No Success without Struggle': Social Mobility and Hardship for Foster Children in Sierra Leone." *Man* 25:70–88.

———. 1990b. "The Politics of Children: Fosterage and the Social Management of Fertility among the Mende of Sierra Leone." In *Births and Power: Social Change and the Politics of Reproduction*, ed. W. Penn Handwerker, 81–100. Boulder, CO: Westview Press.

———. 1993. "Politics of Polygyny in Mende Education and Child Fosterage Transactions." In *Sex and Gender Hierarchies*, ed. Barbara Diane Miller, 170–92. Cambridge: Cambridge University Press.

———. 2002. *Contingent Lives: Fertility, Time, and Aging in West Africa.* Chicago: University of Chicago Press.

Bledsoe, Caroline, and Uche Isiugo-Abanihe. 1989. "Strategies of Child Fosterage among Mende Grannies in Sierra Leone." In *Reproduction and Social Organization in Sub-Saharan Africa*, ed. Ron Lesthaeghe, 442–74. Berkeley: University of California Press.

Bloch, Maurice. 1971. *Placing the Dead: Tombs, Ancestral Villages, and Kinship Organization in Madagascar.* London: Seminar Press.

Bluebond-Langner, Myra. 1978. *The Private Worlds of Dying Children.* Princeton, NJ: Princeton University Press.

Boddy, Janice. 1989. *Wombs and Alien Spirits: Women, Men, and the Zar Cult in Northern Sudan.* Madison: University of Wisconsin Press.

————. 1994. "Spirit Possession Revisited: Beyond Instrumentalism." *Annual Review of Anthropology* 23:407–34.

Boehm, Deborah A. 2008. " 'For My Children': Constructing Family and Navigating the State in the U.S.-Mexico Transnation." *Anthropological Quarterly* 81 (4): 765–90.

Boehm, Deborah A., and Heidi Swank. Forthcoming. "Affecting Global Movement: The Emotional Terrain of Transnationality." *International Migration*.

Boli, John, Francisco O. Ramirez, and John W. Meyer. 1985. Explaining the Origins and Expansion of Mass Education. *Comparative Education Review* 29 (2): 145–70.

Bonney, Norman, and John Love. 1991. "Gender and Migration: Geographical Mobility and the Wife's Sacrifice." *Sociological Review* 39: 335–48

Boocock, Sarane Spence, and Kimberly Ann Scott. 2005. *Kids in Context: The Sociological Study of Children and Childhoods*. Lanham, MD: Rowman and Littlefield.

Booth, George C. 1941. *Mexican School-Made Society*. Stanford, CA: Stanford University Press.

Bourdieu, Pierre. 1977. *Outline of a Theory of Practice*. Cambridge: Cambridge University Press.

Boyden, Jo. 2004. "Anthropology Under Fire: Ethics, Researchers, and Children in War." In *Children and Youth on the Front Line: Ethnography, Armed Conflict, and Displacement*, ed. Jo Boyden and Jo de Berry, 237–61. New York and Oxford: Berghahn Books.

Boyle, Paul. 2002. "Population Geography: Transnational Women on the Move." *Progress in Human Geography* 26 (4): 531–43.

Boyle, Paul, Keith Halfacree, and Vaughan Robinson. 1998. *Exploring Contemporary Migration*. Harlow, UK: Addison, Wesley, Longman.

Brickman, William W., ed. 1964. *John Dewey's Impressions of Soviet Russia and the Revolutionary World—Mexico, China, Turkey, 1929*. New York: Bureau of Publications, Teachers College, Columbia University.

Briggs, Jean L. 1970. *Never in Anger: Portrait of an Eskimo Family*. Cambridge, MA: Harvard University Press.

Brittain, Carmina. 2002. *Transnational Messages: Experiences of Chinese and Mexican Immigrants in American Schools*. New York: LFB Scholarly Publishing.

Brokensha, David. 1966. *Social Change at Larteh, Ghana*. Oxford: Clarendon Press.

Brooks-Gunn, Jeanne, Greg J. Duncan, and J. Lawrence Aber, eds. 1997. *Neighborhood Poverty: Context and Consequences For Children*. New York: Russell Sage Foundation.

Brown, David. 2003. *Santería Enthroned: Art, Ritual, and Innovation in an Afro-Cuban Religion*. Chicago: University of Chicago Press.

Brown, Karen McCarthy. 2001. *Mama Lola: A Vodou Priestess in Brooklyn*. Berkeley: University of California Press.

Brown v. Board of Education. 1954. 347 U.S. 483 (1954) (USSC+).

Bryceson, Deborah, and Ulla Vuorela, eds. 2002. *The Transnational Family: New European Frontiers and Global Networks*. Oxford: Berg.

Bucholtz, Mary. 2002. "Youth and Cultural Practice." *Annual Review of Anthropology* 31:525–52.

Buros, Oscar Krisen, and Alan S. Kaufman. 1970. *The Mental Measurements Yearbook*. Lincoln: University of Nebraska.

Burton, Barbara, and Sarah Gammage. 2009. "*El Envío*: Remittances, Rights, and Associations among Central American Immigrants in Greater Washington DC." In *Border Crossings: Transnational Americanist Anthropology*, ed. Kathleen S. Fine-Dare and Steven L. Rubenstein, 211–29. Lincoln: University of Nebraska Press.

Bushin, Naomi. 2005. " 'For the Sake of the Children?' Children's Experiences of Family Migration to the English Countryside." PhD diss., University of Wales, Swansea.

————. 2007. "Interviewing with Children in Their Homes: Putting Ethical Principles into Practice and Developing Flexible Techniques." *Children's Geographies* 5:235–52.

————. 2009. "Researching Family Migration Decision-Making: A Children-in-Families Approach." *Population, Space, and Place* 15:429–43.

Butler, Ian, Lesley Scanlan, Margaret Robinson, Gillian Douglas, and Mervyn Murch. 2003. *Divorcing Children: Children's Experience of Their Parents' Divorce.* London: Jessica Kingsley.

Capdevila, Manel, and Marta Ferrer. 2003. "Els Menors Estrangers Indocumentats no Acompanyats (MEINA)." *Justicia i Societat*, no. 24. Barcelona: Centre d'Estudis Jurídics i Formació Especialitzada.

Capps, Randy, Rose Maria Castañeda, Ajay Chaudry, and Robert Santos. 2007. *Paying the Price: The Impact of Immigration Raids on America's Children.* Report by the Urban Institute. Washington, DC: National Council of La Raza.

Carsten, Janet. 2004. *After Kinship.* Cambridge: Cambridge University Press.

————. 2000. Introduction to *Cultures of Relatedness: New Approaches to the Study of Kinship*, ed. Janet Carsten, 1–36. Cambridge: Cambridge University Press.

————. 1997. *The Heat of the Hearth: The Process of Kinship in a Malay Fishing Community.* Oxford: Clarendon Press.

Castellanos, M. Bianet. 2009. "Building Communities of Sentiment: Remittances and Emotions among Maya Migrants." *Chicana/Latina Studies* 8 (1/2): 140–71.

Castles, Stephen, and Godula Kosack. 1973. *Immigrant Workers and Class Structure in Western Europe.* London: Oxford University Press.

Chamberlain, Mary. 2006. *Family Love in the Diaspora.* New Brunswick, NJ: Transaction.

————. 2005. *Narratives of Exile and Return.* New Brunswick, NJ: Transaction.

————. 2001. "Migration, the Caribbean, and the Family." In *Caribbean Families in Britain and the Trans-Atlantic World*, ed. Harry Goulbourne and Mary Chamberlain, 32–47. London: Macmillan.

Charnley, Helen. 2000. "Children Separated from Their Families in the Mozambique War." In *Abandoned Children*, ed. Catherine Panter-Brick and Malcolm T. Smith, 111–30. Cambridge: Cambridge University Press.

————. 2006. "The Sustainability of Substitute Family Care for Children Separated from Their Families by War: Evidence from Mozambique." *Children and Society* 20 (3): 223–34.

Chatterjee, Partha. 1999. "The Nation and Its Fragments: Colonial and Postcolonial Histories." In *The Partha Chatterjee Omnibus.* New Delhi: Oxford University Press.

Chávez, Leo R. 2001. *Covering Immigration: Popular Images and the Politics of the Nation.* Berkeley: University of California Press.

————. 2008. *The Latino Threat: Constructing Immigrants, Citizens, and the Nation.* Stanford, CA: Stanford University Press.

Cheever, Susan. 2002. "The Nanny Dilemma." In *Global Woman: Nannies, Maids, and Sex Workers in the New Economy*, ed. Barbara Ehrenreich and Arlie Russell Hochschild, 31–38. New York: Henry Holt.

Cheney, Kristen E. 2007. *Pillars of the Nation: Child Citizens and Ugandan National Development.* Chicago: University of Chicago Press.

Children Act 2004. *www.opsi.gov.uk/acts/acts2004.* Accessed online February 11, 2009.

Clark, Gracia. 1994. *Onions Are My Husband: Survival and Accumulation by West African Market Women.* Chicago: University of Chicago Press.

Clarke, Edith. 1957. *My Mother Who Fathered Me.* London: George Allen and Unwin.

Clegg, Stewart. 1989. *Frameworks of Power.* London: Sage.

Coe, Cati. 1999. "The Education of the Folk: Peasant Schools and Folklore Scholarship." *Journal of American Folklore* 113 (447): 20–43.

————. 2005. *Dilemmas of Culture in African Schools: Youth, Nationalism, and the Transformation of Knowledge.* Chicago: University of Chicago Press.

————. 2008. "The Structuring of Feeling in Ghanaian Transnational Families," *City and Society* 20 (2): 222–50.

————. Forthcoming. "Fosterage, Slavery, and Debt Pawning in the Colonial Gold Coast." In *Fosterage in West Africa Reviewed,* ed. Erdmute Alber, Jeannett Martin, and Catrien Notermans.

————. Forthcoming. "What Is Love? The Materiality of Care in Ghanaian Transnational Families." *International Migration* (special issue, "Affecting Global Movement: The Emotional Terrain of Transnationality," ed. Deborah A. Boehm and Heidi Swank).

Cole, Jennifer, and Deborah Durham, eds. 2007. *Generations and Globalization.* Bloomington: University of Indiana Press.

————, eds. 2008. *Figuring the Future: Globalization and the Temporalities of Children and Youth.* Santa Fe: School for Advanced Research Press.

Colloredo-Mansfeld, Rudi. 2003. "Tigua Migrant Communities and the Possibilities for Autonomy among Urban *Indígenas.*" In *Millennial Ecuador: Critical Essays on Cultural Transformations and Social Dynamics,* ed. Norman E. Whitten Jr., 275–95. Iowa City: University of Iowa Press.

Conant, James Bryant. 1945a. "Public Education and the Structure of American Society: I. The Structure of American Society." *Teachers College Record* 47 (3): 145–61.

————. 1945b. "Public Education and the Structure of American Society: II. General Education for American Democracy." *Teachers College Record* 47 (3): 162–78.

————. 1945c. "Public Education and the Structure of American Society: III. Education beyond the High School." *Teachers College Record* 47 (3): 179–94.

Constable, Nicole. 2004. "Changing Filipina Identities and Ambivalent Returns." In *Coming Home? Refugees, Migrants, and Those Who Stayed Behind,* ed. Lynellen D. Long and Ellen Oxfeld, 104–24. Philadelphia: University of Pennsylvania Press.

Constant, Amélie F., and Douglas S. Massey. 2002. "Return Migration by German Guestworkers: Neoclassical versus New Economic Theories." *International Migration* 40 (4): 5–38.

Cooke, Thomas, and Adrian Bailey. 1996. "Family Migration and the Employment of Married Women and Men." *Economic Geography* 72:38–48.

Coontz, Stephanie. 1992. *The Way We Never Were: American Families and the Nostalgia Trap.* New York: Basic Books.

Corrigan, Phillip, and Derek Sayer. 1985. *The Great Arch: English State Formation as Cultural Revolution.* Oxford: Blackwell.

Counts, George S. 1952. *Education and American Civilization.* New York: Bureau of Publications, Teachers College, Columbia University.

Coutin, Susan Bibler. 2000. *Legalizing Moves: Salvadoran Immigrants' Struggle for U.S. Residency.* Ann Arbor: University of Michigan Press.

————. 2005. "Being En Route." *American Anthropologist* 107 (2): 195–206.

————. 2007. *Nations of Emigrants: Shifting Boundaries of Citizenship in El Salvador and the United States.* Ithaca, NY: Cornell University Press.

————. 2010. "Exiled by Law: Deportation and the Inviability of Life." In *The Deportation Regime: Sovereignty, Space, and the Freedom of Movement,* ed. Nicholas De Genova and Nathalie Peutz, 351–70. Durham, NC: Duke University Press.

Crapanzano, Vincent. 1980. *Tuhami: Portrait of a Moroccan*. Chicago: University of Chicago Press.

D'Andrade, Roy G. 1992. "Schemas and Motivation." In *Human Motives and Cultural Models*, ed. Roy G. D'Andrade and Claudia Strauss, 23–44. Cambridge: Cambridge University Press.

Das, Veena, and Pamela Reynolds. 2003. *The Child on the Wing: Children Negotiating the Everyday in the Geography of Violence*. Baltimore: Johns Hopkins University.

De Genova, Nicholas P. 2002. "Migrant 'Illegality' and Deportability in Everyday Life." *Annual Review of Anthropology* 31:419–47.

———. 2005. *Working the Boundaries: Race, Space, and "Illegality" in Mexican Chicago*. Durham, NC: Duke University Press.

De Genova, Nicholas, and Nathalie Peutz, eds. 2010. *The Deportation Regime: Sovereignty, Space, and the Freedom of Movement*. Durham, NC: Duke University Press.

Dell Clark, Cindy. 2008. "Child-Centered Research." Presentation at the Wenner-Gren Workshop on Migration and Children, New York City, January.

DeLoache, Judy S., and Alma Gottlieb. 2000. *A World of Babies: Imagined Childcare Guides in Seven Societies*. Cambridge: Cambridge University Press.

DeVoe, Dorsh Marie. 1983. "Survival of a Refugee Culture: The Longterm Gift Exchange between Tibetan Refugees and Donors in India." PhD diss., University of California, Berkeley.

Devon County Council. 2007. *Exeter Baseline Profile*. Devon [England] County Council.

Dewey, John. 1902. "Address to the National Council of Education: The School as Social Center." *Elementary School Teacher* 3(2): 73–85.

Diehl, Keila. 2002. *Echoes of Dharamsala: Music in the Life of a Tibetan Refugee Community*. Berkeley: University of California Press.

Dobson, Janet, and John Stillwell. 2000. "Changing Home, Changing School: Towards a Research Agenda on Child Migration." *Area* 32(4): 395–401.

Drayton, Richard. 2002. "The Collaboration of Labour: Slaves, Empires, and Globalizations in the Atlantic World, c. 1600–1850." In *Globalization in World History*, ed. A. G. Hopkins, 98–114. London: Pimlico.

Dreby, Joanna. 2010. *Divided by Borders: Mexican Migrants and Their Children*. Berkeley: University of California Press.

Drieskens, Barbara. 2008. *Living with Djinns: Understanding and Dealing with the Invisible in Cairo*. London: Saqi.

Durham, Deborah. 2000. "Youth and the Social Imagination in Africa." *Anthropological Quarterly* 73(3): 113–20.

———. 2004. "Disappearing Youth: Youth as a Social Shifter in Botswana." *American Ethnologist* 31(4): 589–605.

Duval, David T. 2004. "Linking Return Visits and Return Migration among Commonwealth Eastern Caribbean Migrants in Toronto." *Global Networks* 4(1): 51–67.

Eckert, Paul. 2008. "Tibet Group Urges World Leaders to Raise Crackdown." Reuters, August 5, 2008, *uk.reuters.com/article/idUKPEK10515220080805*. Accessed online July 31, 2010.

Ehrenreich, Barbara, and Deirdre English. 2005. *For Her Own Good: Two Centuries of the Experts' Advice to Women*. New York: Anchor Books.

Ehrenreich, Barbara, and Arlie Russell Hochschild, eds. 2002. *Global Woman: Nannies, Maids, and Sex Workers in the New Economy*. New York: Henry Holt.

Elder, Glen H., Jr. 1994. "Time, Human Agency, and the Life Course: Perspectives on the Life Course." *Social Psychology Quarterly* 57 (1): 4–15.

Elder, Glen H., Jr., and Avshalom Caspi. 1990. "Studying Lives in a Changing Society: Sociological and Personological Explorations." In *Studying Persons and Lives*, ed. Albert I. Rabin, Robert A. Zucker, Robert A. Emmons, and Susan Frank, 201–47. New York: Springer.

Elder, Glen H., Jr., Monica Kirkpatrick Johnson, and Robert Crosnoe. 2003. "The Emergence and Development of Life Course Theory." In *Handbook of the Life Course*, ed. Jeylan T. Mortimer and Michael J. Shanahan, 3–19. New York: Kluwer Academic and Plenum.

Eloundou-Enyegue, Parfait, and C. Shannon Stokes. 2002. "Will Economics Crises in Africa Weaken Rural-Urban Ties? Evidence from Child Fosterage Trends in Cameroon." *Rural Sociology* 67 (2): 278–98.

Empez Vidal, Núria. 2005. "Menores No Acompañados en Situación de Exclusión Social." In *Multiculturalidad y Educación: Teorías, Ámbitos, Prácticas*, ed. Tomás García Fernández and José G. Molina, 314–28. Madrid: Alianza Editorial.

Ensor, Marisa O., and Elżbieta M. Goździak, eds. 2010. *Children and Migration: At the Crossroads of Resiliency and Vulnerability*. Hampshire, UK: Palgrave Macmillan.

Erickson, Frederick. 1987. "Transformation and School Success: The Politics and Culture of Educational Achievement." *Anthropology and Education Quarterly* 18 (4): 335–56.

Erikson, Erik H. 1963. *Childhood and Society*. New York: W. W. Norton.

Escandell, Xavier, and Maria Tapias. 2010. "Transnational Lives, Travelling Emotions and Idioms of Distress among Bolivian Migrants in Spain." *Journal of Ethnic and Migration Studies* 36 (3): 407–23.

Eurostat/NIDI [Netherlands Interdisciplinary Demographic Institute]. 2001. "Push and Pull Factors Determining International Migration Flows." Luxembourg: Commission of the European Communities. *www.nidi.knaw.nl/web/html/pushpull/dest/indexdest.html*. Accessed online February 5, 2009.

"Every Child Matters." *www.dcsf.gov.uk/everychildmatters/*. Accessed online February 11, 2009.

Faier, Lieba. 2007. "Filipina Migrants in Rural Japan and their Professions of Love." *American Ethnologist* 34 (1): 148–62.

Faist, Thomas. 2007. "Migration, Transnationalisation, and Development: An Unfinished Agenda." *Finnish Journal of Ethnicity and Migration* 2 (2): 2–8.

Fallers, Lloyd A. 1969. *Law without Precedent: Legal Ideas in Action in the Courts of Colonial Basoga*. Chicago: University of Chicago Press.

Festinger, Leon. 1957. *A Theory of Cognitive Dissonance*. Evanston, Ill.: Row and Peterson.

Fielding, Anthony. 1992. "Migration and Social Mobility: South-East England as an 'Escalator' Region." *Regional Studies* 26:1–15.

Fischer, Edward F. 2001. *Cultural Logics and Global Economies*. Austin: University of Texas Press.

Flores, William V. 1997. "Citizens vs. Citizenry: Undocumented Immigrants and Latino Cultural Citizenship." In *Latino Cultural Citizenship: Claiming Identity, Space, and Rights*, ed. William V. Flores and Rina Benmayor, 255–77. Boston: Beacon Press.

Flores, William V., and Rina Benmayor, ed. 1997. *Latino Cultural Citizenship: Claiming Identity, Space, and Rights*. Boston: Beacon Press.

Flowerdew, Jennifer, and Bren Neale. 2003. "Trying to Stay Apace: Children with Multiple Challenges in Their Post-Divorce Family Lives." *Childhood* 10:147–61.

Flowerdew, Robin, and Alaa Al-Hamad. 2004. "The Relationship between Marriage, Divorce, and Migration in a British Data Set." *Journal of Ethnic and Migration Studies* 30:339–51.

Foner, Nancy, ed. 2001. "West Indian Migration to New York: An Overview." Introduction to *Islands in the City: West Indian Migration to New York*, ed. Nancy Foner, 1–22. Berkeley: University of California Press.

———. 2009. *Across Generations: Immigrant Families in America*. New York: New York University Press.

Fonseca, Claudia. 2003. "Patterns of Shared Parenthood among the Brazilian Poor." *Social Text 74: Transnational Adoption* 21 (1): 111–27.

Fontaine, André. 1998. "Raise Your Boy to Be a Soldier." In *Children's Culture Reader*, ed. Henry Jenkins, 483–84. New York: New York University Press.

Forde, Maarit. 2007. "Rituals, Journeys, and Modernity." In *Constructing Vernacular Culture in the Trans-Caribbean*, ed. Holger Henke and Karl-Heinz Magister, 101–22. New York: Lexington Books.

———. 2009. "Raha ja rituaalisen vaihdon moraali Karibialla" [Money and the Morality of Ritual Exchange in the Caribbean]. In *Rahan kulttuuri* [The Culture of Money], ed. Minna Ruckenstein and Timo Kallinen, 178–93. Helsinki: Finnish Literature Society.

———. Forthcoming. "The Moral Economy of Spiritual Work: Money and Rituals in Trinidad." In *Obeah and Other Powers: The Politics of Caribbean Religion and Healing*, ed. Diana Paton and Maarit Forde. Durham, NC: Duke University Press.

Forsberg, Hannele, and Tarja Pösö. 2008. "Ambiguous Position of the Child in Supervised Meetings." *Child and Family Social Work* 13 (1): 52–60.

Foster, Geoff, Ruth Shakespeare, Frances Chinemana, H. Jackson, S. Gregson, C. Marange, and S. Mashumba. 1995. "Orphan Prevalence and Extended Family Care in a Peri-Urban Community in Zimbabwe." *AIDS Care* 7 (1): 3–18.

Foucault, Michel. 1979. *Discipline and Punish: The Birth of a Prison*. New York: Vintage Books.

———. 1980. *Power/Knowledge: Selected Interviews and Other Writings, 1972–1977*. New York: Pantheon Books.

Franklin, Sarah, and Susan McKinnon, eds. 2001. *Relative Values: Reconfiguring Kinship Studies*. Durham, NC: Duke University Press.

Freud, Anna. 1965. *Normality and Pathology in Childhood: Assessments of Development*. London: Hogarth Press and Institute of Psycho-analysis.

Friedman, Jonathan. 2002. "From Roots to Routes: Tropes for Trippers." *Anthropological Theory* 2 (1): 21–36.

Furstenberg, Frank F., Jr., J. Brooks-Gunn, and S. Philip Morgan. 1987. *Adolescent Mothers in Later Life*. Cambridge: Cambridge University Press.

Gale, Lacey A. 2006. "The Refugee 'Family': Child Fostering and Mobility among Sierra Leonean Refugees." *International Journal of Sociology of the Family* 32 (2): 273–87.

———. 2008. *Beyond Men Pikin: Improving Understanding of Post-conflict Child Fostering in Sierra Leone*. Boston: Tufts University, Feinstein International Center.

Gamburd, Michele Ruth. 2000. *The Kitchen's Spoon Handle: Transnationalism and Sri Lanka's Migrant Households*. Ithaca, NY: Cornell University Press.

———. 2004. "Money That Burns Like Oil: A Sri Lankan Cultural Logic of Morality and Agency." *Ethnology* 43 (2): 167–84.

Gamio, Manuel. 1916. *Forjando Patria (pro nacionalismo)*. Mexico City, DF: Libreria de Porrúa Hermanos.

Gardner, Katy. 2008. "Diasporic Childhood: Transglobal Children in East London." Plenary lecture, Conference on Migrant Children, University College, Cork, April.

Gardner, Richard. 1989. *The Storytelling Card Game: A Psychotherapeutic Game for Children*. Cresskill, NJ: Creative Therapeutics.

George, Shanti, Nico Van Oudenhoven, and Rekha Wazir. 2003. "Foster Care beyond the Crossroads: Lessons from an International Comparative Analysis." *Childhood* 10:343–61.

Gibbs, Sara. 1994. "Post-War Social Reconstruction in Mozambique: Re-framing Children's Experience of Trauma and Healing." *Disasters* 18:268–76.

Gibson, Margaret. 1988. *Accommodation without Assimilation: Sikh Immigrants in an American High School.* Ithaca, NY: Cornell University Press.

Giddens, Anthony. 1984. *The Constitution of Society.* Cambridge: Polity Press.

———. 1993. *The Giddens Reader.* Edited by Phillip Cassell. Stanford, CA: Stanford University Press.

Gindling, Thomas H., and Sara Poggio. 2009. "Family Separation and the Educational Success of Immigrant Children." UMBC Policy Brief no 7. Baltimore: Department of Public Policy, University of Maryland.

Gitlin, Andrew, Eduardo Buendía, Kristin Crosland, and Fode Doumbia. 2003. "The Production of Margin and Center: Welcoming-Unwelcoming of Immigrant Students." *American Educational Research Journal* 40 (1): 91–122.

Glenn, Evelyn Nakano. 1983. "Split Household, Small Producer, and Dual Wage Earner: An Analysis of Chinese-American Family Strategies." *Journal of Marriage and the Family* 45 (1): 35–46.

Glick Schiller, Nina. 2004. "Transnationality." In *A Companion to the Anthropology of Politics,* ed. David Nugent and Joan Vincent, 448–67. Malden, MA: Blackwell.

———. 2005a. "Transnational Urbanism as a Way of Life: A Research Topic Not a Metaphor." *City and Society* 17 (1): 49–64.

———. 2005b. "Transnational Social Fields and Imperialism: Bringing a Theory of Power to Transnational Studies." *Anthropological Theory* 5 (4): 439–61.

Glick Schiller, Nina, Linda Basch, and Cristina Szanton. 1992. *Towards a Transnational Perspective on Migration: Race, Class, Ethnicity, and Nationalism Reconsidered.* New York: New York Academy of Sciences.

———. 1995. "From Immigrant to Transmigrant: Theorizing Transnational Migration." *Anthropological Quarrterly* 68 (1): 48–63.

Glick Schiller, Nina, and Georges Eugene Fouron. 2001. *Georges Woke Up Laughing: Long-Distance Nationalism and the Search for Home.* Durham, NC: Duke University Press.

Gollop, Megan, Nicola Taylor, and Anne Smith. 2000. "Children's Perspectives on Their Parents' Separation." In *Children's Voices: Research, Policy, and Practice,* ed. Anne Smith, Nicola Taylor, and Megan Gollop. Auckland: Pearson Education.

Gonzales, Nancy. 1970. "Toward a Definition of Matrifocality." In *Afro-American Anthropology,* ed. Norman E. Whitter Jr. and John F. Szwed, 231–44. New York: Free Press.

Gonzales, Roberto G. 2009. "Learning to Be Illegal: The Unauthorized 1.5 Generation and the Construction of Liminal Illegality." Paper presented at "Undocumented Hispanic Migration: On the Margins of a Dream" conference, Connecticut College, October 16–18.

Goody, Esther. 1982. *Parenting and Social Reproduction: Fostering and Occupational Roles in West Africa.* Cambridge: Cambridge University Press.

Gordimer, Nadine. 2001. *The Pickup.* New York: Penguin.

Gordon, Milton M. 1964. *Assimilation in American Life: The Role of Race, Religion, and National Origins.* New York: Oxford University Press.

Gordon, Sally W. 1996 [1987]. " 'I Go to Tanties': The Economic Significance of Child-shifting in Antigua, West Indies." In *Family in the Caribbean: Themes and Perspectives,* ed. Christine Barrow, 106–19. Kingston: IRP, and Oxford: James Currey.

Gottlieb, Alma. 2004. *The Afterlife Is Where We Come From: The Culture of Infancy in West Africa*. Chicago: University of Chicago Press.

Goulbourne, Harry. 2001. "The Socio-Political Context of Caribbean Families in the Atlantic World." In *Caribbean Families in Britain and the Trans-Atlantic World*, ed. Harry Goulbourne and Mary Chamberlain, 12–31. London: Macmillan.

Goulbourne, Harry, and Mary Chamberlain. 2001. "Caribbean Families in the Trans-Atlantic World." In *Caribbean Families in Britain and the Trans-Atlantic World*, ed. Harry Goulbourne and Mary Chamberlain, 2–11. London: Macmillan.

Goździak, Elżbieta. 2008. "On Problems, Dilemmas, and Opportunities in Studying Trafficked Children." *Anthropological Quarterly* 81 (4): 903–24.

Grady, Karen. 2002. "Lowrider Art and Latino Students in the Rural Midwest." In *Education in the New Latino Diaspora*, ed. Stanton Wortham, Enrique G. Murillo Jr., and Edmund T. Hamann, 169–91. Westport, CT: Ablex.

Green, Anne. 1997. "A Question of Compromise? Case Study Evidence on the Location and Mobility Strategies of Dual Career Households." *Regional Studies* 31:641–57.

Greenhouse, Carol J., Elizabeth Mertz, and Kay B. Warren. 2002. *Ethnography in Unstable Places: Everyday Lives in Contexts of Dramatic Political Change*. Durham, NC: Duke University Press.

Grey, Mark A. 1991. "The Context for Marginal Secondary ESL Programs: Contributing Factors and the Need for Further Research." *Journal of Educational Issues of Language Minority Students* 9:75–89.

Grier, Beverly. 1992. "Pawns, Porters, and Petty Traders: Women in the Transition to Cash Crop Agriculture in Colonial Ghana." *Signs* 17 (21): 304–28.

Griffith, David C. 1985. "Women, Remittances, and Reproduction." *American Ethnologist* 12 (4): 676–90.

Grossberg, Lawrence. 2005. *Caught in the Crossfire: Kids, Politics, and America's Future*. Boulder, CO: Paradigm.

Guarnizo, Luis Eduardo. 2003. "The Economics of Transnational Living." *International Migration Review* 37 (3): 666–99.

Guerra, Juan C. 1998. *Close to Home: Oral and Literate Practices in a Transnational Mexicano Community*. New York: Teachers College Press.

Guyer, Jane. 1993. "Wealth in People and Self-Realization in Equatorial Africa." *Man* 18:243–65.

Guyer, Jane, and Samuel M. Eno Belinga. 1995. "Wealth in People as Wealth in Knowledge Accumulation and Composition in Equatorial Africa." *Journal of African History* 36 (1): 91–120.

Haenger, Peter. 2000. *Slaves and Slave Holders on the Gold Coast: Towards an Understanding of Social Bondage in West Africa*. Basel: P. Schlettwein.

Halfacree, Keith. 2004. "A Utopian Imagination in Migration's *Terra Incognita*? Acknowledging the Non-economic Worlds of Migration Decision-Making." *Population, Space, and Place* 10:239–53.

Halfacree, Keith, and Paul Boyle. 1993. "The Challenge Facing Migration Research: The Case for a Biographical Approach." *Progress in Human Geography* 17:333–48.

Hall, Catherine. 2002. *Civilizing Subjects: Metropole and Colony in the English Imagination, 1830–1867*. Chicago: University of Chicago Press.

Hamann, Edmund T. 2003. *The Educational Welcome of Latinos in the New South*. Westport, CT: Praeger.

Hamann, Edmund T., Víctor Zúñiga, and Juan Sánchez García. 2006. "Pensando en Cynthia y Su Hermana: Educational Implications of U.S./Mexico Transnationalism for Children." *Journal of Latinos and Education* 5 (4): 253–74.

————. 2008. "From Nuevo León to the USA and Back Again: Transnational Students in Mexico." *Journal of Immigrant and Refugee Studies* 6 (1): 60–84.

Hart, Jason, and Bex Tyrer. 2006. "Research with Children Living in Situations of Armed Conflict: Concepts, Ethics and Methods." RSC Working Paper. Oxford: Refugee Studies Centre, Queen Elizabeth House, Department of International Development, Oxford University.

Hart, Roger. 1992. Children's Participation: From Tokenism to Citizenship. Florence: UNICEF.

————. 1997. *Children's Participation: The Theory and Practice of Involving Young Citizens in Community Development and Environmental Care.* New York: UNICEF.

Hastrup, Kirsten, and Karen Fog Olwig. 1997. Introduction to *Siting Culture: The Shifting Anthropological Object*, ed. Karen Fog Olwig and Kirsten Hastrup, 1–14. London: Routledge.

Heath, Shirley Brice. 1982. "What No Bedtime Story Means: Narrative Skills at Home and School." *Language in Society* 11:49–76.

Henderson, Sheila. 2005. "Sticks and Smoke: Growing Up with a Sense of City in the English Countryside." *Young* 13:363–79.

Hepburn, Amy. 2006. "Running Scared: When Children Become Separated in Emergencies." In *A World Turned Upside Down: Social Ecological Approaches to Children in War Zones*, ed. Neil Boothby, Alison Strang, and Michael Wessells, 63–88. Bloomfield, CT: Kumarian Press.

Hernández-León, Rubén, and Víctor Zúñiga. 2000. " 'Making Carpet by the Mile': The Emergence of a Mexican Immigrant Community in an Industrial Region of the U.S. Historic South." *Social Science Quarterly* 81 (1): 49–66.

Hernández-León, Rubén, Víctor Zúñiga, Janna L. Shadduck, and María Olivia Villarreal. 1997. "Needs Assessment of the Hispanic Community in Dalton: First Report." Unpublished technical report (computer printout). Universidad de Monterrey.

Hess, Julia Meredith. 2009a. *Immigrant Ambassadors: Citizenship and Belonging in the Tibetan Diaspora.* Stanford, CA: Stanford University Press.

————. 2009b. " 'We Are Not Terrorists!' Uighurs, Tibetans, and the 'Global War on Terror.' " In *International Migration and Human Rights: The Global Repercussions of U.S. Policy*, ed. Samuel Martinez, 184–98. Berkeley: University of California Press.

Hess, Julia Meredith, and Dianna Shandy. 2008. "Kids at the Crossroads: Global Childhood and the State. *Anthropological Quarterly* 81 (4): 765–76.

Hewlett, Barry. 2001. "The Cultural Nexus of Aka Father-Infant Bonding." In *Gender in Cross-Cultural Perspective*, ed. Caroline Brettell and Carolyn Sargent, 42–53. Englewood Cliffs, NJ: Prentice Hall.

Hidalgo, Francisco. 2004. *Migraciones: Un Juego con Cartas Marcadas.* Quito: Ediciones Abya-Yala.

Hidalgo, Francisco, and Ana Lucía Jiménez. 2004. "Una Comunidad Indígena que Emigró a Madrid." In *Migraciones: Un Juego con Cartas Marcadas*, ed. Francisco Hidalgo, 401–18. Quito: Abya-Yala.

Hill, Malcolm, Julia Davis, Alan Prout, and Kay Tisdall. 2004. "Moving the Participation Agenda Forward." *Children and Society* 18:77–96.

Hinton, Alexander Laban, ed. 1999. *Biocultural Approaches to the Emotions.* New York: Cambridge University Press.

Hirschfeld, Lawrence A. 2002. "Why Don't Anthropologists Like Children?" *American Anthropologist* 104 (2): 611–27.

Hochschild, Arlie Russell. 2003. "Love and Gold." In *Global Woman: Nannies, Maids, and Sex Workers in the New Economy*, ed. Barbara Ehrenreich and Arlie Russell Hochschild, 15–30. New York: Metropolitan Books.

Hoffman, Eva. 1989. *Lost in Translation: A Life in a New Language*. New York: Penguin

Hondagneu-Sotelo, Pierrette. 1994. *Gendered Transitions: Mexican Experiences of Immigration*. Berkeley: University of California Press.

———. 2003. *Gender and U.S. Migration: Contemporary Trends*. Berkeley: University of California Press.

Hondagneu-Sotelo, Pierrette, and Ernestine Avila. 1997. " 'I'm Here, but I'm There': The Meanings of Latina Transnational Motherhood." *Gender and Society* 11 (5): 548–71.

Honwana, Alcinda, and Filip De Boeck, eds. 2005. *Makers and Breakers: Children and Youth in Postcolonial Africa*. Oxford: James Currey.

Horst, Heather. 2006. "Building Home: Being and Becoming a Returned Resident." In *Returning to the Source: The Final Stage of the Caribbean Migration Circuit*, ed. Dwaine E. Plaza and Frances Henry, 123–44. Kingston: UWI Press.

Horton, Sarah. 2008. "Consuming Childhood: 'Lost' and 'Ideal' Childhoods as a Motivation for Migration." *Anthropological Quarterly* 81 (4): 925–43.

Huber, Toni. 1997. "Green Tibetans: A Brief Social History." In *Tibetan Culture in the Diaspora*, ed. Frank J. Korom, 51–58. Vienna: Austrian Academy of Sciences.

Instituto Nacional de Estadísticas. 2009. "Inmigrantes por continentes y países más representados, según grupos de edad y sex." *Encuesta Nacional de Inmigrantes* www.ine.es/inebmenu/mnu_migrac.htm.

Isaac, Barry L., and Shelby R. Conrad. 1982. "Child Fosterage among the Mende of Upper Bambara Chiefdom, Sierra Leone: Rural-Urban and Occupational Comparisons." *Ethnology* 21 (3): 243–57.

Isiugo-Abanihe, Uche. 1985. "Child Fosterage in West Africa." *Population and Development Review* 11 (1): 53–74.

Iyer, Pico. 2008. *The Open Road: The Global Journey of the Fourteenth Dalai Lama*. New York: Knopf.

Jacobsen, Karen. 2001. "The Forgotten Solution: Local Integration for Refugees in Developing Countries." Working Paper No. 45. New Issues in Refugee Research. Geneva: UNHCR, Evaluation and Policy Analysis Unit.

James, Allison, and Adrian L. James. 2004. *Constructing Childhood: Theory, Policy, and Social Practice*. New York: Palgrave Macmillan.

James, Allison, Chris Jenks, and Alan Prout. 1998. *Theorizing Childhood*. New York: Teachers College Press.

James, Allison, and Alan Prout. 1990. *Constructing and Reconstructing Childhood: Contemporary Issues in the Sociological Study of Childhood*. New York: Falmer Press.

Jenkins, Henry, ed. 1998. *The Children's Culture Reader*. New York: New York University Press.

Jentsch, Birgit, and Mark Shucksmith, eds. 2004. *Policies and Young People in Rural Europe*. Basingstoke, UK: Ashgate.

Jiménez Álvarez, Mercedes. 2003. *Buscarse la Vida: Análisis transnacional de los procesos migratorios de los menores de origen marroquí en Andalucía*. Madrid: Editorial Fundación Santa María.

———. 2006. "Donde quiebra la protección: las reagrupaciones familiares sin garantías." Report. Taller de Estudios Internacionales Mediterráneos (UAM).

Jiménez Álvarez, Mercedes, and Diego Lorente. 2004. "Menores en las fronteras: de los retornos efectuados sin garantías a menores marroquíes y de los malos tratos sufridos." Report. Federación SOS Racismo.

Johnson, John William, trans. 2003. *Son-Jara: The Mande Epic*. 3rd ed. Bloomington: Indiana University Press.

Jones, Delmos. 1992. "Which Migrants? Temporary or Permanent?" In *Towards a Transnational Perspective on Migration*, ed. Nina Glick Schiller, Linda Basch, and Cristina Blanc-Szanton, 217–24. New York: New York Academy of Sciences.

Kabki, Marjam, Valentina Mazzucato, and Ton Dietz. 2008. "Migrant Involvement in Community Development: The Case of the Rural Ashanti Region, Ghana." In *Global Migration and Development*, ed. Ton van Naerssen, Ernst Spaan, and Annelies Zoomers, 150–71. New York: Routledge.

Kasinitz, Phil. 1992. *Caribbean New York*. Ithaca, NY: Cornell University Press.

Katz, Cindi. 2001. "Vagabond Capitalism and the Necessity of Social Reproduction." *Antipode* 33(4): 709–28.

Kearney, Michael. 1996. *Reconceptualizing the Peasantry: Anthropology in Global Perspective*. Boulder, CO: Westview Press.

Kerrigan, John. 2008. "The Ticking Fear." *London Review of Books*, February 7, *www.lrb.co.uk/v30/n03/kerr01_.html*. Accessed online June 15, 2008.

Khoo, Siew-Ean, Graeme Hugo, and Peter McDonald. 2008. "Which Skilled Temporary Migrants Become Permanent Residents and Why?" *International Migration Review* 42:193–226.

King, Kendall. 2008. "Language Shift and Cultural Change in Indigenous Highland Ecuador: Migration from the Perspective of the Children Left Behind." Paper presented at Working Group on Childhood and Migration, "Emerging Perspectives on Children in Migratory Circumstances," Philadelphia, June 20–22.

Kitwana, Baraki. 2004. "The State of the Hip-Hop Generation: How Hip-Hop's Cultural Movement Is Evolving into Political Power." *Diogenes* 51 (3): 115–20.

Kleinman, Arthur, and Byron Good. 1985. *Culture and Depression: Studies in the Anthropology and Cross-Cultural Psychiatry of Affect and Disorder*. Berkeley: University of California Press.

Knörr, Jacqueline, ed. 2005. *Children and Migration: From Experience to Agency*. Bielefeld, Germany: Transcript.

Kobiané, Jean-François. 2003. "Pauvreté, structures familiales et stratégies éducatives a Ouagadougou." In *Éducation, famille, et dynamiques démographique*, ed. Maria Cosio, Richard Marcoux, Marc Pilon, and André Quesnel, 153–82. Paris: Committee for International Cooperation in National Research in Demography (CICRED).

Kobiané, Jean-François, Anne-Emmanuèle Calvès, and Richard Marcoux. 2005. "Parental Death and Children's Schooling in Burkina Faso." *Comparative Education Review* 49 (4): 468–89.

Kofman, Eleanor. 2004. "Family Related Migration: A Critical Review of European Studies." *Journal of Ethnic and Migration Studies* 30:243–62.

Kohlberg, Lawrence. 1968. "The Child as a Moral Philosopher." *Psychology Today* 214:25–30.

Konrad, Marc, and Vicenta Santoja. 2005. *Menores Migrantes de los Puntos Cardinales a la Rosa de los Vientos*. Valencia: Promolibro.

Korbin, Jill. 2003. "Children, Childhoods, and Violence." *Annual Review of Anthropology* 32:431–46.

Kwamena-Poh, M. A. 1973. *Government and Politics in the Akuapem State, 1730–1850*. Evanston, IL: Northwestern University Press.

———. 2005. *Vision and Achievement: A Hundred and Fifty Years of the Presbyterian Church in Ghana, 1828–1978*. Accra: Presbyterian Church of Ghana Press.

Lambek, Michael. 1993. *Knowledge and Practice in Mayotte: Local Discourses of Islam, Sorcery, and Spirit Possession*. Toronto: University of Toronto Press.

Lancy, David F. 2008. *The Anthropology of Childhood: Cherubs, Chattel, Changelings*. Cambridge: Cambridge University Press.

Lansdown, Gerison. 1995. *Taking Part: Children's Participation in Decision Making*. London: Institute for Public Policy Research.

Leach, Melissa. 1992. "Dealing with Displacement: Refugee Host Relations, Food, and Forest Resources in Sierra Leonean Mende Communities during the Liberian Influx, 1990–91." Brighton, UK: Institute of Development Studies.

Leinaweaver, Jessaca B. 2008. *The Circulation of Children: Kinship, Adoption, and Morality in Andean Peru*. Durham, NC: Duke University Press.

Levin, Paula. 2005. "Changing Childhood in Polynesia: The Impact of Robert Levy's *Tahitians* on Psychological Anthropology in Oceania." *Ethos* 33 (4): 467–74.

LeVine, Robert A. 2003. *Childhood Socialization: Comparative Studies of Parenting, Learning, and Educational Change*. Hong Kong: University of Hong Kong.

LeVine, Robert A., and Karin Norman. 2008. "Attachment in Anthropological Perspective." In *Anthropology and Child Development: A Cross-Cultural Reader*, ed. Robert A. LeVine and Rebecca S. New, 127–42. Malden, MA: Blackwell.

Levinson, Bradley A. 2005. "Programs for Democratic Citizenship in Mexico's Ministry of Education: Local Appropriations of Global Cultural Flows." *Indiana Journal of Global Legal Studies* 12 (1): 251–84.

Levinson, Bradley A., Douglas E. Foley, and Dorothy C. Holland. 1996. *The Cultural Production of the Educated Person: Critical Ethnographies of Schooling and Local Practice*. Albany: State University of New York Press.

Levitt, Peggy. 2001. *The Transnational Villagers*. Berkeley: University of California Press.

Levy, Robert I. 1973. *Tahitians: Mind and Experience in the Society Islands*. Chicago: University of Chicago Press.

———. 1984. "Emotion, Knowing, and Culture." In *Culture Theory: Essays on Mind, Self, and Emotion*, ed. Richard A. Shweder and Robert A. LeVine, 214–37. New York: Cambridge University Press.

———. 2005. "Ethnography, Comparison, and Changing Times." *Ethos* 33 (4): 435–58.

Lipsky, Michael. 1980. *Street-Level Bureaucracy: Dilemmas of the Individual in Public Services*. New York: Russell Sage.

Lopez, Mark Hugo, and Susan Minushkin. 2008. "2008 National Survey of Latinos: Hispanics See Their Situation in U.S. Deteriorating; Oppose Key Immigration Enforcement Measures." Washington, DC: Pew Hispanic Center. *pewhispanic.org/reports/report.php?ReportID=93*. Accessed online December 7, 2008.

López, Susana, and David Villamar C. 2004. "El Proceso Emigratorio en el Sur de Quito." In *Migraciones: Un Juego con Cartas Marcadas*, ed. Francisco Hidalgo, 367–88. Quito: Abya-Yala.

Lubkemann, Stephen. 2008. *Culture in Chaos: An Anthropology of the Social Condition in War*. Chicago: University of Chicago Press.

Lutz, Catherine A. 1988. *Unnatural Emotions: Everyday Sentiments on a Micronesian Atoll and Their Challenge to Western Theory*. Chicago: University of Chicago Press.

Lutz, Catherine A., and Lila Abu-Lughod. 1990. *Language and the Politics of Emotion*. Cambridge: Cambridge University Press.

Luykx, Aurolyn. 1999. *The Citizen Factory: Schooling and Cultural Production in Bolivia*. Albany: State University of New York Press.

Macmillan, Ross, Barbara J. McMorris, and Candace Kruttschnitt. 2004. "Linked Lives:

Stability and Change in Maternal Circumstances and Trajectories of Antisocial Behavior in Children." *Child Development* 75 (1): 205–20.

Maher, Kristen Hill. 2004. " 'Natural Mothers for Sale': The Construction of Latina Immigrant Identity in Domestic Service Labor Markets." In *Immigrant Life in the U.S.: Multi-disciplinary Perspectives*, ed. Donna R. Gabaccia and Colin Wayne Leach, 173–90. New York: Routledge.

Maira, Sunaina, and Elizabeth Soep, eds. 2005. *Youthscapes: The Popular, the National, the Global*. Philadelphia: University of Pennsylvania Press.

Mann, Gillian. 2003. "Not Seen or Heard: The Lives of Separated Refugee Children in Dar es Salaam." Stockholm: Save the Children, Sweden.

———. 2004. "Separated Children: Care and Support in Context." In *Children and Youth on the Front Line: Ethnography, Armed Conflict, and Displacement*, ed. Jo Boyden and Jo de Berry, 3–22. New York: Oxford: Berghahn Books.

Mann, Gillian, and David K. Tolfree. 2003. "Children's Participation in Research: Reflections from the Care and Protection of Separated Children in Emergencies Project." Stockholm: Save the Children, Sweden.

Marcus, George E. 1995. "Ethnography in/of the World System: The Emergence of Multi-Sited Ethnography." *Annual Review of Anthropology* 24:95–117.

Massey, Douglas S. 1990. "Social Structure, Household Strategies, and the Cumulative Causation of Migration." *Population Index* 56 (1): 3–26.

Massey, Douglas S., Rafael Alarcón, Jorge Durand, and Humberto González. 1987. *Return to Aztlán: The Social Process of International Migration from Western Mexico*. Berkeley: University of California Press.

Maússe, Miguel, and Monica Sitoi. 1994. "O papel de família substituta na socialização da criança." Maputo, Mozambique: Ministry for the Coordination of Social Action.

Mayall, Berry, ed. 1994. *Children's Childhoods: Observed and Experienced*. London: Falmer Press.

Maxey, Larch. 2004. "The Participation of Younger People within Intentional Communities: Evidence from Two Case Studies." *Children's Geographies* 2:29–48.

Mayer, Karl Ulrich. 2005. "Life Courses and Life Changes in a Comparative Perspective." In *Analyzing Inequality: Life Chances and Social Mobility in Comparative Perspective*, ed. Karl Stefan Svallfors, 17–55. Stanford, CA: Stanford University Press.

Mazanti, Birgitte. 2007. "Choosing Residence, Community, and Neighbours: Theorizing Families' Motives for Moving." *Geografiska Annaler Series B, Human Geography* 89:53–68.

McKay, Sandra Lee, and Sau-ling Cynthia Wong. 2000. *New Immigrants in the United States: Readings for Second Language Educators*. Cambridge: Cambridge University Press.

McKendrick, John. 2001. "Coming of Age: Rethinking the Role of Children in Population Studies." *International Journal of Population Geography* 7:461–72.

McLagan, Margaret Jane. 1996. "Mobilizing for Tibet: Transnational Politics and Diaspora Culture in the Post-Cold War Era." PhD diss., New York University.

McLeod, Marc C. 1998. "Undesirable Aliens: Race, Ethnicity, and Nationalism in the Comparison of Haitian and British West Indian Immigrant Workers in Cuba, 1912–1939." *Journal of Social History* 31:599–623.

Mead, Margaret. 1961. "Questions That Need Asking." *Teachers College Record* 63 (2): 89–93.

Meillassoux, Claude. 1975. *Femmes, Greniers, et Capitaux*. Paris: Maspero.

Mendoza-Denton, Norma. 2008. *Homegirls: Language and Cultural Practice among Latina Girls*. Malden, MA: Blackwell.

Menjívar, Cecilia, and Leisy Abrego. 2009. "Parents and Children across Borders: Legal Instability and Intergenerational Relations in Guatemalan and Salvadoran Families." In *Across Generations: Immigrant Families in America*, ed. Nancy Foner, 160–89. New York: New York University Press.

Menjívar, Cecilia, and Victor Agadjanian. 2007. "Men's Migration and Women's Lives: Views from Rural Armenia and Guatemala." *Social Science Quarterly* 88:1243–62.

Meyer, Birgit. 1999. *Translating the Devil: Religion and Modernity among the Ewe in Ghana*. London: Edinburgh University Press.

Mintz, Sidney. 1974. *Worker in the Cane: A Puerto Rican Life History*. New York: W. W. Norton.

———. 1989. *Caribbean Transformations*. New York: Columbia University Press.

Minuchin, Patricia. 1985. "Families and Individual Development: Provocations from the Field of Family Therapy." *Child Development* 56 (2): 289–302.

Mishra, Pankaj. 2005. "The Restless Children of the Dalai Lama." *New York Times Magazine*, December 18, *www.nytimes.com/2005/12/18/magazine/18tibet.html*. Accessed online July 31, 2010.

Mitchell, Tony, ed. 2001. *Global Noise: Rap and Hip Hop outside the U.S.A.* Middletown, CT: Wesleyan University Press.

Model, Suzanne. 2001. "Where New York's West Indians Work." In *Islands in the City: West Indian Migration to New York*, ed. Nancy Foner, 52–80. Berkeley: University of California Press.

Moffatt, Michael. 1989. *Coming of Age in New Jersey: College and American Culture*. New Brunswick, NJ: Rutgers University Press.

Montgomery, Heather. 2009. *An Introduction to Childhood: Anthropological Perspectives on Children's Lives*. Malden, MA: Wiley-Blackwell.

Moon, Seungsook. 2003. "Immigration and Mothering: Case Studies from Two Generations of Korean Immigrant Women." *Gender and Society* 17 (6): 840–60.

Mostov, Julie 2008. *Soft Borders: Rethinking Sovereignty and Democracy*. New York: Palgrave-Macmillan.

Nagengast, Carole. 1991. *Reluctant Socialists, Rural Entrepreneurs: Class, Culture, and the Polish State*. Boulder, CO: Westview Press.

———. 1994. "Violence, Terror, and the Crisis of the State." *Annual Review of Anthropology* 23:109–36.

Näsman, Elisabet. 1994. "Individualization and Institutionalization of Childhood in Today's Europe." In *Childhood Matters: Social Theory, Practice, and Politics*, ed. Jens Qvortrup, Marjatta Bardy, Giovanni Sgritta, and Helmut Wintersberger, 165–88. Aldershot, UK: Avebury.

Newton, Velma. 1984. *The Silver Men: West Indian Labour Migration to Panama*. Mona, Jamaica: Institute of Social and Economic Research, University of the West Indies.

Ngai, Mae M. 2004. *Impossible Subjects: Illegal Aliens and the Making of Modern America*. Princeton, NJ: Princeton University Press.

Ní Laoire, Caitriona. 2000. "Conceptualising Irish Rural Youth Migration: A Biographical Approach." *International Journal of Population Geography* 6:229–43.

———. 2007. " 'The Green, Green Grass of Home'? Return Migration to Rural Ireland." *Journal of Rural Studies* 23:332–44.

Norbu, Jamyang. 2008. "Karmapa and the Cranes." Shadow Tibet, May 27, *www.jamyangnorbu.com/blog/2008/05/27/karmapa-and-the-cranes/*. Accessed online August 5, 2010.

Nordstrom, Carolyn. 1999. "Girls and War Zones: Troubling Questions." In *Engendering*

Forced Migration: Theory and Practice, ed. Doreen Indra, 63–82. New York: Berghahn Books.

————. 2003. "Shadows and Sovereigns." In *State/Space: A Reader*, ed. Neil Brenner, Bob Jessop, Martin Jones, and Gordon MacLeod, 326–43. Malden, MA: Blackwell.

————. 2004. *Shadows of War: Violence, Power, and International Profiteering in the Twenty-First Century*. Berkeley: University of California Press.

————. 2006. "The Jagged Edge of Peace: The Creation of Culture and War Orphans in Angola." In *Troublemakers or Peacemakers? Youth and Post-Accord Peace Building*, ed. Siobhan McEvoy-Levy, 99–116. Notre Dame, IN: University of Notre Dame Press.

Notermans, Catrien. 2004. "Fosterage and the Politics of Marriage and Kinship in East Cameroon." In *Cross-Cultural Approaches to Adoption*, ed. Fiona Bowie, 48–80. London and New York: Routledge.

Nowak, Margaret. 1984. *Tibetan Refugees: Youth and the New Generation of Meaning*. New Brunswick, NJ: Rutgers University Press.

Nyangara, Florence. 2004. "Sub-national Distribution and Situation of Orphans: An Analysis of the President's Emergency Plan for AIDS Relief Focus Countries." Washington, DC: USAID, Bureau of Africa.

Oben, W. 1895. "Nneεma horow a etumi siw yεn adwuma kwan" [Obstacles in our Christian work]." *Kristofo Sεnkekafo* 1 (13): 105–6.

Obeyesekere, Gananath. 1984. *Medusa's Hair: An Essay on Personal Symbols and Religious Experience*. Chicago: University of Chicago Press.

Office for National Statistics. 2001. UK Census, *www.ons.gov.uk/census/index.html*. Accessed online August 2, 2010.

Ofori, Immanuel. 1907. "So anyamesεm no renya nkɔso wɔ Akuapεm asase so akyεn aman a edi n'akyi no ana? [Will Christianity bring more progress to Akuapεm than to other nations that came to Christianity later?]" *Kristofo Sεnkekafo* 2 (1): 7–9.

Ogbu, John. 1987. "Variability in Minority School Responses to Schooling: Non-Immigrants and Immigrants." In *Education and Cultural Process*, ed. George P. Spindler, 129–39. Hillsdale, NJ: Lawrence Erlbaum Associates.

Olwig, Karen Fog. 1999. "Narratives of the Children Left Behind: Home and Identity in Globalized Caribbean Families." *Journal of Ethnic and Migration Studies* 25 (2): 267–84.

————. 2002. "A 'Respectable' Livelihood: Mobility and Identity in a Caribbean Family." In *Work and Migration: Life and Livelihoods in a Globalizing World*, ed. Ninna Nyberg Sorensen and Karen Fog Olwig, 85–105. London: Routledge.

————. 2007. *Caribbean Journeys: An Ethnography of Family and Home in Three Family Networks*. Durham, NC: Duke University Press.

Ong, Aihwa. 1999. *Flexible Citizenship: The Cultural Logics of Transnationality*. Durham, NC: Duke University Press.

————. 2003. *Buddha Is Hiding: Refugees, Citizenship, and the New America*. Berkeley: University of California Press.

Ong, Aihwa, and Donald Nonini. 1997. *Ungrounded Empires: The Cultural Politics of Modern Chinese Transnationalism*. New York: Routledge.

Oni, Jacob Bamideli. 1995. "Fostered Children's Perceptions of Their Health Care and Illness Treatment in Ekiti Yoruba Households, Nigeria." *Health Transition Review* 5:21–34.

Opoku, Theophilus. 1893. "Asafo mu nneyεe bi a εsε sε wosiesie [What Some Christians Do That We Should Correct]." *Kristofo Sεnkekafo* 1 (16): 151–56.

Orellana, Marjorie Faulstich. 2009. *Translating Childhoods: Immigrant Youth, Language, and Culture*. Piscataway, NJ: Rutgers University Press.

Orellana, Marjorie Faulstich, Jennifer Reynolds, Lisa Dorner, and Maria Meza. 2003. "In Other Words: Translating or 'Para-Phrasing' as a Family Literacy Practice in Immigrant Households." *Reading Research Quarterly* 38 (1): 12–34.

Orellana, Marjorie Faulstich, Barrie Thorne, Anna Chee, and Wan Shun Eva Lam. 2000. "Transnational Childhoods: The Participation of Children in Processes of Family Migration." *Social Problems* 48 (4): 572–90.

Ortner, Sherry. 2006. *Anthropology and Social Theory: Culture, Power, and the Acting Subject.* Durham, NC: Duke University Press.

Osnos, Evan. 2008. "Letter from China. Angry Youth: The New Generation's Neocon Nationalism." *New Yorker,* July 28, 28–37.

Ossman, Susan, ed. 2004. "Studies in Serial Migration." *International Migration.* 42 (4): 111–21.

———. 2007. *The Places We Share: Migration, Subjectivity, and Global Mobility.* Lanham, MD: Rowman and Littlefield.

Oviedo Campaña, Edmundo. 2002. *Ecuador en España: La Realidad de la Migración.* Madrid: Diseño Gráfico AM2000.

Palmié, Stefan. 2006. "A View from Itia Ororó Kande." *Social Anthropology* 14 (1): 99–118.

Panter-Brick, Catherine. 2000. "Nobody's Children? A Reconsideration of Child Abandonment." In *Abandoned Children,* ed. Catherine Panter-Brick and Malcolm T. Smith, 1–26. Cambridge: Cambridge University Press.

Parish, Steven M. 1996. *Hierarchy and Its Discontents: Culture and the Politics of Consciousness in Caste Society.* Philadelphia: University of Pennsylvania Press.

Park, Robert E., and Ernest W. Burgess. 1970 [1921]. *Introduction to the Science of Sociology: Including an Index to Basic Sociological Concepts.* Abridged student edition. Morris Janowitz, abr. Chicago: University of Chicago Press.

Parreñas, Rhacel Salazar. 2001. "Mothering from a Distance: Emotions, Gender, and Intergenerational Relations in Filipino Transnational Families." *Feminist Studies* 27 (2): 361–90.

———. 2003. "The Care Crisis in the Philippines: Children and Transnational Families in the New Global Economy." In *Global Woman: Nannies, Maids, and Sex Workers in the New Economy,* ed. Barbara Ehrenreich and Arlie Russell Hochschild, 39–54. New York: Metropolitan Books.

———. 2005. *Children of Global Migration: Transnational Families and Gendered Woes.* Stanford, CA: Stanford University Press.

———. 2006. "Understanding the Backlash: Why Transnational Migrant Families Are Considered 'the Wrong Kind of Family' in the Philippines." Research Notes on Childhood and Migration. *www.globalchild.rutgers.edu.* Accessed online July 22, 2010.

Passel, Jeffrey S. 2005. "Estimates of the Size and Characteristics of the Undocumented Population." Washington, DC: Pew Hispanic Center.

Patiño, Agustín, and Ruth Bushi. 2004. "Efectos de la Emigración en Cotopaxi." In *Migraciones: Un Juego con Cartas Marcadas,* ed. Francisco Hidalgo, 389–400. Quito: Abya-Yala.

Pessar, Patricia R. 1999. "Engendering Migration Studies: The Case of New Immigrants in the United States." *American Behavioral Scientist* 42 (4): 577–600.

Pessar, Patricia R., and Sarah J. Mahler. 2003. "Transnational Migration: Bringing Gender In." *International Migration Review* 37 (3): 812–46.

Peutz, Nathalie. 2007. "Out-laws: Deportees, Desire, and 'The Law.'" *International Migration* 45 (3): 182–91.

Phillips, Susan Urmston. 1983. *The Invisible Culture: Communication in Classroom and Community on the Warm Springs Reservation.* Prospect Heights, IL: Waveland Press.

Piaget, Jean. 1968. *Six Psychological Studies*. New York: Vintage Books.

Piaget, Jean, Bärbel Inhelder, and Edith Mayer. 1956. "The Co-ordination of Perspectives." In *The Child's Conception of Space*, ed. Jean Piaget and Bärbel Inhelder, 209–13. London: Routledge.

Pilon, Marc. 1995. "Les déterminants de la scolarisation des enfants de 6 a 14 ans au Togo en 1981: Apports et limites des données censitaires." *Cahiers des sciences humaines* 31 (3): 697–718.

Piore, Michael J. 1979. *Birds of Passage: Migrant Labor and Industrial Societies*. Cambridge: Cambridge University Press.

Plaza, Dwaine E., and Frances Henry, eds. 2006. *Returning to the Source: The Final Stage of the Caribbean Migration Circuit*. Kingston: UWI Press.

Portes, Alejandro. 2000. "Globalization from Below: The Rise of Transnational Communities." In *The Ends of Globalization: Bringing Society Back In*, ed. Don Kalb, Marco van der Land, Richard Staring, Bart van Steenbergen, and Nico Wilterdink, 253–70. Boulder, CO: Rowman and Littlefield.

Portes, Alejandro, and Josh DeWind. 2004. "A Cross-Atlantic Dialogue: The Progress of Research and Theory in the Study of International Migration." *International Migration Review* 38 (3): 828–51.

Portes, Alejandro, Luis E. Guarnizo, and Patricia Landolt. 1999. "The Study of Transnationalism: Pitfalls and Promise of an Emergent Research Field." *Ethnic and Racial Studies* 22 (2): 217–37.

Portes, Alejandro, William Haller, and Luis Eduardo Guarnizo. 2003. *Assimilation and Transnationalism: Determinants of Transnational Political Action among Contemporary Migrants*. Chicago: University of Chicago.

Portes, Alejandro, and Min Zhou. 1993. "The New Second Generation: Segmented Assimilation and Its Variants." *Annals of the American Academy of Political and Social Science* 530:74–96.

Preston, Julia. 2007. "Immigration Quandary: A Mother Torn from Her Baby." *New York Times*, November 17.

———. 2008. "Perfectly Legal Immigrants, Until They Applied for Citizenship." *New York Times*, April 12.

Pribilsky, Jason. 2008. *La Chulla Vida: Gender, Migration, and the Family in Andean Ecuador and New York City*. Syracuse, NY: Syracuse University Press.

Pupavac, Vanessa. 2001. "Misanthropy without Borders: The International Children's Rights Regime." *Disasters* 25 (2): 95–112.

Putnam, Lara. 2002. *The Company They Kept: Migrants and the Politics of Gender in Caribbean Costa Rica, 1870–1960*. Chapel Hill: University of North Carolina Press.

Queen, Stuart A., Robert W. Habenstein, and John B. Adams. 1961. *The Family in Various Cultures*. 2nd ed. Chicago: J. B. Lippincott.

Quinn, Naomi, and Dorothy Holland. 1987. "Culture and Cognition." In *Cultural Models in Language and Thought*, ed. Dorothy Holland and Naomi Quinn, 3–40. Cambridge: Cambridge University Press.

Quiroga, Violeta. 2003. "Els Petits Harraga: Menors immigrants irregulars no acompanyats d'origen marroquí a Catalunya." PhD diss., University Rovira i Virgili, Tarragona, Spain.

Qvortrup, Jens. 1994. "A Childhood Matters: An Introduction." In *Childhood Matters: Social Theory, Practice, and Politics*, ed. Jens Qvortrup, Marjatta Bardy, Giovanni Sgritta, and Helmut Wintersberger, 1–23. Aldershot, UK: Avebury.

Rae-Espinoza, Heather. 2006. "Devoted Abandonment: The Cultural, Social, and

Psychological Effects of Parental Emigration on Children in Ecuador." PhD diss.,
University of California, San Diego.

———. 2010. "Ecuadorian Equilibrium in Consent and Discipline: How to Avoid
Raising an Antisocial." *Ethos* 38:4.

Recio, Maria. 2002. "Recession Hits Hispanics Hard, Study Finds." *Providence [Rhode
Island] Journal*, January 25.

Reddy, William M. 2002. *The Navigation of Feeling: A Framework for the History of
Emotions*. Cambridge: Cambridge University Press.

Redfield, Robert, Ralph Linton, and Melville J. Herskovits. 1967 [1936]. "Memorandum
for the Study of Acculturation." In *Beyond the Frontier: Social Process and Cultural
Change*, ed. Paul Bohannan and Fred Plog, 181–86. Garden City, NY: Natural History
Press.

Reynolds, Rachel. 2002. "An African Brain Drain: Igbo Decisions to Immigrate to the US."
Review of African Political Economy 29 (92): 273–84.

Richman, Karen. 2005. *Migration and Vodou*. Gainesville: University Press of Florida.

———. 2008. "A More Powerful Sorcerer: Conversion and Capital in the Haitian
Diaspora." *New West Indian Guide* 81:1–43.

Rippberger, Susan, and Kathleen Staudt. 2003. *Pledging Allegiance: Learning Nationalism
at the El Paso-Juárez Border*. New York: RoutledgeFalmer.

Roberts, Richard. 2005. *Litigants and Households: African Disputes and Colonial Courts in
the French Soudan, 1895–1912*. Portsmouth, NH: Heinemann.

Robertson, Tatasha. 2002. "An Economic Retreat: Worried about Jobs Some Immigrants
Return to Mexico." *Boston Globe*, February 2.

Rodman, Hyman. 1971. *Lower Class Families: The Culture of Poverty in Negro Trinidad*.
London: Oxford University Press.

Rosaldo, Michelle Zimbalist. 1980. *Knowledge and Passion: Ilongot Notions of Self and
Social Life*. Cambridge: Cambridge University Press.

Rosaldo, Renato. 1980. *Ilongot Headhunting, 1883–1974: A Study in Society and History*.
Stanford: Stanford University Press.

———. 1989. *Culture and Truth*. Boston: Beacon Press.

———. 1997. "Cultural Citizenship, Inequality, and Multiculturalism." In *Latino Cultural
Citizenship: Claiming Identity, Space, and Rights*, ed. W. V. Flores and R. Benmayor,
27–38. Boston: Beacon Press.

Rosaldo, Renato, and William V. Flores. 1997. "Identity, Conflict, and Evolving Latino
Communities: Cultural Citizenship in San Jose, California." In *Latino Cultural
Citizenship: Claiming Identity, Space, and Rights*, ed. William V. Flores and Rina
Benmayor, 57–96. Boston: Beacon Press.

Rosas, Gilberto. 2007. "The Fragile Ends of War: Forging the United States–Mexico
Border and Borderlands Consciousness." *Social Text* 25 (2): 81–102.

Rosen, David M. 2008. "Children's Rights and the International Community."
Anthropology News 49 (4): 5–6.

Rossi, Peter. 1955. *Why Families Move: A Study in the Social Psychology of Urban
Residential Mobility*. Glencoe, IL: Free Press.

Rouse, Roger. 1991. "Mexican Migration and the Social Space of Postmodernism."
Diaspora 1 (1): 8–23.

Rumbaut, Rubén G., and Alejandro Portes. 2001. *Ethnicities: Children of Immigrants in
America*. Berkeley: University of California Press.

Ryder, B. Norman. 1965. "The Cohort as a Concept in the Study of Social Change."
American Sociological Review 30 (6): 843–61.

Sahlins, Marshall. 1972. *Stone Age Economics*. New York: Aldine Transaction.

——. 2004. *Apologies to Thucydides: Understanding History as Culture and Vice Versa*. Chicago: University of Chicago Press.

Samuel, Geoffrey. 1993. *Civilized Shamans: Buddhism in Tibetan Societies*. Washington, DC: Smithsonian Institution Press.

Sana, Mariano. 2005. "Buying Membership in the Transnational Community: Migrant Remittances, Social Status, and Assimilation." *Population Research and Policy Review* 24:231–61.

Sánchez, Betty. 2004. "El Impacto de la Emigración en Loja." In *Migraciones: Un Juego con Cartas Marcadas*, ed. Francisco Hidalgo, 341–66. Quito: Abya-Yala.

Santa Ana, Otto. 2002. *Brown Tide Rising: Metaphors of Latinos in Contemporary American Public Discourse*. Austin: University of Texas Press.

Sassen, Saskia. 1996. "Beyond Sovereignty: Immigration Policy Making Today." *Social Justice: A Journal of Crime, Conflict, and World Order* 23 (3): 9–20.

——. 1998. *Globalization and Its Discontents*. New York: New Press.

——. 2005. "When National Territory Is Home to the Global: Old Borders to Novel Borderings." *New Political Economy* 10 (4): 523–42.

Scheper-Hughes, Nancy. 1992. *Death without Weeping: The Violence of Everyday Life in Brazil*. Berkeley: University of California Press.

Scheper-Hughes, Nancy, and Carolyn Sargent, eds. 1998. *Small Wars: The Cultural Politics of Childhood*. Berkeley: University of California Press.

Schildkrout, Enid. 1973. "The Fostering of Children in Urban Ghana: Problems of Ethnographic Analysis." *Urban Anthropology* 2 (1): 48–73.

Schmalzbauer, Leah. 2004. "Searching for Wages and Mothering from Afar: The Case of Honduran Transnational Families." *Journal of Marriage and Family* 66:1317–31.

——. 2008. "Family Divided: The Class Formation of Honduran Transnational Families." *Global Networks* 8:329–46.

Schneider, David. 1968. *American Kinship: A Cultural Account*. Chicago: University of Chicago Press.

Schor, J. B. 2004. *Born to Buy*. New York: Scribner.

Schwartzman, Helen B., ed. 2001. *Children and Anthropology: Perspectives for the 21st Century*. Westport, CT: Bergin and Garvey.

Serrano, Isidra Albino. 1998. "A Comparative Study of Classroom Coping Behavior in the English and Spanish Classes of Return Migrant and Non-Migrant Puerto Rican Students." *Educación*, August, 93–124.

Shandy, Dianna. 2008. "Irish Babies and African Mothers: Rites of Passage and Rights in Citizenship in Post-Millenial Ireland." *Anthropological Quarterly* 81 (4): 803–81.

Shanley, Mary Lyndon. 2001. *Making Babies, Making Families: What Matters Most in an Age of Reproductive Technologies, Surrogacy, Adoption, and Same-Sex and Unwed Parents*. Boston: Beacon Press.

Shepler, Susan. 2005. "Conflicted Childhoods: Fighting over Child Soldiers in Sierra Leone." PhD diss., University of California, Berkeley.

——. 2006. "Transnational Fosterage of War-Affected Children in West Africa: Immediate Coping Capacities across Borders." Dakar: UNICEF, West and Central Africa Regional Office.

Shipton, Parker. 2007. *The Nature of Entrustment: Intimacy, Exchange, and the Sacred in Africa*. New Haven, CT: Yale University Press.

Shostak, Marjorie. 1983. *Nisa: The Life and Words of a !Kung Woman*. New York: Vintage Books.

Shweder, Richard A. 1985. "Menstrual Pollution, Soul Loss, and the Comparative Study of Emotions." In *Culture and Depression: Studies in the Anthropology and Cross-Cultural Psychiatry of Affect and Disorder*, ed. Arthur Kleinman and Byron J. Good, 182–215. Berkeley: University of California Press.

Shweder, Richard A., and Robert A. LeVine, eds. 1984. *Culture Theory: Essays on Mind, Self, and Emotion*. New York: Cambridge University Press.

Sibley, David. 1995. *Geographies of Exclusion*. London and New York: Routledge.

Sibley, David, and Geoff Lowe. 1992. "Domestic Space, Modes of Control, and Problem Behaviour." *Geografiska Annaler Series B, Human Geography* 74:189–98.

Silk, Joan B. 1987. "Adoption and Fosterage in Human Societies: Adaptations or Enigmas?" *Cultural Anthropology* 2 (1): 39–49.

Smith, Anne, Nicola Taylor, and Pauline Tapp. 2003. "Rethinking Children's Involvement in Decision-Making after Parental Separation." *Childhood* 10:201–16.

Smith, Darren. 2004. "An 'Untied' Research Agenda for Family Migration: Loosening the 'Shackles' of the Past." *Journal of Ethnic and Migration Studies* 30:263–82.

Smith, Michael Peter. 1994. "Can You Imagine? Transnational Migration and the Globalization of Grassroots Politics." *Social Text* 39:15–33.

Smith, Michael Peter, and Luis Guarnizo, eds. 1998. *Transnationalism from Below*. New Brunswick, NJ: Transaction Publishers.

Smith, Raymond T. 1978. "The Family and the Modern World System: Some Observations from the Caribbean." *Journal of Family History* 3:337–60.

———. 1988. *Kinship and Class in the West Indies: A Genealogical Study of Jamaica and Guyana*. Cambridge: Cambridge University Press.

———. 1996. *The Matrifocal Family: Power, Pluralism, and Politics*. London: Routledge.

Smith, Robert Courtney. 2006. *Mexican New York: Transnational Lives of New Immigrants*. Berkeley: University of California Press.

Smock, Pamela J., Wendy D. Manning, and Sanjiv Gupta. 1999. "The Effect of Marriage and Divorce on Women's Economic Well-Being." *American Sociological Review* 64:794–812.

Spener, David. 1988. "Transitional Bilingual Education and the Socialization of Immigrants." *Harvard Educational Review* 58 (2): 133–53.

Sperling, Elliot. 2008. "The Dalai Lama as Dupe: The Dalai Lama Is Being Cast as the Tibetan Leader against Independence." *Los Angeles Times*, April 3. www.latimes.com/news/opinion/la-oe-sperling3apr03,0,6974567.story. Accessed online August 10, 2009.

Spindler, George P. 1997. "The Transmission of Culture." In *Education and the Cultural Process: Anthropological Approaches*, ed. Spindler, 275–309. Prospect Heights, IL: Waveland Press.

Spiro, Melford E. 1967. *Burmese Supernaturalism: A Study in the Explanation and Reduction of Suffering*. Englewood Cliffs, NJ: Prentice-Hall.

———. 1997. *Gender Ideology and Psychological Reality: An Essay on Cultural Reproduction*. New Haven, CT: Yale University Press.

Stack, Carol B. 1997. *All Our Kin*. New York: Basic Books.

Stark, Oded. 1991. *The Migration of Labor*. Cambridge: Basil Blackwell.

Stark, Oded, and Robert E. B. Lucas. 1988. "Migration, Remittances, and the Family." *Economic Development and Cultural Change* 36 (3): 465–81.

Stephen, Lynn. 2003. "Cultural Citizenship and Labor Rights for Oregon Farmworkers: The Case of Pineros y Campesinos Unidos del Nordoeste (PCUN)." *Human Organization* 62 (1): 27–38.

Stephens, Sharon, ed. 1995. *Children and the Politics of Culture*. Princeton, NJ: Princeton University Press.

Stoller, Paul. 2002. *Money Has No Smell: The Africanization of New York City*. Chicago: University of Chicago Press.

Strathern, Marilyn. 1992. *After Nature: English Kinship in the Late Twentieth Century*. Cambridge: Cambridge University Press.

Stryker, Rachael. Forthcoming. "The War at Home: Affective Economies in the American Transnationally Adopted Family." *International Migration* (special issue, "Affecting Global Movement: The Emotional Terrain of Transnationality," ed. Deborah A. Boehm and Heidi Swank).

Suárez-Orozco, Carola. 2004. "Formulating Identity in a Globalized World." In *Globalization: Culture and Education in the New Millenium*, ed. Marcelo M. Suárez-Orozco and Desirée Baolin Qin-Hilliard, 173–202. Berkeley: University of California Press.

Suárez-Orozco, Carola, and Marcelo Suárez-Orozco. 2001. *Children of Immigration*. Cambridge, MA: Harvard University Press.

Suárez-Orozco, Carola, Irina L. G. Todorova, and Josephine Louie. 2002. "Making Up for Lost Time: The Experience of Separation and Reunification among Immigrant Families." *Family Process* 41:625–43.

Suárez-Orozco, Marcelo M., and Carolyn Sattin. 2007. "Introduction: Learning in the Global Era." In *Learning in the Global Era: International Perspectives on Globalization and Education*, ed. Marcelo M. Suárez-Orozco, 1–43. Berkeley: University of California Press.

Sutton, Constance. 2004. "Celebrating Ourselves: The Family Reunion Rituals of African-Caribbean Transnational Families." *Global Networks* 4 (3): 243–57.

Svašek, Maruška, and Zlatko Skrbis. 2007. "Passions and Powers: Emotions and Globalization." *Identities: Global Studies in Culture and Power* 14 (4): 367–83.

Swank, Heidi. Forthcoming. "A Wanderer in a Distant Place: Tibetan Exile Youth, Literacy, and Emotion." *International Migration* (special issue, "Affecting Global Movement: The Emotional Terrain of Transnationality," ed. Deborah A. Boehm and Heidi Swank).

Taylor, J. Edward. 1986. "Differential Migration, Networks, Information, and Risk." In *Migration, Human Capital, and Development*, vol. 4 of *Research in Human Capital and Development*, ed. Oded Stark, 147–71. Greenwich, CT: JAI Press.

Terrio, Susan. 2008. "New Barbarians at the Gates of Paris? Prosecuting Undocumented Minors in the Juvenile Court—The Problem of the 'Petits Roumains.' " *Anthropological Quarterly* 81 (4): 873–901.

———. 2009. *Judging Mohammed: Juvenile Delinquency, Immigration, and Exclusion at the Paris Palace of Justice*. Stanford, CA: Stanford University Press.

Teske, Raymond H., and Bardin H. Nelson. 1974. "Acculturation and Assimilation: A Clarification." *American Ethnologist* 1:351–67.

Thomson, Mark, and Maurice Crul. 2007. "The Second Generation in Europe and the United States: How Is the Transatlantic Debate Relevant for Further Research on the European Second Generation?" *Journal of Ethnic and Migration Studies* 33:1025–41.

Thorne, Barrie. 2007. "Crafting the Interdisciplinary Field of Childhood Studies." *Childhood* 14 (2): 147–52.

Tobin, Joseph H., David Y. H. Wu, and Dana H. Davidson. 1991. *Preschool in Three Cultures: Japan, China, and the United States*. New Haven, CT: Yale University Press.

Tocqueville, Alexis de. 1994 [1831]. *Democracy in America*. London: David Campbell.

Tolfree, David. 2003. "Community Based Care for Separated Children." Stockholm: Save the Children, Sweden.

Townsend, Camilla. 2000. *Tales of Two Cities: Race and Economic Culture in Early Republican North and South America: Guayaquil, Ecuador, and Baltimore, Maryland.* Austin: University of Texas Press.

Trager, Lillian. 2005. "Introduction: The Dynamics of Migration." In *Migration and Economy: Global and Local Dynamics,* ed. Trager, 1–45. Walnut Creek: Altamira Press.

Trouillot, Michel-Rolph. 2003. *Global Transformations: Anthropology and the Modern World.* London: Palgrave Macmillan.

Tsing, Anna Lowenhaupt. 2000. "The Global Situation." *Cultural Anthropology* 15 (3): 327–60.

———. 2004. *Friction: An Ethnography of Global Connection.* Princeton, NJ: Princeton University Press.

Tsundue, Tenzin. 2008. "The Tibet Resolution." *Phayul,* December 29.

Twum-Baah, K. A. 2005. "Volume and Characteristics of International Ghanaian Migration." In *At Home in the World? International Migration and Development in Contemporary Ghana and West Africa,* ed. Takyiwaa Manuh, 55–77. Accra: Sub-Saharan.

Twum Baah, K. A., J. S. Nabila, and A. F. Aryee. 1995. *Migration Research Study in Ghana.* Accra: Ghana Statistical Service.

Uehling, Greta. 2008. "The International Smuggling of Children: Coyotes, Snakeheads, and the Politics of Compassion." *Anthropological Quarterly* 8 (41): 833–71.

UNCRC. See United Nations, Office of the United Nations High Commission for Human Rights.

United Nations, Office of the United Nations High Commission for Human Rights. 1989. "Convention on the Rights of the Child." *www2.ohchr.org/english/law/crc.htm.* Accessed online February 24, 2010.

Vaillant, George E. 1977. *Adaptation to Life.* Cambridge, MA: Harvard University Press.

Valdés, Guadalupe. 2003. *Expanding Definitions of Giftedness: The Case of Young Interpreters from Immigrant Communities.* Mahwah, NJ: Lawrence Erlbaum.

Valentine, Gill. 1997. "A Safe Place to Grow Up? Parents' Perceptions of Children's Safety and the Rural Idyll." *Journal of Rural Studies* 13:137–48.

———. 2003. "Boundary Crossings: Transitions from Childhood to Adulthood." *Children's Geographies* 1:37–52.

Valenzuela, Angela. 1999. *Subtractive Schooling: U.S.-Mexican Youth and the Politics of Caring.* Albany: State University of New York Press.

van Dijk, Rijk. 2002. "Religion, Reciprocity, and Restructuring Family Responsibility in the Ghanaian Pentecostal Diaspora." In *The Transnational Family: New European Frontiers and Global Networks,* ed. Deborah Bryceson and Ulla Vuorela, 173–96. Oxford: Berg.

Van Hear, Nicholas. 1998. *New Diasporas: The Mass Exodus, Dispersal, and Regrouping of Migrant Communities.* Seattle: University of Washington Press.

Verhoef, Heidi. 2005. " 'A Child Has Many Mothers': Views of Child Fostering in Northwestern Cameroon." *Childhood* 12:369–90.

Vygotsky, Lev S. 1978. *Mind in Society: The Development of Higher Psychological Processes,* ed. Michael Cole, V. John-Steiner, Sylvia Scribner, and E. Souberman, 84–91. Cambridge, MA: Harvard University Press.

Waters, Johanna. 2005. "Transnational Family Strategies and Education in the Contemporary Chinese Diaspora." *Global Networks* 5:359–78.

Weisner, Thomas S., and Ronald Gallimore. 1977. "My Brother's Keeper: Child and Sibling Caretaking." *Current Anthropology* 18 (2): 169–90.

Westermarck, Edvard. 1899. "The Nature of the Arab Ginn, Illustrated by the Present Beliefs of the People of Morocco." *Journal of the Royal Anthropological Institute* 29:252–69.

Wilson, Peter. 1972. *Crab Antics: The Social Anthropology of English-Speaking Negro Societies of the Caribbean*. New Haven, CT: Yale University Press.

Wilson, Tamar Diana. 2000. "Anti-Immigrant Sentiment and the Problem of Reproduction/Maintenance in Mexican Immigration to the United States." *Critique of Anthropology* 20 (2): 191–213.

———. 2006. "Strapping the Mexican Woman Immigrant: The Convergence of Reproduction and Production." *Anthropological Quarterly* 79 (2): 295–302.

Wimmer, Andre, and Nina Glick Schiller. 2003. "Methodological Nationalism, the Social Sciences, and the Study of Migration: An Essay in Historical Epistemology." *International Migration Review* 37 (3): 576–610.

Wise, Amanda, and Adam Chapman. 2005. "Introduction: Migration, Affect, and the Senses." *Journal of Intercultural Studies* 26 (1): 1–3.

Wolf, Diane L. 1997. "Family Secrets: Transnational Struggles among Children of Filipino Immigrants." *Sociological Perspectives* 40:457–82.

Wood, Charles C. 1981. "Structural Changes and Household Strategies: A Conceptual Framework for the Study of Rural Migration." *Human Organization* 40:338–44.

Wortham, Stanton, Enrique G. Murillo, and Edmund T. Hamann, eds. 2002. *Education in the New Latino Diaspora: Policy and the Politics of Identity*. Westport, CT: Ablex.

Wylie, Turrell. 1959. "A Standard System of Tibetan Transcription." *Harvard Journal of Asiatic Studies* 22 (December): 261–67.

Wyness, Michael. 2003. "Children's Space and Interest: Constructing an Agenda for Student Voice." *Children's Geographies* 1:223–40.

Yanagisako, Sylvia. 1985. *Transforming the Past: Tradition and Kinship among Japanese Americans*. Stanford, CA: Stanford University Press.

Yeates, Nicola. 2009. *Globalizing Care Economies and Migrant Workers*. Hampshire: Palgrave Macmillan.

Yeh, E. T., and K. T. Lama. 2006. "Hip-Hop Gangsta or Most Deserving of Victims? Transnational Migrant Identities and the Paradox of Tibetan Racialization in the U.S.A." *Environment and Planning* 38 (5): 809–29.

Young, Lorraine, and Nicola Ansell. 2003. "Fluid Households, Complex Families: The Impacts of Children's Migration as a Response to HIV/AIDS in Southern Africa." *Professional Geographer* 55:464–76.

Zhou, Min, and Carl L. Bankston III. 1998. *Growing Up American: How Vietnamese Children Adapt to Life in the United States*. New York: Russell Sage Foundation.

Zilberg, Elana. 2004. "Fools Banished from the Kingdom: Remapping Geographies of Gang Violence between the Americas (Los Angeles and San Salvador)." *American Quarterly* 56:759–79.

Zúñiga, Víctor. 1998. "Nations and Borders: Romantic Nationalism and the Project of Modernity." In *The U.S.-Mexico Border: Transcending Divisions, Contesting Identities*, ed. David Spener and Kathleen Staudt, 35–55. Boulder, CO: Lynne Rienner.

Zúñiga, Víctor, and Edmund T. Hamann. 2009. "Sojourners in Mexico with U.S. School Experience: A New Taxonomy for Transnational Students." *Comparative Education Review* 53 (3): 329–53.

Contributors

Deborah A. Boehm is an assistant professor of anthropology and women's studies at the University of Nevada, Reno (U.S.). Her research with transnational Mexicans has focused on children and youth, transnational and mixed-status families, and gender relations. She is currently conducting a project about deportation and return migration.

Cati Coe is an associate professor of anthropology at Rutgers University, Camden (U.S.). She is working on a book on Ghanaian transnational families tentatively titled "The Scattered Family: Love, Loss, and International Migration in Ghana." She is the author of *The Dilemmas of Culture in African Schools: Youth, Nationalism, and the Transformation of Knowledge* (2005).

Núria Empez Vidal is an associate professor in the Department of Pedagogy, Universitat de Barcelona (Spain), and a PhD candidate in anthropology in the Universitat Autònoma de Barcelona (Spain). She is working on a dissertation about unaccompanied minors migrating from Morocco to Spain.

Maarit Forde is an anthropologist lecturing at the University of the West Indies (Trinidad and Tobago). She is interested in the role of religion and ritual in transnational migration as well as in the politics of religion. Her recent publications include articles on these topics and a volume entitled *Obeah and Other Powers: The Politics of Caribbean Religion*, coedited with Diana Paton, to be published by Duke University Press.

Edmund T. "Ted" Hamann is an associate professor in the Department of Teaching, Learning, and Teacher Education at the University of Nebraska–Lincoln (U.S.) and a visiting professor and associated researcher with the Centro Interdisciplinario de Estudios de Educación y Superación de Pobreza (CIESESP) at the Universidad de Monterrey (Mexico). He has coauthored *Alumnos transnacionales: Las escuelas mexicanas frente a la globalización* (2009), *The Educational Welcome of Latinos in the New South* (2003), and *Education in the New Latino Diaspora: Policy and the Politics of Identity* (2002).

Julia Meredith Hess is a postdoctoral fellow at the University of New Mexico's Department of Pediatrics in the Division of Prevention and Population Sciences and a research adjunct professor in the Department of Anthropology (U.S.). She is the author of *Immigrant Ambassadors: Citizenship and Belonging in the Tibetan Diaspora* (2009).

Heather Rae-Espinoza is an assistant professor in the Human Development Department at California State University, Long Beach (U.S.). Her research with the children of émigrés in Ecuador focuses on cultural internalization, mental well-being, and the changes in rhetoric surrounding migration.

Rachel R. Reynolds is an associate professor in the Department of Culture and Communication at Drexel University (U.S.). She studies ideologies of language in immigrant communities, motivations for language learning, and bilingual families, especially among West African immigrants.

Susan Shepler is an assistant professor in the Department of International Peace and Conflict Resolution in the School of International Service at American University in Washington, D.C. (U.S.). Her research interests include the reintegration of former child soldiers in Africa, youth and conflict, refugee education, and transitional justice. She has worked as a research consultant for the International Rescue Committee, Search for Common Ground, and UNICEF.

Naomi Tyrrell (née Bushin) is a lecturer in social geography at the School of Geography, Earth, and Environmental Sciences at the University of Plymouth (U.K.). In addition to her work on child migration in Britain, she has recently completed the EU-funded Migrant Children Project with colleagues at University College Cork, Ireland, and is currently working on two books related to this research: *Childhood and Migration in Europe: Four Portraits from Ireland* (Ashgate Press) and *Immigrant and Ethnic Minority Children and Youth in Ireland* (Sense Publications).

Víctor Zúñiga is dean of the School of Education and Humanities at the Universidad de Monterrey (Nuevo León, Mexico) and a visiting professor in the School of Education at the Université de Sherbrooke (Quebec, Canada) and the department of sociology at the Université de Provence (France). A Level III member of Mexico's Sistema Nacional de Investigadores in the Social Sciences, some of his recent publications include *Alumnos transnacionales: Las escuelas mexicanas frente a la globalización* (2009) and *New Destinations: Mexican Immigration in the United States* (2005).

Index

acculturation, 157–58
affect. *See* emotion
agency
  adult co-optation of child agency, 8
  of children, 7–9, 18, 25–38, 66, 137–38,
    177, 184
  and children's age, 31–34
  and children's rights discourse, 24–25,
    31, 34
  and children's understanding of
    migration process, 32, 36–37, 38
  cultural constructions of, 8, 9, 41, 43–44
  definition of, 7–8, 41
  and family fragmentation, 35–36
  and intentionality, 41–42, 43, 44
  as limited, among adults, 8, 35, 37
  as meaning making, 9, 137–38
  of migrants, 7, 175
  passive forms of, 7–8, 177
  and power, 25–26, 37, 41, 45–46, 58–59
  and psychological adjustment, 117,
    137–38
  and reasons for migration, 34–35, 36
  as resistance, 7–8, 41, 46
  and technology, 46
  as transformative of discourse, 46–47,
    59–60
  and understanding of childhood, 8–9,
    24–26, 33–38
Appadurai, Arjun, 4, 6, 18, 46–47, 60
assimilation
  and acculturation, 157–58
  critique of, 3–4, 152 (*see also* immigrant)
  definition of, 157–58
  as goal of American schools, 17, 150, 153,
    158–59
attachment theory, 13, 116

Benedict, Ruth, 120
"best interests" of children
  and children's agency, 9, 25, 177
  as constructed by the state, 17, 24–25, 34

  as understood by families, 9, 31–37, 67,
    113–14, 121
bilingual education, 149–50, 151. *See also*
    language
Bluebond-Langner, Myra, 127
Booth, George C., 143, 158
borders
  dangers of crossing, 164, 178
  militarization of U.S.-Mexico border, 166
  patrol of, 178
  and sociopolitical status, 163
  as unimportant, in Africa, 63, 66, 69
Bourdieu, Pierre, 10
Bracero program, 164, 165, 173
Briggs, Jean, 137
Brown, Karen McCarthy, 87, 191n3 (Ch. 4)
Bucholtz, Mary, 2, 49, 57
Buddhism, Tibetan, 43–45

capitalism
  and care work, 10
  and children, 2, 109, 112
  and family life, 97–98, 107–8, 112–13
  and migration, 14, 40, 79–80, 97–98,
    107–8, 175, 176
  and ritual exchange, 191n8
  and social reproduction, 10, 98
care, substitute. *See* fostering
care work
  by children, 192n1
  children's care, 119, 171 (*see also* child care)
  elder care, 90, 105, 106, 113, 192n4 (Ch. 5)
  and global capitalism, 10
  and immigrant labor, 50, 81, 90–91, 106,
    119
  in migrants' households in home country,
    119
  and neoliberalism, 10, 81
  by slaves, 192n4 (Ch. 5)
Carsten, Janet, 85, 88
Chamberlain, Mary, 80, 81, 82, 83, 88, 190n2
Charnley, Helen, 77, 190n8, 190n12

223

Acknowledgments

Thanks to T. J. Berry and Jessica Lavy and all the other wonderful employees at Waldenbooks #1577 in Arlington, Texas. You're terrific!

Thanks, also, to my friend Sandra Welch for bringing my character Cody Jameson from *Lady Deception* to life at the *Romantic Times* Convention Costume Competition in Florida last year. You were wonderful!

And to Sharon Murphy, a true pal. Love ya!

$\mathscr{P}$rologue

$\mathscr{T}$ension filled the air as the two young warriors circled each other, knives drawn. Their expressions were savage as they prepared to do battle.

Word of the fight spread quickly through the village, and a crowd of onlookers gathered. The villagers had known the day would come when the two brothers would challenge one another, for Bear Claw, Chief Ten Crow's oldest son, had long chafed under his adopted brother Wind Ryder's favored status with their father. Many years before, Chief Ten Crow had been impressed by the bravery of the captive white boy and had adopted him. The boy had taken the name Wind Ryder, and in the eight years he had lived as one of them, he had become the best rider in the village and one of the fiercest fighters. The members of the tribe looked on, wondering if Wind Ryder would prove himself to be the best again—now against his brother.

Physically, Bear Claw and Wind Ryder were both fine specimens of Comanche manhood and very evenly matched. Both were tall and strong. Their bodies were sleek and hard-muscled—and they were both determined to win. The villagers knew this would be a true test of their skills.

Bear Claw's hate-filled gaze narrowed as he prepared to make his move. Fury was driving him. Wind Ryder had taken that which should have been his! They had been out raiding when he had seen the white stallion and decided he would have it for his own. But Wind Ryder had reached the magnificent horse first and taken it for himself. The memory fueled Bear Claw's rage. He gave a bloodcurdling cry as he charged.

Wind Ryder had been waiting for Bear Claw to attack, and he was ready. He met him in that charge, and they locked together in a powerful struggle.

Tumbling to the ground, the two young warriors battled fiercely.

Each was fighting for dominance.

Each was determined not to give in.

Bear Claw managed to slash Wind Ryder's upper arm just as they broke apart. Blood flowed from the wound, and Bear Claw smiled, knowing Wind Ryder was in pain. He was proud. He had drawn first blood. Confidence filled him.

Wind Ryder paid little heed to the wound. He ignored the pain as he had trained himself to do since coming to the Comanche. He concentrated only on Bear Claw, anticipating his every move. He saw his brother's arrogant smile and knew his overconfidence was his weakness.

"You are bleeding," Bear Claw taunted.

"It is only a scratch." He smiled back at him, wanting to push Bear Claw's anger to even greater heights.

Hatred surged through Bear Claw.

"I will kill you—" he shouted, rushing at him again.

Wind Ryder moved quickly to avoid the attack. Wielding his knife with unerring accuracy, he cut Bear Claw across his ribs.

Bear Claw was stunned that Wind Ryder had managed to slash him. The shock of the pain drove him beyond all reason.

He despised Wind Ryder! No matter what his father said, this white was no brother to him! Turning, he attacked again, this time blindly.

Blood now covered both of the young men. Neither would give in. Neither would back down. It would be a fight to the death.

Bear Claw tripped Wind Ryder. Wind Ryder fell, but quickly recovered. He rolled away and jumped to his feet just in time to kick out at Bear Claw and knock him to the ground. Bear Claw's knife flew from his grip, and in that instant Wind Ryder made his move. He threw himself upon the other warrior and, knife in hand, held him pinned to the ground.

The furious roar of Chief Ten Crow startled all those who'd gathered around to watch the battle. The villagers fell back as the mighty chief strode forward. The chief grabbed Wind Ryder and hauled him off Bear Claw.

Still caught up in the driving power of his anger, Wind Ryder struggled against the man restraining him; then he looked up into the face of his adopted father and realized what had happened. He stopped fighting and was immediately released. He stood before the chief and met his gaze without flinching.

Chief Ten Crow's expression was unreadable as he stared at Wind Ryder. After a moment, without saying a word, he nodded and then turned to Bear Claw.

"Get up," the chief ordered. "Why were you fighting Wind Ryder?"

Bear Claw flew to his feet in a rage, humiliated that he'd been overpowered. "He is the one to blame!"

The chief sneered, "Wind Ryder returned from the raid with the best horses, and he has just proven himself to be the strongest warrior. Your brother has done nothing wrong."

Bear Claw looked at Wind Ryder, his gaze filled with hatred. "This one is no brother to me!"

"He is my son—as you are."

Bear Claw said nothing more. His anger was too great. He stalked off, pausing only to pick up his knife before he disappeared into the crowd.

A great sadness filled Chief Ten Crow as he watched his son walk away. Only when Bear Claw had moved out of sight did he glance back at Wind Ryder.

"You are bleeding," the chief told his adopted son.

"It is nothing," Wind Ryder answered stoically. He would never allow himself to reveal any pain he was feeling. A proud warrior never showed a sign of weakness.

"The white stallion you brought in is a very fine animal. A mighty warrior deserves such a horse." He nodded to his son in silent approval and walked away.

The chiefs praise pleased Wind Ryder. He'd wanted the horse from the first moment he had seen it. His brother and several of the other braves had wanted it, too, but he'd been lucky enough during the raid to be able to take it for himself. He would ride the stallion proudly once he'd broken it.

Wind Ryder headed to the creek to wash and clean his wound. When he'd first been brought into the camp as a young boy, Wind Ryder had befriended one of the dogs. He'd named the large brown cur Buffalo, because of his size, and it trailed after him now down to the water's edge. It was quiet there by the creek, and he appreciated the peace. He sat down on the bank to pet the dog.

Wind Ryder realized sadly that Buffalo was his one true friend in the tribe. Buffalo never worried that he was white by birth and had come into the tribe as a captive. The dog's only real concern in life was where his next meal was coming from. As long as Wind Ryder provided that, the dog was blindly faithful.

"Where were you when I needed you, Buffalo?" Wind Ryder scolded, even as he smiled down at the dog. "You could have helped me fight Bear Claw."

Buffalo just sat down beside him and leaned slightly against him as if nothing unusual had happened.

"You thought I was good enough to handle Bear Claw by myself, did you?" he said more to himself than the dog.

"And you were," came the sound of a soft feminine voice from behind him.

Wind Ryder looked back and was surprised to see the pretty young maiden Moon Cloud standing there watching him.

"Do you need help?" Moon Cloud asked as she went to him. She knew she was being bold, but she didn't care. Though she was only thirteen, she had been in love with Wind Ryder for a long time. When she'd seen Bear Claw cut him during their fight, she'd been worried that he'd been seriously hurt.

"I am fine," Wind Ryder told her, wanting her to go away. He had come there to be alone. He didn't want to talk to anyone right then. Standing, he moved down to the water's edge and began to wash the blood from his arm.

Moon Cloud was not about to be put off. She'd brought a cloth and healing herbs with her, and she went to the creek and wet the cloth before going to his side. She pressed the cloth to his wound to stop the bleeding. She was surprised when he didn't flinch. The wound had to hurt.

"You fought bravely," she said.

"I did not want to fight Bear Claw," he answered.

"He gave you no choice."

Wind Ryder said no more as she tended his cut. When she finished, the bleeding had stopped. He flexed his arm to test it, and was pleased to find that the pain had lessened.

"It is better. Thank you."

He wanted her to leave, but she remained.

"I am glad I was able to help you." Moon Cloud looked up at him, thinking him the most handsome of all the young warriors. True, he was white, but that didn't really matter to her. He had proven himself to be the strongest and the best.

Wind Ryder felt uncomfortable under her scrutiny. He deliberately moved away.

"I must go back and see to the horses," he told her. Buffalo came quickly to his side.

Moon Cloud was disappointed that he didn't want to linger there with her a little longer. She walked back to the camp with him, but he said little to her on the way back.

Bear Claw's anger did not lessen as he sat alone some distance from the village. If anything, the hatred he felt for Wind Ryder grew as he tended his own wound. The fight between them was not over. He doubted it ever would be.

His fury burned hot within him. He longed to find some way to get back at Wind Ryder.

It was growing dark when he finally decided to return to the village.

As he made his way back, he spotted Wind Ryder's dog.

Bear Claw smiled.

Wind Ryder passed the evening sitting by the campfire with the warriors, listening to tales of their raids and telling a tale or two of his own. Bear Claw never joined them, and Wind Ryder was glad.

It was late when Wind Ryder decided to bed down for the night. As a young warrior, he had his own tipi, and he made his way there ready to seek rest. He was surprised that there was no sign of Buffalo. The dog was usually waiting for him outside the lodge.

Then he went inside.

Wind Ryder had suffered much in his fourteen years of life. He had forced much of the horror he'd witnessed from his mind, not wanting to remember the pain of losing his white family in the Comanche raid on their ranch when he was six. But the sight of Buffalo lying dead within the tipi, his throat slashed, brought it all back in a violent rush. The pain tore at him physically and mentally, and he fought not to cry out in horror.

"Buffalo—"

Wind Ryder dropped to his knees and stared at the lifeless dog.

Only Bear Claw could have done something so vicious. Only Bear Claw would think of killing a gentle animal to take revenge on an enemy.

Wind Ryder wanted to go after the man who was supposed to be his brother and take his own revenge, but he had no real proof.

Wind Ryder reached out to stroke Buffalo's rough fur. The dog's body was cold and stiff.

The finality of death struck him again. The loss of yet another loved one tore through him.

Wind Ryder bit back the cry that threatened as long-suppressed memories tormented him. It took all the strength he could muster to repress them.

Gathering Buffalo in his arms, he carried him from the tipi and out into the dark of the night. He was glad that no one saw him as he found a secluded spot and buried his one friend.

Wind Ryder remained alone there throughout the night and did not return to the village until dawn.

Any trace of youth within him had been destroyed.

He was a solitary man—a lone warrior.

Chapter One

Ten Years Later

*F*rom a distance, Chief Ten Crow and his raiding party kept watch over the way station. He knew his braves would take many horses during this raid.

Soon the time would be right—very soon he would give the order to attack.

Marissa Williams exchanged a weary smile with her friend and traveling companion, Louise Bennett, as their stagecoach slowed to a stop before the lonely way station.

"I never thought I'd be this excited to see a way station," Marissa remarked, looking out the window at the forlorn structure in the middle of the wild Texas countryside.

"Me, either," Louise agreed, feeling battered from the rough ride in the cramped interior of the stage.

"It's been a long ride today, ladies, that's for sure," put in Thurmond Atwood, a heavyset traveling salesman. "I didn't know dawn could come as early as it did this morning. Seems to me the birds were still sleeping and we were already on the road."

"Quit all your jabberin' and open the door so we can get out of here," crotchety, white-haired Blake Randolph ordered

from where he sat next to Thurmond. He had no intention of spending another minute in these close quarters, sitting on a hard seat, crammed in next to the overweight Atwood. The stage had stopped. He wanted his freedom, and he wanted it now.

Just as Blake finished speaking, Matt Hogan, the stage driver, appeared outside the door and opened it. Marissa was the first to climb out, and Matt took her hand to help her step down.

"Thank you," she told him with an appreciative smile.

"My pleasure, Miss Williams," Matt answered.

Marissa Williams was the prettiest female he'd seen in ages. She was blond and downright beautiful, not to mention friendly. Her bright smile could charm any man, and he was charmed. Her friend Louise Bennett was an attractive woman, too, though she was older than Marissa. He couldn't help wondering what two ladies of quality were doing heading for Dry Springs. He'd heard the women talking about New Orleans, and thought by the looks of them that that was where they belonged—in a sophisticated, civilized city, not in West Texas.

"We'll be spending the night here," he went on, "so you and Miss Bennett go on inside and make yourselves comfortable."

"Will we be starting at the same time tomorrow morning as today?" she asked as she waited for him to help Louise down.

"Yes, miss, we will—bright and early."

Matt ignored the mumbled complaints of the men still sitting in the stage as he aided Louise in her descent. Once Louise had gotten down, he moved off to unload the bags and take care of the horses, leaving the men on their own.

Louise went to join Marissa. They walked slowly toward the way station, taking their time, enjoying the chance to stretch and move around a bit. Louise paused to stare out across the land. She was accustomed to the sights of New Orleans, and though Marissa had warned her that West Texas was nothing like Louisiana, she

hadn't expected it to be this desolate or this empty. Marissa had made the trip to Dry Springs before with her father and had always come home with wonderful tales of the beauty and excitement of her Uncle George's ranch. Right now, though, the beauty and excitement were eluding Louise. She glanced at the younger woman in amazement.

"So this is what the Wild West looks like. Do you really like this place?"

"It's beautiful, don't you think?" Marissa was gazing off in the distance.

The sun was painting the land golden with its glow as it sank lower in the western sky.

"It's certainly ... untamed looking," Louise remarked uneasily. She was feeling a bit apprehensive as she looked around at the stark landscape dotted only by some low-growing shrubs and a few trees. It was so vast—so deserted—so isolated.

"You'll come to love it, I promise." Marissa tried to sound encouraging. "It grows on you."

Even as she spoke, sudden memories of her last visit to the Crown Ranch brought the sting of tears to her eyes. That had been a joyous, exciting trip in the company of her father. This journey, however, was anything but joyous. Her father was dead. He had died tragically and unexpectedly, and now her uncle was her only living relative; her mother had passed away several years before. Marissa had wired her uncle the news of her father's death, and he had insisted she come to Texas to live with him. She loved the ranch, and she was looking forward to seeing Mark Whittaker again. He was a handsome ranch hand who worked for her uncle. They had enjoyed each other's company during last year's visit, and she hoped he was still working there.

"If you say so," Louise replied less than enthusiastically. From the looks of things, she was not at all sure that she would find

anything about this place to love. "But right now, as far as I'm concerned, we can't reach your uncle's ranch soon enough."

"You aren't enjoying our travel accommodations?" Marissa asked quietly, giving Louise a quick, knowing smile.

"Let's just say that I'm looking forward to having a clean bed again," Louise said, suppressing a shudder as she thought about the less-than-pristine bed she'd slept in the night before. Heaven only knew who had slept in it last and whether or not they had been infested with vermin. She'd found herself longing for her own bedroom in her home in New Orleans and for her maid and her freshly laundered linens.

"I'm sorry it's been so difficult." Marissa said.

"Oh, darling, there's no need to apologize. It's been an exhausting trip, but that was to be expected. I'm trying to think of this as an adventure."

"Then you're not sorry you came with me?"

"I never considered *not* coming with you," Louise insisted. She had been a close friend of Marissa's mother and had stayed in regular contact with the family even after her death. She was devoted to Marissa. She thought of her as the daughter she'd never had, and she knew how devastated the young woman was by father's passing.

"Thank you," Marissa said as she glanced at Louise.

"There is no need to thank me. Until I see you safely to your Uncle George, my place is with you," Louise reassured her, giving her a quick hug.

They started on toward the building once again, eager to go inside for the night.

The waiting was over. The time had come.

Chief Ten Crow gave the signal to the warriors waiting to raid the way station and claim the horses as their own.

They attacked.

Marissa and Louise were about to enter the station when suddenly shots rang out and chaos erupted around them. Louise grabbed Marissa's arm in panic at the sound of the war cries of the Comanche warriors.

"What's happening?" Louise asked, staring wide-eyed and fearful.

"Comanche raid!" the station master shouted.

Shocked, Marissa and Louise froze in the midst of the deadly confusion. The guards who manned the way station ran for their rifles. Several of the them were cut down by the gunfire of the attacking warriors before they could arm themselves. The two men passengers on the stagecoach were also shot where they stood, helpless before the deadly onslaught.

"Get inside!" the stage driver ordered the two women as he raced past them on his way to retrieve his own rifle from the stagecoach.

Matt's fierce command jarred Marissa and Louise from their stunned state. Terrified, they ran for the safety of the building.

A guttural scream rent the air.

At the sound, they looked back to see Matt lying in the dirt. He was writhing in agony, and blood was streaming from a gaping chest wound.

"Mr. Hogan!" Without a thought for her own safety, Marissa tore away from Louise and rushed to help the fallen man.

"Marissa—don't!" Louise gave chase, trying to stop her as the bloodcurdling war cries of the Comanche sent chills of terror through the very depths of her being. No wonder she'd felt that terrible sense of apprehension earlier. Somehow, she had sensed the danger that surrounded them. But it was too late to help Matt now—they could only try to save themselves. "Marissa! We have to get inside."

"No—I have to help him—I can't just leave him there to die! You go on!"

Marissa kept running, and she'd almost made it to Matt's side when she heard a war cry behind her. She turned to see a warrior taking aim at Louise. Marissa had no time to react as the Indian fired his weapon. She watched in horror as Louise collapsed.

"Louise!" The scream erupted from her.

"Get my gun," Matt called out to her. He had no strength to move or to help her, but he could see what was happening around them and knew she had to have some way to protect herself. It was her only hope of survival.

Marissa needed no further encouragement. She ran for the stage, suddenly filled with violent emotions she'd never experienced before. Hatred. The need for revenge. She had just seen innocent people murdered—and Louise shot down in cold blood! She was going to get that gun and shoot the savages!

But the Comanche raiding party was too close.

By the time Marissa reached the side of the stage, the blood-thirsty warriors were circling ever nearer.

Chief Ten Crow saw the woman with the golden hair climbing onto the stagecoach to grab up a gun. In that instant, a jolt of recognition shot through him. He had seen this woman before—in a vision.

The chief wheeled his horse around and rode in her direction. Snake, one of his best warriors, was ahead of him, and Chief Ten Crow watched as he closed in on the woman.

Matt could feel his life's blood draining from him; he was growing weaker by the minute. He knew he was going to die, but when he saw the Comanche charging toward Marissa, he knew he had to do something. He tried to raise himself up on an elbow as he called out another warning to her.

"Look out!"

His shout took Snake by surprise. He turned quickly and shot the white man again, this time making sure he was dead. Then he

turned his attention back to the woman. She was what he wanted. She was the prize he was after.

Marissa had just grabbed up the weapon as she heard the stage driver's warning. Rifle in hand, she turned.

It was too late.

Snake was already upon her. He struck quickly, snaring her around the waist to pull her away from the stage. She fought to hang on, but Snake jerked her forcefully free.

The warrior's grip was brutal, and Marissa began to scream as she struggled in wild fury. The rifle flew from her hands as she twisted and turned, trying to break free. Marissa knew he might kill her, but she didn't care. She knew from tales her uncle had told her about the Comanche that death was preferable to being taken captive by them.

Snake fought to control both her and his horse. He was furious at the woman's fierce resistance. He shifted his powerful hold on her to try to bring her fully before him on his horse.

Marissa saw her one and only chance to escape the warrior, and took it. She viciously kicked the side of his mount and, at the same time, jerked herself sideways with all the force she could master. The horse shifted unexpectedly, and when she made her violent move, Snake momentarily loosened his hold on her.

Suddenly Marissa found herself free, tumbling to the ground. Pain jolted through her as she landed heavily, but she surged to her feet and looked around for the rifle. It had fallen too far away for her to reach it. She looked up at the warrior, and in that moment her gaze met his. Marissa knew by the fury in his war-painted face that she was looking into the face of death. She turned to run, but before she could take more than a step, another Comanche was there, snatching her up.

Marissa was silenced as the wind was knocked out of her. She fought to get away, but the Indian who held her in his grasp was far more powerful than the first. Her captor shouted something to the other warriors as he urged his horse to a run, and they galloped off.

A short distance from the way station, Chief Ten Crow reined in to wait for the rest of his warriors to join him. The building was engulfed in flames. The fierce fire cast a golden glow upon the night. The chief nodded to himself as he saw his son Bear Claw riding toward him, a silhouette with the light of the fire at his back.

It was as he'd foreseen in his vision—the flames—Bear Claw—the golden one.

The other warriors came then, too, driving the horses ahead of them, and they all raced off into the night.

Marissa managed a quick last look back at the death and devastation they were leaving behind. She could see the lifeless bodies strewn about the grounds, and pain ripped through her soul.

They were all dead—slaughtered at the hands of this deadly Comanche raiding party.

And Louise—

Memories of their last conversation tortured Marissa:

"*My place is with you.*"

Her dear friend was dead.

It was all her fault.

If only they'd never come to Texas—

If only—

Anger and fear warred within Marissa. She offered up a tormented prayer as she tore her gaze away from the sight of the destruction. A terrible sense of hopelessness overcame her.

She wished that she had been the one to die, not Louise. She wished she were dead right then.

If she had had a weapon and had been able to use it, she would have killed herself in that moment.

Marissa was glad that the cover of night was claiming the land, for the Comanche who had taken her prisoner would not be able to see the tears she could no longer deny.

Chapter Two

The raiding party rode long into the night.

Chief Ten Crow was more than pleased with the success of the raid. His warriors had claimed many horses, and he had claimed the golden one.

The chief smiled to himself in satisfaction.

Until now, Chief Ten Crow had not understood the full meaning of the vision that had come to him some weeks ago. In it, he had seen his sons Bear Claw and Wind Ryder engaged in a life-or-death struggle, silhouetted by flames and blood. He had also seen a white woman with hair the color of the sun draw Wind Ryder away from that deadly battle. He had not been able to see her features clearly in his vision, but when he saw her for the first time during the attack, he had instinctively known she was that woman. Wind Ryder had not accompanied them on this raid, but when they returned to the village, Chief Ten Crow was certain all would be as he'd envisioned.

Chief Ten Crow realized what he had to do. He would protect the golden one and keep her safe until he could present her to Wind Ryder. The rest of his vision would then come to pass as well—the violent hatred between his sons would cease and peace would come to his people.

There was another part of the vision he deliberately didn't dwell on, but now that fate had set everything in motion, Ten

Crow knew he had to face it. Soon he would be going to the spirit world. His vision had not told him how he was going to die, only that the time was coming. It was important that he see peace established between his sons before he left this world.

Marissa's fear heightened anew when the raiding party finally stopped for the night. She had managed to hold her fear at bay by keeping her mind blank, but facing the reality of being a captive terrified her.

When her captor dismounted, Marissa stiffened. She was ready to fight him, but got no chance. He pulled her down from the horse before she could react, and quickly bound her wrists tightly in front of her. He dragged her along to where the other warriors had already started building a fire, and pushed her down to sit on the ground before it. Marissa made sure not to let her terror show. She glared defiantly up at the Comanche.

Chief Ten Crow studied the white woman for a moment as she met his gaze without flinching. Finally, without saying a word, he turned and walked away to tend to his horse.

Marissa breathed a silent sigh of relief as he left her, but then she noticed the other warriors watching her. The sight of so many of them, so close, made her want to scream. In the flickering light of the flames, the war paint on their faces made them seem even more ghoulish. With an effort, she fought down her panic. She remained unmoving, her expression impassive in spite of the looks the Comanche were giving her. They were speaking in their native tongue and laughing as they watched her.

"Snake! I thought you were a brave warrior! You let this little woman escape you?" Bear Claw chided as he looked at the white woman sitting before them. She wasn't very big and didn't look very strong either. He had little use for white women and was certain he could have controlled her with only one hand.

Snake's expression turned ugly as he responded to Bear Claw's challenge. "She did not escape me. I did not want her. I let her go."

"If you did not want her, you should have given her to me," Running Dog put in, laughing.

"Perhaps we can all have her," Hooting Owl suggested, drawing his knife and walking toward her.

Marissa sat still as the warrior approached. She fought to keep her expression from revealing what she was feeling as she stared at the wicked-looking blade he held in his hand. The way they were watching her, she could just imagine what they were saying.

Desperation filled her.

She looked around for a way to escape. She wanted to jump up and run. She wanted to save herself from the horrors she was certain they planned to inflict on her.

But there was no way out.

Forcing herself to appear calm, Marissa waited. She prayed fervently that the opportunity would come and she would be able to get away from them.

Hooting Owl came to stand over her. A sneering smile twisted his lips as he leered down at her. He was surprised when she looked up at him, seemingly unafraid. He decided she needed to learn what fear was. Ever so slowly and with great deliberation, he ran his knife down the buttons at the front of her gown, slicing them free and leaving her dress gaping open.

The other warriors called out lewd comments to him, urging him on, enjoying the scene. Each expected to have a turn with her once he was through.

Snake went to stand with Hooting Owl. He reached out to grab the dress where the other man had cut it. In one harsh move, he ripped it open, revealing the shoulder strap of her chemise.

Marissa had managed to control her terror so far, but she cried out in shock when he tore her dress. She jumped to her feet to try to flee from the two men.

Snake grabbed her by the arm, ready to begin teaching her a few lessons.

"No!" Marissa screamed. Her flesh was crawling from his vile touch.

It was then that Chief Ten Crow returned to the campfire. He was furious to see what was going on.

"Release her!" the chief ordered angrily.

Snake and the others were surprised by their chief's fury. She was only a white captive. Snake immediately dropped his hand from her and moved off.

Marissa was startled to find herself suddenly free again. She had no idea what the man who was her captor had said to them, but they were backing away from her. She was relieved at the reprieve. She clutched the shreds of her torn bodice to her.

"You have plans for this white woman?" Snake asked.

"We thought she was only a captive," Hooting Owl explained to Ten Crow, not wanting to further anger their chief.

Ten Crow's expression was cold and commanding as he looked at them. "The golden one is mine. I have taken her for my own. You will not touch her again."

The warriors were shocked by his declaration, but they knew better than to challenge him. They moved away. Hooting Owl slid his knife back into its sheath as he sat down across the campfire from where the chief and the woman stood.

For a time, Marissa hadn't known what to expect from the Comanche warriors. She wasn't sure if they were about to rape her or torture her and kill her. Her captor's sudden appearance had been timely, and her relief was great as he motioned for her to sit back down. She obeyed, her legs trembling.

A short time later, they all bedded down. Her captor came to Marissa's side. Absolute terror gripped her again as she imagined what was to come next.

The Comanche stared at her for a moment, then took a length of rope and bound her ankles tightly together. He said nothing, but lay down a short distance from her.

Conflicting emotions warred within Marissa—ridiculous joy that the warriors had not raped or harmed her and pure horror over the hopelessness of her situation. She was trapped with no possible chance to get away. She lay awake for a long time until exhaustion finally claimed her.

The dawn of the new day brought no relief for Marissa. For a moment when her captor gave her a horse of her own to ride, she hoped she could make a run for it, but then he took her reins to lead her mount as they got ready to move out. Sadly she realized that even if she had controlled the reins, she wouldn't have gotten very far without a saddle. She had never ridden astride before, and her skirts were a terrible hindrance as she struggled valiantly to keep her seat at the quick pace the Comanche warriors set.

The miles were endless. The sun beat down mercilessly all day long as the raiding party continued on. They stopped only to rest and water the horses, then rode off again.

A blessed numbness settled over Marissa. She focused only on staying on the horse's back and staying alive.

They made camp again, and her captor treated her in the same way as he had the previous night. This night, however, the other warriors did not come near her.

Only when the darkness surrounded her and Marissa closed her eyes, pretending to be asleep, did the pain return. She cried silently into the night for all that had been lost and the utter hopelessness of her situation.

Chapter Three

Meanwhile, at the Crown Ranch

George Williams saw the rider coming and walked out of his stable to greet him. Even at this distance, he recognized Ken Thompson, the deputy from Dry Springs, and he was suddenly concerned. It was a rare thing for a lawman to ride out to the Crown. He wondered if there was trouble.

"Morning, Ken," George called out. "What brings you out this far?"

"We need you in town," the deputy told him, his manner serious as he reined in and dismounted.

George was instantly cautious. "What's wrong?"

"Sheriff Spiller and I rode out to the way station. The stagecoach was over a day late, so we went to check on it and see if there was any kind of trouble. It's a damned good thing we did. A Comanche raiding party has burned the way station to the ground."

George went still, fearful of what the deputy was about to tell him. His niece Marissa had sent word that she would be arriving in Dry Springs soon, depending on travel conditions, and he'd made arrangements with the stable in town to have her brought out to the Crown when she got there. "Why do you need me?"

"There was one survivor of the attack—a woman. She was shot and left for dead. I don't know how she did it, but she managed to hang on. She's been delirious and talking crazy, but she did call your name."

"Is it my niece Marissa?" George asked tightly.

"No, I met your niece the last time she came to visit you. This woman is older than Marissa. The sheriff and I transported her back to town. It wasn't easy, but we managed. Doc Harrison's taking care of her now."

"She could be my niece's companion, Louise Bennett. Did she tell you her name?"

"No, she was too weak to say much of anything. We were just shocked when she called for you."

"Is she going to make it?"

"Doc didn't know."

"What about Marissa?" He asked the question slowly. He was deathly afraid that his niece had been killed in the raid and the deputy was just trying to avoid giving him the bad news. "Was there any sign of her?"

"We found one other woman at the way station—"

George's heart sank.

"But it wasn't your niece," Ken finished quickly. "It was the station master's wife. She was dead, and so were all the men."

George felt as sick as he felt relieved. If the woman who'd survived was Louise Bennett, then where was Marissa? The thought that she might have been taken captive by the Comanche tore at him. He knew how captives were treated.

"I'll ride with you to town. Just give me a minute to take care of things here."

George left the deputy and went back into the stable to speak with Claude Collins, his foreman. Leaving him in charge, he hurriedly saddled his horse and was ready to head out. They rode for Dry Springs at top speed.

George made no attempt at conversation with the deputy, who kept pace at his side. His mood was too dark. Terrible thoughts haunted him, and his deepest fear ate at him: Had Marissa been taken captive? It seemed there could be no denying it, but first he had to talk to the injured woman and make sure. If this was Louise Bennett and Marissa had been taken, there was going to be hell to pay. He would see to it personally.

They reached Dry Springs and rode straight to the doctor's office. George dismounted and tied his horse out front. He hurried inside to speak with Dr. Harrison, leaving Deputy Thompson to follow after him.

"Is the woman who was found at the way station still alive?" George asked. He was as ready as he would ever be to face the terrible truth.

"Yes. She's an amazing woman. She's quite a fighter," the physician told him.

"Thank God. Can I see her—talk to her?"

Dr. Harrison stood and led the way to the sickroom at the rear of his office. The doctor paused before the closed door to speak with George for a moment before they went in.

"She's in a bad way, George. She was shot in the back and lost a lot of blood. She's been drifting in and out of consciousness since they brought her in. To tell you the truth, I don't know how she managed to stay alive long enough for Sheriff Spiller and Deputy Thompson, to find her." He nodded proudly toward the lawman. "It's a miracle, that's for sure, and I'm going to do everything I can to help her pull through."

"Deputy Thompson said she called my name. Has she said anything else? Has she told you who she is? My niece Marissa was due in town, and she was traveling with a woman named Louise Bennett."

"No, except for calling your name, she hasn't said anything else that's made sense. Would you recognize this Louise Bennett if you saw her?"

"No, I've never met the woman before."

"Well, let's see if she's awake."

The deputy waited in the outer office as the doctor quietly opened the door and went in to check on his patient. George paused, hesitating in the doorway at the sight of the woman lying deathly still on the bed. He'd always pictured Louise Bennett as a gray-haired, elderly matron, and he was surprised to see that this woman was much younger than he'd imagined. Her hair was a vibrant auburn, and though her color was ashen now, she was a delicate beauty.

"How is she?" he asked the doctor in a quiet tone as he stood there staring at her.

At the sound of a voice, the woman stirred and opened her eyes. She stared around herself blindly for a moment, frightened by her unknown surroundings. Then suddenly she tried to sit up.

"No!" she cried out.

George rushed to her side as Doc Harrison pressed her back down and spoke to her in a comforting voice.

"You're safe now, ma'am. You're in town, and you're going to be all right," the doctor reassured her gently.

She looked at the two men hovering over her. The terror that had scarred her soul screamed a warning to her to flee, that danger was everywhere. She struggled to get away for a moment, but what little strength she had quickly gave out.

"But the Indians—they were everywhere—" she managed frantically, looking between the two men in desperation. Tears filled her eyes as she remembered the carnage she'd witnessed.

"It's all right now. No one is going to hurt you. The Comanche are gone," George reassured her as he took her hand in his.

She clung to his hand and gazed up at him. It felt good to hold on to his strength. She fought hard to focus as pain ravaged

her. Something about this tall, dark-haired man standing over her seemed familiar. "Who are you?"

"I'm George—George Williams. And this is Dr. Harrison," he told her. He saw the sudden look of recognition in her eyes as she studied him.

"You're Uncle George," she said, her expression turning even more tormented when she realized she was facing Marissa's uncle. It had been her job to see Marissa safely to him. "Oh, God," she whispered. Terror once again overcame her as she thought of Marissa running to the stage driver's side. "How is Marissa? Is she here with me? Where is she?" Louise tried to sit up and look around, needing to reassure herself that Marissa was safe. "I have to see her!"

The emotions that flooded George at her words were over-whelming. His greatest fear had been realized. "So, you are Louise."

Her gaze met his, and they shared a moment of horrible comprehension.

"Yes—I'm Louise—and Marissa?" Her grip on his hand tightened even more as she started to ask, "Is she—"

"She's not dead," George told her quickly, wanting to ease her suffering.

"Thank God. Where is she? I want to see her," Louise insisted, desperate to know that Marissa was safe. "I tried to get her to go inside the way station, but she wanted to help the driver. He'd been wounded—"

George nodded in understanding. That was just like Marissa. She was always helping everyone. He could just imagine now what that act of kindness had cost her.

Grim acceptance of his niece's fate came to George. There could be no denying it any longer: The Comanche had taken her.

Louise went on quickly, wanting to explain, "I told Marissa to stay with me—I told her we had to get inside where it was safe—"

She started to get hysterical again. "But she wouldn't come back! She kept going—"

"Easy," the doctor said.

Louise struggled to draw a breath as she looked up at both men, slowly shaking her head. "I'm sorry—I don't remember anything more after that. If she's not dead, then where is she? I want to see her."

George looked over at the doctor. They both knew there was no point in lying to her or trying to deny what had happened.

"Marissa was taken captive," George said quietly. "But I'm leaving right now to go after her."

"You'll find her, won't you? You'll bring her back—"

"I'm going to do everything in my power to find her, Louise. I promise you that."

Their gazes met, and Louise saw in the depths of his dark eyes the intent look of a man of his word.

"You will. If anyone can find her, it will be you," she whispered. A profound weariness overcame Louise then, and she closed her eyes against the brutal memories.

George stayed at her side for a moment longer. When her breathing became normal and her hold on his hand relaxed a little, he gently laid her hand down and quietly left the room with the doctor. They stepped out into the outer office and closed the door behind them. Deputy Thompson had taken a seat in the office, and he looked up questioningly.

"Is she your niece's companion?" he asked George.

"Yes," George answered grimly as he glanced back at the closed door.

"And your niece?"

"The Comanches must have taken her captive," he ground out as a fierce and terrible determination filled him.

"What are you going to do?"

"I'm going after her." George looked at the deputy, a deadly resolve showing in his eyes. He turned back to the doctor. "I'll take full responsibility for Miss Bennett's care. As soon as she can be safely moved, I want her out at the ranch. Send word if there's any change in her condition."

"I will."

George started to leave, then turned back to the doctor. "And you might want to say a few prayers for my niece."

Dr. Harrison nodded to him in silent understanding.

Without another word, George headed off with Deputy Thompson to speak with Sheriff Spiller.

The sheriff looked up as George barged into his office.

"I'm glad Ken brought you to town. Do you know the woman?" Spiller asked, concerned.

"Yes, she was my niece's traveling companion," George told him. "Her name is Louise Bennett."

"Damn. So Marissa was there at the way station, too." Sheriff Spiller's expression reflected his sudden fears. He'd met George's niece on one of her previous trips to Dry Springs. She was a lovely young lady, but he had seen no trace of her at the site of the raid.

"Yes. Marissa and Louise were making the trip to the Crown together." He looked the lawman straight in the eye. "The Comanches must have taken Marissa, Harry. I've got to go after her—I've got to find her."

The sheriff was sickened by the news, but he understood the rancher's feelings. "I know, George, but it won't be easy."

"I didn't think it would be." His tone was cold.

"I've already notified the Rangers."

"I can't wait for them. It might be weeks before they show up, and it's already been too long. I've got to head out as fast as I can while their trail is still fresh. Who's the best tracker you know? Is there anybody here in town?"

"Hawk Morgan," Spiller answered without hesitation.

"The half-breed who works at the livery stable?" George asked sharply, not feeling the least bit kindly toward anybody with Indian blood right then.

"That's right. Hawk's as good as they come. He's helped me in the past whenever I needed him."

George nodded. "Thanks."

He turned to go, fighting down the anger he was feeling at having to deal with a half-breed, yet knowing he had a much better chance of finding Marissa with his aid. If he was going to save her, he needed the man's help.

"George."

George looked back at Sheriff Spiller.

"Be careful."

They shared a look of complete understanding. George nodded tightly, then left the office and made his way straight to the stable. He met Jim Watson, the owner of the stable, first and talked briefly with him.

"I need to speak with Hawk Morgan."

"Hawk's working out back," Jim told George. "Let me get him for you."

"I'd appreciate it." He was tense as he readied himself to speak with the half-breed.

"Hawk—someone out here needs to talk to you!" Jim Watson called out.

Hawk had been working with a horse in a corral behind the stable. At Jim's call, he went inside to see what was wanted. Hawk saw George Williams standing with Jim. He knew of the successful rancher and wondered what he wanted. "What is it?"

George eyed the tall, dark-haired half-breed coolly. He judged him to be about thirty, but he couldn't be sure and didn't care. He didn't want to take any time with niceties or trying to be polite. "Sheriff Spiller tells me you're the best tracker around. I need to hire you."

Hawk frowned. "For what?"

George quickly related all that had happened. "I've got to go after my niece while there's still time to pick up the trail. Will you do it? I'll pay you whatever you ask."

"How soon can you be ready to ride?" Hawk asked, understanding the rancher's fury and desperation.

George realized that Hawk was agreeing to go. "I want a couple of hands from my ranch to ride with us. We can be ready in a matter of hours."

Hawk asked his boss, "This all right with you, Jim? Will you be shorthanded without me?"

"I'll manage," Jim returned.

George looked at Hawk. "You didn't say how much you wanted. Name your price."

"Let's find your niece, Mr. Williams. We'll worry about the money later."

George was shocked. He would have paid whatever amount the man wanted. He would spare no cost trying to save Marissa. "Are you sure?"

Hawk nodded.

"Hawk—"

The man looked at him questioningly.

"Call me George."

Hawk nodded and shook the hand George offered him.

Jim smiled grimly, glad that things were working out. "Good luck," he told George.

"We're going to need it."

"If anyone can track them down, Hawk can," Jim said. "He's the best."

Hawk and George set up the time and place where they would meet, and then George rode for the Crown.

They all realized time was of the essence if they were to rescue Marissa from the Comanche.

Chapter Four

Chief Ten Crow was glad when the Comanche village came into view. It had been a long, arduous trip back, but at last they were home. He shouted out to his men in triumph, and they responded with shouts of equal joy. The villagers heard the sound of their cries and ran to greet them, cheering their success. The chief and his warriors were pleased with the rousing welcome.

Marissa stared about her as they rode into the camp. It was alien to her—the tipis and open campfires, the half-naked children and the buckskin-clad women who were staring and pointing at her as she passed by. Once again she faced the fear of the unknown, and a shiver of terror trembled through her. She fought it back with fierce denial. One thing she'd come to learn in watching these Comanche who had taken her captive. They showed no fear, and they respected those who were fearless as well. Determination filled Marissa. She would face them and her future as bravely as she could.

Her captor reined in before a tipi where a woman stood. Marissa held on to her mount and waited in silent expectation to see what was going to happen next. Her gaze swept over the village again, a part of her desperately seeking help, but there was no sign of any whites—no sign of anything familiar. She was alone in a foreign and dangerous world.

Chief Ten Crow dismounted. Dropping the reins of both horses, he went to greet his wife, Laughing Woman.

"You are back, my husband," Laughing Woman said with a smile, glad to see him.

"It is good to be home."

"Your raid was successful?" she asked, looking up at the white woman. She had already seen the many horses they'd herded in.

"Very."

"You have a captive?" Laughing Woman moved closer to get a better look at the female.

"Yes."

She studied the woman intently, especially her blond hair and pale skin.

"Is she the one?" Laughing Woman asked knowingly. Ten Crow had told her of his vision of the golden woman before he'd left on the raid.

"She is." He nodded. "And she is very brave."

"It would seem so," Laughing Woman agreed, seeing how quiet the girl was. She expected her to cower, and she was surprised when the captive met her regard without showing any fear. White captives usually screamed and cried when they were brought into the village.

Chief Ten Crow came to the horse's side and pulled Marissa down from its back. Images of his vision came to him as he stared down at her for a moment.

"Have you given her a name?"

"I will call her Shining Spirit, for her hair is the color of the sun."

"It is fitting."

"Where is Wind Ryder?" Chief Ten Crow asked, surprised that his adopted son had not come to greet him.

"He left on a raid with Rearing Horse and the others. They have been gone many days, as you were."

The news troubled him. He had plans for the woman, but could do nothing until Wind Ryder returned.

"See to the woman," he directed.

"I will," Laughing Woman answered obediently.

"And keep her away from the others—except for Crazy One. I will have her come to you."

"That is good." She led Marissa into the tipi.

Chief Ten Crow was disappointed at Wind Ryder's absence. He wanted to see his vision fulfilled. He wanted to ensure the peace of his tribe.

Chief Ten Crow went to join the other warriors to celebrate the success of their raiding. He would anxiously await his other son's return.

Marissa's imagination had conjured up all kinds of terrible images of what was about to happen to her. She'd felt certain that the fate she'd been dreading during the trek to the village was about to befall her. Her surprise had been real when a woman led her away into the tipi. Any relief she'd felt quickly gave way to panic when the woman began trying to pull her clothes off her.

"No!" Marissa fought back as best she could, but it was difficult with her wrists bound.

Laughing Woman was not laughing over the captive's resistance. She was tempted to beat her into submission, but restrained herself. She knew how important Ten Crow believed this white woman to be to the future of their tribe. Pulling out her knife, she saw for the first time a glimmer of fear in the woman's eyes. That pleased Laughing Woman. She moved in on her, and with a few quick strokes cut away most of her skirt and petticoats.

Marissa was truly terrified as her garments were slashed and torn from her. She stood before the Comanche woman, half-unclothed, valiantly trying to be brave as she wondered if she was

to be stripped completely naked and paraded through the camp. Horror and dread filled the very depths of her soul.

Was she to be beaten? Or given over to the warriors for their pleasure?

Laughing Woman gestured toward the rest of the clothing she still wore.

"Undress yourself," she ordered in her native tongue.

Marissa didn't know what the other woman was shouting or what she wanted her to do.

Laughing Woman repeated her command, this time gesturing toward the garments Marissa still had on.

Marissa had no intention of taking off what little was left of her clothing. She stood her ground.

Frustrated, Laughing Woman wished Crazy One would hurry. She knelt and sorted through her own clothing to find a garment for the captive to wear. When she found the one she'd been seeking, she rose and held out the fringed, buckskin dress to the white woman.

Marissa looked from the woman to the dress and back. Laughing Woman shoved it toward her again, and then Marissa understood. She grabbed it and clutched it to her breast, trying to cover herself. Once more, Laughing Woman motioned for her to undress.

Marissa finally understood what she wanted, but knew she couldn't change clothing with her hands bound as they were. She stepped forward and held out her arms so the Comanche woman could see the problem.

Laughing Woman realized she would have to free the girl, and with one sure motion cut the rope.

Marissa rubbed her sore wrists, grateful for at least that much freedom. She kept her gaze focused on the woman as she quickly shed the remnants of her gown. Taking up the buckskin dress,

she started to pull it on over her underthings, but the Comanche woman grabbed her arm to stop her, gesturing for her to strip those off too. Embarrassed, Marissa turned her back and quickly did as directed. She was glad when she finally pulled on the fringed and bead-trimmed buckskin dress. She noticed immediately that it smelled very much like a dead cow, but right then, that didn't matter to her. At least she wasn't naked. The dress modestly covered her, and the buckskin was surprisingly soft against her skin.

Laughing Woman stared at Shining Spirit's feet. The captive was still wearing shoes. Laughing Woman went through her own belongings again and took out a pair of moccasins, offering them to her.

Marissa took the moccasins, but did not really want to wear them. She glanced at the Comanche woman and found that she was watching her closely. She sat down and pulled off her own shoes and stockings, then donned the other footwear.

Laughing Woman studied Shining Spirit thoughtfully. Seeing how filthy she was, she decided to allow her to bathe. Her husband wanted the white woman to be ready for Wind Ryder when he returned. She motioned for Shining Spirit to get up so they could leave the tipi. Laughing Woman wondered why Crazy One hadn't come to them yet. She could not trust the white woman alone and could have used her help. As it was, she would have to be the one to go with her to the stream and keep watch over her.

Marissa stared at the Comanche woman, trying to understand what she wanted her to do. After a moment, she finally understood and got up to follow her from the tipi. They made their way down to the creek.

Marissa eyed the clean water, longing for a hot bath. The endless days on the trail had taken their toll. She had never been this dirty before in her entire life. She wished there was some way to scrub every inch of herself clean, but even as she wanted to bathe,

Marissa wondered if she would ever feel really clean again. Still, if she was going to have the chance to wash up at all, it was now.

"Wash!" Laughing Woman ordered, pointing at the water.

Marissa watched as the Indian woman squatted down and pretended to wash herself.

"Wash!" Laughing Woman said again.

Marissa looked around, torn between her innate sense of modesty and her desperate yearning to be clean. The shrubbery on the bank of the stream provided some privacy, so she quickly stripped off the buckskin dress and moccasins and stepped into the water. It was chilling, but she didn't care. She waded out until the stream was waist deep, then dipped beneath the water and hid as she washed.

The cool, clean water washed the dirt and grit away, but even as Marissa took what small pleasure she could from feeling clean again, the reality of her situation did not change. Always in the back of her mind, torturing and haunting her, were Louise's death and the horrors of what she'd witnessed during the raid. Why had she been the only one left alive? At that moment, if the water had been deeper, she might have considered suicide. Her mother was dead, and her father, and now Louise ...

The painful memories overwhelmed her again, and Marissa slipped under the water to hide her tears. After washing her hair and wringing the water out of the sleek, heavy length of it, she made her way back to the bank where the Indian woman awaited her.

Donning the buckskin dress again, Marissa followed the woman's lead back to the encampment, where this time she was directed to go into a different tipi. Marissa wondered whom it belonged to as she stepped inside. She waited to see what would happen next, and was relieved when the woman did not bind her hands again. The woman simply looked around and walked back outside, leaving her alone.

Marissa started to follow her back outside, but the woman turned and shouted angrily at her, gesturing for her to stay inside. She retreated into the tipi. Unsure of what she ought to do, Marissa sat down on the blankets on the far side of the lodge, across from the opening, to wait.

Bear Claw had not known the white captive would be bathing in the stream, but as he'd made his way back to his tipi he had seen the captive heading toward the stream, accompanied by his mother. He had tended to his business, and then on his return deliberately made his way past the stream. Though his mother was standing guard, he eluded her detection and watched the golden one in the water. When the captive finally emerged from the stream, her long golden hair fell around her in a natural, shimmering shield, hiding her breasts from his view. Heat had stirred within him as his hungry gaze devoured the sight of her rounded hips and long, shapely legs. Bear Claw was surprised by his own reaction to her. He usually felt no attraction to white women, but this one seemed different. He remained where he was, enjoying the view until the captive dressed again and left the stream bank. Only when she had gone from sight did he go on to the village and seek out his father.

"Father, what will you do with the new captive?" Bear Claw asked, trying not to sound too interested.

"She will serve her purpose here," Chief Ten Crow answered mysteriously.

Bear Claw did not recognize the strangeness of his answer. He thought his father was just going to keep her in camp as he would any other white captive. "I will buy her from you," he offered.

"You do not like the whites," his father pointed out, frowning at his son's show of interest. There had been white female captives in their village before, but Bear Claw had never shown interest in any of them.

"This one is different."

"She is not for sale." Chief Ten Crow's frown darkened. The woman was meant for Wind Ryder—not Bear Claw. She was to somehow encourage peace between his sons, not cause more trouble.

"As you say, Father." Bear Claw was angered by his refusal, but struggled not to show it. He was not accustomed to being denied anything he wanted, but this was his father—the chief—so he had to accept his answer as final.

Frustrated, Bear Claw fell silent. His body was still on fire, so he bided his time, waiting for the late hours so he could find a village girl who was willing to ease the ache within him. Bear Claw knew, though, that all the while he was taking her he would be thinking of the golden one.

Marissa remained alone in the tipi. As the hours passed, her uncertainty grew. Darkness was just beginning to claim the land when she decided to take a look outside and see if there was anyone around. The thought of trying to escape taunted her as she pushed the flap farther back and looked out. She saw no one nearby, and, feeling bolder, she started outside. She didn't know how far she could get, but she had to try.

Laughing Woman had not trusted the captive. She'd sent one of the small boys in camp to keep watch over the tipi while she went to find Crazy One. She had had no success in finding Crazy One and was still looking for her when the boy rushed to alert her that the white captive had come out.

Marissa hadn't gotten very far when Laughing Woman confronted her.

"Go back!" Laughing Woman commanded in the Comanche tongue, giving her an angry look as she pointed toward Wind Ryder's tipi. Her husband had directed that Shining Spirit was to stay there until Wind Ryder returned from his raid.

Marissa's hope of slipping away undetected was ruined. She went back into the lodge, wondering if she would ever get a chance to try to save herself. As she stepped inside, she gasped in shock. There was another woman in the tipi. The woman was hunched down, visibly shaking, her face averted, a shawl covering her head.

"Who are you?" Marissa demanded, frightened. She didn't know how the woman had been able to get inside without being seen. Even as she was speaking, she realized miserably that the woman couldn't understand her.

At the sound of her voice, the woman stopped shaking and went completely still. Ever so slowly, she lifted her head to stare at the woman before her.

"Who are you?" Crazy One demanded in English, still staying huddled down.

"You speak English?" Marissa was stunned. Tears of relief burned in her eyes as she tried to get a better look at the woman.

"You speak English?" Crazy One repeated as she peered up at her.

When the woman said that, Marissa feared she was mocking her with her own words. Her spirits had momentarily soared, but now they died again. She stood there staring down at the old woman as she answered wearily, "Yes, I speak English."

Marissa did not expect an answer.

"Why are you in Wind Ryder's lodge? It is not good to be here! I must leave—quick—quick—before he returns! I must go." She stood, ready to flee, the expression on her face one of pure panic and fear.

"What?" Marissa was even more shocked as she looked into the haggard old woman's leathery face and realized she was a white woman. "You're white! Who are you?"

"They call me Crazy One."

She was taken aback by her name. "I'm Marissa—"

"No," Crazy One interrupted her. "You are Shining Spirit. Chief Ten Crow said so."

"Shining Spirit? No, my name is Marissa Williams, and I was taken captive—"

"Doesn't matter—doesn't matter," she said quickly, cutting Marissa off again as she looked nervously toward the doorway. "Wind Ryder may be coming."

"Who is Wind Ryder? Why are you so afraid of him?"

"You will see," Crazy One answered slowly, knowingly. "He is a fierce warrior—an angry warrior. I must go."

She fled the tipi.

Behind her, Marissa called out as she started to follow her, "Wait! Don't go! Can you help me? Why did you come here?"

Crazy One didn't stop to answer that she had only come because Chief Ten Crow and Laughing Woman had insisted. She wanted only to stay away from Wind Ryder's tipi.

Marissa watched Crazy One run off into the gathering darkness; then she looked around to find others in the village watching her. She went back inside.

Marissa's emotions were in turmoil as she sank down on the blankets. The relief she felt at having discovered that someone in the village spoke English was destroyed by the knowledge that the old woman had obviously been a captive for a long time and that she had a very real fear of this warrior named Wind Ryder. The very warrior whose tipi she was staying in.

Wind Ryder.

Marissa wondered who he was and what he had done to instill such terror in Crazy One. Was this Comanche warrior—this Wind Ryder—the most vicious and savage of them all? And would he really be returning soon? She had no answers. The one person who could have told her was gone.

Uneasy and greatly disturbed by Crazy One's visit, Marissa tried to rest, but sleep, again, was long in coming.

Chapter Five

At the sighting of riders approaching the village, a shout went out, and the people rushed from their lodges to see who it was.

"I hope it's Wind Ryder!" Moon Cloud told her friend Soaring Dove as they joined the others going to meet the incoming warriors.

Soaring Dove laughed at her friend's excitement. "Somehow I knew you were going to say that. It is the same thing you said three days ago when Chief Ten Crow returned."

Moon Cloud ignored her as she strained to see who was coming.

"Look!" she cried out in delight, seeing Wind Ryder riding at the front of the raiding party. "It is Wind Ryder!"

Her gaze was hungry upon the tall, handsome brave. He was broad-shouldered, powerfully built, and darkly tanned, and he rode his horse as if they were one. From the distance, there was no evidence of his white blood. He appeared the fine warrior that he was. Her heartbeat quickened at the sight of him.

"Wind Ryder will be mine. You will see." Moon Cloud was confident.

"I am not the one you have to convince," Soaring Dove advised cautiously. "*He* is the one."

"I will do it."

Soaring Dove knew Moon Cloud was determined, but wondered if her friend really could win Wind Ryder's favor. He had shown little interest in her or any of the young maidens, and there were many who found him attractive. Still, she knew how dogged Moon Cloud could be.

They went forth to welcome the returning warriors.

Wind Ryder and the other warriors were proud of their accomplishments as they returned to the village. They had taken many horses and knew their chief would be pleased.

Wind Ryder saw his father coming to welcome them, and he reined in before him. He paid no attention to the women who crowded around, speaking only to Chief Ten Crow.

"Hello, my father."

"It is good that you are back," Chief Ten Crow told him. "I see you did well."

Wind Ryder nodded. "We took many horses. No one was injured or lost. And your raid? Were you successful?"

"All went as I had foreseen," the chief answered cryptically.

Wind Ryder nodded, assuming he meant everything had gone well. "I will tend to my horse and then come to tell you of our raids."

Chief Ten Crow watched him go and smiled to himself. He did not doubt that his son would return to him quickly.

Crazy One had hidden behind a tipi to watch the raiding party's return. She looked on nervously as Wind Ryder spoke briefly with the chief and then left him, striding toward his own lodge. Conflicting emotions filled her. She was torn between the desire to flee from the fury she was sure would come and the need to stay and try to help Shining Spirit. During the past three days, she

had tended to the captive as Laughing Woman had ordered her to do, taking meals to her and guarding her when she went to the stream to bathe. She hadn't wanted to. She didn't want to have anything to do with Wind Ryder, but now, seeing that he was returning to his lodge, she wondered what was going to happen to the woman. She knew how he'd felt about having her around—as a boy he'd chased her away any time she'd come near him and she had learned through the years that he avoided her because she was white. She could only imagine how he was going to react to finding Shining Spirit in his tipi.

Crazy One crept away.

She did not want to witness his fury.

Marissa was surprised by all the excitement she heard outside the tipi. In the time that she'd lived with the Comanche, the village had been very quiet. She wondered what had happened to cause such a celebration.

The temptation to take a look outside was strong, but Marissa knew there was always someone nearby, keeping watch over her. The moment she showed herself, her guard would descend and force her back inside. She was only allowed to leave the lodge to bathe and to take care of her private needs. Otherwise, she was as much a prisoner in the tipi as she would have been in any jail, visited only by Crazy One several times a day when she brought her food.

Once she had discovered that Crazy One was white, Marissa had hoped she would help her, but the old woman had offered no help at all. She did not say much, but when she did, she only babbled about how she had to stay away from Wind Ryder.

Marissa was constantly praying for someone to rescue her, but she was losing heart. Surely her uncle had received word of her disappearance by now. That knowledge gave her one last hope she

could hold on to—that Uncle George had put together a search party and he and Mark were trying to find her even now. But the raiding party had traveled so many miles so quickly after attacking the way station, she wondered if anyone would ever be able to track them down.

Being helpless this way didn't suit Marissa. She hated being afraid. She hated being at the mercy of the Comanche. She hated this idleness that left her sitting alone, worrying about the fate that awaited her.

Anger stirred within her breast and emboldened Marissa. In a moment of brazenness, she decided to tempt fate and go outside. She moved forward ready to throw open the flap.

Marissa had taken only one step when suddenly the door covering was drawn aside and a tall, powerful Comanche warrior stepped into the lodge. She stopped, startled by the intrusion. The sun was at his back, so it was difficult for her to make out his features. Uneasiness gripped her. Since she'd been kept captive in the tipi, no men had been permitted to come near her—and now this warrior had walked in.

Wind Ryder entered his tipi completely unaware of what he was about to discover. He straightened, letting the flap close behind him, and found himself face to face with a woman—a white woman with hair the color of golden sunshine.

"Who are you?" Wind Ryder demanded curtly in the Comanche tongue. It was shocking enough to find a female there, but the fact that she was white and beautiful disturbed him even more.

At the harshness in his deep voice, Marissa gasped and stepped back. She got her first good look at him then as he stood before her clad in the traditional Comanche loincloth and moccasins, and she realized she had never seen this warrior before. If she had, she certainly would have remembered.

The warrior's presence was overwhelming. He was tall, his shoulders broad, his body lean and hard-muscled. On his upper arm Marissa could see a wicked scar, pale against his darkly tanned flesh, a silent testimony to the violent life he led. The warrior's black hair was long and held back by only a headband. Slashes of war paint colored his features, and his expression was fiercely arrogant as he glared down at her. He seemed to fill the entire tipi as he loomed over her.

A shiver of fear trembled through Marissa as she realized this might be the warrior Crazy One had warned her about. This man might be Wind Ryder. She could understand the old woman's fear of him. He exuded an aura of danger. Marissa took another step back, wanting to get as far away from him as she could.

"What are you doing here?" Wind Ryder demanded, again in the Comanche tongue. He knew everyone in the village, but he had never seen this woman before. He was irritated by her presence in his lodge.

He sounded so angry that Marissa wanted to turn and flee, but she knew there was nowhere to go, nowhere to run. Drawing upon what little bravery she had left, she lifted her chin and glared back up at him.

Wind Ryder grew even more angered by her show of defiance. He closed on her and grabbed her by the upper arm to drag her to him.

Fear—sudden and real—tore through Marissa.

Was this the moment she'd been dreading all this time?

Was this the moment when she was to be sacrificed to a Comanche warrior's lust?

Had she been offered up to this man as some prize to be claimed—to be taken and used as he desired?

"No! Let me go!" she cried as she fought wildly against his hold. She was desperate to break free, to try to save herself. The

fear she'd held at bay for so long erupted into pure terror. She would not surrender easily.

Wind Ryder was surprised by the fierceness of her resistance, but he was just as determined not to let her get away. He pulled her tightly to him, and a shock of instinctive physical awareness jolted through Wind Ryder at the feel of her soft body molded to him.

Crushed against the hard-muscled width of his chest, Marissa gasped. She looked up at him and found herself staring into a pair of green eyes. Her eyes widened in shock at the discovery.

This Comanche warrior was a white man!

How could that be?

"You're white!" Marissa's gaze locked with his. She remained frozen in his arms as she tried to understand.

Her words stunned Wind Ryder. Hearing English after all this time had a powerful effect on him. He released her immediately and moved away, denying any knowledge of the language of his childhood.

"Please!" she began desperately, a faint glimmer of hope sparking within her for the first time. This man could help her! This man could save her!

Wind Ryder didn't show any reaction. He just stared at her, seeing her frantic desperation and wondering how she had come to be in his tipi.

Marissa came toward him, pleading, "You're white, so you understand. You've got to help me!"

He still did not respond.

She went on, her desperation growing, "They murdered everyone at the way station! They killed Louise. Please—can you do something to help me? Can you help me get away?"

For an instant, a distant, fragmented, painful memory threatened to surface, but Wind Ryder savagely denied it. Without a word, he turned his back on the woman and left.

Wind Ryder strode back toward the tipi where his father was waiting for him. He remembered his father's earlier statement— "*All went as I had foreseen.*" He wondered now if there had been a secret meaning behind his father's words.

Chief Ten Crow had been sitting before his own tipi, awaiting Wind Ryder's return. When he saw his son striding across the camp in his direction, he smiled inwardly, but revealed nothing in his expression. He looked up as Wind Ryder came to stand over him. Seeing his son's stony expression, he got slowly to his feet.

"You have found the present I have given you?" Chief Ten Crow asked.

"I have no need for a white woman," Wind Ryder answered tersely.

"You would refuse my gift?" The chief pinned him with a penetrating gaze.

"Why have you given this woman to me?" he challenged.

"It came to me in a vision. This golden woman was meant for you."

"Your vision was wrong," Wind Ryder said angrily, refusing to believe him.

"My visions are never wrong," the chief responded with confidence. "There is much you do not know, my son."

"Then help me. Tell me what it is I do not know, but do not put this white woman in my care."

"You will guard Shining Spirit well." He stated it as fact, ignoring Wind Ryder's protests.

"Shining Spirit?"

"It is the name I have given her."

"But I have no need of a slave."

"I have spoken. Come, let us join the others and hear the tales of your raids."

Wind Ryder knew there was nothing more he could say or do. He accompanied his father to the fire, where the other warriors had gathered to speak of their feats of daring.

Even as he passed the long hours with the other men, Wind Ryder found images of the golden woman drifting into his thoughts. He decided he would stay away from his tipi for as long as he could.

Marissa's thoughts were racing as she sat alone in the lodge. Darkness had come, but still the warrior had not returned. When the flap was thrown open, she looked up, startled, unsure of what to expect.

"I must hurry," Crazy One said as she came in carrying the evening meal. She was glancing behind herself as if fearful that someone was following her.

"Is something wrong?"

"I told you he would be back." She was nervous as she put the food down. "Wind Ryder has returned to the village."

"Is Wind Ryder the white warrior?" she asked.

"Yes, and he is a fierce one." The old woman started to back away, wanting only to be gone from his tipi. "And now you are his."

"What?" Crazy One's words shocked Marissa.

"I must go."

"Will you tell me—?"

Marissa got no further. Crazy One slipped outside and was gone. She was alone again.

Wind Ryder was back—

And she was his—

Marissa's confusion was real. Her nerves were on edge as she tried to understand what Crazy One had meant.

Wind Ryder was back—

The knowledge that he was a white man still shocked her. Over and over, she found herself wondering how he had come to be there with the Comanche, living as one of them. Had he been taken captive and raised in the village, or had he joined the tribe of his own free will? She couldn't imagine any white man going there of his own free will, yet he seemed so natural in this setting, so attuned to the Comanche ways, that he must have lived among them for a long time.

And she was his—

Marissa's imagination conjured up images of what might happen in the long hours of the night ahead that left her trembling. She knew she had to find a way to communicate with Wind Ryder, yet having witnessed Crazy One's fear of him, she was unsure of what to do. When he returned to the lodge, she would try to talk to him again in hopes that some part of him remembered his life in the white world and would be able to understand her desperation.

Even as she allowed herself that small hope, Marissa realized that little had really changed. The man who had stood before her in the tipi had been as much a Comanche warrior as any of the other men in the village. He had been fearsome, and the look in his eyes—no matter that they were green in color, a testimony to his white heritage—had been cold and unfeeling. A shiver trembled through her as she remembered the way it had felt when he'd held her prisoner in his arms.

Emotionally exhausted, Marissa lay down and pulled the blanket up over her. It was a meager defense against the dangers that threatened, but somehow she felt safer that way.

The hours dragged on, and a great weariness settled over her. When at last she could fight no more, she closed her eyes and fell into a troubled slumber.

Wind Ryder sat with his father and the other braves before the campfire. Many stories had been told and many feats of courage recounted, including the tale of the raid on the way station and taking the white woman captive.

"She was almost Snake's captive, but she was too quick for him," Running Dog taunted Snake. "We will find out soon if Wind Ryder is a better warrior than Snake. We will find out if she can get away from him, too."

The warriors laughed.

"Your father has given you a fine prize," Snake said, looking coldly at Wind Ryder across the fire. He had been wondering ever since they'd returned why Chief Ten Crow was giving the woman to his adopted son. Wind Ryder was no real Comanche. Though some of the others had come to accept him as one of them, Snake never would. To him, Wind Ryder would always be white—and he hated him for his white blood.

"Yes, he has," Wind Ryder agreed, but did not say more. He was in no mood to discuss the woman.

Bear Claw grew angry as he listened to the talk of Wind Ryder and the captive white woman.

He had wanted her.

He had offered to buy her from his father, and his father had refused to sell her to him.

Finding out now that she had been a gift to Wind Ryder left him furious. He had wondered why his father had kept her in Wind Ryder's tipi since they'd returned to the village, and now he knew. Hatred seethed within him.

His father had never given him such an important gift. He stared at the man his father claimed as a son. Nothing had changed between them since that day when they had fought all those years ago. Bear Claw had no brother.

The talk among the warriors continued until the hour grew late.

Wind Ryder stayed away from his lodge for as long as he could without drawing attention to himself. When at last the hour came to retire for the night, he made his way slowly back to his tipi. His mood was as dark as the moonless night that surrounded him.

Chapter Six

Wind Ryder walked silently to his lodge. He drew back the flap and went in. It was dark and very quiet inside. The weather was warm, and no fire had been lit, so he stood there with the flap held up to give him just enough light to see the woman asleep on the far side of the lodge. She was a vision as she slept, her long, golden hair unbound and spread out around her in a shimmering halo.

The golden one—

Shining Spirit—

Wind Ryder understood why his father had called her these things. In sleep, she looked soft and delicate, but he caught himself in that self-deception. He knew what a fierce fighter this woman was. She had been a she-cat when he'd held her earlier, and he'd heard how she'd escaped from Snake during the raid.

He could imagine how she'd respond if he tried to touch her now. As quickly as the thought had come to him, he dismissed it.

He would not touch her—not now—not ever.

Wind Ryder was glad that she was asleep. He needed peace in his soul. He didn't want to hear her speak English. He didn't want to be reminded of things he'd long ago put from him—memories that were powerful enough to destroy the life he'd created for

himself. He was Wind Ryder, Comanche warrior, son of Chief Ten Crow and Laughing Woman.

Dropping the flap, Wind Ryder settled in on his own blankets to get some much needed rest. He would deal with the woman in the morning. For now, he just wanted to sleep. He stretched out and closed his eyes, trying to put all thoughts of Shining Spirit and his father's troubling vision from him.

Marissa's dreams were tormented. During the past few nights she'd managed to get some rest, but the warrior's unexpected appearance today left her frightened and desperate again. Bloody visions of the raid at the way station returned. In her mind, she heard the screams of the dying, along with the sounds of the gunfire and the smell of the fire.

And then Marissa saw Louise—

Louise calling out; Louise warning her and trying to protect her—

Then finally, the gunshot that had taken her life.

Marissa awoke with a start and sat up quickly. Terror surrounded her in the darkness. She didn't know where she was or why she was there.

"No!" she cried out, and tears fell freely as she relived the horror of Louise's death. Her heart was pounding and her breathing was ragged. She stared around her, trying to understand what was real and what was not.

At the sound of her cry, Wind Ryder was instantly awake. Expecting trouble, he was on his feet, knife in hand, ready for whatever danger was near.

Still caught in the grip of her nightmare, Marissa screamed at the sight of the warrior standing over her.

Wind Ryder moved instinctively, pulling her to her feet and clamping a hand over her mouth to silence her.

Mindlessly, Marissa fought his hold on her. She kept scream-ing even though the sound was muffled by his hand.

"Be still!" Wind Ryder commanded harshly in a low voice, using English with her for the first time.

She continued to struggle for a moment until the realiza-tion that he'd actually spoken English penetrated her terror. She stopped.

The moment she gave up the fight, Wind Ryder released her. He stood there staring down at her, his expression revealing the anger he felt at being so awakened.

Marissa thoughts were still chaotic. Memories of the raid and Louise's death tormented her. She was shaking as she looked up at him.

Marissa saw the fury in his face and backed as far away from him as she could. What little bravery she'd felt earlier vanished as she wondered whether he would attack her now. The night had become a living nightmare.

Horrified, Marissa waited for him to make his move—to begin beating her or to rape her. He hadn't responded to her earlier pleas for help in any way, and she could only imagine that he had no sympathy for her plight.

"Don't kill me," she whispered in a frightened voice, unable to deny her fear any longer.

Her words struck savagely at Wind Ryder, and the memory they awoke in him angered him even more. He pushed the painful vision away, turning his anger on Shining Spirit.

"Lie down," he ordered.

Marissa was stunned.

So this was to be her fate. He was going to rape her. She didn't know what to do—Should she try to flee or should she obey him?

Panic filled her. Mindlessly, she tried to dodge past him, to escape from the tipi and the fate she was certain was about to be hers.

Wind Ryder was shocked by her daring move, but he reacted quickly. He snared her around the waist when she would have darted by and brought her against him, her back to his chest.

Marissa went instantly still when his arms closed around her. She waited for what she believed was to come next. Understanding Crazy One's fear of this man, she began to tremble as he walked toward the side of the tipi where she'd made her bed.

Wind Ryder released her.

"Lie down!" He pointed at her blankets.

The look on his face was as frightening as the tone of his voice. Marissa knew there was no way out. She did as he commanded and sat down on her blankets, but she never took her gaze off him. Instinctively, she clutched one of the blankets to her breast as she stared up at him, waiting—expecting him to attack her, for though his skin was white, his heart was Comanche.

Wind Ryder appreciated that she was a beautiful woman, but the look of pure terror in her expression left him cold. He knew what she was thinking and silently cursed the fact that his father had put her in his care. He wanted nothing to do with her. The farther away from him she stayed, the better. If he could have taken her to another tipi in the village, he would have.

"Sleep." The word was harsh.

Marissa blinked in confusion, shocked by his order.

"What?" she choked out.

"Sleep." He didn't want to say anything more to her. He just wanted her to be quiet.

Relief swept through Marissa. She couldn't believe what was happening, but quickly did as he'd ordered. She wrapped the blanket tightly around her, for it was her only defense. She did not say another word and remained quiet, fearful that any move she might make would stir his wrath again.

Wind Ryder looked on and gave a grunt of some satisfaction when she obeyed him. He went back to his own bedding and lay down. He shut his eyes and sought sleep. He wanted to rest. But the pain of hearing her words ate at him.

Don't kill me—

How old had he been when his mother had cried those same words? How old had he been when he'd seen her murdered before his very eyes?

Don't kill me—

As much as he wanted to, Wind Ryder wondered how he could deny the reality behind Shining Spirit's fears. She had seen the other warriors raiding and knew the terror of being helpless before them—just as he had been all those years ago.

The unexpected thought jarred him.

Everything Shining Spirit had said to him earlier returned to haunt him. Long-denied, unwanted memories of his own past crept back into his consciousness—of how he'd felt when he'd been brought into the Comanche camp for the first time. He tried to remember how old he'd been. He had a vague recollection of being about eight years old, but he wasn't sure.

It had been many years ago.

Wind Ryder realized, too, that it had been almost that long since he'd spoken English. The language did not come easily to him now, but that did not surprise him. It pained him to draw upon his knowledge of his past. That was why he had refused to speak English to her earlier.

More memories assaulted him now even as he tried to deny them. In order to survive his ordeal, he had pretended that none of his life before the Comanche raid had really happened. He'd told himself that he hadn't really lost his white father, mother, and brothers to the savage raiding party—that the boy he had been had never existed. Zach Ryder, the oldest

son of Michael and Catherine Ryder and the brother of Jeff and Will, was dead.

Zach Ryder had died the day he'd watched his family slaughtered by the Comanche who had taken him with them as they rode away.

In his place, Wind Ryder, the fearless warrior, had been born. He had focused all his energies on becoming the best warrior in the village. It had been hard for him, for the Comanche boys had hated and resented him, but that had only spurred him to work harder. He had been fortunate that Chief Ten Crow had taken such a liking to him or he probably would have been dead by now or traded off to another tribe.

Zach Ryder—

Just thinking of his white name tore at Wind Ryder, and it took all his considerable willpower to force the thoughts of that time away. As he gave in to the weariness that gripped him, he did allow himself to remember how he had quietly celebrated every time one of the warriors who'd murdered his white family had been killed on a raid.

Wind Ryder slept, but not before he had taken one last look at the golden captive asleep across the lodge from him.

Marissa lay unmoving, barely breathing, making no sound. She was acutely aware of the warrior's powerful presence so close to her within the confines of the lodge. As the hours dragged on, Marissa found herself wondering if dawn would ever come. Yet even as she longed for the start of the new day, she feared it.

Wind Ryder had returned to take command of the tipi—and of her. What did he want with her? What was to become of her?

Marissa had no idea what her future held, and it was that uncertainty that left her unable to sleep. Anxiety was her only companion there in the darkness. She prayed that her uncle would find her.

Wind Ryder awoke with the dawn. He glanced over at Shining Spirit and was glad to see she was still asleep. Rising soundlessly, he left the tipi.

The village was just stirring to life as he made his way down to the stream to bathe. He stripped off his clothing and waded out into the water.

The cold water was refreshing, and Wind Ryder took his time. His thoughts were troubled as he scrubbed the war paint away. He did not know what he was to do with Shining Spirit. Beauty though she was, he did not want her. She meant nothing but trouble for him. She was a complication he did not need. The restless night he'd just passed was proof of that.

But his father had decreed that she was to be his as had been foreseen in his vision. In irritation, Wind Ryder wondered what else his father had seen in the vision.

Annoyed, Wind Ryder left the water and dressed. He strode through the village, deliberately not returning to his tipi. He sought out the other warriors, wanting to stay as far away from Shining Spirit as he could. The less time he spent in the company of the white woman, the better.

Marissa awoke to find the warrior gone. Relief swept through her, and amazement filled her at what had transpired during the night just past. The man Crazy One tried so hard to avoid had returned and spent the night in the tipi with her, but he had not harmed her in any way. She had remained untouched. After witnessing the old woman's fear of being near him, Marissa had expected the worst from him, and yet nothing had happened.

Marissa rose, but she was unsure of what she should do. Crazy One always came for her early in the morning, but she wasn't sure if she'd appear now that Wind Ryder had returned. Marissa

wondered if she was free to move around the village on her own. She decided to wait awhile to see if anyone came.

Laughing Woman was eager to reach Wind Ryder's tipi to find out what had happened overnight. She had told Crazy One that she would tend to the captive today, and, as she'd suspected, the old woman had been relieved. Laughing Woman knew Crazy One wouldn't want to chance seeing Wind Ryder.

Ten Crow had said Shining Spirit was the woman from his vision, so Laughing Woman wanted to make sure all was going as it should. If it did, her worries would soon be over. There would be peace in the village.

Peace. Laughing Woman smiled at the thought. She knew how much Bear Claw hated Wind Ryder, and she understood. The white captive had disturbed the tribe and her family. She had tried to convince her husband not to adopt the boy, but he had been too impressed with the white youth's fearlessness and his abilities. Once he had become their son, Wind Ryder had stolen that which should have been Bear Claw's—he had stolen Ten Crow's favor.

Laughing Woman had tried all these years to accept Wind Ryder as her son, but she had never fully succeeded. Though the white boy had grown into a strong and powerful warrior, she could never forget that he was not Comanche. Others in the tribe had been able to, but she could not.

Reaching the tipi, Laughing Woman saw that the door flap was thrown back. She called to Wind Ryder, but when he did not come out, she looked inside and saw that Shining Spirit was alone. She wondered where Wind Ryder had gone so early in the day. She gestured for the white woman to come out and was pleased when the captive obeyed her.

Marissa found she was almost glad to see the Comanche woman instead of Crazy One this morning. After the night just

past, she wasn't sure she was ready to listen to the old woman. Marissa was puzzled, though, by the strange look this woman gave her when she stepped outside. She felt almost as if the Comanche were inspecting her for some reason.

Laughing Woman eyed Shining Spirit closely, trying to guess what had transpired during the night. It puzzled her that the white woman seemed no different after spending time alone with Wind Ryder. She had expected the warrior to use the captive the way her son or Snake would have if she had been theirs. Laughing Woman motioned for Shining Spirit to follow her, and they started off.

Marissa trailed after her. As they walked through the village, she found herself looking around for some sign of Wind Ryder. She was nervous about seeing him again.

Wind Ryder was sitting with the warriors when he caught a glimpse of Shining Spirit following his mother through the camp. Satisfied that there was no need for him to concern himself with the troubling female, he turned his attention back to the other warriors. As they were talking, Chief Ten Crow and Bear Claw came to join them.

"Good morning, Father, Bear Claw," Wind Ryder greeted them.

Chief Ten Crow asked, "Where is your woman?"

Wind Ryder didn't like hearing the woman called 'his,' but did not argue. "She is with my mother."

The chief nodded.

"How was your night?" Bear Claw asked. His thoughts were lewd as he imagined what must have gone on between captor and captive. He certainly would have enjoyed having the white woman for his own. "Is the talk true that screams were heard coming from your lodge? She must have fought you as hard as she fought Snake."

Wind Ryder looked at him steadily. His expression was closed as he answered, "But Shining Spirit did not get away from me."

Bear Claw smiled thinly at him as he thought, *Yet.*

Wind Ryder saw his sneer and knew what Bear Claw would have done with Shining Spirit had she been his. The terror that had possessed her last night would have been merited. Shining Spirit had been worried he might kill her—but Wind Ryder knew there were many fates worse than death, and she would have suffered them all at Bear Claw's hands.

Wind Ryder pushed thoughts of Shining Spirit from his mind.

It did not matter what she suffered. She was a captive. Her destiny was to submit to his will.

"They are coming," Chief Ten Crow told him some time later when he saw the two women returning.

Wind Ryder turned to look their way. Across the distance his gaze met Shining Spirit's.

Chapter Seven

Wind Ryder noticed a change in Shining Spirit's expression as their gazes locked, but he did not understand it. What he did understand was the sudden physical reaction he had to the sight of her. There was no doubt she was a beautiful woman. The golden mane of her hair tumbled down her back in a mass of soft curls, and she moved with an easy grace that drew all eyes to her. As Shining Spirit and Laughing Woman came toward them, Wind Ryder felt his desire grow. He frowned and fiercely denied the feelings she was stirring within him.

A shock ran through Marissa at the sight of Wind Ryder standing with the other warriors. She was stunned by the change in his appearance. She would never have imagined that he could look like this without the harsh camouflage of his war paint. Though his dark hair was long and he was wearing a loincloth and moccasins, there was no mistaking his heritage. Her warrior was truly a—

Marissa stopped, startled by the way she'd thought of him—

Her warrior.

He wasn't *her* anything!

Wind Ryder might look like a white man, but that was where it ended. His appearance didn't change his actions.

She knew what he was.

He was a Comanche.

The memory of how he'd treated her the night before, however, slipped into her thoughts and tempered them, for he had not
harmed her in any way.

Marissa dropped her gaze away from Wind Ryder as Laughing
Woman led her to where the men had gathered.

Bear Claw and Snake were both staring at the captive hungrily. Snake, in particular, wanted to get his hands on her so he
could teach her a lesson. The screams everyone had spoken of last
night would be nothing compared to what he would rouse from
her if he got the chance. He looked on in silence as Wind Ryder
went to speak with his mother and the woman.

"I have been keeping her safe in your lodge, but there is no
need now that you have returned."

"You are right, Mother," Wind Ryder agreed. "Can you teach
her the ways of our women?"

"It is what you want?"

"Teach her well." Wind Ryder nodded, though he really didn't
care if Shining Spirit learned the Comanche ways or not. He just
wanted to keep her away from him.

"I will do this," Laughing Woman agreed, glad to have extra
help with her work.

Marissa wished she knew what they were saying, but the
Comanche tongue was still foreign to her even after being in their
midst for all these days. The older woman took her arm to draw
her away. Marissa glanced up at Wind Ryder to find that he was
already walking back to rejoin the men. Unsure whether to be
relieved at being taken away from him or concerned about where
the woman was leading her, Marissa went along without resistance.

"She does not have any bruises," Bear Claw taunted Wind Ryder
as he joined them again. "Why was she screaming in your lodge
last night if you were not beating her?"

Wind Ryder cast a quick glance at him, then smiled slightly. "It is you who said she was screaming because I was beating her."

The rest of the men laughed loudly at Bear Claw's expense.

Bear Claw grew angry.

Chief Ten Crow sensed the growing tension and stood. "Let us see to the horses. There is much to be done."

Snake looked at Bear Claw as Wind Ryder and the others went off after the chief to break the new horses.

"She is a beautiful one, this captive," Snake remarked, staring after Shining Spirit. His expression turned to a leer as he watched the sway of her hips and imagined her lying naked beneath him as he ..."I am sorry she got away from me."

"My father should never have given her to Wind Ryder," Bear Claw snarled. Then an idea occurred to him. He glanced at Snake, his eyes narrowing. "You still want this woman. Together, we could find a way to take her from him."

Snake did not like Wind Ryder. He never had. Like Bear Claw, he had always resented the white man's presence among them, but he knew what a fierce warrior Wind Ryder was. He knew better than to challenge him. Wind Ryder would make a deadly enemy.

"No, I will not go against Wind Ryder."

"You are a coward?"

"I do not want to die. Wind Ryder protects what is his. If you go after the woman, you will do it on your own."

Bear Claw was disgusted by Snake's refusal and stalked away.

Marissa wasn't sure which was worse, sitting alone in the tipi for days on end or doing the women's work in the camp. Under Laughing Woman's tutelage, she learned how to sew buffalo hides together and had been working at it since they'd left the men

that morning. Activities went on around her, and she kept watch, hoping to come up with a plan to escape now that she was being given a little more freedom.

Marissa's hope of returning to the white world was the only thing that kept her from complete despair. She could tell that the other women were watching her and talking about her, and for once she was glad she could not understand what they were saying. Mostly, they seemed to be laughing and sneering at her. She tried to ignore them, but occasionally one of them would get up and come over to poke her or yank on her hair. She fought to stay calm and concentrated on doing the task set before her.

"She is ugly," Moon Cloud sneered to Soaring Dove, jealousy filling her as she watched the golden-haired captive working with Laughing Woman.

"She is very ugly," Soaring Dove agreed. "I am sure Wind Ryder only took her because she was a gift from his father and he could not refuse."

"But I want Wind Ryder for my own. She is the one sharing his tipi."

"As his captive," Soaring Dove insisted. "Shining Spirit is not his wife. *You* will be his wife."

"That is what I have wanted for as long as I can remember, but he has never asked me."

"Then perhaps it is time for you to go to him," Soaring Dove suggested.

Moon Cloud smiled at the prospect of humiliating the white woman that way. "Soon. Yes, very soon."

"And perhaps it is time for this captive to learn her place in the village."

The thought intrigued Moon Cloud and her smile broadened. "That would be good."

Word came to them that the men were about to start breaking the horses. The women knew it would be a challenge. They quit what they were doing and hurried off to watch.

Marissa had been hard at work, and she was surprised when the other women got up and left. She had no idea what was going on, so she decided to follow them. She trailed after them to what she discovered was a corral made of posts and surrounded by brush and branches that were stacked high against the posts to discourage the horses from jumping out. The other villagers were already there, shouting and yelling, and as she drew closer she saw what all the excitement was about. A brave was in the corral trying to break one of the wild stallions. The stallion was bucking and twisting wildly, trying to dislodge the warrior Black Eagle from his back. Then with one particularly violent move, it threw the man off.

A roar of laughter went up from the other warriors as Black Eagle landed heavily in the dirt. He scrambled to his feet and ran to get away from the angry, rearing stallion.

"Where is Wind Ryder?" someone shouted. "Only Wind Ryder can break this one!"

Wind Ryder heard them calling him and went forward, eyeing the powerful stallion knowingly. It was a fine-looking horse, and Wind Ryder knew it would prove a challenge. He approached the animal slowly and took up the rope that was serving as its bridle. The stallion was watching him, rolling its eyes nervously as it waited for him to make his move. Wind Ryder knew what it expected, though, and he wasn't going to comply. Drawing on the rope, he led the resisting horse from the corral and down to the stream nearby. He waded out into the middle of the water, bringing the stallion with him. It wasn't too deep there, but deep enough to slow the horse's movements, and that was just what Wind Ryder wanted. In one fluid movement, he vaulted onto its

bare back and prepared himself for the violent ride he knew was to come.

Marissa found herself caught up in the drama unfolding before her. Wind Ryder seemed so calm and deliberate as he took charge. She had to admit he looked magnificent as he sat on the stallion's back. His expression was serious, and his body was tense and ready. The black stallion and the proud warrior looked evenly matched, and she wondered which would prevail. Marissa could feel the excitement growing in the crowd around her, and a thrill went through her.

The stallion stood unmoving for a moment, tension etched in every quivering, taut muscle of its sleek body. Then the horse erupted in fury, rearing and bucking with all its might, trying to rid itself of the man who dared ride him. Arching, twisting, turning, the horse was determined not to surrender.

Wind Ryder was equally determined to win the confrontation. He held on tightly as the stallion fought both him and the water. He had broken many horses in the past, but this one was proving particularly stubborn. Even with the help of the water, the stallion was testing his abilities.

Marissa watched in awe as Wind Ryder kept his seat, staying with the bucking, surging stallion.

The whole scene suddenly seemed unreal to her. Here she was in the midst of the West Texas wilderness watching a Comanche warrior break a horse.

She felt almost dazed as she wondered how she had come to this. Just weeks ago she had been living the life of a lady in New Orleans, and now here she was living in an Indian village, dressed in buckskin, watching Wind Ryder attempt to tame a stallion.

The horse reared suddenly, pawing at the air as it tried with all its might to throw Wind Ryder from its back.

Marissa gasped in awe as he kept his seat.

She didn't want to admire anything about this man. She hated the Comanche for what they had done. They were killers, cold-blooded murderers.

But as she watched, Wind Ryder continued to amaze her with his ability to stay with the horse. He held on, the powerful corded muscles of his arms straining as he fought for control over the animal.

The horse continued to battle his domination. The hindrance of the water drained its strength, though, and made it harder and harder for the stallion to move.

Wind Ryder felt the weakening of its resistance, and he smiled confidently to himself. Soon it would be over. The stallion was an excellent, spirited animal. Whoever ended up with it was going to be well served.

After fighting a few minutes more, the horse realized the battle had been lost. Its sides were heaving as it stopped bucking and stood in the stream, trembling and sweaty from the exertion of its lost fight for freedom.

Wind Ryder reached down and patted the proud horse's lathered neck.

Cheers arose from those who'd gathered round to watch the challenge.

Marissa looked on as Wind Ryder rode the exhausted horse from the stream up into the corral. He dismounted and handed the reins to another warrior.

Around Marissa, the villagers hurried forward to congratulate him on his hard-fought victory. She did not join them. She stayed back to watch. It was then she noticed that two of the warriors had walked away without saying a word. Their backs were to her, so she could not see who they were. She found it strange that they alone did not want to share in Wind Ryder's victory celebration.

After a time, another wild horse was brought forward, and another brave prepared to mount. The crowd backed away once more to give them room.

Wind Ryder went to stand with his father.

"As always, you have made me proud, my son," Chief Ten Crow told him, smiling at his accomplishment.

"The stallion will make some warrior a fine raiding pony," Wind Ryder said.

"He was a stubborn one," the chief agreed. "You have once again proven your ability. You are the best horseman in the village."

Wind Ryder was pleased by his praise, but before he could say anything, Black Eagle joined them.

"Wind Ryder—it was good that I wore the stallion down for you, wasn't it?" Black Eagle laughed.

"It was very good," Wind Ryder answered, laughing good-naturedly with him.

They turned their attention back to the corral where the brave was trying to mount the new horse.

Marissa quietly moved to the back of the crowd. Glancing around, she noticed that no one was keeping watch over her, and it looked like the villagers would be busy watching the warriors with the horses for some time to come.

The lure of freedom called to her.

She wondered if she dared try to get away now while everyone was so distracted. She quickly made her decision. Without drawing undue attention to herself, she edged her way through the gathering. As the villagers concentrated on the drama in the corral, Marissa slipped off.

Determination filled her as she walked calmly away. She wanted to break into a run, she wanted to flee as quickly as she could, but she forced herself to walk slowly. She headed

back toward where she had been working with the women earlier, hoping that by going in that direction, she would fool anyone who might see her into thinking she was returning to her work.

Marissa tried not to appear nervous, but a part of her wanted to keep looking around to make certain that the way was clear. Somehow, she controlled the desire. She walked at an even pace, appearing outwardly calm, while in truth her heart was beating a frantic rhythm. She was imagining herself away from the Comanche—

Free at last—

Going home.

Bear Claw and Snake had seen enough of Wind Ryder breaking the stallion. The cheers of the villagers had driven them away in disgust. They went to sit on the far side of the encampment. They did not want to listen to everyone singing his praise.

"Snake! Look!" Bear Claw spotted the white captive walking alone through the village. "Shining Spirit is by herself."

"No one's watching her," Snake agreed, surprised.

"I wonder where she is going. If she wanders away from the camp, she might not be found again."

"What of Wind Ryder? Should we tell him?"

Bear Claw gave him an angry look. "Why? He is the one who let her out of his sight. If she disappeared, no one would know what happened to her."

"There isn't much time." Nervousness took Snake as he thought about what Bear Claw wanted to do. Snake knew the fierceness of the revenge Wind Ryder would exact if he ever found out what had happened to her.

"I will do this alone." Bear Claw was disgusted that Snake was still worried about angering Wind Ryder. He didn't have the time

to argue with him. He knew what he wanted to do, and he was going to do it.

Bear Claw trailed after the white woman, watching her as she wandered farther from the gathering by the corral, heading ever away from the village.

Wind Ryder looked up from where he'd been standing with his father and Black Eagle to discover that Shining Spirit was nowhere to be seen. She had disappeared. His gaze swept over the villagers gathered there, and he found no trace of her. Knowing how badly she wanted to escape, he went to look for her without a word to the other men.

Chapter Eight

*M*arissa knew her plan might be dangerous. She didn't care. This might be the only chance she ever got to make her escape. She wished she could find a way to take a horse without being noticed, but that was impossible. The horses were the Comanche's most prized possessions. She resigned herself to the fact that whatever she was going to do, she would have to do on foot. Offering up a silent prayer, she forged ahead and never looked back.

Bear Claw followed Shining Spirit easily. He stayed behind her, silently stalking her, letting her get farther and farther away from the village. He would take her, but in his own good time. He did not want to risk anyone finding them.

The warrior smiled to himself as he imagined what he was going to do to Shining Spirit. He could not let her make any sound, though. No one could ever know what had happened, and when he was finished with her, he would make sure her body was never found.

Marissa tried not to get too excited as she stayed along the bank of the stream where the foliage was the heaviest and would shelter her passing. Her pace quickened as she drew away from the village.

Time was of the essence.

She had to get away while she could.

The terrain grew rockier, and Marissa was glad. It gave her more places where she could hide if necessary and made her trail harder to follow. She rushed on and kept her thoughts focused on being reunited with her uncle. She did not allow herself even to consider that Wind Ryder might discover she was missing and come after her. She permitted herself to have hope that she could do this.

And then the fierce-looking warrior stepped out in front of her.

Marissa stopped, horrified. She recognized the man as one of the savages from the raiding party, and she would have screamed, but he moved too quickly for her. Grabbing her, he covered her mouth with his hand before she had time to utter a sound. His hands on her body were brutal as he dragged her behind some bushes and wrestled her to the ground.

Bear Claw couldn't believe that he had taken Shining Spirit so easily. He had worried that she would fight him as she'd fought Snake, but she had offered little resistance. He grew even more confident. Things had gone better than he'd hoped. He smiled coldly down at her as he kept her mouth covered.

"My father should never have given you to Wind Ryder," he taunted in his native tongue as he roughly groped her breasts with his free hand.

Marissa had never been touched so intimately before. The shock of his hated hands upon her jarred her and started her fighting him in earnest. She struggled against his overpowering strength.

She had to get away from him!

She had to save herself, for there was no one else to do it.

Marissa swung out at him with her fists, trying to knock his hands away.

Bear Claw was more amused by her struggles than threatened by them. He was already hard with wanting her, and her resistance just heightened his lust. He was eager to take her, to abuse her.

"You will be a fine one to mount," he said, leering at her as he reached down to pull up the skirt of her buckskin dress. He was more than ready to bury himself between her thighs.

Marissa didn't know what he was saying, but she had a good idea. She kicked with all her might, trying to dislodge him, trying to keep him from touching her. She screamed against his hand and moved as violently as she could to escape his assault. His touch was painful and deliberately cruel, and she could only imagine what he was going to do to her next.

From the moment she'd been taken prisoner, she had lived in terror of just this moment—of being completely helpless before a Comanche attacker. The vicious warrior was far more powerful than she was, and he was intent upon his deed. It was her worst nightmare realized.

Thoughts of Wind Ryder came to Marissa. Her warrior hadn't exactly been kind to her, but he had not abused her in any way. Not like this. Her attacker pawed at her thighs and roughly shoved her legs apart in spite of her best efforts to keep them together. Marissa continued to try to resist him, but he was too strong for her.

She was helpless.

Still, Marissa fought on. No one would be coming to save her. She was alone. Her arms were free, and she desperately groped about on the ground beside her, hoping to find some weapon to use against him.

And then her hand closed on a rock.

Without any pause or thought, Marissa grabbed the rock and swung at him. Her blow caught him alongside the head and stunned him for an instant. Shocked as he was, he drew his hands

away, giving Marissa time to utter only one sharp cry for help before he viciously backhanded her.

"You will pay for that!" Bear Claw snarled, grabbing her wrists and pinning her arms above her head. Blood trickled from a cut high on his cheek, infuriating him even more.

Marissa was terror-driven. She continued to resist him, but there was little she could do except try to twist free.

Bear Claw laughed at her feeble efforts now. He could tell her strength was failing, and he was glad. He wanted her completely submissive beneath him.

Wind Ryder might have mounted and tamed the stallion, but he was going to mount and claim this woman.

Bear Claw knelt between her legs and leaned forward, pinning her body to the ground as he shoved her skirt up even higher and groped at her with cruel hands.

At first, Wind Ryder had not been too concerned that Shining Spirit was gone. He thought she might have returned to work with one of the other women. As he crossed the village looking for her, though, he saw no sign of her anywhere. The village was nearly deserted, for most of the people had gone to watch the men with the horses. He checked in his tipi, but found it empty. Finally he began to suspect that she might have tried to get away. He decided to circle the encampment and search for signs of her passing. It didn't take him long to discover her tracks. He immediately set out to bring her back.

Wind Ryder hadn't gone far when he noticed that another set of tracks covered hers, tracks belonging to a man. Tension grew within him. He stood silently for a moment looking ahead, frowning as he tried to imagine where she was going and who might be following her. Wind Ryder took care to be as quiet as possible as he hurried on. He hoped Shining Spirit hadn't gotten too far ahead.

The realization that he was worried about her startled Wind Ryder. He told himself he didn't care, that he was only going after Shining Spirit to bring her back because his father had given her to him. In truth, though, just the thought that someone might harm her infuriated him. A vision of the golden captive played in his mind as he tracked the path she'd taken.

The sound of a distant cry came to Wind Ryder, and he charged forward. The scene he came upon put him in a mindless rage. There before him was Bear Claw with blood on his cheek, attempting to rape Shining Spirit. Wind Ryder threw himself bodily at the other warrior and knocked him away from the help-less woman. The two men grappled in the brush in their fight for supremacy. Wind Ryder won easily, having taken Bear Claw by surprise. He pinned him to the ground and glared down at him with pure hatred in his eyes.

"She is mine!" Wind Ryder growled. "You do not take what is mine!"

"She wanted me. She lured me out here." Bear Claw lied, the lust he'd felt for the captive vanishing in the face of Wind Ryder's attack.

Wind Ryder knew different. He looked at Shining Spirit, who was trying to cover herself. She was dirty, her clothing was in disarray, and there was a mark on her face where she'd been struck. He knew she had not been trying to lure Bear Claw anywhere.

"The blood on your face and your trail tell me otherwise," he said with deadly intent.

Bear Claw realized his mistake too late. Wind Ryder was an expert tracker and would have known just by checking the trail that he had been following her, not walking by her side. He went still, trapped by his own lie and by the blood on his cheek where Shining Spirit had hit him.

Wind Ryder was furious. He wanted to draw his knife, but managed to control his rage as he stood up. He remained standing over Bear Claw, looking down at him, his expression savage.

"Go. Now." It was all Wind Ryder could say. He had been angry in the past with this man who was supposed to have been his brother, but never as angry as he was at this moment.

Bear Claw slowly got to his feet and, without looking back at the white woman, walked away. Fury filled him, too, but his need for revenge would have to wait.

Marissa had been visibly trembling as she'd watched Wind Ryder face down the other warrior. She had never thought she would be relieved to see him, but he appeared a savior to her right now as he stood there so tall and magnificent before her. He had driven the evil warrior away.

When Bear Claw had disappeared from sight and Wind Ryder looked her way, she suddenly felt naked and vulnerable before him. She struggled to cover herself again, but still felt exposed. Worse, Wind Ryder had seen the other man's hands upon her.

Wind Ryder stared down at Shining Spirit and saw the uncertainty in her eyes. He went to her.

Marissa was unsure of what to expect next. She wondered if he was going to finish what the other warrior had started. She waited, huddled and frightened, as he came toward her. When he bent down, she cowered away from him even more.

He understood her terror. In one move, he scooped her up into his arms and stood, carrying her much as he would a small child.

"I can walk," Marissa gasped in protest and looked up at him.

"I will carry you."

Their gazes locked.

For a long moment, they stared at each other. She searched his expression for some sign of danger, but found none. She sensed he

was no threat to her—she was safe. She drew a strangled breath as a shudder wracked her.

"Thank you," Marissa managed in a choked voice.

Wind Ryder did not respond, but turned back toward the village.

As he began to walk, Marissa looped her arms around his neck to steady herself. She allowed herself to lean against him, her emotions in turmoil. Anger over her failed escape attempt ate at her. She had believed she was going to get away, but she'd been terribly wrong. If Wind Ryder hadn't appeared, there was no telling what might have happened to her.

Thank God Wind Ryder had shown up when he did.

Marissa was shocked by the revelation that she truly was grateful to this warrior.

The power of her turbulent emotions was nearly overwhelming as she tried to accept her failure. She had to accept, too, that her fate was now sealed.

She was Wind Ryder's.

Wind Ryder's own thoughts were deeply troubled as he made his way back to his lodge with the golden one in his arms. He had not wanted to care about Shining Spirit. He had not wanted to get close to her. In truth, he'd wanted as little to do with her as possible; he had wanted to keep a physical distance between them. The less time he spent with this white woman, the better. But then he'd heard her cry out and had found Bear Claw about to rape her. In that moment, any semblance of indifference within him had been destroyed. It had jarred him to discover that he did care what happened to her, that he would protect her with his life.

Now, carrying her close to his heart, Wind Ryder felt a stirring of some strange emotion within him. The awakening disturbed him. He had guarded his heart and his soul for so long

now, he feared allowing himself to feel any tender emotion toward anyone—and especially toward a white woman.

It had been difficult enough for him through the years just seeing Crazy One around the camp. He had deliberately been harsh to her so she would stay away from him. He hadn't wanted to be reminded of his past life. He hadn't wanted to remember his white family and all that had been lost to him.

But that was over now.

This woman had changed everything.

Shining Spirit had proven herself to be a fierce fighter, yet as he held her in his arms right now, he was amazed at how delicate and fragile she was. Though he was angry with her for trying to escape, he had to admit that he was impressed by her courage. There were not many captive women who would have been brave enough to try.

They drew near the tipi, and Wind Ryder was glad it was late in the day. Once they returned to the lodge, he would make sure Shining Spirit did not leave it again that night. Though she was quiet now, he did not trust her to give up her attempts to reclaim her freedom. He had been the same way—at first. He did not trust Bear Claw, either, to accept the fact that Shining Spirit would never be his. He was going to stay with her and keep watch over her to make sure she was safe from all harm.

As Wind Ryder entered his lodge, he did not notice Snake watching him from across the campsite.

Snake saw Wind Ryder return, carrying the white captive, and he was instantly curious about what had happened to Bear Claw. Obviously, his friend's plan to take Shining Spirit had failed.

Snake went looking for Bear Claw to find out what had gone wrong. He found him a good distance from the camp, sitting alone, staring off into the gathering darkness.

"Bear Claw?" he called as he drew near. "What happened with Shining Spirit? I saw Wind Ryder take her back into his lodge."

The warrior turned to look at him. His expression was ugly, filled with hatred.

"Wind Ryder was tracking the white woman, too." He would not tell the other warrior any of what had happened. He would not admit his humiliation.

Snake could see the injury to Bear Claw's face, but did not remark on it. He knew just how ugly his friend's temper could be. "There will be another time," he reassured him.

"And I will be ready," Bear Claw snarled, the promise of violence in his voice.

Wind Ryder set Shining Spirit on her feet once they were inside the tipi.

Marissa looked up at him, uncertain of what was to come. "What do you want of me?"

"Lie down." His order was terse.

Marissa's reaction was immediate. She did as she was told, but she was surprised when he turned around and walked out of the lodge. He was gone for only moments, then returned with a rope in hand. Marissa swallowed nervously, knowing he was probably going to tie her up to keep her from trying to run away again. She had sealed her own fate with her failed attempt to escape.

Wind Ryder picked up his bedding and moved it next to hers, then sat down beside her. He saw her eyes widen as he reached for her leg, taking her by the calf just above the ankle.

Marissa stiffened, expecting him to be as rough with her as the other warrior had been. She was surprised when his hands were gentle upon her.

Wind Ryder pushed her skirt up a little. She tensed even more, and then he started to tie the rope around her ankle.

Wind Ryder stopped when he saw the bruises already forming on her legs. He knew they were from Bear Claw's rough handling of her, and his anger renewed itself, along with his determination never to let any harm come to her again.

"There is much danger here in the village," he told her, staring first at the bruises, then lifting his gaze to hers. "Do not try to run again."

He finished tying the rope to her ankle, then knotted the other end around his own. He lay back on his blankets and tried to relax, closing his eyes. It was still early in the evening, but he had no desire to leave her again that night.

Marissa stared at Wind Ryder, startled by this development. He seemed oblivious to her presence as he lay there beside her. She sat on her bedding for a moment, not certain what to do. Finally she stretched out next to him.

Marissa scooted away until the rope that bound them together brought her up short. She glanced nervously at the warrior to find his green-eyed gaze steady upon her. He made no move toward her, though, so she stopped where she was and lay still, closing her eyes. She knew that sleep would be long in coming, though.

Chapter Nine

Wind Ryder had known he wouldn't sleep much that night, but he had never imagined he would still be lying wide awake in the predawn darkness. The night had been long and troubling for him. Shining Spirit's presence disturbed him deeply. Several times he'd wanted to get up and leave the lodge, but bound to her as he was, he could not.

Glancing over at her now, Wind Ryder could make out the beauty of her features as she slept. She was relaxed, not wary or frightened, and looked even more lovely than before. He studied her, visually caressing her features. He thought of all the hardships she'd endured and survived. He understood her misery far better than she would ever know.

Wind Ryder stared off into the darkness, refusing to allow himself to think about his life before that fateful day when he'd been taken captive. He had long ago put the memories from him, for they caused too much pain.

Much had happened in the years since. He had managed to make a life for himself as one of the tribe. It had not been easy, but he had done it. His youth had helped him to adapt.

Shining Spirit, though, was older than he had been when he was captured. He wondered how she would deal with what had happened to her. How long would she mourn the life she'd left

behind? How long would it take her to accept that she would not be going back?

As if sensing that he was thinking of her, Shining Spirit stirred in her sleep. There was a chill in the night air. Unconsciously, she shifted closer to the warmth beside her, instinctively drawn there.

Wind Ryder all but groaned at the jolt of sensual awareness that went through him as she nestled against him. He would have moved away, but the rope bound them together. He was caught in a trap of his own making.

The powerful feelings Shining Spirit aroused in him were confusing. He found the innocent press of her body against him almost unbearable. Wind Ryder swallowed tightly, trying not to think about the softness of her breasts against his side.

His jaw locked as he fought for control, and sweat beaded his brow. He did not want to desire her. He did not want to care about her.

He looked down at the sleeping golden one and realized she was completely, blissfully unaware of his inner turmoil.

Wind Ryder wondered what the future would bring. He knew he would have to keep as much distance—physically and emotionally—between them as he could.

It would be better that way.

Marissa awoke slowly. She had found forgetfulness in sleep. She had been at peace.

She smiled, still keeping her eyes closed to enjoy the sensation. She was warm. She was safe. And she was—

Marissa almost gasped out loud as she finally opened her eyes to find herself staring at the broad expanse of Wind Ryder's tanned, hard-muscled chest. Suddenly she realized why she was so warm—she was curled up next to him! She thought about bolting, but the feel of the rope around her ankle held her immobile.

Wind Ryder hadn't moved, so she lifted her gaze to his face and discovered that he was still sleeping. Relief swept through her, and her tension eased. He had slept beside her all night, and no harm had come to her. If anything, she had been safer because of his nearness. After the attack by the other warrior, she was tempted to stay tied to Wind Ryder forever.

Marissa hadn't meant to smile, but the thought of being physically bound to this man, and riding double with him as he broke a stallion like he'd done the day before, almost made her laugh.

Wind Ryder awoke to find Shining Spirit watching him, a soft, gentle smile curving her lips. He had never seen her smile before, and he was amazed by the way it transformed her. He realized then that he wanted to see her smile more often.

"Oh! You're awake," Marissa gasped as she found his gaze upon her. Her smile instantly disappeared.

"I have not seen you smile before," he said in a quiet voice.

"There has been nothing to smile about."

"Perhaps that will change."

"You'll take me back?" she asked hopefully, quickly sitting up to face him.

"No. This is where you are to stay."

"But I don't belong here."

"You are mine."

"But you don't belong here either," she countered.

"This is my home."

"But it hasn't always been your home, has it? Where is your family?"

"Chief Ten Crow is my father, and Laughing Woman is my mother."

"But you're white. Where's your real family? Your white family? Were you taken captive, too, like I was?"

Wind Ryder's expression turned stony at her questions.

But Marissa wasn't about to be deterred.

"My name is Marissa Williams. What's yours?"

He did not answer, but sat up and worked at untying the rope that bound them together. He had to get away from her.

"One of the women will come for you." The tone of his voice had gone cold.

"But, Wind Ryder—why won't you—"

With that he was gone, leaving her alone in the lodge and her questions unanswered.

Marissa did not smile as she stared after him.

She wondered if she would ever smile again.

Louise lay in the bed in her room at the boardinghouse, staring listlessly out the window. Dr. Harrison had moved her there when she had begun to recover from her wound. He wanted her to stay in town for another week until she was physically strong enough to make the trip out to George Williams's ranch. So she was biding her time, waiting, worrying, and agonizing about Marissa.

A knock sounded at the door.

"Come in," Louise called out. It wasn't often she got visitors, and she was hoping it was someone with good news for her.

"Mrs. Bennett?" Sarah Collins let herself in. Her husband, Claude, worked for George and had ridden with him to find Marissa.

"Sarah, it's so good to see you," Louise said, her spirits lifting at the sight of her. Sarah had been coming to see her regularly, and Louise appreciated her visits very much. "Have you heard anything new? Has there been any word about Marissa at all?"

"No, none," Sarah answered honestly, knowing there was no point in lying. "It's too soon. They've barely been gone a week."

"How long could this take?" Louise asked, fearful of the answer.

"It could take months." Sarah saw Louise's devastated expression and empathized. "I'm sorry."

"There's nothing for you to be sorry for. It was foolish of me to hope we'd hear something already, but I've been so frantic, worrying about Marissa."

"We all have been, Mrs. Bennett," Sarah said kindly.

"Please, call me Louise."

"All right, Louise." They shared a warm smile, a silent acknowledgment of friendship formed in trying circumstances. "I just wanted to come to town to see how you were feeling. I spoke with the doctor, and he thought you might be recovered enough by the end of next week to make the trip out to the Crown. Are you about ready to come stay with us at the ranch?"

"I am more than ready."

Louise was relieved by the doctor's report. There were days when she wondered if she really was getting any better. The pain was great, and she was very weak, barely able to get up and move around by herself. It was good to know the doctor saw some improvement in her condition. He checked on her daily, and Tildy, the woman who ran the boardinghouse, kept a close eye on her, too.

"Sarah, have you ever been through anything like this before with the Comanche?" she asked. "I've heard terrible stories of how captives are treated. Do you honestly believe they'll be able to find Marissa and bring her home?"

Sarah was quiet for a long moment, then answered, "If anyone can find them, it will be George. He loves Marissa very much, and he's going to do everything in his power to track her down."

"But he's only a rancher going up against an entire tribe of Comanche."

"No, he's George Williams, and that's saying a lot in this country. Everyone knows what a determined man George can be when

he wants something. He took my husband, Claude, and Mark, one of the hands from the ranch, with him. Mark is quite fond of Marissa and was looking forward to seeing her again. George also hired a man named Hawk from the livery in town to help with the tracking. I've heard he's very good at it."

"I wish I had been more help to them." Louise sighed. Her memory of meeting George was vague, for she'd been very weak and feverish that day. She just remembered he was a determined, angry man.

"There was nothing more you could do. George was just thankful you were alive," Sarah said kindly as she smiled at Louise. She wanted to offer her what comfort she could.

"When will we know for sure that I can make the trip out to the ranch?"

"Dr. Harrison said he'd make the decision the first of the week."

"Good. At least that gives me something to look forward to."

"I'll see about finding you some clothes, too."

Louise suddenly realized her desperate and destitute situation. "But I don't have any money. Everything I brought with me was lost in the raid."

"Don't worry about a thing. It'll be fine. George is taking care of everything."

"I'll have to find a way to pay him back."

"I wouldn't worry about it. He told me to take care of you while he was gone, and I intend to do just that."

Louise was touched by his kindness, and tears shone in her eyes. "Thank you."

Sarah stayed on to visit with her for a time, then left when Louise showed signs of tiring. She promised to return later in the week or sooner if she received any word from the men.

George Williams's mood was grim as the search party continued on across the vast, untamed expanses of West Texas. The days they'd spent tracking Marissa had been hell for him. He longed to find her quickly, to bring her safely home, but with each passing day and each passing mile, he knew his chances of finding her safe and unharmed were lessening.

"I don't like the look of those storm clouds up ahead," Hawk told George as he dismounted to check the trail. "We've been lucky so far, but if we get rain ..."

The two men shared a knowing look.

If the trail washed out, they would be lost. There would be no way to track the raiding party that had taken Marissa.

"We'd better keep moving, then," George said, his determination never fading.

Hawk nodded and mounted up. He led the way, following the trail they hoped would lead them to the missing girl.

Hawk had realized George had had trouble dealing with him at first, but he was used to that kind of reaction from folks. There weren't many white people who could ignore his Indian blood. Over the course of the last week, though, as they'd worked together to find the stolen woman, the two men had come to regard each other with mutual respect.

"Let's ride," George urged.

George knew the other men were tired, but he was not about to give up on his niece. He would not rest. He wanted to stay on the trail of the raiding party while they could. He wouldn't quit until he had Marissa back.

As they continued on, George's thoughts turned to Louise Bennett, and he wondered how she was doing. He hoped her recovery was going well. Doc Harrison was a good man, and George was sure the physician would do all he could to help her.

George felt sorry for the woman—for all that she'd been through. She was a lady, and life was hard in West Texas. She'd found that out firsthand. He hoped he could show her it wasn't all bad when he returned with Marissa.

George was trying to convince himself that that day would come when the storm hit.

Hawk had feared the threatening weather, and with good reason. The power the storm unleashed was brutal. Violent lightning strikes exploded an around them, but Hawk refused to stop until they absolutely had to. When the torrent hit full-force, there could be no continuing. The four riders sought what shelter they could find in overhangs among the rocks. They hoped that it would hit quickly and move on.

But the storm was a vicious one, lasting nearly an hour. It was a gully-washer. The downpour scoured the land with its torrential rains and high winds.

With every passing minute, George's rage against the heavens grew. His scowl darkened, and his mood turned as black as the sky overhead.

Mark and Claude could see the change in their boss's expression, and they understood. After a storm like this, there would be nothing left for them to follow. Hawk was one of the best trackers they'd ever seen, but he wasn't a miracle worker.

Hawk studied the clouds, looking for a sign that the storm would be letting up soon, but it continued. He stared out across the rain-soaked land, his expression stony. There was nothing they could do but wait it out.

And finally the storm started to let up.

The parched land had been thirsting for a good rain. Streams flowed now, where earlier there had only been rock beds. The sky overhead lightened as the cloud cover lifted.

"Wait here," Hawk told George and the others.

They understood. They stayed with the horses as Hawk moved out alone in an effort to find any trace left of the trail they'd been following.

The time passed slowly for George. He knew that the longer it took Hawk to come back for them, the worse the news was going to be. It was nearly an hour later when Hawk returned.

"What did you find?" George asked hopefully, but deep inside he already knew the answer.

"Nothing. Everything's been washed away," Hawk told him. "We can ride on a mile or so in the direction we were heading and check there. It might not have rained so hard farther out, and we might get lucky and be able to pick up the trail again."

"Let's go." George was ready.

Hawk didn't have much hope as he led the way. It had been difficult enough tracking the Comanche over the rocky terrain before the heavy rainfall, but now it was proving impossible.

Several hours passed before they stopped their search.

"George—there's nothing more we can do," Hawk told him, his own frustration as great as the rancher's.

"No!" George argued. "I'm not giving up."

"We have to keep going!" Mark insisted.

Claude knew, as Hawk did, that they had reached a dead end. There was no way of knowing which direction the raiding party had gone.

"They could be anywhere out there," Claude said, looking across the vast, empty land.

"I'll go on alone," George declared. Miserably, he knew Hawk was right. The storm had been too severe, but his desperate need to save Marissa was driving him. He couldn't abandon her to the torturous life he knew would be hers in a Comanche village. "You go on back. I'll be fine."

He kneed his horse onward, not looking at the other men.

"You're not going without me," Mark said, riding to his side.

Hawk glanced at Claude, then nodded toward George and Mark.

They fell in behind them.

Chapter Ten

*M*arissa had been nervous and uneasy for most of the morning as she'd worked with the women. She'd been fearful that Bear Claw might come after her again. Wind Ryder seemed to have left camp, and she felt vulnerable.

As the morning aged, thoughts of Wind Ryder drove Marissa to seek out Crazy One. She'd hoped the old woman would join her in working with the others, but it seemed she liked to keep to herself. Marissa supposed that was part of the reason why they'd given her the name Crazy One. The old woman was sitting alone by the stream, working with some hides when Marissa found her.

"You are working hard," Marissa noted as she went to stand beside her.

"Always—always." Crazy One suddenly looked a little worried. "Wind Ryder isn't coming after you, is he?"

"No," Marissa said.

"Good. He's starting to trust you."

Marissa wondered how he could trust her after her escape attempt the day before, but no one had tried to stop her when she'd left the tipi. "I haven't seen him since early this morning."

Marissa wanted to understand him, but was finding it difficult. That was why she wanted to talk to Crazy One. She hoped she

could learn something about Wind Ryder's past that would help her deal with him.

"May I sit with you for a while?" Marissa asked.

Crazy One nodded as she continued her work.

Marissa sat down on the bank beside her. It was a peaceful place, shady and quiet. She understood why the other woman liked to work there.

"I wanted to ask you about Wind Ryder," Marissa began hesitantly.

Crazy One gave her a cautious look. "What about him?"

"How long has he been with the tribe? Was he very young when he was taken?"

"I have watched him grow."

"So he was young," she said thoughtfully.

"He was only this tall," Crazy One went on, holding her hand at the height of about a six- or seven-year-old child. "And he was so afraid." Her expression turned sad.

"Why are you sad?"

"I went to him. I knew what he was going through, and I wanted to comfort him."

Marissa could imagine how terrifying his capture must have been to a small boy. She was a grown woman, and she was still frightened. "That was kind of you."

"He was a warm child—a gentle child. He reminded me of my own son—"

"You had a son?" Marissa was shocked by the news. She stared at Crazy One, trying to envision her as she'd been all those years ago.

Crazy One nodded. "I had a husband and two children—a boy and a girl. My husband was killed by the raiding party that attacked our ranch. They took me and the children, but they separated us. They traded me to Chief Ten Crow, and I never saw my son or daughter again."

Marissa's heart was breaking for her. She reached out to touch her hand in sympathy.

Crazy One jerked her hand away as if she'd been burned. She turned back to her work, holding herself rigid.

"If Wind Ryder reminded you of your son, why are you so frightened of him now?"

"It was Chief Ten Crow," she said as she looked up again. "He beat me when he found me with the boy. He told me to stay away from him."

"Why would he do that?"

"The chief wanted him to forget his white past. He wanted him to become a Comanche—and Wind Ryder did. Later, as he grew older, whenever Wind Ryder saw me, he would chase me away."

Marissa's heart ached for her and the horror that her life had been. Her heart ached for Wind Ryder, too, who as a small boy had been torn from his family and forced to survive in a world foreign to him in all ways—a world without any warmth or love. She could only guess that Wind Ryder chased Crazy One away because her presence reminded him of what it had been like when he'd first come to the village and of all that had been lost to him.

"Do you ever think about running away?" Marissa asked.

"Oh no," Crazy One answered seriously. "I couldn't go back. Not now. Oh, no. But Wind Ryder—he tried to escape when he was little. But they found him each time and brought him back. He was a brave one—Chief Ten Crow saw that in him. That's why he took him as his son."

It surprised Marissa to learn that Wind Ryder had tried to escape, and it also gave her a glimmer of hope that that same little boy still existed somewhere inside the fierce warrior Wind Ryder had become. All she had to do was find a way to reach that part of

him and make him understand how badly she wanted to return to her family in the white world.

Marissa remained there with Crazy One for a little longer, then left to make her way back to the camp.

"Look, Moon Cloud! There she comes now," Soaring Dove told her friend as she saw Shining Spirit returning.

"I was hoping she had run away or maybe drowned in the creek," Moon Cloud snarled.

"The water is not deep enough." Her friend laughed.

"That is a shame."

"So, have you made your plan."

"Oh yes. Tonight I will go to him. Tonight I will tell Wind Ryder of my love."

Soaring Dove smiled. "It is good. You have waited long enough."

"I want him and I will make him mine," Moon Cloud declared.

She grew excited as she thought of the night to come. Among her people, if a maiden was interested in a particular warrior, she could sneak into his lodge at night and let him know of her feelings. That was her plan for tonight. By morning, she was certain she would have Wind Ryder's heart.

Moon Cloud glanced toward the white captive who shared Wind Ryder's lodge, and her lip curled in disgust. She hated the white woman.

Tonight she would teach Shining Spirit her place in the village.

Tonight she would make Wind Ryder hers.

Wind Ryder deliberately stayed away from the village for most of the day. He had ridden out early to hunt with several other

warriors. While on the hunt, he'd found himself thinking about Shining Spirit and worrying about her, and that had irritated him. He wasn't used to caring about others or fearing for anyone's safety. Wind Ryder wanted to believe that Bear Claw would not try to harm her again, but a sense of distrust and uneasiness stayed with him, distracting him.

Returning to camp late in the afternoon, Wind Ryder was anxious to seek out Shining Spirit and reassure himself that she had come to no harm during his absence. He saw no sign of Bear Claw in the village and was glad. He didn't know where his adopted brother was, and he didn't care. He just wanted to make sure the other man stayed away from Shining Spirit.

Wind Ryder walked toward the group of working women.

Marissa had been scraping hides ever since she'd returned from her visit with Crazy One. She had not seen Wind Ryder anywhere in camp, and so she stayed there, passing the time and honing skills she had never, even in her wildest dreams, thought she would master.

As Wind Ryder strode across the camp, he saw her safely working with the women. The feeling of relief that filled him annoyed him even more than his earlier anxiety. When she looked up and saw him, he again felt a strange emotion tug at him. He scowled.

Marissa had somehow instinctively known that Wind Ryder was near. At the sight of him striding toward her, her heart actually skipped a beat, surprising her. Her gaze went over him. He was tall and powerful, and there was an air of arrogance about him that set him apart. He was a man to be reckoned with. She could understand why Chief Ten Crow had wanted to adopt him. Marissa tried to imagine him walking toward her dressed as a gentleman would dress in New Orleans. She pictured him with his hair cut, wearing a suit and tie. The image was striking, and she looked away.

"Come, Shining Spirit," he dictated as he came to stand before her.

Delighted to be away from the women, Marissa quickly rose to obey him. He nodded and led her to the chief's tent. There, they shared the evening meal with Ten Crow and Laughing Woman. Wind Ryder only spoke Comanche with them, so again Marissa was at a loss. She merely sat in silence, eating and waiting for the visit to end.

"Bear Claw is not here?" Wind Ryder asked his father.

"He left with a raiding party this afternoon," Ten Crow told him.

"This is good. I do not want him near Shining Spirit," he told his father. He went on to explain what his brother had done to Shining Spirit the day before.

Chief Ten Crow's expression darkened at the news. Again he found himself worrying about what was going to happen in the future between his sons. Shining Spirit was supposed to make things better—not worse.

Night came far too quickly for Wind Ryder's peace of mind, and he realized he could linger there no longer. He stood to go, and Marissa did the same. She followed him outside.

Wind Ryder led the way to his own tipi. He knew there could be no avoiding it—it was time for them to bed down for the night.

While he'd had his father's conversation to distract him, he'd been able to ignore Shining Spirit's presence. Alone with her in the darkness now, her hair silvered by the moon's pale glow, he was acutely aware of her. Soon he would be lying with her in the privacy of his lodge. Wind Ryder was concentrating so hard on convincing himself that he could make it through the night without touching her, he did not notice Moon Cloud watching him as they passed through the village.

Marissa walked quietly by Wind Ryder's side, unaware of his inner turmoil. She was nervous in her own right. It was time again to bed down for the night. She wondered if he would insist on sleeping beside her again. She glanced up at him as they reached the tipi, and he brushed aside the door flap to enter.

"Will you bind me to you again tonight?" Marissa asked as she followed him inside.

"Yes." Wind Ryder's answer was terse.

"There is no need. I will not run away again," she said.

Wind Ryder managed to give her a cold look of distrust as he reached for the rope.

"Lie down," he directed, going to her.

Marissa lay down on the blankets as he'd ordered and waited as he tied the rope securely around her leg. The night before, she'd been afraid, thinking about what might happen, but tonight the warmth of his hands upon her leg sent an unexpected thrill through her. She looked on without saying anything more as he tied the other end of the rope to his own leg and then made himself comfortable.

"Did the Comanche tie you up like this when you were little to keep you from running away?" she asked quietly.

"Captives must be trained to obey," he answered without emotion.

"That must have been hard for you—as a child."

"Go to sleep," he ordered, not wanting to discuss his past with her. He was already far too aware of her....

"Good night," she said softly as she closed her eyes, pulling the blanket up over herself.

Her gentle words touched a chord within him, but he did not let on. He kept his eyes closed and only grunted in response.

He made sure to lie so he was not touching her in any way.

He wanted to sleep.

He hoped he could.

Moon Cloud waited breathlessly for the village to quiet. She had watched Wind Ryder return to his lodge and couldn't wait for the moment to go to him. She knew the white woman would be there, but she didn't care. If anything, she would humiliate Shining Spirit tonight when she made the handsome warrior hers and hers alone.

Smiling at the thought, Moon Cloud gazed up at the night sky. The moon and stars shone brightly above her. Everything was perfect. All she had to do was go to Wind Ryder and declare her love for him. She had wanted him for what seemed like forever, and now she was going to have him.

Moon Cloud admitted to herself that her experience with other warriors should help her. She had met a few of the other men under the cover of night to taunt and tease them, but she had never wanted any of them the way she wanted Wind Ryder.

An ache grew deep within her in anticipation of the long, hot, exciting hours to come.

Soon she would be lying with him.

Soon she would feel the heat of his flesh next to hers.

Moon Cloud wandered away into the darkness to calm herself.

It was not quite time yet—

But it would be soon.

Wind Ryder stirred at the press of the lush feminine body against him. He did not open his eyes, but gritted his teeth against the unbidden desire that pounded through him. Shining Spirit must have rolled over in her sleep to end up pressed so tightly to him. He told himself that if he didn't move and just stayed quiet, he would be able to keep himself under control until she moved away again. He thought it odd that the close contact with him hadn't awakened her, but then realized she was probably too exhausted to awaken easily tonight.

And then the woman's hands were upon him—aggressively.

The caress was very intimate and very knowing as a woman's voice—not Shining Spirit's—breathed in his ear, "Wind Ryder—I want you."

He tensed at the sound of her voice, and his eyes flew open to find it was Moon Cloud who had slipped beneath his blanket— Moon Cloud who'd been caressing him. She was raising herself up over him now as she gave him a knowing, hungry smile.

"You want me, too—I can tell," she purred with confidence as she hiked her skirt up and ground her naked hips against the hardness of his need.

Moon Cloud gazed down at him, a look of pure hunger on her face. She knew the white woman was in the tipi, but she didn't care.

All she cared about was Wind Ryder.

All she wanted was Wind Ryder.

She was offering herself to him completely—freely. She wanted him to lose control and make love to her. It surprised her more than a little when he did not instantly grab her and bring her beneath him to make her his.

"Wind Ryder—" Moon Cloud said his name breathlessly, wanting him—needing him—urging him on. She leaned down and kissed him fully and hungrily.

Wind Ryder took her by the upper arms and pushed her away from him. "Moon Cloud? No."

Marissa had been sleeping, but awoke when she felt the rustling beside her.

Sitting up in confusion, Marissa found the Comanche woman with her dress hiked up to her waist, sitting astride Wind Ryder. He was holding her by the arms and seemed to be enjoying that very intimate contact.

Moon Cloud was startled when Marissa sat up right next to them. She had been so intent on making love to Wind Ryder that

she hadn't noticed the other woman sleeping so close beside him. She had expected her to be bedded down across the lodge.

"Moon Cloud—you must go. Leave now!" Wind Ryder told her, lifting her off him. He quickly got to his feet and stood, glaring down at her.

"You want me! I could feel your desire," she said defiantly. "It does not matter that the white one is here. She could watch us and learn how to please a man—for I would please you well." She murmured the last in a suggestive tone and ran the tip of her tongue across her lips.

"The desire you felt was not for you," he said, showing her the rope that bound him to Marissa. "Go now."

Moon Cloud stood up, her humiliation complete. She jerked her skirt back down and started to storm from the lodge. She paused to look back once in the hope that Wind Ryder might have changed his mind, but he was staring after her, his expression cold and inscrutable. Moon Cloud glanced down at the white woman and found her watching, smiling triumphantly. Shining Spirit's smile only made Moon Cloud's rejection more complete. She stomped away into the night, filled with fury.

Chapter Eleven

*M*arissa was glad Moon Cloud had gone. The other woman had obviously wanted Wind Ryder, but for some reason he'd turned her down. When he sat back down on the blanket beside her, Marissa looked over at him.

"You are smiling," Wind Ryder pointed out, remembering how the night before she'd said there was little to smile about.

"She is gone," Marissa replied.

"You are glad?" he asked. The heat that had risen in his body was still with him.

"Yes."

Their gazes met. A silence stretched between them there in the intimate confines of the lodge.

The recognition of the power of his desire shocked Wind Ryder even as he realized he'd wanted Shining Spirit all along. He could deny it no longer after his reaction to Moon Cloud.

Moon Cloud was an attractive woman. She could have been his for the taking. But he had not wanted her. He wanted Shining Spirit.

Marissa was entranced by the wonder of Wind Ryder's gaze. The jealousy she'd felt when she'd seen the other woman trying to seduce Wind Ryder had shocked her. She'd thought this man meant nothing to her, but now Marissa wondered what she truly

did feel for him. What she had learned about Wind Ryder from Crazy One had touched her deeply. There was much more to him than just the fierce and fearless warrior.

"Do women throw themselves at you that way often?" Marissa asked.

He gave a slight shrug.

"You could give me my own tipi. Then you would be alone so you could—"

"You will stay here with me," he stated firmly, his gaze still upon her. His voice lowered as he added, "This is where I want you to be."

Wind Ryder was drawn to Shining Spirit. He shifted closer to her, wanting to kiss her, wanting to taste the sweetness of her. The need he felt for her was overpowering, undeniable. He lifted one hand to gently cup her cheek, and then his lips sought hers in a tender-soft caress.

A thrill shot through Marissa at the touch of his lips. She held her breath as Wind Ryder took her in his arms. She was so caught up in the moment that she almost succumbed to the temptation, but then the memory of Moon Cloud's brazen attempt to seduce him returned. She drew back, pulling away from him, ending the embrace.

"No," she whispered, unsure that the desire he was feeling was really for her and not left over from the other woman's passionate ploys.

Wind Ryder stared down at Shining Spirit, surprised by her withdrawal from him. He said nothing as she lay down with her back to him and drew the blanket up over herself.

The fire of his need burned within him. He had felt her response to him. He was tempted to go to her and take her in his arms, to kiss her again and force her to admit that she desired him as much as he desired her, but he held himself back.

Marissa lay quietly beside him, waiting to see what he would do. She knew she was taking a chance. If Wind Ryder wanted to take her, he was certainly strong enough to force her to his will. She would not be able to fight him off for long. She was tense as she anticipated what was to come.

Wind Ryder fought down the heat in his body and lay back on his blankets. There were still many hours until sunrise, and he hoped to somehow find a way to sleep. Shining Spirit's presence beside him was both arousing and comforting. He wanted her, and he also wanted to be sure she was safe. In frustration, he closed his eyes to await the dawn.

Several hours passed, and still Wind Ryder could find no rest. His body was on fire with the hunger he felt for the golden one, and he reached out idly to caress one soft golden curl. Even that simple touch proved a mistake. Her hair was silky and begged a man's caress, and yet he was forbidden that pleasure.

He wanted to kiss her.

He wanted to caress her.

He wanted to slip between her silken thighs and possess her fully—to lose himself within her and seek the perfection that only their union could bring.

But she had said no.

Fighting for control, Wind Ryder carefully sat up and untied the rope from his own leg. There was no way he could spend the rest of the night so close to her without making love to her. She stirred slightly as he got up and she murmured something in a soft voice, but she did not awake.

Wind Ryder was glad.

He left the tipi and went straight to the stream. Stripping, he walked out into the flowing water. Its iciness cut through him like a knife, but the pain was worth it to him. The cold water did what

he'd hoped it would do—it successfully killed the fiery, passionate need within him.

The relief he felt was great.

When he finally left the stream, Wind Ryder dressed and remained sitting there on the bank for the rest of the night. He did not trust himself to return to the lodge—not after having kissed her.

Marissa was surprised when she awoke and found it was morning. As upset as she'd been, she hadn't expected to get much rest that night. But eventually she had fallen asleep, and the hours had flown. Girding herself for a confrontation with Wind Ryder after all that had happened, she rolled over.

Marissa was shocked to discover her warrior had already left the lodge. She must have been sleeping deeply not to have awakened when he'd left her side. She wondered when he'd gone and where.

For an instant, she wondered if he'd gone after Moon Cloud, but then she remembered the kiss he had given her. If he had wanted Moon Cloud, he could have taken her last night. Certainly, the other woman had been ready and willing. But he had sent Moon Cloud away.

Wind Ryder had kissed *her*.

Even as she thought about Wind Ryder's kiss, she smiled. She had told him no, and he had stopped. He could have taken her against her will—certainly he was strong enough to force her, but he had not. Warmth filled her as she found, to her amazement, that she was beginning to trust him, and with that trust also came respect.

Marissa arose to start the new day.

Soaring Dove had been anxiously watching for Moon Cloud to appear that morning. She could hardly wait to hear all about the night just past. She had no doubt that Wind Ryder would soon be taking Moon Cloud as his wife. When she saw her friend come out of her tipi, she hurried over to speak with her. She saw that Moon Cloud looked tired and believed that was a good sign.

"You had a good night, Moon Cloud?" Soaring Dove asked, giving her a knowing smile.

Moon Cloud scowled at her.

"Is something wrong? What happened? I thought you had it all planned."

"I will tell you later," Moon Cloud answered curtly.

"It was not good?"

When Moon Cloud gave her a discouraging look, Soaring Dove fell silent, shocked by her unspoken message.

Moon Cloud was glad that she'd managed to silence Soaring Dove's questions. The last thing Moon Cloud wanted to do was stand there in the middle of the village talking about what had happened between her and Wind Ryder. Her fury was still raging, and she had yet to give vent to her tears.

The pain she felt over Wind Ryder's rejection was real. She had loved him for a long time and had always believed that one day he would be hers. Now, it seemed that dream would never come true.

She felt humiliated and angry, and she hated the white captive with a passion. The woman had dared to smile at her humiliation! Somehow, Moon Cloud vowed to herself, she would find a way to exact revenge upon her.

Moon Cloud and Soaring Dove went to join the other women, only to find that Shining Spirit was already there, working beside Laughing Woman. Moon Cloud was angered by her presence, but knew she could do nothing about it.

They settled in to work. The hours passed slowly.

Marissa was well aware that Moon Cloud had come to join them and that the other woman was watching her closely. She pretended to ignore her, concentrating on the task Laughing Woman had given her. She had to admit to herself, though, that she was glad everything had gone as it had the night before. She could just imagine her own embarrassment if Wind Ryder had taken Moon Cloud up on her offer and she'd had to witness their lovemaking.

Moon Cloud stared at Shining Spirit.

"She is truly the ugliest white woman I have ever seen," she said to Soaring Dove.

"And she is stupid, too," her friend agreed, laughing at the way Shining Spirit was doing her work.

A few of the other women chuckled at her remark, for they knew the captive was still learning their ways and was not very proficient at her tasks.

Marissa sensed they were laughing at her and again cursed the barrier of language that kept her from understanding all that was going on around her. She'd been trying to pick up words and phrases, but was having little success. When Laughing Woman gestured for her to come along, she was glad of the reprieve. Rising, she started to follow Laughing Woman.

Moon Cloud saw her opportunity for revenge, and she took it. As the captive walked past her, she deliberately stuck her foot out. She laughed uproariously as Shining Spirit tripped and fell face down in the dirt. Soaring Dove was laughing, too.

"Not only is she ugly and stupid, she is clumsy, too!" Moon Cloud said loud enough for everyone to hear.

Marissa had been born a lady.

She had been raised a lady.

But there came a time when enough was enough.

Any semblance of the Marissa Williams who'd charmed New Orleans society vanished in that instant. She was mad—fighting mad. She surged to her feet in righteous fury and without pausing, launched herself at the laughing Moon Cloud.

Marissa knew very little about physical fighting, but she didn't care. With all her might, she began to pummel the other woman. She landed several punishing blows to her face before Moon Cloud got over her shock at being attacked and began to fight back.

Soaring Dove and the other village women scrambled to get out of their way as the two grappled in the dirt.

Marissa and Moon Cloud rolled on the ground, kicking and punching, each shrieking in anger.

"Should we stop them?" one of the women asked.

"Why?" Soaring Dove returned smugly. "Shining Spirit will get what she deserves."

Laughing Woman, however, thought differently. She was too old to pull them apart herself, so she ran to find Wind Ryder.

Marissa had never been in any kind of physical confrontation before. Moon Cloud's blows were painful, but they were not enough to stop her.

They continued to battle, scratching and clawing, yanking and punching. They were both bleeding and filthy, but neither thought of quitting.

Moon Cloud had been shocked by Shining Spirit's attack. She had thought the woman would be easily intimidated and tormented, but she realized now, as she snared a handful of her blonde hair, that she'd been wrong.

Marissa responded with a cry of pain and hit out at her rival, bloodying her lip. Moon Cloud grabbed a handful of dirt then and tried to throw it in her face, but Marissa was able to block her arm just in time to stop her.

"Wind Ryder was to be mine!" Moon Cloud shrieked as she tried to throw off her opponent.

Moon Cloud had just spoken those words when suddenly the white captive's weight was lifted from her. She looked up to see Wind Ryder standing over her, holding Shining Spirit with her back against his chest. The white woman was trying to break free of him, but his grip on her was as ungiving as iron.

"No, Moon Cloud. I was never yours. If I had wanted you, I would have taken you," Wind Ryder told her. His tone was angry, but the words were only loud enough for her to hear. He did not want to debase her any further than he already had the night before, but he did want to discourage her from thinking that he cared anything for her. He also wanted to warn her away from Shining Spirit. "Shining Spirit is my woman." He said the Comanche words to her first, and then looked up at those who were gathered around. "Know this—Shining Spirit is my woman. I have taken her as my wife."

He was making the announcement to let everyone know that Shining Spirit was not to be abused in any way. As his captive, she had been his property, but by proclaiming her his wife, he was giving her his complete protection. He didn't want a wife, but then he hadn't wanted a captive either. Now, no one would dare try to harm her. She would be safer this way.

"Shining Spirit is Wind Ryder's woman—" A murmur of interest spread through the onlookers.

Marissa was totally unaware of what Wind Ryder had just said. She didn't want to listen to all this Comanche talk. She just wanted to get loose and go after Moon Cloud again.

"Let me go!" Marissa was shouting, swinging her fists and violently trying to twist free.

Wind Ryder ignored her command and walked away with her, carrying her easily in spite of her protests.

The villagers watched them go, smiling to themselves at the sight.

Moon Cloud struggled to her feet and stared after him.

"You would have beaten her," Soaring Dove told her, trying to be supportive. "Too bad Wind Ryder showed up when he did."

"It does not matter," Moon Cloud said, and in that moment she meant it. She was thoroughly disgusted with Wind Ryder, and angry with herself for having thought he was worthy of her love. She had been foolish. He was not worth it. Wind Ryder was welcome to his ugly, stupid white wife. "It does not matter any more about Wind Ryder."

"It doesn't? You don't care?" Soaring Dove was surprised.

Moon Cloud smiled at her friend. "If he wants a white wife, he can have her. I will waste no more time on him." She lifted her gaze to look around the camp.

"You won't?" Soaring Dove's tone was disbelieving.

"No. I want to see Running Dog. Do you know where he is?"

"Running Dog?" Soaring Dove's eyes widened in surprise at her friend's complete change of heart. "When I last saw him, he was working with the horses."

"Good. As soon as I have cleaned myself up, I think I will have to run an errand by the corral." She moved toward her own tipi.

Soaring Dove was surprised that Moon Cloud had set her sights on another warrior so quickly, but then she realized she shouldn't have been. Moon Cloud wanted a man, and since she wasn't going to get Wind Ryder, she was ready to go after her second choice. Soaring Dove smiled to herself and returned to her work with the women.

Chapter Twelve

arissa was still wriggling against Wind Ryder's hold as he crossed the village, but he tightened his grip around her waist and she stopped. She felt almost like a recalcitrant child as he stormed back toward the lodge. She didn't know what was about to happen, but she knew he was angry.

And this time he was angry with her.

Once they were inside the tipi, Wind Ryder released Shining Spirit. He stood there glaring down at her. She was filthy from head to toe, and her hair was in disarray. A bruise was forming on her cheek, and one of her knees was cut and bleeding.

Wind Ryder had to admit he was proud that she'd held her own with Moon Cloud. Judging from the way the other woman had acted, he could imagine how the fight had come about. It surprised him and pleased him that Shining Spirit had been so fierce.

And he had claimed her as his wife—

He did not regret his words, for they would keep her safe, but he had no intention of telling her what he'd done. She had no interest in being his wife, and he had no interest in having a wife. Things would continue as they had between them, but the rest of the tribe didn't need to know that. In the eyes of the village, they were married.

Wind Ryder found that Shining Spirit was looking up at him now, defiantly meeting his gaze straight on. It seemed as if she were ready to fight him, too.

"You are bleeding," Wind Ryder said, unthinkingly speaking to her in Comanche.

Marissa was angry already.

She had just been forced to fight another woman, and now he was speaking to her in the foreign tongue and that made her even more furious.

"Speak English!" Marissa all but shouted at him.

"You are bleeding," Wind Ryder repeated in English, realizing his mistake.

"Well, Moon Cloud is bleeding more," she shot back at him, lifting her chin.

"And you are dirty," he pointed out.

"Moon Cloud's dirtier!" she countered again.

"Well, I am not sleeping with Moon Cloud," Wind Ryder pointed out. "Let's go."

"Go where?" She eyed him cautiously.

"We're going to the stream so you can get cleaned up," he dictated, starting toward the door of the lodge.

"I'm not going to take a bath in front of you!"

"Yes, Shining Spirit, you are," he stated easily, confident of what he was about to do.

"My name's Marissa—not Shining Spirit!" she ground out. "Say it! Marissa!"

Wind Ryder ignored her as he crossed to where she was standing. In one easy move, he lifted her up and threw her over his shoulder.

Marissa grunted at being so manhandled.

"What do you think you're doing?" She shouted, the wind knocked out of her by his unexpected ploy. "Stop!" She started

pounding on his back as he left the tipi and headed for the stream. "Put me down! How dare you?"

Wind Ryder didn't pause or bother to argue with her. Her protests meant nothing to him. He barely felt her blows. She needed a bath, and she was going to get one. He hoped the shock of the cold water would cool down her temper. She was certainly a wild one when she got angry. He suppressed an unbidden smile.

Word of the fight between Moon Cloud and Shining Spirit had spread through the village, along with the news that Wind Ryder had taken the white captive as his wife.

When Crazy One heard this, she grew worried about Shining Spirit. She went to hover near Wind Ryder's tipi, fearful that something bad might have happened to Shining Spirit. She was still afraid of Wind Ryder, but she was concerned for the other captive woman.

Crazy One knew that Shining Spirit would be more respected and protected in the village as Wind Ryder's wife, but she also knew that Shining Spirit wanted to go home to her family. There would be no chance of that happening now.

When Wind Ryder came out of the lodge carrying Shining Spirit over his shoulder, Crazy One gasped and darted away to hide. She admired the white captive even more as she watched them. For although Shining Spirit was dirty and bruised, she was fighting him as best she could—considering her position.

Trailing after them, the old woman was ready to go to the younger's aid if he tried to harm her in any way. It was the bravest thing she'd done in years, but she'd come to like Shining Spirit and didn't want to see her hurt.

Others in the village heard Shining Spirit shouting at Wind Ryder, and they came rushing out to see what was going on. They found the sight of the warrior carrying his female captive amusing

and decided to follow the pair. They all stayed back a distance, fearful of angering Wind Ryder by appearing too eager to know his business. He was a mighty warrior, a man to be reckoned with, and nobody wanted to make him mad.

Wind Ryder was so preoccupied with keeping Shining Spirit under control that he didn't pay any attention to those around him. He stalked straight down to the water's edge.

"Put me down! What do you think you're doing?" Marissa yelled. "Put me down now!"

Without ceremony or warning, Wind Ryder did just what she had demanded. He lifted her off his shoulder and tossed her straight into the deepest pool in the stream.

Marissa let out a scream as she landed with a big splash in the ice-cold water. Furious and indignant, she struggled to her feet. Her knee was stinging where it had been injured, and her buckskin dress was a heavy, sodden weight upon her. Her expression was one of pure outrage as she pushed her wet hair out of her eyes and glared up at him, arms akimbo.

Wind Ryder stood on the bank, gloating.

"Wash," he ordered smugly.

"Why you—"

This was Marissa's day to lose any and all semblance of civilized behavior. Without another thought, she attacked the arrogant, overconfident man standing over her. She started splashing him with all the force she could muster. She didn't just do it once. She kept on splashing water at him, wanting him to be just as wet as she was. She was delighted when he was drenched.

Wind Ryder was shocked by the iciness of the water, and it took him a moment to react to her unexpected and continued assault. When he finally did react, he moved quickly, charging forward into the stream to stop her.

Marissa saw him coming after her and turned to run.

As with the stallion Wind Ryder had broken the day before, the water slowed her efforts to escape. He was there before she could reach the far bank.

"I'm sorry!" Marissa said quickly, trying to hide her smile. She'd seen the determination in his expression and wanted to discourage him from doing whatever it was he had in mind for revenge.

"Sorry? You're going to be sorry all right! You're going to pay for that!"

Wind Ryder grabbed her up and deliberately tumbled backward into the deeper water, taking her with him.

They both surfaced sputtering and choking.

Amazingly, Marissa found herself laughing at his antics. She'd feared he was going to beat her, and instead he had only dunked her again.

"You think this is funny?" Wind Ryder asked in a threatening voice, even as he was smiling back at her. He didn't give her a chance to escape. He snared her around the waist before she could run and brought her tightly against him.

The moment was startling—and revealing for them both.

They went still as the shock of sensual recognition hit them. Sleek and wet, they clung together.

They were suddenly and completely oblivious to the real world around them. It was just the two of them, standing hip to hip, breast to bare chest in the waist-deep water of the stream.

Marissa was stunned by the power of her physical reaction to Wind Ryder's nearness. She was breathless as she looked up at him, her eyes wide, her lips parted in anticipation of ... She didn't know what, but she did know that being this close to him left her breathing labored and her pulse pounding.

Wind Ryder remained unmoving, completely caught up in the unexpected arousal of the moment. The feel of her breasts

crushed against him sent heat pounding through his body. It settled in his loins and left him aching.

He had never felt this way about a woman before.

Even when Moon Cloud was sitting so brazenly atop him the night before, offering herself freely to him, he hadn't felt this kind of desire.

What was there about Shining Spirit that affected him so profoundly? He wanted to lay her down and make her his own. He was ready. He needed her. He had taken her as his wife—

And then Wind Ryder heard the muffled laughter.

The sound of chuckling jarred him back to the reality of where he was and what he was doing. He looked up toward the bank of the stream to find nearly half the villagers standing there, watching them and laughing at their antics.

Marissa had been in the grip of a sensual daze. It took her a moment to realize that they had become the center of attention in the village. When she saw the people gathered around laughing at them, she blushed and looked nervously away from the onlookers. It embarrassed her that she had completely forgotten herself in his arms.

And then Wind Ryder released her and stepped away.

Marissa felt suddenly lost without his powerful arms around her, supporting her, warming her. She looked up at him to find his gaze riveted upon her for a moment before he looked away.

Wind Ryder faced those who were watching them from the banks of the stream.

"Have you never seen anyone take a bath with clothes on before?" he asked in the Comanche tongue as he smiled wryly up at them.

Everyone roared at his humor. People began to wander away, now that the excitement was over.

Even Crazy One found herself actually smiling a little bit. She was relieved that Shining Spirit was unharmed.

Wind Ryder was glad when the villagers began to move away from the stream. Fighting to bring his desire for Shining Spirit under control, he turned back, ready to help her out of the water. He stared down at her, seeing the way the wet dress clung to her every curve and seeing how her golden hair was a sleek cascade down her back. Neither observation helped quell his need. He lifted his gaze to hers and saw confusion mirrored there. He wondered if she was as troubled as he was by what had happened between them.

Then he noticed the small smudge of dirt that remained on her cheek.

"You need to wash your cheek," he told her, unable to resist gently lifting one hand to touch the spot.

"Oh—" she said nervously.

Marissa didn't understand why Wind Ryder had such an effect on her, but his simple touch sent a thrill through her unlike anything she'd known before. Desperate to distract herself, she scrubbed at her cheek until she'd washed away the last trace of the dirt.

Marissa looked up to find his gaze still upon her. What she saw mirrored in the depths of his gaze unsettled her so much, she quickly started from the stream on her own. Marissa had only made it a few steps when she slipped.

Her loss of footing gave Wind Ryder just the excuse he needed to sweep her up into his arms. He carried her from the water and on toward their tipi.

Their return to the lodge was far different from their earlier exit. Though they were both dripping wet, Wind Ryder was

carrying her with the utmost tenderness, and he was thoroughly enjoying the feel of her body against him. She was not pounding on his back or shouting at him to put her down. She was quiet in his arms, although she was shivering a little. He thought that was probably from the dampness of her dress. He ducked to enter the lodge and set her on her feet once they were inside.

"Take off your dress," Wind Ryder ordered.

Chapter Thirteen

$\mathcal{M}$arissa looked up at Wind Ryder quickly, eyes widening at his command. "No—I can't—"

"You're wet, and you're shivering," he pointed out.

"Well, you're the one who threw me in the water," she returned, not wanting to admit the real reason she was trembling. True, the dress was damp and cold, but it was his overpowering nearness and the excitement he'd created within her that were taking their toll on her peace of mind.

"Give me your dress."

"But I ..." The thought of being naked before him unnerved her completely. She started to tremble even more. "I don't have any other clothes."

"Here." Wind Ryder scooped up one of his own blankets and held it out to her. "Use this."

She took it and clutched it to her breast, eying him warily.

"Turn around," she insisted.

Marissa was surprised when he responded to her request without argument. Wind Ryder acted in a most civilized manner, turning his back on her. She realized that if he'd been dressed in a white man's clothing and had had his hair cut, he would have seemed the perfect gentleman.

With great relief, she started to peel off the clinging, sodden garment.

Wind Ryder stood facing away from Shining Spirit, his shoulders set, his posture rigid. He did not peek as she struggled out of the wet clothing, but he wanted to.

Marissa was glad to be rid of the dress, but she longed for something more to cover herself than just a simple blanket. She wrapped it around her as best she could, then tucked the end in over her breasts to secure it. As decent as she could be, she picked up the wet clothing and went to Wind Ryder.

"Here." She held the dress and shoes out to him.

Wind Ryder turned back to her and felt another powerful jolt of desire at the sight of her wrapped in the blanket. The blanket did cover most of her, but it left her shoulders bare to his gaze. He reached out to take the garments from her, and as he did, his hand touched hers.

Wind Ryder stopped and stood staring down at her. He saw a beautiful woman—a brave woman—a woman who had survived many terrible trials and still was able to laugh. The memory of the sound of her laughter echoed in his mind. He wanted to hear her laugh again. He wanted to see her smile more. His gaze roved over her face, stopping at the bruise on her cheek. He tenderly reached out to touch it.

"Moon Cloud hurt you," he said quietly.

Wind Ryder was surprised by the sudden anger that flared within him at the thought of the Comanche woman hitting her. Ever so slowly, he bent toward Shining Spirit and pressed a soft kiss to the injury.

Marissa went still at the touch of his lips on her cheek. When he moved to really kiss her, she did not resist or pull away. She met him in that exchange, tentatively at first, then turning toward him and welcoming him warmly.

It was a wondrous moment of pure discovery and pleasure for both of them as they gave themselves over to the desire they'd each tried so hard to deny.

Marissa reached up to link her arms around Wind Ryder's neck and draw him closer to her. Her encouragement emboldened him. He crushed her to him, reveling in the softness of her lush body against his.

Wind Ryder deepened the kiss. He sought the sweetness of her, parting her lips to taste of her.

Marissa was enraptured. A part of her told her to end the embrace now, while she still had the willpower to do it. But her heart overruled her. She relaxed in his arms and gave herself over to the power of his kiss.

Wind Ryder felt her surrender. He broke off the kiss to seek the softness of her throat and neck, pressing heated kisses there.

Marissa shivered at the sensations coursing through her. She had never been so intimate with a man before. She had kissed a few men while courting, but their kisses had never evoked any feelings in her like she was experiencing now. The excitement building within her thrilled her even as the power of it frightened her a bit. When Wind Ryder picked her up and laid her upon the bedding, she could only gaze up at him in wonder.

Wind Ryder followed her down, joining her there, stretching out fully beside her.

A small logical voice within Marissa cried out that Wind Ryder was a Comanche—

She should run from him while she still could—

She should try to save herself—

But another part of her looked up at him and saw the white man he could have been. She saw the passion in his eyes and knew her passion matched his.

Wind Ryder sought her lips in a wild exchange, and Marissa responded fully. She drew him down even closer to her, and he went eagerly. Their kiss was long and hungry, and as he was kissing her, his hands began a gentle foray over her sweet curves. One hand skimmed the top of the blanket over her breasts, drawing a gasp of excitement from her.

Wind Ryder freed the blanket from where she'd secured it and brushed it aside to bare her breasts to his caress. Marissa was shocked by his move and by the intimacy of his touch. She tried to cover herself.

Wind Ryder only smiled down at her, amused by her innocent efforts.

"Don't," he told her in a husky voice. "You're beautiful. I want to look at you."

He took her in his arms. Marissa reveled in being held against the hot, hard-muscled strength of his chest. His warmth and nearness ignited fires of desire within her. She sought his lips again as he began to caress her more intimately. With each touch, he created new and thrilling feelings within her.

Marissa reached out to him, wanting to touch him as he was touching her. Her hands skimmed over the hard planes of his chest and back, sculpting the rock-hard muscles. As she let her hands move lower down his back to his waist, she felt him shudder in excitement. It gave her a sense of power to know that she could arouse him, too.

Wind Ryder was on fire for her. With every touch and kiss, his desire grew. He moved away only long enough to take off his loincloth, and then he returned to her, ready to know the fullness of her love. He moved over her.

Marissa was caught up in a haze of delight. She opened to him like a flower to the sun.

Wind Ryder felt her unspoken invitation. He fit himself to her in love's perfect union.

She tensed as he moved to make her his own. She was surprised by the intimacy of their joining and by his power. She cried out softly as he breached her innocence.

Wind Ryder shuddered at the power of the emotions that surged through him at the proof of her virginity.

She was his wife.

He had made her his own.

Unable to deny himself what he wanted most, Wind Ryder pressed his entry home, making her his in all ways. He began to move within her. He was careful to be gentle, caressing her and kissing her until she, too, was caught up in the perfection of what was happening between them.

They moved together in love's ageless dance. The rapturous rhythm swept them away from reality. They were two lovers seeking only the pure pleasure that complete surrender could give.

With Wind Ryder's every touch, Marissa's excitement grew. Her body was on fire. She was being consumed by the heat of her need. Mindlessly she clutched at him, holding him close, thrilled at being one with him. It seemed she couldn't get close enough to him.

And then ecstasy burst upon her.

She was lost to the myriad of sensations that throbbed through her as she clasped Wind Ryder to her heart.

Wind Ryder felt the tension in her as she attained the heights of passion. Knowing he'd pleased her heightened his own already driving desire. He quickened his pace, wanting to join her in that sweet release.

"Marissa—" He groaned her name as his own rapture claimed him.

Wrapped in each other's arms, they gave themselves over to bliss.

Later, in the aftermath, they lay quietly together, their bodies still joined. Neither spoke. There was no need for words between them.

Later, they would talk.

Wind Ryder rested with Shining Spirit in his arms, savoring the contentment of the moment. He had not been surprised that she was a virgin; he had sensed an innocence and a purity about her. What he was surprised about was the power of his need for her. Even now, as he lay quietly holding her, he could feel the fire stirring within him again. The touch of her bared breasts, her long, slender legs entwined with his, just thinking about taking her another time aroused him.

Marissa gazed up at him, her eyes widening as she felt the proof of his renewed arousal deep within her. He bent ever so slowly down to her and captured her lips in a devastating kiss that erased any thought of stopping from her mind. She became a creature of the flesh, wanting only to be one with Wind Ryder again.

Darkness claimed the land, but they did not notice. They were too entranced by the beauty of what they were sharing. It was well into the night before they slept, exhaustion claiming them in the aftermath of their spent passion.

Marissa awoke slowly to find herself curled against Wind Ryder's side, her head resting on his shoulder, her hand splayed upon his chest. It was dark in the tipi, and he was sleeping soundly. She was glad he was still asleep, for her sanity had returned with a vengeance and she was trying to come to terms with what she'd done.

She had made love to Wind Ryder.

Her emotions were in turmoil as she relived in her mind their passion-filled night. How could she have given herself to him so wantonly?

She had never desired any man the way she desired Wind Ryder. He had had only to kiss her and caress her, and she'd been lost in the wildfire of passion that had flamed to life between them.

Marissa studied her warrior as he slept. He looked even more handsome in the dark shadows of the lodge—the dark curve of his brows, his straight nose and high cheekbones. Her gaze dropped to his lips, and her heart stirred as she remembered his kiss and the feel of his hands tracing paths of ecstasy over her.

Was this love? Did she love him? Marissa didn't know.

He was a Comanche warrior. She was his captive.

It seemed impossible that she could love him. They had only known each other a short time.

She was filled with conflicting feelings. A part of her couldn't believe she'd surrendered her innocence to him, and yet she found, deep inside, that she still wanted him—

She wanted to touch him and hold him.

Her turbulent emotions tormented her. Their lovemaking had changed everything.

Marissa was agonizing over her need for Wind Ryder when he rose on one elbow to gaze down at her.

"You're awake—" She was startled by his unexpected move.

"And I want you," he told her. "Again."

Before Marissa could say anything, Wind Ryder kissed her. It was a deep, soul-searching exchange that stirred to life her hunger for him. He was ready for her, and she welcomed him passionately. He took her quickly, their union exquisite. They reached the heights together and crested there, clinging to one another as they drifted slowly back to reality.

They quieted.

Marissa lay in his arms, her head pressed to his chest, listening to the powerful beat of his heart. As she rested there, she could see

a scar on his arm. It must have been a bloody gash and caused him much pain. She wondered how it had happened. She wondered, too, if his heart and soul had been scarred as deeply as his body. She lifted her gaze to his face to find him watching her.

"How did you get that scar?" Marissa asked, reaching out to gently trace the mark with one finger.

"In a fight with Bear Claw when we were young," he answered without emotion.

"Did you win?"

"Bear Claw was far bloodier than I was," he said, echoing her words about Moon Cloud.

"Good." And she meant it. Her mood turned somber as she thought of the other warrior. "That must have been hard for you—coming to the village when you were so young. How old were you?" She wasn't sure he would answer her, but she wanted to know. She wanted to learn everything she could about him.

"Six."

"Only six," she said sadly, his answer confirming her fears. Her heart ached for him. "What was your name?"

"My name is Wind Ryder," he answered, balking at revealing any more about his past.

"But who were you then?" she asked, watching his expression, trying to read his thoughts.

Her questions, though softly asked, tore at him. He finally managed, "My name was Zach. Zach Ryder."

"Zach." She repeated his name gently.

Wind Ryder liked the way it sounded on her lips, but quickly denied the feeling.

"And your family, Zach? What were they like? I'm sure they still miss you."

At her words, she could feel him tense.

"They're all dead," he said tightly as he moved her away from him and sat up. "Everyone in my family was killed that day."

She was stunned by his revelation. Tears burned in her eyes as she wrapped her arms around him and held him. "I'm sorry, Zach."

"My name is Wind Ryder," he repeated, holding himself rigid.

"You can still go back—"

"No. That life is over."

"Your life isn't over. It doesn't have to be this way. We can go back together."

"You don't understand," he said, tearing himself from her arms. "Zach Ryder died that day. He died with his parents and his brothers."

Wind Ryder donned his breechcloth, then stood up and left the lodge.

Chapter Fourteen

Wind Ryder stalked through the dark village. He was used to being by himself, but he had never felt more alone.

Zach Ryder—

Feelings he had long refused to acknowledge stirred within him.

He had convinced himself that Zach Ryder was dead. He had created a new life for himself with the tribe, and he had come to be accepted as one of them. Chief Ten Crow had adopted him. It had been hard, but he'd survived.

But now Shining Spirit was threatening to destroy the world he'd created for himself and what little inner peace he had.

Wind Ryder made his way out of the village and stood alone, staring up at the heavens. The moonless night was clear, the sky a star-spangled canopy above him. He thought of the hours just passed in Shining Spirit's arms. He had never known that loving could be so beautiful. He remained lost in thought, trying to understand all he was feeling.

Laughing Woman was in a bad mood when she arose just before dawn. She had not slept well. It seemed to her that the captive who was supposed to bring peace to the tribe was causing more trouble than ever. The fight with Moon Cloud had been bad enough, but

the news that Wind Ryder had taken Shining Spirit as his wife troubled her even more deeply.

Ten Crow awoke to find his wife moving about the tipi, her expression troubled. "Is something wrong?"

"I was thinking of all that's happened since Shining Spirit came into the village. I thought she would bring peace to our people, but it seems there is to be no peace for Bear Claw."

"Our son tried to take what was not his," Ten Crow said flatly.

"He wanted her. He even offered to buy her from you. Why could you not give her to him?"

"In the vision, it was not so."

"I hope your vision proves true."

"As do I."

"Sometimes I think bringing Wind Ryder into the tribe was wrong. Look at the trouble he has caused!"

"Wind Ryder is our son," Ten Crow said.

"Wind Ryder is not *my* son," Laughing Woman denied angrily.

"You raised him as your own."

"Only because you took him in. Bear Claw is our one true son. Wind Ryder doesn't belong here—he never has."

Ten Crow had always known his wife resented Wind Ryder, but she had never stated it so bluntly before. He defended his adopted son. "He is a fine brave."

"So is Bear Claw, and yet you have always favored Wind Ryder over him! Wind Ryder should have remained a captive. If he had, there would be no worry right now about peace in our tribe."

Ten Crow stood up. His expression was angry as he towered over her, but she did not back down or cower before him.

"We will speak of this no more," he ordered. "All is as it should be."

With that, the chief started from the lodge. He did not want to listen to his wife speak of Bear Claw's bravery anymore. Time and

again through the years, the son of his flesh had proven himself to be less than a man.

As he emerged from the tipi, Ten Crow did not see Wind Ryder disappear into the shadows.

He did not know that Wind Ryder had heard their every word.

When the eastern sky had begun to brighten, Wind Ryder had made his way toward his father's lodge. He knew the chief always got up early, and he'd wanted to talk with him. As he'd drawn near the tipi, he'd heard his father and mother talking inside. He'd been glad that they both were awake, but as he'd started to make his presence known to them, he'd overheard what Laughing Woman was saying.

"Wind Ryder is not my son."

"You raised him as your own."

"Only because you took him in. Bear Claw is our one true son. Wind Ryder doesn't belong here—he never has."

Her words had been like a lash upon him. He'd considered this woman to be his mother, and yet now he'd learned the truth of her feelings for him. He had remained there, listening to the rest of their conversation, until he had realized that Ten Crow was about to leave the tipi.

Tormented by all that he'd learned, Wind Ryder had moved away before his father could see him. He wandered a distance from the camp, not wanting to see or speak to anyone. He couldn't go back to his own lodge, for Shining Spirit was there. He sought solitude and returned to the secluded spot where he'd been earlier. As he sat there, the memory of his parents' talk replayed in his mind.

"Wind Ryder is not my son."

"You raised him as your own."

"*Only because you took him in. Bear Claw is our one true son. Wind Ryder doesn't belong here—he never has.*"

The words tortured him.

Wind Ryder realized now that all along he'd had doubts about the way Laughing Woman had treated him. She had never been outwardly cruel to him, but she had always taken Bear Claw's side against him.

Laughing Woman had said he didn't belong there.

Slowly, painfully, Wind Ryder was coming to believe that the woman he'd thought of as his mother might be right—he truly didn't belong with the tribe.

He thought about Shining Spirit's words and realized he did have an alternative now.

He was a man full-grown.

He could walk away—if he wanted to.

The confusion he'd felt earlier deepened. And with the confusion came the memories he'd so long suppressed.

In his mind's eye, Wind Ryder saw his true parents—his white mother and father. Their names came to him in a painful rush—Michael and Catherine Ryder. Images of his brothers played before him, too—his big brother, Will, and his younger brother, Jeff. He remembered playing with them and working with his father and saying grace together before eating dinner.

It came to him bitterly that he'd continued to pray after he'd been taken by the Comanche. He had prayed for his family—that somehow, in spite of the murderous attack, they'd survived. He had prayed to be rescued. But no one had ever come to rescue him. After endless months, he'd given up praying. After endless months, he'd realized Zach Ryder was dead.

Until now.

Until this moment.

"Zach." He said his own name out loud.

Again memories overwhelmed him.

He heard his mother screaming his name, and he saw far too clearly his mother running toward him, her arms out, trying to save him from the warrior who'd grabbed him. He saw, too, how she'd been struck down by an arrow in her back—how she'd fallen, yet had tried to get back up to keep coming after him, until finally her strength had failed and she'd collapsed and lain unmoving.

Silent rage filled him.

The burning house—

The screams of his brothers trapped inside—

The sight of his father, lying dead by the stable.

He had witnessed it all as the Comanche had ridden off, taking him with them as their captive. The scenes were seared into his consciousness.

Wind Ryder had denied the memories because he'd been just a boy and had needed to adapt to survive. But they could never be forgotten. They were still a part of him—of the man he'd become.

He thought about his first days as a captive, of the terror and abuse he'd suffered. His rage intensified as he remembered his own hopelessness and fear. Crazy One had been the only white person in the village. She had sought him out to try to help him, but Ten Crow had been furious when he'd caught her tending to him. Ten Crow had beaten Crazy One severely and had forbidden her to go near him. He had seen the chief beating her, and he had been horrified by the violence done to her. From that day on, he had done everything in his power to make sure Crazy One didn't come near him, for he hadn't wanted her to be hurt in any way because of him.

His thoughts turned to Shining Spirit. He could only imagine how difficult it was to be taken captive as an adult. He had been a mere boy when he'd been brought into the village. He had been young enough and strong enough to fit in. But Shining Spirit was

a grown woman. She had had a life of her own, and they had taken it from her.

Wind Ryder wondered about her life. He knew she wasn't married, for he had been the one to take her innocence, but he wondered if she had left behind someone she'd loved. And if she had—what right did he have to take her life from her? And what right did he have to make her stay?

Shining Spirit had begged him to take her back to her world. She had told him he could return to the white world.

Wind Ryder didn't know if that would be possible. He had no life there, no family.

But then, he had no family here either.

There was only Ten Crow—the man who'd taken him as his son, the man who had raised him in the tribe and taught him what he needed to know to become a warrior. Wind Ryder cared about Ten Crow; he admitted to himself that he loved him. It was because of the chief that he was still alive today.

But was there anything holding him in the village now that he knew the truth of Laughing Woman's feelings?

Was there any hope of his returning to the white world after he had lived as a Comanche for so long?

Instead of being able to clear his thoughts as he'd hoped, Wind Ryder found they grew even more troubled.

Daylight had come, and he knew what he had to do. He needed time alone, time away from everyone.

If he returned to his lodge and Shining Spirit, he did not know if he would be able to keep himself from her, not after the pleasure he'd found in her arms during the night, not after knowing the beauty of her love.

Wind Ryder returned to the village and went straight to get his mount. One of the other warriors was there working with the horses as he prepared to ride out.

"Are you going on a raid?" Black Eagle asked. "Wait, and I will ride with you."

"No. I am riding alone."

"You will be back soon?"

Wind Ryder swung up on his horse's back and looked down at the other man. "I do not know when I will return. Tell my father."

Before Black Eagle could say more, he wheeled his mount around and rode off.

Unnoticed, Crazy One had been watching and listening a short distance away.

Black Eagle finished what he was doing, then went to find the chief. He gave him Wind Ryder's message.

Ten Crow was troubled by the news that Wind Ryder had left the village. He thought of all Laughing Woman had said earlier, and he wondered for the first time if his vision could have been wrong. His visions had always been proven right in the past, but the sense of foreboding he felt could not be easily ignored.

He thought of his vision again—of Bear Claw and Wind Ryder fighting, of the blood and flames, of the golden one drawing Wind Ryder away, and of peace for his people. Was the golden one going to bring that peace? He was no longer certain.

It was already daylight when Marissa stirred. She awoke slowly, clinging to the serenity she'd found in sleep. But as she opened her eyes, she was forced to face reality—to remember what had transpired the night before.

"*That life is over. Zach Ryder died that day.*"

Even now, pain filled her as she remembered how tortured Wind Ryder had sounded. She had hoped, after all they'd shared,

that she would be able to reach him, but he had refused to listen to her pleas. He had walked out after the passionate night of loving they'd shared, and he hadn't come back.

Marissa got up, determined to find him. After dressing, she left the lodge and went looking for him. She was surprised when she could find no sign of him anywhere in the village. She returned to the tipi and was about to go back inside when Crazy One approached her.

"He's gone," Crazy One told her solemnly.

"Yes, he is. You're safe."

"No. No." She shook her head as she drew closer. "He's gone. He left the village. He rode away by himself. I saw him. Don't know when he'll be back."

"You saw Wind Ryder leave?"

"Yes."

"When?"

"At dawn. I heard him tell Black Eagle he didn't know when he'd be back."

Marissa was stunned—and heartbroken.

How could Wind Ryder have left her without saying a word?

Had last night meant so little to him that he could just ride away and not look back?

"Is that all he said?" she asked Crazy One.

"That is all I heard. He's gone. Now I have to go, too. I have work to do."

She walked away without saying anything more.

Marissa went back inside the lodge and stood alone, staring down at the blankets where she and Wind Ryder had made love just hours before—where she had given him her innocence. She wanted to get a horse and go after him, but she couldn't. She would be forced to wait there for his return—whenever that would be.

As she considered remaining alone in the village, Marissa thought of Bear Claw and fought down a shiver of fear. She would have to be watchful every minute, for she did not trust the other warrior to stay away from her. Without Wind Ryder's protection, she was vulnerable.

A thought came to her, and Marissa knelt down to quickly go through the few personal belongings Wind Ryder kept in a buckskin bag in the tipi. She was hoping to find a weapon of some kind so she could defend herself against Bear Claw if the need arose. Digging through his belongings, she was glad to find a small knife. She secured it in her waistband and had just started to put everything back when she saw something shining in the bottom of the bag. Marissa reached down and drew out a gold chain and cross.

A shiver went through Marissa as she stared down at the cross. The cross belonged to Zach. This was the only connection to his family he had left. Despite his words, he had not severed all ties with Zach Ryder.

There was hope.

Marissa carefully put the cross and chain back in the bag.

Tears threatened, and she paused, waiting to regain control of her emotions before she went back outside to join the women at work. She did not know if the tears were tears of joy at the knowledge that she might be able to convince Wind Ryder to leave the village or tears of sorrow at knowing he still kept that one connection to the past he so vehemently denied.

He was Zach Ryder.

She had to find a way to convince him of that truth when he returned.

Chapter Fifteen

Bear Claw's mood had not improved with the passing of the days, and he was glad to be heading out of the village with his father and the raiding party. He needed time to plan what to do next. He wanted to take the golden one, but he now knew that he would have to kill Wind Ryder to claim her.

He smiled to himself. He found the thought quite pleasant.

He hoped Wind Ryder would be back in the village when they returned. He was looking forward to their next encounter.

It was useless.

Everyone riding with the search party knew it, but no one wanted to be the first to admit it.

They continued on day after day, doggedly searching, always hoping, scouring the land looking for a trail, for some clue as to where the Comanche had taken Marissa, but there was nothing. There was only the vast, deserted Texas wilderness.

They made camp and settled in for the night—hot, dirty, exhausted, frustrated, and angry.

"What do we do now, Hawk?" George asked as they sat around the campfire. His mood was black, for he realized how desperate their situation was.

"There is nothing more we can do, unless you just want to keep searching in ever widening circles. But even if we keep on another week or another month, there's no guarantee we'll ever turn up any trace of them."

"That's what I was afraid of."

Hawk looked up at George, his expression troubled and sympathetic. "I wish there was some way to give you hope. Hell, I wish there was some way to give myself hope that we'd find her if we kept on, but there isn't."

"I know."

George had come to respect and trust Hawk's opinions. Though it was painful to admit it, he knew Hawk was right. The storm had destroyed their only hope of locating Marissa quickly. Now it would be a matter of pure luck if they ever found her. He'd offered up silent prayers every night for help, but all his praying seemed to have come to nothing.

"So, what do you want to do? Do you want to keep heading west in the morning?" Hawk asked.

George was silent as he searched his soul for an answer. He would have ridden on forever if he believed there was even the slightest chance of finding the Comanche's trail. The long days in the saddle and the endless hours of tracking would be worth it if they could found a clue to Marissa's whereabouts, but since the storm, they hadn't found a thing. It was as if she and the raiding party had disappeared off the face of the earth.

George could hide from the truth no longer. They were defeated. It was time to give it up.

George looked up at the man who'd become his friend. They shared a look of painful understanding as he answered, "No, we'll head back at first light."

"We can't just quit!" Mark argued. The thought of Marissa as a helpless Comanche captive angered him.

George looked up at his young ranch hand and understood his anger. Marissa was George's blood relation; no one wanted her safe return more than he did.

"Mark—we've done everything we can. Hawk's right. There's no point in going on."

"There's got to be something more we can do! We can't just give up," Mark argued.

"Nobody's giving up on her," George told him.

"But you want to go back!"

"There's nowhere else to go right now. Hawk's the best tracker around, but we could search every inch of West Texas for the next six months and not find a thing. You know that."

Mark fell silent. Though logic told him George was right, a part of him didn't want to quit. He considered going on by himself, but if even Hawk couldn't find their trail, Mark knew he didn't stand a chance.

"You all right?" George asked when Mark remained silent.

"Yeah." His answer was terse. He turned and stalked away from the campsite.

George and Hawk watched him go, knowing what he was feeling, knowing he needed time alone.

Claude had kept his silence as he'd listened to their exchange. He realized how difficult making that decision had been. But their course had now been decided.

In the morning, they would turn back.

Mark walked a distance away, needing time to sort out his feelings. When he'd first learned that Marissa was coming to live at the ranch after her father's death, he'd been glad. She was an attractive girl, and they had spent some time together during her last visit. He'd been seriously considering courting her when she arrived.

Marrying George's only heir would be a smart move, for the Crown Ranch was very successful.

Now, though, Mark wondered about his plan. If they had managed to find Marissa, he would have won George's favor by marrying her. Certainly, no one else was going to want her after she'd been held by the Comanche. He smiled at the thought. There would be no competition for her hand in marriage. But their failure to find her had ruined everything. He didn't know what he would do next, but he was sorry they weren't going to keep looking for her.

Louise was moving slowly and painfully, but at least she was moving, and for that she was grateful. She made her way down the hall of the boardinghouse, leaning heavily on Dr. Harrison's arm.

"Are you certain you're up to this?" the doctor asked, concerned.

"Oh, yes," she said with determination.

The endless days of lying in bed had taken their toll on Louise. Her worries about Marissa were consuming her. She wasn't the type of person to sit idly by when others were in trouble. She had to get up and try to do something to help.

It took a great effort, but she made it down the stairs and into the physician's buggy.

"Sarah has things all ready for you out at the Crown. I'll have you at the ranch in no time," the doctor promised as he climbed in beside her and took up the reins.

"Thank you for everything you've done for me," Louise told him, truly grateful for his compassionate care.

"I'm just glad you're doing so well. There was a time early on when I wasn't sure you were going to make it." He smiled over at her, glad that she was looking so much better. "You're a strong woman, Louise Bennett."

"I've been told that before," she said quietly, sitting back and trying to make herself comfortable.

She noticed that the doctor had a rifle in the buggy, and she was glad. She had made up her mind to learn how to ride astride and how to fire a gun when she got to the ranch. There would never be another time in her life when she would be left defenseless the way she had been in the raid on the way station. If she'd had a gun that day and had known how to use it, she might have been able to save Marissa from the Comanche. Louise had vowed to herself never to be helpless again.

The trek to the ranch passed far too slowly for Louise. Lingering terror from the Comanche attack left her nervous and unsure as they traveled the long miles across the open country.

"You're on Crown property now," Dr. Harrison told her after they'd been on the road for over an hour.

Louise was tremendously relieved some time later when the Crown ranch house and outbuildings finally came into view. She'd had no idea the ranch was so successful. She was impressed by the empire that George had carved out of the wild Texas land.

As they drove up the main road toward the house, Louise saw Sarah come out on the front porch and wave to them in welcome. Once they'd drawn to a stop, Sarah approached the buggy.

"It is so wonderful that you're finally here," Sarah told Louise, smiling brightly.

"Have you heard anything from George and the others?" Louise asked quickly, desperate for news about Marissa.

"Not a word in all this time," Sarah answered honestly. "I wish I could tell you different, but there's been nothing."

Dr. Harrison climbed down from the buggy and then assisted Louise in her descent.

Louise realized all too painfully how weak she still was. She was forced to cling to the doctor's arm just to make it inside the house. With the doctor's and Sarah's help, she settled on the sofa in the parlor.

"Will you be all right now?" the physician asked Louise once he'd made sure she was comfortable.

"Yes, thank you."

"Don't worry about her, Doc. We'll take good care of her," Sarah promised.

"I'll be holding you to that," he said.

"Can you stay for a while?" Sarah invited.

"No, I've got to get back. But if there's any change at all in Miss Louise's condition, you send word to me right away. We don't want to take any chances."

"I'll do that."

"You take care of yourself," Dr. Harrison said to Louise. "I'll check back in on you in about a week."

Sarah went out to see him off, then returned to join Louise.

"I turned the dining room into a bedroom for you so you wouldn't have to climb the stairs," Sarah explained.

"Thank you. And, Sarah?" When the other woman turned to her, "Thank you for providing all the personal things for me." The doctor had told her that Sarah had left money with him to buy the personal things she needed.

"No need to thank me. George was the one. He told me to make sure you were taken care of, and I knew you would be needing clothes and such. I'm just glad that you're finally well enough to be here. Now all we have to do is pray that they return soon with Marissa. It's been far too long already."

Their gazes locked.

"I've been praying for that since the day they left," Louise admitted.

"So have I."

It was almost dusk when Marissa returned to the tipi for the night. She was just about to go inside when she saw a warrior in the distance.

She stopped, her heartbeat quickening at the sight of the brave riding in.

Was it Wind Ryder?

Had he finally returned to her?

She waited, unsure what to do. Her first impulse was to run forward and greet him, but she stayed back, uncertain of his response.

Marissa grew nervous. She hated to admit it, but she had missed Wind Ryder desperately. She'd been worried about him, too. As excited as she was about the chance to see him again now, doubt held her in place. He'd been angry when he left, so she did not know what to expect. She walked slowly in the warrior's direction, trying to ignore the quickening of her heartbeat.

Marissa was almost holding her breath as she watched the warrior draw nearer, but finally she realized it was not Wind Ryder. She was surprised by the surge of disappointment that filled her.

Turning away, she quickly returned to the lodge and settled in for the night. She had heard that Bear Claw had ridden out with a raiding party, but even so, she fell asleep with Wind Ryder's knife close at hand.

Chapter Sixteen

*I*t was more than a week before Wind Ryder made the return trip to the village. Time held little meaning in the wilderness. He'd deliberately lost himself, seeking solitude and peace.

He had found the solitude, but the peace had been harder to achieve. It seemed that Shining Spirit haunted his thoughts every moment. He'd tried to put the memories of the last night they'd spent together from his mind, but whenever he attempted to fall asleep, images of her were there before him—images of her naked in his arms, taunting him with her beautiful body and tempting him with her innocent love.

He had realized quickly there would be no forgetting Shining Spirit.

The understanding had come to him in the dark of night when he had stirred in his sleep and reached out for her, only to discover she was not there.

It had been a revelation for Wind Ryder to discover that he no longer wanted to be by himself—to be a lone warrior.

He wanted Shining Spirit.

As he accepted that truth, another realization struck him. Feeling as he did, he did not know if he still belonged with the tribe. Laughing Woman's words had been like a knife in his heart, severing the ties he'd believed he'd had with her and the people.

During his time alone, Wind Ryder considered all that Shining Spirit had told him about the white world. He was not a man who admitted to fear. He faced any and all challenges straight on. He had learned to do that under Ten Crow's tutelage, but the thought of trying to make a life for himself among the whites troubled him.

He was a Comanche warrior. How would he ever fit into the white world? Did he want to?

Wind Ryder looked up as he neared the village. All was calm. He knew the village was the same as when he'd left, but somehow it appeared almost alien to him.

The village might be the same, but he had changed.

He quietly greeted the brave keeping watch, then tended to his horse before making his way to his tipi.

Silently Wind Ryder lifted the door flap and let himself into the lodge. Shining Spirit was asleep, and he stopped just inside the entry to stare down at her. In his thoughts and dreams, she had been beautiful, but as he gazed down at her now in the semidarkness, she was even more lovely.

Wind Ryder let the door flap fall down as he moved closer to her. He had been a driven man on the ride back to the village. He had thought of nothing except losing himself in the heat of her passion. He wanted to take her in his arms, to feel her against him. He stretched out beside her and drew her to him.

Marissa had been deeply asleep, but when she felt a man's hands upon her, she jerked awake in a panic. Fearing it was Bear Claw, she reached for the knife and scrambled away to crouch across the lodge. She was trembling, but she was ready to fight if she had to.

And then Wind Ryder whispered her name.

"Marissa—"

He moved nearer, wanting to calm her, wanting to reassure her.

At the sound of his voice, a shiver of a different kind trembled through Marissa.

"You're back," she breathed, and lowered the knife.

"You were afraid?" He saw the weapon, and he was glad she had it to defend herself, but a sudden fear raged through him. "Has Bear Claw tried to harm you?"

"No, but I did not know when you would return. You've been gone for so long." The days had seemed endless.

"I missed you," he said simply.

Then, unable to resist her any longer, he lifted one hand to caress her cheek as he bent to capture her lips in a sweet, soft kiss.

The knife fell unheeded from her hand as Marissa surrendered willingly to his embrace.

Wind Ryder had returned to her. And he wanted her.

She welcomed him to her now without question.

Their time apart had only heightened the desire they felt for each other. They came together in a rush of passion. Clothes were quickly stripped away in their need to be close to one another. They lay together upon the softness of their blankets, completely caught up in the glory of their nearness.

Wind Ryder moved over her, claiming her as his own. The excitement of their union swept them both away. They were alone in the world they'd created, lost in the splendor of their loving.

Marissa responded wildly to his every touch, and she returned his every caress, wanting to please him as he was pleasing her. They crested together, ecstasy sweeping over them, taking them to the heights of pleasure.

Afterward, Marissa lay quietly in Wind Ryder's arms, her head resting on his chest.

He had come back to her. She hadn't been sure that he would.

"I'm sorry I upset you," Marissa said in a soft voice as she trailed one hand across the width of his chest. It felt good to touch him, to have him near. "I only wanted to learn more about you—about who you really are and what your life was like before—"

His long days alone had changed the way he felt. The anger was no longer there.

"I know," Wind Ryder finally answered after a long pause. "I remember a little about my family—my parents and my two brothers. We had a ranch near San Antonio. Life was good then—until the raid."

"I understand," she said, thinking of Louise and all that she'd witnessed at the way station. "I lived in New Orleans with my father until he died. That was when I decided to make the trip to Dry Springs to live with my Uncle George on his ranch. Louise Bennett, a friend of my parents, was making the trip with me. I was the only one who survived the attack on the way station." Her voice was choked. "I don't know why I had to be the one. I saw everything. I saw Louise die."

"I understand," Wind Ryder said quietly. "I saw everything, too."

"Then why do you stay?" She remembered what Crazy One had told her, but she didn't want to let him know she'd spoken to the old woman about him.

"I did try to get away in the beginning, but Ten Crow found me every time. After a while, I gave up and did what I had to do to survive."

"You became one of them."

"There was no other way. Then Ten Crow took me as his son, and I was accepted." He did not tell her what he'd heard Laughing Woman say.

"But you're a man full-grown now. You could leave the tribe if you wanted to."

"There's nothing for me in the white world. My family is all dead."

"If you took me back, I would be with you. You wouldn't be alone. We could go to my uncle's ranch."

Wind Ryder could just imagine the reception he'd get in the white world. He would be an outcast.

"I don't belong there."

Marissa fell silent. She wanted to press Wind Ryder, but this wasn't the time. He had opened up to her a little, and for now she would be thankful for that much. He had returned to her. She would wait and hold on to the hope that maybe, in time, she could find a way to convince him to take her to her uncle.

Wind Ryder said nothing more, for he was lost deep in thought. The days alone in the wilderness had proven to him that he wanted her with him. He wondered if he could bear to be parted from her.

Rising up on an elbow over her, he kissed her.

He didn't belong in the white world. Nor did he belong in the village. The only place he felt he did belong was in her arms.

"The boss is back! They're riding in!"

"They're back?" Louise asked Sarah, her hopes soaring at last.

With each day that had passed during the weeks since she'd come to stay at the ranch, her fears had increased that she would never see Marissa again.

"Thank God!" Sarah said as she got up to look out the window. She'd been worrying about them, too, fearing for her husband's safety.

Louise had regained most of her strength, and she rushed from the house, desperate to see Marissa. Sarah followed her outside on the porch. The ranch hands were coming up to the house to greet the newcomers, too.

Louise shielded her eyes against the sun as she stared down the road. She could see a group of riders in the distance, and her heart leapt in excitement.

Marissa was back!

Joy filled her, and she offered up a prayer of thanks for Marissa's safe return. George had told her he was going to find her, and he had.

And then she heard one of the ranch hands mutter, "Damn. There's just the four of them."

"What?" Louise went still at his words, every fiber of her being denying the truth of he'd just blurted out.

Sarah reached over to take her hand in a supportive gesture, but said nothing as the riders drew closer. Sarah knew there was nothing more to be said. The fact that it was just the four men returning after all this time said it all.

Louise began to tremble. Sarah clutched her hand even more tightly, but still said nothing. She understood what Louise was feeling.

Tears welled up in Louise's eyes. "George was going to find her. He promised me he would."

The men reined in before them, tired, dirty, and defeated.

"Boss, you're back," the hands greeted him.

George only nodded to his men, then turned to meet Louise's gaze. He was thrilled that she was looking so well. She appeared fully recovered, but he hated giving her the bad news.

"How did it go?" one of the hands asked. "Did you find anything?"

"No." The word was dragged from him. "A storm came through and wiped out the trail. We kept searching as long as we could, but there was no use. The trail was gone."

Louise had been watching him, trying to read his expression. At his answer, all the pain he was feeling was revealed in the depths

of his eyes. She had lain awake night after night, agonizing over what she would do if the worst came to pass.

And now it had.

She wanted to scream and cry and rant and rave, but she drew upon her deepest inner strength and left the porch to go to George. Her heart ached for him and for all that he had suffered and lost.

"George——" She said his name softly, reaching his side just as he dismounted.

"We did everything we could, Louise." George was not a man who admitted defeat easily, and the words were choked from him.

She saw the torture in his eyes, the pain in his soul. Her own sorrow and misery matched his. Her worst fears had been realized.

Louise's voice was tight as she asked, "Is Marissa dead?"

"No—I don't think so," he answered quickly, but in his heart he wondered if she might not have been better off dead than living as a captive. He would never say that aloud, though.

"Then there's still hope." Louise was relieved that she still had something to cling to—and that George did, too. She put her hand reassuringly on his arm. "If it's possible, I know Marissa will come back to us."

George knew the odds were against that eventuality. He was trying to accept what he believed was the inevitable truth—that he would never see his niece alive again—but he did not have the heart to deny Louise her one last, slender thread of hope.

"Marissa's a strong girl," he said.

"Yes, she is," Louise agreed.

"Let's go inside," George said, then turned to the men who'd ridden with him. "Hawk, you're more than welcome to spend the night."

"Thanks, but I'd better be getting back to town," he said. "If you hear anything more, let me know."

"I will," George promised. "And, Hawk—"

Hawk had started to mount up again, but paused to glance his way.

"Thanks."

George left Louise's side for a moment and went to offer Hawk his hand in friendship. Hawk nodded solemnly. The bond they'd formed was a strong one. Then he swung up in the saddle and rode out, lifting one hand in a farewell gesture.

"I'm glad you're back," Sarah said as she went to her husband and hugged him in welcome. She was devastated over the news that they hadn't found Marissa, but relieved that Claude had returned safely.

"I just wish things had turned out different," Claude remarked.

"We all do," Sarah agreed.

"I'll take care of the horses," Mark offered, knowing Claude wanted time to be with Sarah, and George would want to talk more with Marissa's aunt.

"We got 'em," the other hands spoke up, helping him with the horses.

Mark appreciated their help. It wasn't in his nature to give up, but there had been no choice. His mood was dark as he walked with them to the stable.

Chapter Seventeen

Word spread that the raiding party was riding in, and the villagers went to meet them. There was always a great celebration when Chief Ten Crow returned, for he always led the most successful raids. The welcoming mood changed quickly when they saw the chief being brought in on a travois.

Laughing Woman rushed to kneel at her husband's side. She was shocked to find him unconscious.

"Was he wounded during the raid?" she asked, looking up at Bear Claw when he dismounted and came to her.

"No, a rattlesnake struck at his horse two days ago, and he was thrown."

"Take him inside. I will send for the medicine man," Laughing Woman ordered.

With the help of another warrior, Bear Claw moved his father into the lodge. When he came back outside to see if the medicine man was coming, Snake approached him.

"What do you want to do with the captive?" Snake asked.

Bear Claw didn't care if the young white boy he'd taken captive lived or died.

"Tie him to the pole at the center of the village. I will see to him after we have cared for my father."

Snake went off to do as Bear Claw had directed. He dragged the bound and beaten captive through the village to the center pole. He tied him there, his arms extended above his head, and left him alone to be subjected to the ridicule and taunting of the villagers.

Wind Ryder had been working with the horses when word came to him that the raiding party was back, and that his father had been seriously injured. He rushed to the tipi to find Laughing Woman and Bear Claw waiting outside.

"What happened?"

"A rattlesnake struck at his horse, and he was thrown. The medicine man is with him," Laughing Woman told him.

Wind Ryder was shocked by the news, for Ten Crow was one of the best horsemen in the tribe. He looked at Bear Claw and Laughing Woman worriedly, "Will he be all right?"

"We do not know. The medicine man will call us in when he is ready."

Conflicting emotions tore at Wind Ryder as he awaited word of his father's condition. He did not want to be with Bear Claw and Laughing Woman, but his concern for Ten Crow held him there. The chief had cared about him and loved him as if he were his own. He could do no less.

Except for the ecstasy and forgetfulness Marissa found during the long, dark hours of the night in Wind Ryder's arms, the days and weeks of her captivity were passing with agonizing slowness. There were times when she wondered if she would ever be reunited with her uncle. She made the best she could of things, and this day sought out Crazy One to visit with her near the stream. They were there talking when they heard shouting coming from the village.

"I wonder what's happening," she said, looking in that direction.

Crazy One listened for a moment, and then her expression changed. Her eyes widened as a tremor of terror shook her.

"What is it?" Marissa asked, puzzled by her reaction.

"We cannot go there," she said, her fear obvious.

"Why? Is something wrong? Should we go see if we can help?"

The older woman's expression grew more fearful. She grabbed Shining Spirit forcefully by the arm, her fingers digging into her flesh. "Do not go there."

Her insistence left Marissa even more worried. She tore herself loose and started off toward the village.

Crazy One stood uncertainly where she was. She knew what was happening, and she feared for Shining Spirit's safety. A part of her wanted to run, to find a place to hide, but her heart was moved by Shining Spirit's daring. She thought her aptly named. She was brave and courageous, and her goodness shone for all to see.

But ever since the early days when Wind Ryder had come into the tribe, Crazy One had made it a point never to care for anyone. Somehow, though, this strong, determined young woman had found a place in her heart. Though her mind screamed at her to go hide, her heart led her.

Crazy One went after Shining Spirit; she knew her friend was going to need help.

The closer Marissa came to the center of the village, the faster she ran. Something was telling her that there was trouble.

The sight that greeted her shocked her to the depths of her already tortured soul.

There, tied helplessly to a pole, was a young white boy. He was bloodied and nearly unconscious. The Comanche children

were throwing rocks and sticks at him, and they cheered when they hurt him.

Outrage filled her, and she reacted without thought. She ran screaming at the children. She was shocked when she heard someone behind her shouting and looked back to see Crazy One following her. At that moment, she loved the old woman.

Crazy One grabbed up the biggest stick she could find and waved it at the children, who stayed just out of range. She deliberately acted wild and insane, wanting to keep them away as Shining Spirit worked at freeing the injured youth from his bonds.

"Do you need help to get him down?" Crazy One asked.

"No, I can do it," Marissa told her with determination.

The boy was barely conscious, but at the feel of gentle hands upon him, he opened his eyes. His expression was both pained and dazed as he tried to focus on her. His terror eased a little at the sight of her blond hair.

"Who are you?" he asked, his voice barely above a whisper.

"A friend," she told him. She knew there would be serious consequences for her actions, but she didn't care. All that mattered was saving the boy from further abuse.

One of the boys ran to find Bear Claw to let him know what was happening. He found the warrior at his father's lodge.

"Bear Claw! Hurry!" the boy shouted.

"What is it?" he asked, jumping to his feet when he heard the urgency in the boy's tone. He had been waiting outside the tipi for word of his father's condition.

"Your captive! Shining Spirit is trying to free him from the pole!"

Wind Ryder had been standing nearby. He had not known that Bear Claw had taken a prisoner, and he could only imagine

Shining Spirit's reaction to witnessing the torture of a captive. He knew he had to get to her before Bear Claw did.

Wind Ryder reached the women just as Shining Spirit finished untying the boy's hands.

Crazy One saw him coming. For a moment, she started to run, then stood her ground, stick in hand.

"Stay back! You will not harm them!" she shouted at him.

He looked from the two women to the boy. A jolt of recognition seared him to the depths of his being. The pain was unlike anything he'd experienced. Wind Ryder could tell the boy was young, not even ten. His face was battered, and he was cut and bloodied. His wrists were raw from being bound. Shining Spirit had her arm around his shoulders, trying to help him stand, but he was sagging weakly from the abuse he'd suffered.

Wind Ryder remembered when he had felt the same way—when he had been beaten and abused—when he had been alone and desperate. Crazy One had been the only person to help him—in the beginning.

Wind Ryder knew what he had to do. He started to walk past Crazy One, unafraid that she might hit him. He knew only that he had to help this boy.

Crazy One stood her ground for a moment, then backed off and let him pass without attacking him.

"What are you going to do?" Shining Spirit asked, not wanting the boy to come to any more harm.

The boy looked up at Wind Ryder.

Wind Ryder didn't answer. In one move, he picked the youth up in his arms and started back toward his own tipi with him, leaving the women to follow.

Wind Ryder had gone only a short distance when Bear Claw confronted him. Fury was etched in the other warrior's face.

"The captive is mine. Put him down," Bear Claw snarled.

Wind Ryder faced him without fear. "I will buy him from you. Name your price."

"The boy is not for sale," he said coldly. He was glad to be having this confrontation. He had made it a point to bring the boy back just so he could taunt Wind Ryder with him. It pleased Bear Claw to see his brother so angry.

Wind Ryder had known Bear Claw would challenge him, and he was prepared to fight him. He turned and set the boy on his feet near Shining Spirit and Crazy One.

"What are you doing?" Marissa asked, unable to understand what was being said.

"Do not worry," Wind Ryder answered in English. He turned back to Bear Claw.

"If you will not sell or trade him to me, then I will take him from you," Wind Ryder said simply.

Bear Claw had not wanted to fight Wind Ryder, at least not face to face. He'd lost to him in fair fights too many times already. If he fought Wind Ryder again, he wanted to have an advantage over him—like surprising him in an ambush. But all eyes were upon him now. He was trapped. He could not back down from Wind Ryder's challenge.

"You can try," he sneered.

Wind Ryder looked over at the women. He was proud of their courage in coming to the boy's aid. "Take him to our lodge."

Marissa and Crazy One led the injured boy away. Marissa kept an arm around him, for he was staggering and barely able to stay on his feet.

"What's going to happen to me?" the boy asked weakly.

"Wind Ryder has claimed you," Marissa told him.

"Is he a white man?"

"Yes." Marissa nodded. "And he wants to keep you safe."

She could feel how weak and unsteady he was, and she was glad when they reached the tipi. After casting one nervous look back toward the men, she led the way inside. The boy and Crazy Woman followed her in.

Wind Ryder remained calm as he faced Bear Claw.

"The boy is mine now," he stated confidently.

Wind Ryder's arrogance infuriated Bear Claw. He was ready to erupt in fury when the crowd that had gathered around them suddenly parted and Laughing Woman appeared before them.

"Come," Laughing Woman said, rushing to Bear Claw and taking his arm. "There is no time for this. Your father—he has awakened and wants to see you."

Bear Claw looked at Wind Ryder. "It is not over between us," he threatened. "We will settle this later."

Wind Ryder only stared at him. There was no need to say anything more. For now, the boy was safe.

"He wants to see you, too," Laughing Woman told Wind Ryder, though it angered her to do so.

They started toward the lodge.

"Stay here," Crazy One told Shining Spirit. "Tend to the boy. I will go see what is happening."

Crazy One hurried back to watch Wind Ryder.

Marissa stood over the boy, who was trying to put on a brave face in spite of all he'd suffered.

"Don't worry," Marissa said. "Wind Ryder is the best warrior in the tribe. You will not be returned to Bear Claw."

At her words, he began to tremble. "I want to go home. I want my ma and pa."

"I know," she said sadly. "I know."

Kneeling down beside him, she took him in her arms and held him to her, offering what solace she could.

"What's your name?" Marissa asked gently. "My name is Marissa."

"I'm Joe. Joe Carter." Tears welled up in his eyes as he leaned back a bit to gaze up at her. "Thanks for helping me."

"You're welcome. Let's see what we can do to get you cleaned up a bit."

Marissa tried to distract herself by tending to the boy, but all the while she was straining to hear what was going on outside. She prayed fervently that if there was fighting, Wind Ryder would prevail.

As she bathed the youth's wounds, she began to understand how Crazy One had felt all those years ago when she'd tried to help Wind Ryder. There was no way she could let Joe return to Bear Claw's keeping.

Wind Ryder reached the chief's tipi first and went in. Bear Claw and his mother followed.

Chief Ten Crow lay unmoving on the blankets. His eyes were closed and his breathing was shallow and labored. His coloring was gray and lifeless.

Wind Ryder stared down at the man he had called father for so many years. He wondered what would happen if Ten Crow didn't recover. The question haunted him.

"Father—" he said quietly as he went to his side.

At the sound of his voice, Ten Crow opened his eyes. He stared up at Wind Ryder as if seeing him for the first time. There was a distant look in his eyes for a moment before he focused.

"No—I need to see my son—I need to see Bear Claw." Ten Crow struggled to speak in a weak voice.

At Ten Crow's words, Wind Ryder stepped away. Pain stabbed him at being denied by the chief.

Bear Claw smiled confidently and went to his father's side.

"Yes, Father, I am here," he said triumphantly.

Laughing Woman, too, felt a moment of exhilaration. Her son was Ten Crow's favorite. The chief wanted Bear Claw by his side, not Wind Ryder.

Ten Crow gathered what little strength he had left to speak. He grabbed his son's arm for emphasis.

"Bear Claw—you must bring peace to the tribe. You and Wind Ryder."

Ten Crow turned his head and looked over at Wind Ryder. The effort cost him. Their gazes met for only an instant, and then his eyes closed.

The chief's hand fell away from Bear Claw's arm as his spirit left his body.

His fight was over.

"My husband!" Laughing Woman cried out in agony and threw herself across his chest.

Wind Ryder and Bear Claw remained silent as they realized their father was dead.

Wind Ryder knew in that moment what he had to do. There would never be peace in the tribe as long as he was there, and without Ten Crow, there was no reason for him to remain.

"I will leave the village. Now. Today," Wind Ryder said, breaking the silence.

Laughing Woman looked up at him. Her face was distorted and tear-stained in her grief. She was shocked by her husband's death, but a surge of perverse delight filled her at Wind Ryder's words. She was glad that she would never have to see him again.

"It was a bad thing that you were ever brought here," she spat out angrily. Now that Ten Crow was dead, she could finally give vent to her true feelings about this interloper.

Wind Ryder was more than ready to ride away and never look back, but he wanted to make his point before he left. He looked at Laughing Woman, his expression cold.

"You forget, woman, that I never asked to be brought here. I came to this village as a captive." Then he looked at Bear Claw. "Shining Spirit, Crazy One, and the boy will go with me when I leave. I will not be back."

"Good," Laughing Woman said. "Go now. Leave us. You are no son of mine!"

Wind Ryder looked at them both and realized she was right—very right.

He left the tipi and walked away.

Bear Claw was furious.

"He cannot take my captive!" he raged as he started to go after Wind Ryder.

"Let them go!"

"The boy is mine!"

"Your father is dead, my son," she admonished. "Do you care more about some white captive? Let him go with Wind Ryder. Be glad they are gone."

Bear Claw longed to go after Wind Ryder, to somehow get the better of him.

"Remember, son, Wind Ryder is leaving, never to return. That is good—very good."

Bear Claw's anger knew no bounds, but he stayed with his mother as she mourned Ten Crow's passing.

Later there would be time to seek his revenge.

Chapter Eighteen

W ind Ryder returned to his own tipi to find the boy there with Shining Spirit.

Marissa looked up and was relieved to see Wind Ryder unharmed.

"You're all right," she breathed, quickly going to him. "Did you fight Bear Claw?"

"No. Laughing Woman came for us. Ten Crow is dead."

Marissa was shocked. "I did not know he had been hurt."

Wind Ryder explained what had happened.

She wasn't sure how to react to the news. She knew Wind Ryder had cared about Ten Crow, but somehow he seemed almost unaffected by the chiefs death. "I'm sorry."

"Where is Crazy One?" he asked, not mentioning Ten Crow again. He wondered if he ever would.

"I don't know. She left us to find out what was happening with you and Bear Claw. She was afraid for you."

"We must find her."

"Why?"

Wind Ryder looked down at her and saw her questioning look. "We are leaving the village. We will take Crazy One and the boy with us."

Marissa was stunned by his announcement.

"We're leaving?" she repeated in a whisper. Her hopes were soaring, but she still wasn't sure she'd heard him right.

"There is no reason to stay here in the village any longer."

She wanted to throw herself in his arms. She had prayed for this moment but feared it would never come—and now it was here. She was going back to her own world.

"Is the boy strong enough to travel?" Wind Ryder asked.

Though he was weak, Joe jumped to his feet at this question. Excitement was coursing through him at the prospect of returning home. "I'm strong enough!"

"Strong enough to ride alone?" Wind Ryder asked.

"Yes."

Wind Ryder gave the youth an approving look. It was good that he was strong and willing to fight. A child of lesser strength might not have been able to survive the trek they were about to make.

"Good." He glanced at Shining Spirit. "Find Crazy One and bring her here. I will get the horses."

"Wait for us here," Marissa told Joe.

Marissa hurried from the lodge, ready to search for the older woman. Wind Ryder followed her. She stopped and turned back to look at him.

"Thank you," she said softly.

He stood, staring at her for a long moment, then nodded once. He remained where he was, watching as she rushed off. When she'd gone from view, he let his gaze sweep over the village, committing to memory all the sights and sounds that had been so much a part of him for so long.

But this part of his life was over now.

Ten Crow, the man who had been like a father to him, was dead. There was nothing left to bind him there, nothing to hold him.

He was going to leave, and he would never come back.

Wind Ryder did not know what he would find in the white world. But even if he himself never fit in there, he knew he was doing the right thing. What mattered was returning the boy and Shining Spirit to their own people.

Wind Ryder realized that once they left the village, everything between him and Shining Spirit would change. He had taken her as his wife, but she did not know it, and in the white world he could make no claim on her. That realization saddened him, and he tried to prepare his heart for the loss.

"I cannot go!" Crazy One cried, backing away from Shining Spirit. "Leave me alone! Leave me alone!"

"Crazy One," Marissa said quietly, gently. "There is no reason to be afraid. This is Wind Ryder—the boy you cared about. He wants to take you with him. He wants you to return to your own people."

"No! No!"

"I will be with you, and so will the boy. Wind Ryder will take us to my uncle's ranch. We'll be safe there, I promise you."

Crazy One had been in the Comanche village for more years than she could count. Any dream she'd had of going home had been destroyed long ago. The thought that she might actually be able to leave the tribe was as frightening to her as it was thrilling.

Home—Could she really go back?

"You will be with me?" Crazy One asked, calming a bit.

"And the boy. He needs your help, too."

It seemed so simple, yet the older woman's terror held her frozen as she fought all her demons.

"Come with me, Crazy One."

"But who would want me now? No one. No one." She shook her head in abject sorrow. She knew how the white world reacted

to captives who were returned. They were made outcasts and subjected to all kinds of humiliation.

"Wind Ryder wants you. He asked for you. He said to find you and bring you to him."

"Wind Ryder said that?" She looked up, shock showing on her face.

"Yes. He wants you to go with him, and he is waiting for us with the horses at the lodge right now."

"He is?" Crazy One still sounded frightened.

"Yes. There is no reason for you to be afraid, but we must go now."

Finally, the old woman calmed. She was amazed by what Shining Spirit had told her.

Wind Ryder wanted to take her along. Wind Ryder wanted her with him.

"Yes. Yes, I will go with you. I will leave this place. We will go together." Crazy One smiled.

Marissa was startled, for she had never seen the other woman smile before. It transformed her, and for just an instant Marissa had an image of what Crazy One had looked like when she was young.

Crazy One moved to Shining Spirit's side, and together they walked toward Wind Ryder's lodge.

The nightmare that had been their captivity was about to end.

Wind Ryder had returned with four horses and was waiting for them. It took them only a short time to gather their belongings. They mounted up and started to ride out.

The mourning for the dead chief had begun. The wails of those who had loved and respected him echoed through the village.

Joe was frightened by the sounds. "Are they gonna come after us?"

"No," Wind Ryder reassured the boy. "No one will bother us."

In his heart, Wind Ryder, too, was mourning Ten Crow's passing. He looked back only once, then put his heels to his mount and rode away from the village for the last time.

Louise stood on the porch of the ranch house, staring out across the night-shrouded land. Her mood was as dark as the night. In the weeks since the search party's return, there had been no word about Marissa.

It was truly as if she'd vanished.

It was almost as if she'd never existed at all.

But Louise knew that wasn't true. Marissa was very much alive in her heart. If only they could find her!

A single tear traced a forlorn path down her cheek, and she brushed it angrily away. What good did it do to cry? Crying wouldn't bring Marissa back. It seemed that nothing would bring her back.

Louise sighed and turned around.

"Oh," she gasped when she found George standing just outside the front door, watching her.

"Are you all right?" he asked, crossing the distance between them.

He'd noticed that she had been very quiet at dinner and had excused herself to come outside as soon as they'd finished eating. He'd stayed indoors to give her some privacy, but then he'd started to worry when she hadn't come back in.

Louise drew a ragged breath at his question. She answered honestly, "I don't know, George. I don't know if I'll ever be all right again." She turned away from him to look back out into the night. "There are times when I think I should leave. I've gotten my strength back. Maybe I should go back to New Orleans. But then I realize I'd have to board a stagecoach again, and the thought

terrifies me. I know I can't stay here forever, living on the hope that Marissa is going to return. At some point..."

Louise stopped, emotion overwhelming her as she was about to voice the horrible truth that was threatening to destroy her. George went to her and put a gentle hand on her shoulder, urging her to turn back to him. She resisted for a moment, not wanting him to see her this way, but then faced him. George gazed down at her, seeing her tears in the pale light that shone from the house.

"Don't cry, Louise," he said in a husky voice.

She lifted her gaze to his. "But I feel so helpless—I want to do something. I want to find Marissa and bring her home, but I have to accept that we may never see her again. She truly may be lost to us—especially after all this time. Oh, it's been so long, George, and with each day that passes ..."

George gathered her tenderly in his arms. "We've done everything we can. If there was anything else that could be done, I would do it in a heartbeat, but there isn't. I know Marissa. If she's alive out there and there's any way she can come home to us, she'll do it. She's a strong, intelligent young woman. She's a survivor. I can't believe she's dead. I won't allow myself even to consider it."

"But what should I do? I don't belong here. I was her companion. I was supposed to keep her safe."

George had long suspected that Louise was feeling guilty that she had survived while her charge's fate was unknown. It hurt him deeply that she was so sad. He wanted to make things better for her. He wanted to help her and support her in any way he could. He wanted to make her smile, but he knew that only one thing could do that—seeing Marissa again.

"You almost died in the attack," he told her fiercely. "Don't ever feel that you failed Marissa in any way. You were trying to save her when you were wounded. I'm just thankful you're alive."

"You are?" Her breath caught in her throat at his unexpected declaration.

"Yes." George's answer was almost a groan.

In that moment, the careful control he'd been keeping over his own turbulent emotions was destroyed. He sought her lips in a hungry kiss.

Louise was stunned by the power of his embrace. He had kept himself so distant from her that she'd had no idea he harbored tender feelings toward her. When he broke off the kiss and stepped away from her, she found she was a bit lost.

"I'm sorry, Louise. That should never have happened," George told her.

"Are you really sorry?" she asked a bit breathlessly as she stared up at him.

He looked down at her in the moonlight and found himself smiling gently at her. "No. No, I'm not sorry. I've wanted to do that for some time now, but..."

"I know," Louise said a bit sadly. "It's hard to allow ourselves any bit of happiness while we're worrying about Marissa."

"But we both know that at some point we have to go on with our lives."

They fell silent, standing together there at the porch railing surrounded by the West Texas night.

"Tell me about yourself," Louise finally said. "Here I am, living in your home, taking advantage of your wonderful hospitality, and I know so little about you—only what Marissa told me." She smiled up at him as she remembered. "Marissa said you were—and I quote—wonderful and perfect and the best uncle in the whole world."

He returned her smile as he imagined his niece saying that. "She's one special girl. But considering that I'm her only uncle, there wasn't a lot of competition." He paused, then went on,

"There's not much to tell about me. I was married many years ago, but my wife, Julie, died in childbirth. The baby, too."

"I'm sorry."

"It was a rough time for me, but it's been almost twenty years now." It surprised George to realize that he didn't think of Julie very often anymore. He supposed it was true that time was a great healer. "Since then I've just concentrated on building up the Crown."

"Well, you've done a magnificent job. It's a wonderful ranch."

"I'm proud of it."

"Marissa told me West Texas would grow on me, and she was right." As she thought of Marissa again, her smile faltered.

"What about you, Louise?" George asked, wanting to distract her. "I know so little about you. Were you ever married?"

"No—although I was engaged once, but then I found out that he was only marrying me for my money, so I broke off the engagement. My parents left me a substantial inheritance. Now I spend most of my time working for social causes and helping the poor."

"You're a very special woman, Louise."

At his gentle words, she looked up at him again and was mesmerized by the look in his eyes. "Thank you."

George really wanted to kiss her again, but knew he should wait. With an effort, he forced himself to be a gentleman.

"Well, it's getting late. I guess we should call it a night," he said.

Louise had been hoping that he might kiss her again, and she had to fight to hide her disappointment. "You go on in. I'm going to stay out here a little while longer."

"All right. If you need anything, just let me know."

She wanted to tell him that she needed him to kiss her, but the thought so surprised her that she only nodded in response. When George had gone inside, Louise stood there alone, wondering what had come over her.

She had always been prim and proper. She was a lady. Why was she thinking about George this way?

Louise frowned into the darkness, even as she remembered his embrace, and she smiled a bit. His kiss had certainly been wonderful. And he was so strong and so supportive, not to mention handsome.

For the first time in all the weeks she'd been there, her heart lightened a bit.

George lay in his bed angry with himself for having been so forward with Louise. He did not want to take advantage of her in any way, but at the time kissing her had seemed so right. And it had certainly felt right.

He rolled over and sought sleep, but the memory of how wonderful she'd felt in his arms was burned into his consciousness. Louise had been with him on the ranch for weeks now, and he'd discovered that he liked having her there. She was a calming presence, a gentle woman. She was pretty, too, there was no denying that. George thanked God that she had made a full recovery from her wound.

He thought of Marissa then. He missed his niece, longed to have her there with him, too. She had suffered so much losing her father, and then to have witnessed the horror of the raid and been taken by Comanche ...

Happy memories of Marissa played in his mind, and he smiled in the darkness. She had been a beautiful little girl, and she'd grown into an even more beautiful woman. He prayed Marissa would come back to him. He vowed that if she did, he would protect her and make sure she was never in any danger again.

Sleep was long in coming for George that night.

Chapter Nineteen

Laughing Woman was devastated by the loss of her husband. She mourned him deeply. The only good she could find in all that had happened was that Wind Ryder was gone. It did not matter that he had taken the other whites with him. They meant nothing. Wind Ryder had been the one to cause all the trouble for Bear Claw, and now they were rid of him.

"Laughing Woman!"

She heard another woman call her name from outside her lodge, and she got up to see who wanted her.

"What is it?" she asked as she found Soaring Dove waiting there for her.

"It is Bear Claw—"

"What about my son?" Laughing Woman frowned. Was something wrong? She knew the young woman cared for Bear Claw.

"He is getting ready to leave the village."

"Why?"

Soaring Dove looked nervous as she spoke, but she had to tell Laughing Woman. "Bear Claw is still angry with Wind Ryder. He says he wants to get his captive back."

Laughing Woman was instantly furious with her son. Wind Ryder was gone! Bear Claw should have been jubilant, not angry over a stolen captive. She was going to find him and tell him so.

"Where is he now?"

"By the horses," Soaring Dove told her.

Without another word, Laughing Woman hurried off to confront her son. She reached him just as he was about to leave.

"Bear Claw! I must speak to you!"

When Bear Claw looked at her, Laughing Woman could see the rage within him.

"What do you want, Mother?" He was irritated by her interference.

"Where are you going?"

"It is none of your concern where I am going, woman. I am no youth to be watched over and coddled," Bear Claw snapped, wishing she would go away and leave him to his plan.

Laughing Woman was hurt and infuriated by his dismissal of her. "You are my son. We have just buried your father. He has been dead only two days, and now *you* want to leave me, too?"

"There is something I must do," he told her seriously.

"Are you going after Wind Ryder?"

"Yes. There is much I have to settle with him."

"You are wrong! There is nothing for you to settle with him. He is gone! That was always our hope—that he would leave, and he finally has. Why do you chase after him? Your father's vision was right! There can be peace in the village now that Wind Ryder is no longer here."

"There can be no peace for me," Bear Claw said angrily. "He has stolen that which is mine! I will have the captive back!"

"Let them go! The whites have caused nothing but trouble for us here in the village. We are well rid of them. You are a fine and mighty warrior. There is no need for you to go after Wind Ryder!"

"There is every need, Mother," he said tersely. The humiliation he had suffered at Wind Ryder's hands through the years

had only intensified after Wind Ryder had taken the boy from him in front of the entire village. He had waited a day to mourn his father's death, but now he would find his enemy and seek his revenge.

"You have nothing to prove!" Laughing Woman insisted, her desperation growing. She feared that if he left her, he might never come back.

"I have everything to prove," he said, swinging up on his horse's back.

"Bear Claw—my son—you should stay here and celebrate your newfound peace. There is no need for you to go after him."

"Out of my way, woman," Bear Claw ordered coldly.

He felt no tender emotion for his mother as he wheeled his mount around and galloped away. He needed no nagging woman trying to keep him from his destiny.

Wind Ryder had stolen his captive. Everyone in the tribe had seen it.

Too many times he had suffered embarrassment at Wind Ryder's hands. He was going to hunt Wind Ryder down. And he was going to kill him. And the boy. And Crazy One.

And Shining Spirit, too—but only after he'd had his way with her.

Bear Claw was smiling as he raced off, following Wind Ryder's trail.

"The ranch is west of Dry Springs," Marissa told Wind Ryder. "About an hour's ride out of town. Have you been there before? Do you know the area?"

Wind Ryder nodded. "The tribe has traveled that way. It will be a long trip."

"That doesn't matter," she said, smiling at him. "What matters is that we're going."

Wind Ryder stared at her, seeing the delight in her smile. He had always thought her lovely, but she had never seemed more beautiful to him than she did now. She truly was a shining spirit. His father had been very wise in naming her.

At that moment, Wind Ryder had a great desire to rein in and pull Shining Spirit from her horse. He longed to make love to her right there in broad daylight in the middle of the countryside. He fought down the impulse. It would be a little difficult to do with Crazy One and Joe looking on.

Wind Ryder started to smile at the thought, but stopped. It was then he realized that they might never make love again.

Everything was different now that they had left the village. He had protected Shining Spirit by claiming her as his wife, but soon she would no longer need his protection. He was taking her home—back to her own people. They would never be alone again.

He scowled, wondering what he would do after he had seen her safely home.

Marissa had been watching him, and she saw the change in his expression.

"Are you sorry we left the village?" she asked. She feared he was regretting his decision.

"No. All is as it should be," he answered without emotion. He did not want to betray the turmoil and pain that had arisen within him at the thought of never knowing her love again.

Wind Ryder did not want to talk anymore. He kneed his horse and rode ahead, leaving the rest of them to follow. In the mood he was in, he did not want to be too close to Shining Spirit. He needed to keep some distance between them.

Joe was unaware of Wind Ryder's mood. He had come to admire Wind Ryder greatly, and he wanted to stay by his side all the time. He hurried to catch up with him.

"Wind Ryder—" Joe looked up at him as he reached Wind Ryder's horse's side.

Wind Ryder glanced at the youth.

"Thanks for helping me get away," Joe said.

He hadn't had time to talk with Wind Ryder much or to get to know him. He was still feeling the pain of his injuries, but just being away from the Comanche village had lifted his spirits, so he could ignore the physical discomfort.

"It is good that we are gone from the village," Wind Ryder said. "There will be peace now."

"How long did you have to stay there? It musta been awful for you," the boy said, unable to imagine spending years with the Comanche. Just the short time he'd spent with them had been hell. He couldn't imagine how Wind Ryder and Crazy One had managed to survive.

"I was brought to the village when I was six," he answered.

"Were you scared like me?"

"Yes. It was not an easy time."

"Did you want to go home?" Joe shuddered at the thought of being forced to spend the rest of his life with the Comanche.

"I tried to run away, but each time they found me and brought me back."

"Well, they aren't gonna find you and take you back this time," Joe said with confidence. "You don't ever have to go there anymore. Now you can go home, just like me."

Wind Ryder was almost certain he knew what the boy was going to find when they returned, but he said nothing. At least Joe was still alive. If he'd remained Bear Claw's captive much longer, there was no telling what torture the other warrior would have inflicted on the boy.

"How come your name's Wind Ryder?" Joe asked with a child's curiosity.

"Chief Ten Crow called me that because I could ride like the wind," he answered simply.

"Really?" Joe's eyes rounded in awe. "I want to be a good rider like you some day."

"You will be," Wind Ryder said with confidence.

The boy beamed up at him as they continued on.

Bear Claw rode hard as he followed the tracks of his quarry. It was good that Wind Ryder was not trying to hide his trail. It made what he planned to do very simple. True, he was a full day behind Wind Ryder, but with any luck, he would catch up to him soon.

The warrior's smile was feral as he thought of the pleasure he would get out of killing Wind Ryder. He had hated him from the moment his father had taken him into their family all those years ago. Bear Claw had been the oldest, and yet his father had always favored Wind Ryder.

The rage Bear Claw had harbored for all these years was now full-blown. Soon Wind Ryder would cower in submission before him. Soon Wind Ryder would die by his hand.

Just thinking about having that much power over Wind Ryder gave Bear Claw a rush of intense satisfaction, and the thought that Shining Spirit would be watching all the while made him feel even more powerful.

Soon he would find them.

Very soon.

Wind Ryder was still awake long after everyone else had fallen asleep. He lay unmoving, staring up at the star-studded night sky.

His thoughts were troubled, for it would not be long until they reached the white world, and it was then that he would have to begin thinking of himself as Zach again. It would not be easy.

Disturbed, Wind Ryder faced the truth: He was alone. His family had been murdered. And now Ten Crow was dead, too.

Wind Ryder had been forced to become self-sufficient. He had not allowed himself to care for anyone until now—until Shining Spirit. And he did care about her deeply, but he knew they could have no future together. She was excited about returning to the white world, but he had heard how the whites treated returning captives. He would do her more harm than good if he stayed with her. Though his skin might be white, they would always look upon him as a Comanche warrior.

More than anything, Wind Ryder wanted Shining Spirit to be safe and happy again. She had made it clear she wanted to return to the life she was accustomed to. He had nothing to offer her, and he had no idea what his future held. She would be better off without him.

Wind Ryder shifted to his side, and he immediately regretted his action, for there, directly in his line of vision, was Shining Spirit. She was sleeping just across the campfire from him. She was close—so very close.

Biting back a growl of frustration, Wind Ryder rolled back over. He was glad the others were sound sleepers or he would have awakened them by now with all his tossing and turning. He glanced back at Shining Spirit once more and could see that she slept peacefully next to Crazy One, completely unaware of his tormented thoughts.

Frustrated, Wind Ryder got up and moved silently out of the glow of the campfire. It was going to be a long night. He would regret the lack of sleep the next day, but he could not force slumber to come. He sat down some distance away with his back to the campsite; there was no reason to continue to torture himself by watching her sleep.

Marissa did not know what had disturbed her rest, but she awoke sensing that something wasn't right. She immediately noticed that Wind Ryder was gone. Worried, she got up to look for him.

She moved quietly, not wanting to wake the others. It didn't take her long to find him.

Wind Ryder sensed someone behind him and turned to find Shining Spirit making her way toward him. His expression was intense as he watched her. Cast in a golden glow by the low-burning campfire, she was a vision of loveliness.

"Is something wrong?" she asked softly.

"No. Nothing's wrong. Go back to sleep," he answered tersely as he stood up.

"You look worried." Marissa went to him.

Before he could move away from her, she put her arms around him and started to kiss him. At the touch of her lips, Wind Ryder tensed. He took her by the upper arms and held her away from him.

Marissa was stunned by his move. He had never treated her this way before. The change in him troubled her. He seemed so distant to her—so cold.

Before she could say anything more, the sound of Joe's worried call rent the night. "Wind Ryder?"

"We'd better go back," Wind Ryder told her, grateful for the boy's interruption.

He turned away from her and went back to where the boy was bedded down.

"Are you all right?" he asked Joe as he knelt down beside him.

Joe nodded sleepily. "Now that you're here, I am. I was worried about you 'cause you were gone. I was scared."

"I'm here."

Joe yawned and, secure once more, let his eyes drift shut.

Wind Ryder glanced at Shining Spirit; she had already lain down on her own blankets next to Crazy One, her back to him.

Wind Ryder did not try to sleep. There was no point. He returned to sit in the darkness alone. Peace was not his that night.

Marissa lay awake, trying to understand what had been troubling Wind Ryder. He had acted so strangely, putting her from him. She glanced toward where he should have been bedded down, but he was not there. He had gone off into the night again. For a moment, she considered going after him again, but she didn't. He obviously needed some time by himself.

Closing her eyes, she sought sleep. Her last thought as she drifted off was of the pleasure she always found in Wind Ryder's arms.

Chapter Twenty

"Wind Ryder is in a strange mood today," Marissa remarked to Crazy One as they watched him and Joe riding ahead of them the following day. He had had little to say to either one of them that morning.

"Yes, his mood is strange," Crazy One agreed. "Perhaps he is afraid."

"Wind Ryder? Afraid?" Marissa was shocked by the very idea. He was fearless and brave. She couldn't imagine that anything could trouble him, but then she remembered how she'd found him awake and sitting alone in the middle of the night. She realized Crazy One might be right.

"I am frightened. Aren't you?"

"No. I'm excited. I can't wait to get to my uncle's ranch. Don't be afraid. I'll be with you to help you."

"But all the whites will hate us now."

"No, they won't."

"Yes, they will. We are squaw women. They will think we are lower than dogs," Crazy One warned her.

Marissa had been thinking only of the joy of being reunited with her uncle, but now she faced an ugly truth she hadn't considered.

The whites would think her a ruined woman.

"I don't think it will be that terrible," Marissa said hesitantly.

"There will be some who will want us dead."

"It doesn't matter what they want, and we don't care what they think," Marissa said, realizing she truly didn't care what anybody thought of her. "The only thing that matters is that we are free again."

"Yes, we are," Crazy One agreed, an almost dreamy look coming into her eyes. She had never thought she would live to see the day.

Marissa admired her strength. "I don't know how you managed it—being all by yourself in the village for so many years."

"It was not easy, but once they thought I was crazy, they left me alone."

"Well, I just thank heaven that Wind Ryder is taking us back. Even if the whites do consider me an outcast, I'd rather be an outcast in the white world than a slave in a Comanche tribe."

"Slave?" Crazy One looked at her, a bit confused. "You were not Wind Ryder's slave. You are his wife."

"What?" Complete shock stunned Marissa to silence.

Crazy One saw the younger woman's look of surprise. "He did not tell you?"

"Tell me what?"

"After your fight with Moon Cloud, he claimed you as his wife to keep you safe. No one would dare harm the wife of one of the tribe's fiercest warriors. It was a fine thing for Wind Ryder to do—protecting you that way."

The whole time Crazy One was talking, Marissa's mind was racing. Wind Ryder had claimed her as his wife?

"It does not matter that he did not tell you. What matters is that he kept you safe."

Marissa looked at Wind Ryder as he rode so proudly and confidently ahead of them. He was a tall and powerful warrior. And, according to Crazy One, he was her husband.

"You have come to love him, haven't you?" Crazy One asked.

Love him? Marissa asked herself. Did she love him?

Why else would she have given herself to him with such abandon? Why else would his kiss and caress leave her weak with wanting him?

"Many women wanted to be Wind Ryder's wife," Crazy One went on, "but you were the one he chose." She smiled at her, thinking Shining Spirit would be happy about the news.

"I—I have to talk to Wind Ryder."

Marissa's thoughts and emotions were in turmoil as she put her heels to her horse's sides and rode to catch up with him. It seemed so clear to her now. She loved him—he had protected her—he had saved her—and now he was taking her home. She was ready to tell him of her love for him, but first she wanted to know why he hadn't told her of their marriage.

"Joe, I need to speak with Wind Ryder alone for a moment."

The boy was surprised, but reined in and fell back to ride with Crazy One. Crazy One made sure they stayed a good distance back.

Wind Ryder looked at Shining Spirit. He could see that she appeared upset about something, and he wondered what could be wrong.

"Crazy One just told me that we're married. Is that true?"

In her heart, she was hoping he would declare his love for her. She waited almost breathlessly for his answer.

Wind Ryder had never intended for her to learn that he had taken her as his wife in the tribe. He was glad that she was angry, for he needed to put distance between them. It was going to hurt him to face her, but he was doing it for her own good.

"I claimed you as my wife to keep you safe while we were in the village, but you are not bound to me in any way. A Comanche marriage means nothing in your world."

Marissa had expected declarations of love and devotion. She stared at him, her expression frozen. She couldn't believe their loving had meant so little to him.

"Did you really take me as your wife to protect me—or just so no other warrior could have me?" she challenged angrily.

"I did not force you. You came to me willingly."

His statements were cold, and her heartbreak and misery were complete. What they'd shared had only been sex to him. She could never let him know that it had meant much more to her.

"I had no choice," she said. "I did what had I to do to survive—to stay alive."

Wind Ryder's mood turned black as he recognized his own words—his own desperation from his early days as a captive. She had submitted to him because she had had no other choice. She had surrendered to him out of fear. She thought of him just as he knew all the others would once they reached the white world.

To Shining Spirit, he would always be a Comanche warrior.

"I will see you to your uncle, and then I will take care of Crazy One and Joe."

Wind Ryder did not know what he would do once he'd made sure the captives were safe and settled.

He didn't belong in either world—Comanche or white.

He would truly be alone.

Marissa said nothing more, but slowed her horse's pace. She almost wished that Crazy One wasn't there, for she didn't want to speak with anyone. But she took her place by the old woman's side, while Joe returned to ride with Wind Ryder.

"All is well with Wind Ryder?" Crazy One asked.

"Yes," was all she answered.

Crazy One was curious about their conversation and glanced at Shining Spirit. The younger woman's dark expression surprised her. As a warrior's wife—especially Wind Ryder's—she should

have been proud. Crazy One wondered what had transpired between them, but she did not ask.

Bear Claw's rage drove him relentlessly. He was glad Wind Ryder had the women and the boy with him. It slowed his pace and made him more vulnerable. He could tell their tracks were fresher, that he was closing in. If all went as he hoped, he would catch up with them that very night. The anticipation excited him.

The day passed quickly for Wind Ryder. There wasn't a lot of conversation, but Marissa did speak of how her uncle had worked to establish his ranch and make it a success.

Joe told them about his family and their spread near Sidewinder.

Wind Ryder and the women shared a pained look, thinking about what the boy was going to face when they found out the truth, hoping someone in his family had survived.

Crazy One remained quiet. The years of living in fear and misery with the Comanche had taken their toll on her. Fear was eating at her, and she still had trouble believing they were going back. It would be a difficult transition for her. She just hoped that once they were among the whites, she would find some measure of peace.

Wind Ryder glanced over at the older woman and saw her troubled, haggard expression. He had always known that life was hard for her in the village, but for the first time now, he realized how strong a woman she was to have survived her captivity. He had never forgotten the savage beating she'd gotten for trying to take care of him as a child.

"Everything will be all right," he said to her.

Crazy One glanced at him.

Their gazes met, and the fear in her eyes faded.

"You would not lie to me." It was a statement of fact. She trusted him.

"No."

For the first time in many years, she smiled at him.

The smile touched his heart, and he smiled back. He was going to do everything he could to make life better for her.

Wind Ryder glanced at Shining Spirit. She had said little directly to him, and he doubted that she ever would again. He had wanted to distance himself from her. He knew it was best to let her go. But he wondered if he could bear the pain.

They made camp near a small stream that night. They had covered a good distance, and they all were tired. They fell asleep quickly, even Wind Ryder. His lack of rest the night before had taken its toll on him.

Bear Claw knew he was closing on Wind Ryder. He was about to bed down for the night when he caught sight of the glow of a campfire ahead in the distance. Leaving his horse behind, he moved forward on foot. He did not want to risk making any sound that would alert Wind Ryder to his presence.

He was certain Wind Ryder had no idea he was being followed. The thought left him smiling. He wanted that element of surprise.

Bear Claw went close enough to see the four people bedded down around the fire.

An immense feeling of power overcame him. He would kill Wind Ryder first, then worry about the others.

Crazy One did not know what had awakened her from her sound sleep. There were many nights when she woke up and lay for hours, unable to rest. She didn't bother to stir or get up. There was nowhere to go. It would be dangerous to wander around in the

wilderness this late at night. She glanced at the fire, but it was still burning, so there was no need for her to tend to it. She tried to relax. She closed her eyes again.

And then she heard it—

The sound of a small rock dislodged in the distance.

Crazy One held her breath. She knew it might be nothing more than an animal hunting in the night, but the chill that shivered up her spine warned her otherwise. She waited, wishing she had a weapon close at hand. Ever so cautiously, she turned her head to look out into the darkness in the direction the sound had come from.

The light of the campfire glinted off a gun barrel, aimed in their direction.

"Wind Ryder!" The scream erupted from her just as the first shot was fired.

He reacted instantly. He threw himself sideways and, by a miracle, avoided being shot dead as he slept. The rifle bullet slammed into his blankets. Wind Ryder grabbed up his gun and dove into the darkness for cover.

Marissa and Joe were both shocked from their sleep by Crazy One's warning shout and the gunshot. Joe scrambled away into the night, all the horrors of the Comanche raid on his home fueling his mindless panic.

"Run!" Crazy One was shouting as she herself started to flee.

Bear Claw was furious at the old woman's interference. In that moment, he had never hated anyone as much as he hated her. He knew what he was going to do. He took careful aim.

Crazy One was turning, ready to follow Joe, as the second shot rang out. The bullet tore through her. She cried out in a bloodcurdling scream that rent the night. She looked once toward Marissa as she collapsed to the ground.

Marissa was horrified by what she'd just witnessed.

First Louise—

Now Crazy One—

Time seemed to pass in slow motion as she turned toward the older woman, wanting to help her.

She heard the sound of someone running toward her and thought it was Wind Ryder.

He would come to save her.

He would help her.

And then she looked up.

Horror unlike anything she'd ever felt before filled her at the sight of Bear Claw charging toward her.

Chapter Twenty-one

"*N*o!"

Bear Claw was there before she could grab her knife. In a violent, punishing move, he jerked Shining Spirit to her feet. He pinned her savagely against his chest and held his knife to her throat as he backed away to stand before some rocks. He didn't want to give Wind Ryder the chance to sneak up on him from behind.

It would have been a simple thing to shoot her down like Crazy One, but he wanted Wind Ryder to suffer.

Marissa tried to fight him.

He jerked her even more tightly against him and pressed the sharp blade harder against her throat. A line of blood appeared on her fair skin.

She went still.

Bear Claw chuckled evilly in her ear. He lifted his gaze to stare out into the night. Wind Ryder was out there somewhere watching, and Bear Claw planned to give him quite a show.

"Well, *brother*, where are you? Can you not show your face? Or are you too afraid of me now?"

"I fear no coward." Wind Ryder's voice echoed through the night.

Bear Claw glanced around but couldn't determine where the voice had come from. "Show yourself or watch your woman die!"

Silence reigned as Bear Claw waited and listened. He felt no fear of Wind Ryder. He had Shining Spirit. There was no way Wind Ryder could take a shot at him and not hit her. He was safe.

Wind Ryder would have to come out—

And when he did—

Bear Claw pressed the knife harder against her throat, wanting to encourage Wind Ryder to take action. He smiled at Shining Spirit's whimper. The power he had over her made him feel invincible.

"Wind Ryder! You hide in the darkness. Shall I go ahead and slit Shining Spirit's throat as I did your dog's?" he called out. "Your dog did not fight much. Do you think your woman will?"

Wind Ryder's blood ran cold at Bear Claw's words. Hidden in the darkness with Joe huddled by his side, he watched and waited for a chance to make his move against the man he'd once considered a brother. He knew Bear Claw's threats were real, and he knew he had to take action. He could not let Shining Spirit suffer at this man's hands. His grip tightened on his rifle.

Joe looked up at Wind Ryder, his expression questioning as he waited for his hero to save Shining Spirit. Wind Ryder picked up a stone and handed it to the boy, motioning for him to throw it to the far side of the campsite on his signal. The boy nodded in understanding, ready to do whatever he could to help.

Marissa could feel the blood seeping from the mark Bear Claw had made on her neck, and she was desperate for some way to help Wind Ryder. He was out there watching. She knew he was trying to save her.

Her only hope was her knife. Bear Claw didn't know she had it. The way Bear Claw was holding her with one arm across her chest, pinning her against him, her lower arms and hands were

free. If she could pretend to sag weakly just a bit and somehow manage to get a hand on her weapon, she might be able to stab him. Then she could get away, and Wind Ryder would be able to get a clear shot at him.

The pain of the knife on her throat convinced her to take the chance.

Marissa readied herself.

"Wind Ryder! Are you too afraid to show yourself?" Bear Claw called out. "Are you mourning Crazy One? I enjoyed watching Father beat her whenever she was kind to you. There were times when I would chase her down and hit her myself. She is dead now."

Marissa did not understand what Bear Claw was saying in the Comanche tongue, but she could restrain herself no longer from trying to get away. She let herself go limp for an instant and snatched the knife from her waistband.

Bear Claw shifted his hold on her, trying to tighten his grip, as Wind Ryder ordered Joe to throw the rock.

At the sound of the rock tumbling in the distance, Bear Claw turned in that direction, expecting to see Wind Ryder.

Marissa knew the time was right, and she attacked. With all the force she could muster, she swung her lower arm back, stabbing at any part of his body she could reach. She heard him grunt in pain as she buried the knife in his thigh. For an instant, his hold on her loosened. She jerked free and threw herself to the ground.

In that moment, Wind Ryder's shot rang out in the night.

Bear Claw stood motionless for an instant, his expression one of disbelief as he stared in the direction the shot had come from. His knife dropped from his hand. Blood poured from the knife wound on his thigh and from the bullet wound in his chest.

Wind Ryder stood and showed himself.

Across the distance in the pale light of the campfire, their gazes met and locked.

"Wind Ryder—" The name was a curse on his lips as Bear Claw crumpled to the ground.

Dead.

Wind Ryder ran forward, rifle in hand. He could think of nothing except getting to Bear Claw and making sure he was dead. He knelt beside him and turned him over. He stared down into the face of the man he had come to hate. He did not understand how a man like Bear Claw could be born of a father like Ten Crow. It saddened him to know that he had taken his life, but Bear Claw had left him no choice. It had been kill or be killed.

Certain at last that Bear Claw would never harm anyone again, Wind Ryder stood up and went to Shining Spirit.

"Are you all right?" Wind Ryder asked, his voice gruff. He wanted to hold her, to tell her of his feelings, but he held himself back.

"Yes," she answered tightly, the injury to her neck very slight. She wanted to go into his arms and stay there for eternity, but she knew it wasn't to be. Instead, she looked worriedly for the boy. "Where's Joe?"

Joe came out of hiding when he heard them talking.

"She's dead," Joe said, staring down at Crazy One, who lay unmoving.

Marissa and Wind Ryder hurried to console him.

"Are you all right?" Marissa asked Joe, worried about him. He was so young to have witnessed so much death.

"Yes—I think so," Joe said hoarsely. "Crazy One saved us." He looked up at them. "She saved all of us."

"Yes, she did," Wind Ryder answered.

He knelt beside the old woman and took her lifeless hand in his. He was tormented by the promise he'd made to her that very

afternoon. He had told her everything was going to be all right. He had believed they would be safe on the trip to the ranch. He had never suspected that Bear Claw would come after them. He had never thought he was putting her in any danger.

Guilt and anger assailed Wind Ryder.

He had promised Crazy One a better life, and now she was dead.

Marissa was as torn by the older woman's death as he was. She did not understand why fate had spared her again. The only thing that kept her from breaking down was her firm belief that there was a better life after this one—that Crazy One would find peace in heaven—far more peace than she'd ever known on Earth. There, she would at last be reunited with her family.

"Oh, Crazy One, I'm so sorry."

Marissa gave vent to her tears.

Wind Ryder almost took her in his arms, but he stopped himself.

"What are we gonna do?" Joe asked. He was trying to be brave, but he was visibly shaking. He looked around nervously. "Are there any more Comanche coming after us?"

Marissa went to hug the boy.

Wind Ryder shook his head. "Bear Claw came alone. He is dead. There will be no more bloodshed."

Joe looked relieved.

"You did a fine job," Wind Ryder praised him. "Without your help, I might not have been able to get off that shot."

The boy brightened a bit at the praise. "Can we go home now?"

His question was so pitiful, it tore at Wind Ryder.

"Yes, Joe. We're going home."

Wind Ryder hoped, for the boy's sake, that when they got back they would discover he had a home to go to.

They did not sleep the rest of the night.

Marissa tended to Joe, trying to calm and reassure him, while Wind Ryder buried Crazy One and Bear Claw.

At first light, Wind Ryder rode out to look for Bear Claw's horse. It was a fine animal. When he found it, he was tempted for a moment to take the mount for Joe, but then changed his mind and turned it loose. He wanted no reminders of the man who'd tried to kill them while they slept.

He returned to the campsite, and they said their final goodbyes to Crazy One. They stood over her grave, and Marissa offered up a prayer.

Joe looked up at her when they'd finished praying.

"We never knew her real name," he said sadly, tears welling up in his eyes.

"I know it," Wind Ryder said softly.

They both looked at him expectantly.

"When I first came to the village, I remember she told me her name was Elizabeth."

"Elizabeth," Marissa whispered as she gave Joe a loving hug.

They stood over her grave a little longer, then Wind Ryder quietly went to get their horses.

His mood was dark. Any connection he'd had to the tribe had died with Crazy One and Bear Claw. He was leaving that part of his life behind forever.

He led the horses back to where the others were waiting for him, eager to leave this place of heartache.

"Let's go home, Wind Ryder," Marissa said wearily.

"From now on, my name is Zach, Marissa," he told her.

She was startled, but as their gazes met, she understood. "Let's go home, Zach."

They mounted up and rode for the Crown Ranch.

The terror of the night had taken its toll on Marissa. She had honestly believed that things were going to be all right for all of them—that they were all going to find happiness once they returned to the white world. But now Crazy One—Elizabeth—was dead. Marissa wondered what else the future held for them.

Zach looked back toward the graves one last time. Sorrow filled him. He had wanted to protect Crazy One, and yet she had been the one to protect him—just as she had when he'd first come to the village.

He turned away and stared out across the wide expanse of land. His future lay somewhere out there before him. He kneed his horse to a quicker pace. He was done with the past.

The days and miles passed slowly.

At first, Marissa couldn't stop looking back, fearful someone else might be following them but with each passing mile she grew calmer, and her spirits lightened as they shortened the distance to her uncle's ranch. At the ranch, she would find peace.

Marissa was proud of how well Joe was handling himself. She prayed that they would find a way to put his life back together. He had already suffered enough.

Marissa often found herself watching Joe and thinking that Zach must have been much like him as a boy. She was glad that they had gotten Joe away from the village so quickly. Life had been hard on him, but not as hard as it had been on Zach.

The days and nights were difficult for Marissa. As angry as she'd been with Zach, she could not forget the intimacy they'd shared. Nor could she forget that he had taken her as his wife to protect her and now he had given up everything—his whole life—to see her home.

They had been traveling for two weeks when one night, as they were getting ready to bed down, Zach came to her.

"We passed near the way station where you were taken captive today," he told her.

"We're that close to Dry Springs?" Marissa asked excitedly.

"Yes. We should be at your uncle's ranch very soon."

"That's wonderful," she said as a torrent of emotion tore through her.

"It will be good to see you returned to your family."

He stood there staring at her. The last thing he wanted to do was give her over to her family. What he really wanted was to take her in his arms and kiss her and know the beauty of her love again.

But since the day of their confrontation, everything had changed between them. He had never dreamed it would be so difficult to be with her, and watch her, and want her, and yet have to stay away from her.

"If only—" she began, then stopped, knowing there was no point in speaking of Louise again. She couldn't change what had happened. She could only pick up the pieces of her life and try to go on. But at least she was going on—in the white world, and it was all thanks to Zach. She looked up at him, a myriad of emotions showing in her eyes. "Thank you."

He managed to nod in response, then turned away to busy himself with Joe.

Marissa lay down. She was exhausted from the long days of riding, but this night, sleep would not come. As much as she tried to fight them and keep them at bay, memories of the raid tormented her. The turmoil kept her tossing and turning long into the night. It wasn't until the early morning that she finally drifted off. Her sleep was filled with disturbing visions of violence and death.

Chapter Twenty-two

"You're sure you want to do this?" George asked Louise as they rode away from the ranch.

"I'm sure," she answered with conviction.

George nodded and said nothing more for the time being. He'd learned what a fighter she was. Her recovery had been amazing. He'd been even more impressed when she'd asked him the week before to teach her how to ride astride. Louise had been a quick study and had already mastered the technique on the quiet mare he'd given her. But her request this morning had still shocked him.

Louise was aware of George's silence and wondered if it meant disapproval. "I have to do this, George. I have to make sure I can take care of myself. I don't ever want to be afraid again."

George wanted to tell her that he would take care of her, but he knew she wasn't ready to hear that yet.

"All right, we'll start with a handgun, and once you've mastered that, we'll practice with a rifle."

She nodded her approval. "Good. And, George—"

He looked over at her.

"Thanks for taking me seriously."

"Most of the women who live out here know how to use a gun, so it's good that you're interested in learning," he said.

They rode on companionably to a place down by the creek where he figured it was safe enough for her to start practicing. They reined in there and dismounted, tying up their horses.

George took out the handgun he'd brought along in his saddlebag and the tin cans she'd use for targets. He checked to make sure the gun was loaded.

"Let me set up these cans, and we'll see what you can do," he said.

They walked to a fallen tree and he lined the tin cans up along the trunk. Moving back a ways, he handed the sidearm to her.

"Be careful, it's loaded."

"It's heavy." Louise was surprised by the weight of the weapon.

"You can use two hands if you need to."

"No, I'm going to learn to do this right. There wouldn't have been time during the raid to worry about aiming with both hands. I've got to get good at this."

"All right, let's see what you can do."

George went to stand behind her. He lifted her arm to help her take aim.

"Just remember to squeeze the trigger slowly," he advised, trying to ignore the scent of her perfume as it drifted around him.

A shiver trembled through Louise at his touch. She told herself it was because she was nervous. But it did feel wonderful to have George standing so close to her. She thought fleetingly of the kiss they'd shared, then remembered the purpose of their excursion. This was no time to think about kissing. She needed to learn how to use a gun—and not just for target practice.

Louise took her time as she aimed at a can. She got off her first shot. It went wide, not even coming close to the can.

"Oh, no. I'm horrible at this! I missed all of them by a mile!" she cried in embarrassment.

"It wasn't quite that bad."

"No wonder you brought me out here so far away from everything. If we'd tried this near the house, I might have shot somebody." She had to laugh.

"Let's try it again," George said, smiling. She was only partly right about why he'd brought her away from the house. The truth was, he'd wanted some time alone with her, and this seemed the perfect place. "It's not easy. It takes a lot of practice and a lot of patience to get it right."

"I'm ready. I've waited too long as it is." Louise turned back to look at the cans. Her expression grew serious. There was an almost deadly glint in her eyes.

George understood her mood. Once more he went to stand behind her. This time he leaned in even closer to help improve her aim. Again he forced himself to ignore her sweet perfume and the soft press of her body against him. It wasn't easy.

"What do you think?" Louise asked.

"You're fine. Go ahead and shoot," he told her, but he wondered what she would have thought if she'd known exactly what he was thinking just then.

Louise fired and came much closer this time.

"Is the third time the charm?" she asked over her shoulder, not quite as embarrassed as the last time, but still not satisfied with her performance.

"Let's find out," George said encouragingly, stepping back. "Why don't you try it on your own?"

He didn't want to tempt himself too much. She was a lady, and it was broad daylight.

Louise was fiercely determined. With utmost care she took aim at the tin can and pulled the trigger.

The can went flying.

"I did it!" Louise cried out in complete and utter surprise.

She wheeled around and threw her arms about George, taking care to keep the gun pointed away from both of them.

He was a bit taken aback by her display of excitement, but enjoyed every moment of it. This was the first time he had seen her truly happy.

As he gazed down at her, the mood between them suddenly changed.

"Yes," he said solemnly, "you did do it."

George had never expected to fall in love again. After the death of his wife and child, he'd deliberately kept himself so busy with building up the ranch that he'd never thought about getting seriously involved with another woman.

And now Louise had come into his life.

Every day George gave thanks that she'd survived the Comanche raid. He still remembered how she'd looked when he'd seen her at the doctor's office that first day. She had looked so beautiful, so fragile, so delicate, but he had learned what a strong woman she was. Now that she was back in good health, he found himself fearing that she might start making plans to return to New Orleans. He decided it was time to let her know the truth of what he was feeling for her—that he'd fallen in love with her.

Ever so slowly, George lowered his head and kissed her.

"Are we there yet?" Joe asked. The seemingly endless days on the trail were wearing on him.

"Not yet, but we're getting close," Zach told him.

"How much farther do we have to go?" Joe asked.

"We should be there very soon, maybe even today," Marissa said, even more eager than he was to reach the ranch.

"Today? Really?" He looked over at her, his eyes wide with excitement.

"Really," she answered, smiling at him.

Marissa could only imagine how wonderful it was going to feel to see her uncle again. Overnight, she had managed to deal with all the horrible memories of the raid and Louise's death.

Marissa missed Louise terribly. If there were some way to turn back time and change everything that had happened that day, she would have done it, but there wasn't. She couldn't change the past. With an effort, she fought back the sorrow that threatened to overwhelm her.

This was to be a happy time.

She was almost home.

It was then they heard gunshots echoing in the distance.

"What's happening?" Marissa reined in and looked at Zach worriedly.

"I don't know," he answered, studying the horizon. He wasn't sure what they might be riding into. "Stay here. I'll go see."

"Be careful," she said nervously. She knew how any white in the area would react to seeing him.

"Who do you think it is, Marissa?" Joe asked.

"It's probably just some folks out hunting. Zach will check for us."

"White people?" The boy's expression grew hopeful.

"Yes. Why?"

Before she could say more, Joe turned his horse and urged it to a run, galloping after Zach, needing desperately to see white people again.

Louise had been mesmerized by the wondrous feeling of being in George's arms. As his lips met hers, her eyes drifted shut, and

she gave herself over to the myriad of delightful feelings that were coursing through her.

Louise had not forgotten the kiss he'd given her on the porch. But when he had made no further romantic advance, she'd come to believe that he'd thought it was a mistake. The way he was kissing her now, though, she knew it hadn't been a mistake.

She started to draw him nearer when the weight of the gun in her hand reminded her of where they were and what they'd been doing.

"Oh—the gun." It startled Louise that she'd completely forgotten she was holding it.

George gave her a lopsided grin as he let her go. "It wouldn't be too good if it went off when we weren't expecting it."

He took the revolver from her and laid it carefully aside.

"Now—where were we?"

"I think we were celebrating," Louise said, blushing at her own brazenness. She told herself she was a mature woman, but there was something about George that made her feel young again—young and happy.

"I like celebrating with you," George said in a husky voice as he took her back in his arms.

They came together a bit timidly at first, for they were finally fully acknowledging their attraction to each other. But the moment their lips met, all awkwardness was forgotten. His mouth moved over hers in a possessive brand, evoking feelings within her she'd never known before.

"Louise—"

She opened her eyes to look up at him when he broke off the kiss.

"I think we'd better head back now," he told her regretfully.

"Don't I need more practice?" she asked with a teasing smile, not wanting to be out of his arms.

"I would love to stay here and practice with you, but I'm not sure it's safe."

"Safe?" She frowned.

He smiled even more. "I wasn't talking about the gun. I was talking about keeping you safe from me."

"Are you dangerous?"

"Right now I feel like I am," he said tightly. Then deciding to be honest, he went on, "I've been taking care to keep my distance from you since that night I kissed you on the porch, but it hasn't been easy. I didn't want to take advantage of you, but then I didn't believe I could ever feel this way again."

She was afraid to let herself hope what he was going to say. "Feel what way again?"

"Louise, I love you," he declared earnestly. "I want you to marry me and stay here with me. I don't ever want you to leave me."

"Oh, George." His name was a heartfelt whisper on her lips. "I love you, too. You've been my strength. I don't know how I would have gotten through all this without you."

She found herself back in his arms.

"I don't even want to think about it," George said. "All that matters is that we're together."

He kissed her once more, deeply, passionately.

"Louise—will you marry me?" he repeated, wanting to hear her say it.

She had never believed this moment would come in her life. She had resigned herself to her spinsterhood, but now George had changed all that. She wanted him as she had never wanted another man. She loved him.

"Yes, George, I'll marry you." Louise lifted her lips to his, ready to seal her answer with a kiss.

As she did, she happened to glance over his shoulder, and she went still.

There on the hilltop across the way, silhouetted against the sky, was a Comanche warrior.

And he was staring down at them.

"Oh, my God!" Louise gasped as she froze in George's arms.

"What?"

He had been ready to kiss her when he felt the sudden change in her. He released her and turned to see what had frightened her.

"Get on your horse and ride out of here, now!" he ordered as he grabbed up the gun she'd been using for practice. "Don't look back!"

"No! I will not leave you here!" She stood her ground. "Give me that gun!"

She all but snatched the revolver out of his hand. They looked at each other for an instant. It seemed almost an eternity before he nodded.

"Get down behind the tree trunk," he ordered.

"Where are you going?"

"To get my rifle."

George ran for their horses and got his rifle and saddlebags before racing back to join her where she was taking cover behind the fallen tree.

"Why hasn't he attacked?" Louise asked. She was frightened, terrified actually, but she wasn't helpless—not this time. Her grip tightened on the gun as she waited.

"I don't know—I—"

As George spoke, a rider came charging past the warrior, galloping down the hill in their direction. George feared it was an attack. He lifted his rifle and took careful aim—

But he stopped before pulling the trigger.

He dropped the gun and stood up.

"What is it? Why didn't you shoot?" Louise demanded.

"Look," was all George could mutter as he watched the young white boy racing toward them with the warrior following.

Louise went still as she realized the rider was only a child. "Why, it's a boy—a white boy." She looked at George, incredulous. "But why is he with that warrior?"

As soon as Joe rode past him, Zach gave chase. He was afraid someone might take a shot at the boy and wanted to warn him to go slowly so he wouldn't threaten the white people.

"Joe—wait. Be careful, they don't know who you are!" Zach called out to him.

But Joe was in no mood to listen to Zach. He had no intention of slowing down. There were white people here!

He was almost home!

Louise and George were watching their approach cautiously.

"What should we do? That warrior is right behind him," Louise said, still holding her gun in a death grip.

George had his rifle in hand, too. "We wait. Neither one of them has a weapon that I can see."

And then they heard the boy's frantic calls.

"Don't shoot! Don't shoot!" Joe was gasping for breath as he rode at full speed toward their hiding place.

George stood up, showing himself to the boy.

"George! What are you doing?" Louise grabbed his arm, wanting to pull him back down to safety.

He stood his ground and hoped his instincts were right.

Joe saw the white man stand up, and his heart leaped for joy. He rode straight toward the man, tears streaming down his face.

Zach slowed his pace and stayed a short distance behind. He did not want the whites to feel threatened, but he wanted to make sure Joe was not harmed. He reined in as the boy stopped and all but threw himself from the horse's back to run to the white man who'd come forward to meet him. Zach was still worried. The white man had a gun.

Joe stopped right in front of the stranger and looked up at him. He knew he was dirty and battered and bruised, but he also knew he was almost back home.

"We're coming home—Zach brought us back," he blurted out.

George had no idea what the boy was talking about, but he could see that the child had been through a rough time. "Easy, son."

"We been riding for weeks now. I didn't think we'd ever get here." Joe was gasping in his excitement.

"What happened to you?" George asked.

"I was taken captive in a raid, but Zach's bringing me home."

"Zach?" George could not make much sense out of what the boy was saying. He looked up at the warrior who had stopped a distance away, wondering whom the boy was talking about.

"Yes, he knew the way. He brought us." He was babbling.

Before George could respond, he heard Louise cry out in shock.

"George! Look!"

He turned toward Louise, expecting more trouble. He didn't know what had frightened her, but he would defend her with his life. He would shoot to kill if need be.

Louise had come to her feet and was staring off toward the crest of the hill again, her expression one of complete amazement.

George turned back to look, expecting to see an entire raiding party there, expecting to face death.

Instead he saw only a solitary mounted figure—

A woman—

And the sun was glistening off her golden hair—

Chapter Twenty-three

"Oh, my God," George muttered as he began to tremble with the force of the emotions that besieged him.

He feared he was dreaming. He feared if he blinked she would be gone.

But she was still there.

"Mister—are you all right?" Joe asked, a little frightened by the way the man looked—almost as if he'd seen a ghost.

George was too numb to answer.

His rifle dropped from his hand, and he started running past the warrior and up the hillside.

Louise still couldn't believe her eyes.

There was the boy—

And the Comanche warrior—

But on the hilltop—

Was it really Marissa? Had she returned to them?

Suddenly she didn't care about her gun or the warrior.

Suddenly all that mattered to Louise was getting to Marissa— touching her and holding her—and reassuring herself that she was truly alive.

Louise laid the gun down and started to run after George.

Marissa had reined her horse in at the top of the hill to see what was happening below.

The sight that greeted her touched her to the depths of her soul. There below, standing with Joe, was her uncle. When Uncle George looked her way, she knew he recognized her almost immediately, for he started running toward her.

"Marissa!"

She heard him call her name, and a thrill unlike anything she'd ever known filled her heart.

"Uncle George!" She put her heels to her horse's sides and raced down the hill.

Joe looked at Zach, who had ridden down to his side and dismounted to stand with him.

"He's her uncle?" Joe asked, confused by all that was happening.

"I think so, Joe."

They waited and watched as Marissa quickly dismounted and threw herself into the white man's arms.

"You're alive!" George said over and over as he held her to his heart. "You're alive!"

He leaned back a bit to stare down at her, his expression both joyous and wondrous. He didn't know how this had come to pass, and it didn't really matter. All that mattered was that Marissa was there. She was alive and had come home to him.

"Uncle George—it really is you! It is! I never thought I'd see you again!" Marissa was crying as she clung to him frantically, unable to believe that she had really found him.

"Oh, yes, sweetheart, it's me—and you're home. At last you're home and you're safe! We searched for you for weeks! We thought we'd never see you again. We were so afraid you were dead."

"We?" Marissa asked.

"Yes, we," he replied. Gently he took her by the shoulders and turned her a little so she could see Louise.

Marissa's breath caught in her throat at the sight of her friend—alive and well and rushing toward her at that very moment.

"Louise," she whispered in a strangled voice. "Dear God—" Marissa looked up at her uncle, awed, stunned, almost speechless. "She's alive? You saved her?"

"Yes, darling, Louise is very much alive."

At that moment, Louise reached them.

She stopped a few steps away to stare at Marissa. She remembered the last time she'd seen her as the Comanche had grabbed her up. Pain stabbed her at the bloody, vivid memory, and her tears fell silently.

"Marissa—I thought I'd never see you again," Louise said in a voice just about a whisper.

"I thought you were dead," Marissa returned before rushing to hold her.

They came together in an embrace of love and desperation, of pure loving reunion. The two women stood wrapped in each other's arms, crying in joy over the gift of life they'd been given.

George went to them and put his arms around them both. It was a long moment before they even thought about moving apart, so great was their need to reassure themselves that this was reality and not a dream.

"Come, you have to meet Joe and Zach," Marissa said when they finally stopped crying and were calm enough to talk. She looked over to where the two stood watching them.

They followed her to meet the strangers.

"Uncle George—Louise—this is Joe Carter, and this is Zach Ryder. Zach brought us back."

"Zach?" George was stunned when he realized the warrior was a white man. He looked at him critically, fighting to control

his initial feelings of hatred and violence toward this man who, to all outward appearances, was a Comanche warrior. Finally he stepped forward and offered him his hand.

"Thank you, Zach, for saving my niece," George said earnestly. He clasped Zach's hand in a firm handshake. "Thank you for bringing her back to me."

"You are welcome," Zach returned.

The two men looked each other in the eye, and each recognized the other as a worthy opponent and an honorable man.

"And, Zach, this is Louise," Marissa said, her eyes welling up with tears again as she accepted the wonderful truth that her friend was alive.

"Louise?" Zach said in surprise as he faced her for the first time. "You survived the raid—"

Louise was staring at him, frightened yet trying to fight her fear. "You're not an Indian—"

"He was a captive—like me, Louise," Marissa quickly explained.

"Oh—" Louise suppressed a shiver at standing so close to him. She tempered her terror by telling herself he really was a white man—not a warrior. "Yes, I survived the raid. I was the only one. It wasn't easy, but I had George to help me."

George understood her fears and kept a supportive arm around her to give her the strength she needed to accept all that was happening.

"This is Joe," Marissa continued, going to the boy. "He was brought into the village right before Zach decided it was time for us to leave. Zach got us all away from the tribe and brought us safely here." Marissa thought about telling them of Crazy One and her tragic death, but decided against it. She would talk of her friend later, when things had settled down.

George faced Zach. He wasn't sure of the right way to phrase his question, so he decided to come out and ask forthrightly. "Are you staying here with us or returning to your tribe?"

"Zach is staying," Marissa answered before Zach had a chance. "He's not going back."

George was a bit surprised by the answer, for he knew how difficult it would be for Zach to fit in, but that didn't matter. Zach had saved his niece, and in doing that he had earned George's eternal friendship. He would help him in any and every way he could.

"Well, let's get on back to the ranch. I think it's time for a celebration."

Zach went to Joe. "Are you ready?"

"Oh, yes. Soon I'll be home!"

George went to get their horses. He stopped only long enough to pick up the weapons and then returned to where everyone was waiting. They mounted up and rode for the ranch.

Marissa rode between George and Louise. She kept looking from one to the other, wanting to reassure herself that she was truly home.

"When we get near the house, I'll ride in first," George told them, catching Zach's eye. "We don't need any trouble today."

When the house came in sight, George galloped ahead to tell everybody the news.

"Marissa's back?" Sarah repeated, staring at George as he tied his horse to the hitching rail.

"She's coming right now," he told her, pointing to where the four riders were approaching. "A man named Zach, who was raised by the tribe, is the one who led her here. He brought a young boy who'd been a captive, too."

"This is so wonderful. Our prayers have been answered," Sarah said tearfully.

"Yes, they have," George agreed gruffly. Then, thinking how his men were going to react to Zach, he added, "We'll have to find them some clothes."

"I'll take care of that as soon as I've seen Marissa. How is Louise?"

He smiled. "Louise is beside herself. Who would have thought they'd just come riding in this way?"

"I'll go get Claude and Mark."

She rushed off to find the men and give them the exciting news.

George knew Mark would be thrilled. He remembered how hard it had been on him when they'd had to give up the search.

Sarah, Claude, Mark, and all the other men who were working in the stable came up to the house to join George in welcoming Marissa back.

"Marissa!" Sarah cried out excitedly when she saw her riding up.

Though Sarah had cautioned the men that the travelers were in Comanche dress, there was still some tension among them at the sight of the warrior riding in with the women and boy.

"Easy, boys," George said in a low voice. He knew a few of the hands had short tempers and no love for the Comanche. He didn't want any trouble.

The men relaxed at his order. They prepared to welcome Marissa home.

Sarah rushed forward and hugged Marissa the minute she dismounted.

"Damn—I ain't never seen no white warrior before," one of the men said in a low voice to Claude.

"It'll be fine. He's the one who got Marissa and the boy out of there alive."

The men heard the comment, and their opinion of the stranger went up, but white or not, they wouldn't be comfortable around him as long as he looked like an Indian.

Mark was standing back, watching everything. His gaze went over Marissa as she hugged Sarah. It surprised him that he was both disgusted and aroused by the sight of her wearing the buckskin Indian dress. It reminded him far too clearly of where she'd been and of what had, no doubt, happened to her there. Still, he was glad she had returned. It looked like his fortunes had changed. His prospects were bright again—as long as he could manage to hide his reaction to seeing her this way.

"It is so good to see you!" Sarah was crying. "You have to tell me everything that happened. We were so worried about you. And when we thought you were lost ... well, George and Louise have been inconsolable. We all have."

Marissa was warmed by Sarah's affection. "I'm glad to be here, believe me."

"And who is this?" Sarah asked as she looked past Marissa to the boy and man standing by their horses.

Marissa quickly made the introductions.

"I'm gonna be going home soon," Joe piped up as Sarah took him under her wing. "Zach promised."

Marissa and Zach glanced at each other but said nothing.

As Sarah took charge of Joe, Louise and Marissa started inside. It was then that Mark stepped forward.

"Marissa—" Mark's voice was deep and his expression earnest as he went to her.

"Mark—" She stopped and gazed at him, delighted to see him. She'd been so busy with Joe and Sarah, she hadn't noticed him standing back with the ranch hands.

"I'm glad you're back," he said.

She smiled at him. "I am, too."

She had no time to say more as Louise drew her on toward the house.

"Let's all go inside and celebrate!" Louise urged.

"That will be wonderful, but I really have to have a bath first," Marissa told her.

"That's fine. You can all get cleaned up first, and then we'll have our celebration."

They went inside.

Zach had been standing off by himself watching Marissa's reunion. He'd expected the whites to be suspicious of him, and they had been. Nothing had troubled him, though, until one man had stepped forward and stopped Marissa to talk to her. Something about the way he'd looked at her—and she had looked at him— bothered Zach.

It startled him when he recognized his reaction as jealousy. He scowled to himself. He had no reason to be jealous. He had no claim on Marissa.

Now that she was 'safely back with her family, he could be moving on as soon as he took care of Joe. But seeing how the woman named Sarah had taken over tending to the boy, he was tempted to cut his ties and ride out right away. He wasn't needed or wanted at the ranch.

"Why don't you give us about an hour and then come on up to the house?" George said to his men after the women and the boy had gone inside. "We're going to have us one fine party."

"We'll do that, boss," Claude said. "Come on, boys, let's take care of their horses and go back to work for a while."

Claude stopped before Zach and stuck out his hand. "Thanks for bringing our Marissa home."

Zach nodded.

None of the others came over to speak to him.

"Coming, Zach?" George called from the bottom of the porch steps where he was waiting for him.

Zach followed him inside.

Chapter Twenty-four

"Let's see what we can find for you to wear," Louise said as she started to go through the closet in the bedroom she was using. "All of our possessions were destroyed during the raid. George was kind enough to buy me some new clothes. I know they'll be a little bit big on you, but we can go into town tomorrow, if you want, and buy everything you need."

"I don't care how big everything is. I just want to be out of this buckskin."

"Here." Louise laid out one of her prettiest day-gowns along with shoes and the necessary undergarments. "While you start getting undressed, I'll go help Sarah bring up the water for your bath."

"You don't know how delicious having a bath sounds."

"What did you do in the village?"

"There was a stream nearby, and everyone washed up there."

"I promise you will enjoy this bath much more."

"I have no doubt about it," Marissa said, actually laughing a bit.

"I'll be right back."

Left alone in the bedroom, Marissa sank down on the edge of the bed. She stared at Louise's bathtub, thinking of how, very shortly, she would be soaking luxuriously in a tub of hot water and

using real soap. As her thoughts drifted, memories of her "bath" after the fight with Moon Cloud returned. She remembered the icy water, her fury with Wind—Zach—and the way it had felt when he'd held her in his arms in the middle of the stream.

That had been their wedding night.

The thought took her by surprise.

She'd had no idea that he'd claimed her for his wife that day. And then—when he'd taken her back to the tipi—

Marissa got up and went to the window to look out. She had to distract herself. She had to banish those memories once and for all.

As she waited for Louise's return, she let her gaze sweep over the panoramic view of the countryside, and then she glanced toward the stable. She could see Mark working with one of the unbroken horses in the corral. Claude was holding the horse's bridle as Mark mounted and prepared to ride it. She couldn't hear what they were saying, but she grew excited as she waited for Claude to release the mount.

He did.

The horse spun crazily and bucked once.

Mark went flying off and landed heavily in the dirt.

Marissa knew that Zach would never have been thrown. He would have broken the horse in no time.

When she realized the direction of her thoughts, she turned away from the window. It was time to put Zach and her time in the village in the past.

Louise and Sarah returned shortly, and after filling the tub and making sure she had the linens she needed, they started from the room. Louise stopped at the door and went back to Marissa to take her in her arms.

"You have no idea how thrilled I am that you're here—safe and healthy and—"

Marissa hugged her back. "Oh, yes, I do." She smiled at her. "Because I feel the same way about you. When I saw you coming toward us, it was a dream come true. I was so sure you were dead—It was so terrible—"

"I know. I still don't know how I managed to hang on long enough for them to find me. But once they brought me into town, George found out who I was, and he took care of everything from then on. He even hired the best tracker in the area to help him try to find you, but a bad storm came through and washed out your trail. They didn't want to come back without you, but there was no way for them to keep going."

"Uncle George is a very special man."

"Yes," Louise agreed. "He is."

Something in her friend's tone of voice made Marissa look at her questioningly.

"I have to tell you—" Louise said quickly, unable to keep the secret any longer.

"Tell me what?"

"The good news. Your uncle—George and I—well, he's proposed to me, and I've accepted."

With that, Marissa threw her arms around Louise again in absolute joy. "That's wonderful! Now you truly will be family!"

"I know." Louise could think of nothing better. "You hurry and take your bath now, so we can really celebrate."

"I'll be down as soon as I can."

"We'll be waiting."

Louise left her to her privacy, and Marissa took off the buckskin dress for the last time. She stepped into the steaming water and sank down into its welcoming heat. The soap Louise had given her was scented, and Marissa felt as if she were in heaven. She gloried in the silky lather, and once she'd finished bathing, she

washed her hair, too. The towels were soft against her skin, and she was eager to put on real clothes again—to feel like a lady.

"I think I can find some clothes to fit you," George told Zach as he took him to his own bedroom at the back of the sprawling ranch house.

Zach had known the time would come when he would have to dress as a white man again, and it seemed that time had arrived. He wasn't certain he was going to like it.

"I will find a way to repay you as soon as I can," Zach told George.

"Don't worry about it. After what you did for Marissa, this is the least I can do to help you," he answered.

George went through his dresser and took out the things he thought would work for Zach.

"Here—these should fit you," George said, handing him the clothing he needed along with a pair of boots.

"Thanks."

"And you can have this room over here." He directed Zach to a bedroom across the hall from his own. "You'll be needing a bath, too. There's a bathhouse out back that the men use. I can show you where it is now, if you want."

"All right."

Zach knew that things would be more comfortable around the ranch once he was dressed as a white man. The way the whites felt about the Comanche, he was surprised that none of the hands had tried to start a fight with him. From the looks they'd given him, he was certain a few of them had thought about it.

"So, how did you come to be living with the Comanche?" George asked as they walked out to the bathhouse. He was curious

about this strong young man who'd been brave enough to help Marissa and Joe.

"I was taken captive when I was young. I was about the same age as Joe. Then I was adopted into the tribe."

"So you've lived most of your life with them."

"Yes, I did."

"Do you remember anything about your own family? Where your home was?"

"Somewhere near San Antonio, I recall, but I doubt there's anything left of it—not after all this time."

"We can check for you, if you want," George offered.

"No. There's no need. My family was killed in the raid."

"Are you sure?" he asked.

For an instant, Zach looked haunted; then he hid his emotion. "Yes, I'm sure. I do want to check on Joe's family. Is there any way to find out if he has any relatives?"

"We can go into Dry Springs and wire the town nearest his family's ranch. The law there might know something."

"Good. If there's any chance he's got family left, I want to find them for him."

"That's kind of you."

"He's a good boy."

"And what about you? What do you intend to do once you've taken care of Joe?" George asked.

"I'm not sure. I was mostly worried about bringing Marissa back. Now that she's here with you, I can move on."

"There's no reason for you to go. You're welcome to stay here at the Crown for as long as you want. And if you want a job, I can always use an extra hand."

"Thanks."

George left him at the bathhouse.

Zach went in and quickly bathed. When he'd finished, he dried himself off and began to dress, donning the clothing George had given him. Everything felt foreign to him—the underwear—the denim pants—the shirt that buttoned—the socks and boots. He felt awkward and unable to move quickly, but he knew he would have to adjust. He cut a narrow piece of leather from his loincloth and used it to tie back his hair. He started to gather up his few things before leaving the bathhouse, then stopped and stuck the knife in the waistband of his pants. He did not want to be completely unarmed. Zach drew a deep breath as he opened the door and stepped outside.

In that moment, he left his time with the Comanche behind.

He was once again Zach Ryder.

As soon as George returned to the house he sought out Louise.

Sarah was tending to Joe, so Louise had taken over in the kitchen. She was just starting to prepare dinner when she heard someone behind her and turned to see George. She didn't say a word but went straight into his arms and laid her head upon his chest.

"She came back to us," Louise said in a tear-choked voice.

"Yes, thank God, she's back."

They stood that way for a long moment, offering up thanks for Marissa's safety.

"Is she all right? Really all right?" George asked quietly when they finally moved apart.

His expression was dark and concerned as he looked down at Louise. He had put on a good face for everyone until now, but deep inside, his worries about Marissa were eating at him. It was no secret how the Comanche treated their captives, and it sickened him to think she had been tortured and abused.

Louise understood what he was thinking as she lifted her gaze to his. "She seems fine, George. We haven't talked about any of what actually happened, but she was acting as if she was all right."

He swallowed tightly. "I want to help her. I want to do everything I can for her."

"You are," Louise told him, kissing him softly. "You're loving her, and that's all she needs right now—your love and the safety of being here with you."

He nodded, feeling a little better. He was a man who liked to fix things, to make things better when he could. But in a situation like Marissa's, he was helpless to change what had happened.

"Well, she certainly has my love," he said gruffly. "She's suffered so much lately—"

"She has, but she's a strong young woman. Marissa will do just fine, you'll see."

George gathered Louise near again and kissed her warmly. She watched him as he left the room, then turned back to her work. In her heart, she was hoping and praying that she was right—that everything would be all right—with Marissa.

Only time would tell.

George saw Zach coming up to the house and went out to meet him. The change the clothes made in him was amazing.

"Everything fit all right?" George asked as Zach drew near the porch.

"Fine, thanks."

"You want to take your other things to your room? We're just sitting in the parlor."

"I'll be right back," Zach said.

George watched him as he walked inside and down the hall. He seemed a bit uncomfortable in the clothes, but that would pass. Smiling, George returned to the parlor to join the others.

Zach entered his bedroom and stopped dead as he looked up. Directly across from the door was a dresser and its mirror, and he found himself staring at his reflection.

His mirror image startled him.

So this was what Zach Ryder looked like.

The shirt he wore was a bit tight across the shoulders and the pants fit more loosely. The change was dramatic. He looked like the other white men he'd seen today.

Feeling as ready to begin his new life as he ever would, Zach left his old clothes in the room and turned back to join the celebration.

"Here he is!" George called out when he saw Zach standing in the doorway of the crowded room. "Come on in, Zach."

Zach went to his side, and George pressed a glass of whiskey into his hand.

"Here, relax a little," he said in a low voice.

Zach nodded and took a quick drink. He had had whiskey before in the village and knew its powers. He would have to be careful not to drink too much, for he had seen how it made some of the warriors crazy.

Joe ran over to talk with him.

Mark was there with the other hands, enjoying a drink and waiting for Marissa to appear. It had been a good day—a very good day. His plans were going to work out after all. There was no way of telling what had happened to Marissa while she was a captive of the Comanche, and none of the men had dared to bring up the subject. They were too loyal to George to question her reputation. And Mark would play that game, too. He would do

whatever it took to make his own dreams come true. He smiled to himself and glanced toward the hall, wondering when Marissa was finally going to join them.

Marissa sat at the dressing table and worked at pinning her hair up. It felt good to look like a lady again. It had been so long that she'd forgotten how much she enjoyed dressing up. After the months she'd spent living the life of a Comanche woman in buckskin and moccasins, it was definitely a change to be wearing petticoats and shoes.

When she had finished with her hair, she paused to stare at her reflection. Except for the fact that she was tan now instead of pale, she looked no different from the young woman she used to see in the mirror at her home in New Orleans. But she knew better. Inwardly, everything had changed.

Marissa found herself wondering how Zach was doing. She was certain Uncle George was helping him, but she knew this was going to be a difficult time for him. She wanted to do all she could for him, but she didn't know if he even wanted her help.

After one last glance in the mirror, Marissa left the bedroom. She was eager to spend time with her uncle and Louise. She wanted to relax and to laugh again.

Instinctively, Zach knew Marissa was near. He had been standing with his back to the doorway and turned when he felt her presence. He stood there, drink in hand, staring at her.

Zach had always thought Marissa was lovely—beautiful, in fact—but seeing her this way, dressed as a lady, he was amazed. Her hair was done up on top of her head, revealing the slender arch of her neck. Heat centered low in his body at the thought of pressing kisses along the sweet line of her throat. He took a drink of whiskey as his gaze dropped lower. The gown she wore was simple

and modest. It was a little big on her and so it only hinted at the sweet curves he knew lay beneath it. She looked a perfect lady, a far cry from the Comanche maiden he'd ridden in with—a far cry from the fierce, fighting woman he'd taken as his wife.

"Here she is!" George said happily as he went to embrace her.

Sarah and Louise bustled in from the kitchen where they'd been busy putting together a big meal while George had been serving up the drinks. At his announcement, all eyes turned to Marissa.

"Thank heaven, you're back!" the men were saying as they all came forward to talk with her.

Marissa made small talk with them, but found herself looking around for Zach. She didn't see him at first and thought maybe he hadn't joined them yet.

And then Marissa caught sight of him. Standing across the room was a tall, handsome white man. Her eyes widened in shocked recognition as he looked up at her and their gazes met.

Zach Ryder was there.

Chapter Twenty-five

Mark had been getting himself a drink when Marissa came into the room. He went straight to speak with her, glad to see that she was back to looking like herself. There was no telling what had happened to her while she'd been gone, but he wasn't going to worry about that. He had his eyes set on a bigger prize than any woman's virginity. Money and power were what mattered in life, and that was what he was after. He would get both by marrying her.

"Evening, Marissa," Mark said, coming to her side.

"Hello, Mark." She smiled at him a bit distractedly.

She had been watching Zach, trying to reconcile the man standing across the room from her with the warrior she'd known and loved. Zach looked so different—so wonderful—this way. She was hard put not to just walk away from Mark and go to Zach. It took an effort, but she managed to give the other man her full attention.

She'd always thought Mark nice-looking. He was tall and lean and blond. It surprised her to find that the attraction she'd felt for him during her last visit to the ranch had faded. She didn't let her reaction show as they talked, though. She pretended to listen to his every word, while in truth she was longing to be with Zach.

From across the room, Zach was keeping watch over Marissa. She appeared happy, and he was glad. Deep within him, though, an

ache had grown, for he knew they would soon be parting. It saddened Zach to think he would never see her again, but he knew it was for the best. He was an outcast among these people. When Mark had approached Marissa, Zach had been hard put to stay where he was and keep his distance. There was something about the man that troubled him, but Mark wasn't his concern. Marissa was home. She was no longer his to protect.

"Zach!"

Joe's call distracted him, and he was glad to be drawn away to join the boy and Sarah outside on the porch.

"Miss Sarah says we can go into town tomorrow and send a telegram to my family," Joe told him excitedly.

"We'll do that," Zach agreed. "With any luck, we'll hear back from them right away."

"We will," the boy said with certainty.

"Well, while you're here with us, let's have some fun. What do you say?" Sarah said with a smile.

"Yeah." Joe's eyes lit up, and he sounded like an eager, innocent child once again.

Sarah and Zach smiled. Zach seemed a little uncomfortable, and she wanted to make him feel welcome.

"Would you two like to walk down to the stable and take a look at the horses?" she asked.

"Sure," Joe answered quickly.

The three of them got up to go.

Zach cast one quick glance back inside to see that Marissa was still talking with Mark before following Sarah and Joe. His gaze lingered on Joe, and he found himself wondering what his own life would have been like if he had been rescued from the Comanche early on as Joe had been. Zach put the thought from him. There was no point in thinking about it. He couldn't change the past.

Marissa had watched Zach disappear outside. She wanted to excuse herself from Mark to follow him, and she was just about to do that when Claude and several other hands came over to talk with her, and the opportunity was lost.

Some time later, after walking through the stable and seeing the Crown's fine horses, Sarah and Joe decided to return to the house. Zach wanted to remain outside awhile longer.

"Are you sure you don't want to come with us?" Sarah asked.

"I want to see Marissa," Joe said happily. "Don't you, Zach?"

"I'll be in later," Zach said.

He wanted to see Marissa, too. He wanted to be with her, but he knew it was best if he stayed away—especially while Mark was hovering over her. He didn't like the way he felt when he saw the other man with her.

"Well, the food will be ready soon. Don't miss out."

She led Joe up to the house, leaving Zach alone with his thoughts down by the corral.

Zach appreciated all the work George had done to carve his empire out of the West Texas wilderness. He was sure it hadn't been easy fighting nature and the Comanche, but George had done it and survived. The Crown Ranch was a beautiful spread.

As he thought of the Comanche, Ten Crow slipped into Zach's thoughts. He realized Ten Crow's vision had been real. He was certain there was peace in the tribe now that both he and Bear Claw were gone.

He found he did not miss anything about the village. His only regret was Crazy One's death. She had suffered so much in her life, and he had hoped to somehow make it up to her. All he could do now was to make sure things turned out better for Joe. He wanted him returned to his family, just as Marissa had been returned to hers.

Thinking of the boy, Zach headed back toward the house to be with him.

The rest of the day passed quickly and pleasantly for Marissa. George and Louise made their happy announcement, and everyone was thrilled by the news of their upcoming marriage. The company was wonderful, the food was delicious, and just being back with Uncle George and Louise made everything seem perfect.

Joe stayed with her, needing the security she offered, and she enjoyed having him near. He only left her when Zach came back inside.

When it grew late and everyone was ready to call it a night, the men went to the bunkhouse and Sarah and Claude retired to the small outbuilding where they lived.

"Are you sure you're up to going into town tomorrow?" George asked Marissa.

"Oh, yes," she answered. "I think it's important we send the wire about Joe as quickly as we can."

"All right, then, we'll leave first thing in the morning."

"I'll be ready. Good night, Uncle George," Marissa said, kissing him on the cheek.

"Good night, sweetheart," he said, all the love he felt for her shining in his eyes.

"And I am truly thrilled about you and Louise," she said as she looked from one to the other. "I think it's wonderful."

"So do I." George gave Louise a grin.

Louise kissed him good night, and went with Marissa to her room for a chat.

"Did you enjoy yourself?" Louise asked as she helped Marissa out of her dress.

"Oh, yes. I'm still finding it hard to believe I'm actually here with you."

"I feel the same way. Joe seems to be doing quite well, considering all he's been through."

"I only hope that when we send that wire tomorrow, we get some good news back."

"What will you do if ... you don't?"

"I haven't talked to Zach about it, but I would want Joe to stay here on the Crown with me. I don't think Uncle George would mind."

"Oh, no. Of course not. Your Zach ..." Louise paused for effect. "He's quite an interesting man. He looked like a different person dressed in George's clothes, don't you think?"

"I didn't even recognize him for a moment," Marissa admitted.

"Well, he's quite handsome."

"Yes." She was reluctant to say anything more, fearful of revealing the truth of her feelings. Louise had a way of reading her mind sometimes, and this was one time when she didn't want her friend to know what was in her heart.

"Marissa—when you were in the village—what was it like? What happened?" Louise asked, sitting down on the side of the bed.

Marissa sat beside her. She had known they were going to have to talk about it eventually, and this was as good a time as any. "After the raid, we rode for days on end."

"Was Zach part of the raiding party?"

"No."

"Oh, good." Louise was visibly relieved. As much as she'd appreciated his bringing Marissa back to them, the thought that he might have been in the raiding party that had killed so many people had disturbed her.

"I wasn't given to Zach until we reached the village."

"You were 'given' to Zach?" Louise was shocked.

"Yes, I was his captive. He was very good to me," she added quickly when she saw Louise's horrified expression.

"What happened next? Were you hurt in any way?"

"No. Zach protected me. One of the other warriors tried to hurt me, but Zach saved me."

"So you really are all right?" Louise desperately wanted to believe that nothing bad had happened to Marissa, that she hadn't been raped or abused.

"I'm fine. I really am. Nothing happened to me," she answered, her heart breaking as she said it.

She was lying. Something had happened. She had fallen in love with Zach.

"I'm just so glad that you're back with us, safe and sound." Louise gave her a loving kiss and a warm hug. "Good night, darling. Sleep well."

"I will," Marissa murmured as Louise left her alone.

She had honestly thought she would sleep well that night. She was exhausted, and she was back at the ranch, resting in a comfortable bed. But sleep eluded Marissa, and she lay awake long into the night.

George looked over at Zach and Joe. "How are you two doing?"

"We're fine," Zach answered. "Thank you for everything you've done."

"No, Zach, it's like I told you before—thank *you*."

"Good night."

Zach and Joe went together to the room George had given them. A cot had been brought in for Joe to sleep on, and it didn't take the boy long to undress and seek its comfort.

"Zach—I'm sleeping in a real bed again," Joe said, grinning as he pulled the covers up to his chin. "G'night, Zach."

"Good night, Joe."

Zach blew out the lamp, then got ready for bed himself. Still feeling a bit uncomfortable and uneasy, he decided to sleep with his pants on just in case there was any kind of trouble. He sat down

on the edge of the bed and marveled at its softness. He tried to remember the last time he'd slept in a real bed. A vague and distant memory of his mother tucking him in and saying a prayer came to Zach as he settled back on the pillows and pulled the blanket up.

Closing his eyes, Zach sought rest. It had been a long and adventuresome day. He was glad that everything had turned out so well and that Marissa was home safely. He wanted only her happiness.

As he lay there in the dark thinking of Marissa, pain filled his heart. He would soon have to leave her. He didn't want to, but there was no future for them together. He had seen her with Mark and knew the cowboy was the kind of man she deserved—not someone like him, a man raised in the wild by the Comanche—a man without a future or a home.

He'd felt awkward and unsure of himself at the celebration, so he'd remained quiet, keeping to himself. There was no point in making friends at the ranch. He would be leaving soon, and he wouldn't be back.

He would be leaving Marissa.

Hot, exciting memories of their nights together in his lodge assailed him. Her kiss, her caress, the claiming of her innocence. The pure pleasure of making her his own.

Zach bit back a miserable groan as he fought down his desire for her.

She was his wife—

But not with her consent, he argued with himself. And only in the Comanche world.

Louise went to look for George and found him outside, sitting on a bench on the porch.

"Enjoying the peace?"

"Yes. Join me?"

"I'd love to." Louise went to sit beside him.

"You were right about Marissa. She seems fine."

"I think so. It's been a difficult time for her, but she's a strong young woman. We're so blessed to have her back."

George looked over at her in the moonlight, then leaned down and kissed her softly. "Just yesterday, I would never have believed we'd be sharing this moment—but we are."

She smiled up at him. "It's a dream come true for both of us."

"Will you help make the rest of my dreams come true?"

"I'd love to."

"How soon do you want to get married? Let's set a date."

"Tonight?" Louise asked, her voice a soft purr.

George chuckled. "Don't tempt me, woman."

"Why don't we speak with the reverend when we go into town tomorrow?"

"I guess I can wait that long."

They kissed one last time before going inside for the night.

Zach lay in the darkness, unable to sleep. His surroundings were too strange; his thoughts were too troubled.

In frustration, he finally got up.

It was well past midnight. After checking to make sure Joe was sleeping soundly, he took his own blanket and left the room. He silently went out of the house. He bedded down some distance away and lay there, staring up at the stars. The night sky and the hard ground were familiar to him, and he relaxed a little.

Many thoughts plagued him. As a boy, he had longed to escape from the village. He had prayed to be rescued. He had waited and hoped, but he had finally been forced to give up his dream of going home. He had accepted his fate and done what he'd had to do to survive. Yet even after he'd become a fearless warrior, he acknowledged that in the deepest recesses

of his heart, a secret part of him had always longed to go home again.

And now he was free.

He was back among the whites.

But he felt no joy.

He only felt alone.

In irritation, he got up. He didn't like the direction of his thoughts. He was not a man who felt sorry for himself. He was a man who took action. Restless as he was, he knew there would be no sleep for him that night. He had just resigned himself to that when he heard Marissa say his name.

"Zach—"

The sound of Marissa's voice so close behind him sent a thrill through Zach. He turned, surprised to find her there within arm's reach. He had been caught up so deeply in his own troubled thoughts that he hadn't been aware of her approach.

"Marissa—what are you doing out here?" he asked softly, knowing the sound of their voices would carry in the night.

"I was awake and looked out my window, and I saw you here. I was worried about you. I thought something might be wrong. I wanted to make sure you were all right."

He longed to tell her that he was all right—now that she was with him—but he didn't. "I'm fine. I'm just not used to sleeping indoors yet."

She nodded thoughtfully, understanding. "It is quite a change after all we've been through. I was sorry we didn't get any time to talk tonight—"

"You were busy." He deliberately sounded as if it were of no importance to him.

His tone of voice was so cold and indifferent that it put Marissa off a bit.

"I know. I wanted to spend as much time with my uncle and Louise as I could."

He held his tongue, but he wanted to mention all the time she'd spent with Mark.

"Zach—" Marissa took a step closer to him. She sensed that he was angry with her about something. "I really never got the chance to thank you properly for bringing me home. I never really allowed myself to believe that it was going to happen until today."

She boldly went to Zach and lifted her arms to encircle his neck.

"Thank you." Her words were a hushed whisper upon her lips.

Ever so gently, she drew him down to her, seeking his lips in a cherishing, loving exchange.

The sweetness of her embrace sent a shaft of almost painful desire jolting through Zach.

He wanted her—

How he wanted her—

Zach responded instantly, any restraint he'd had upon himself destroyed by the touch of her lips on his. He crushed her to his chest, deepening the kiss to a hungry, devouring exchange. He needed this. He needed her.

He didn't know how he was going to stay away from her, but he had to. Because he cared so much about her, because he loved her.

The cold emptiness of the despair that besieged him gave Zach the strength he needed to end the kiss. He put her physically from him.

"Go back inside now, Marissa. It's where you belong."

She belonged in a soft bed in a safe, comfortable ranch house, not out here, sleeping under the stars with him.

She didn't need to be worrying about where the next meal was coming from or what danger the next day might bring.

Marissa was startled and confused. She had felt the flame of their passion for an instant while in his arms, but, just as quickly, the passion had vanished and now he was sending her away.

She stared up at Zach in the starlight. In that moment, he was her warrior again—strong, powerful, and determined. But no trace of emotion played on his handsome features. He looked cold and distant. And he had sent her away from him.

Heartbroken, Marissa turned away from him without another word and made her way back to the ranch house. She took care not to make any noise as she entered her room and lay down for the night.

Zach remained standing, watching her until she was out of sight. Only then did he lie back down.

In the distance, down by the stable, Mark had been watching all that transpired. Fury and disgust had filled him at the sight of Marissa kissing Zach. The woman was a slut.

He'd hoped that she hadn't changed too much while she'd been a captive, but now he knew the truth.

As annoyed as he was by what he'd witnessed, he would not change his plans. His feelings for her had certainly changed. It was hard to care for any white woman who would let herself be kissed by a Comanche. Mark didn't care if Zach was white or not. He'd been raised a Comanche. Nothing could change that. And Marissa had acted like some kind of whore, going to him in the middle of the night.

He wondered if he could live with the knowledge of what she'd done. He decided he could. The prize that awaited him made it all worthwhile.

Chapter Twenty-six

*I*n the past, Marissa had never thought much of Dry Springs, but today it appeared a booming metropolis to her as they rode down Main Street toward the mercantile. She had made the trip in the buckboard with Louise and Joe, while Uncle George and Zach accompanied them on horseback.

Sheriff Spiller happened to be making his rounds when he saw George coming up the street. He didn't pay any attention to who was in the buckboard. He'd heard back from the Rangers and wanted to let George know that they had no new information on his niece.

"George!" the sheriff called out as he flagged him down.

"Morning, Sheriff," George said, grinning as he reined in before him.

Sheriff Spiller was surprised by how happy the rancher looked. Ever since Marissa had disappeared, George had been a very somber man.

"I got some news from the Rangers," he began.

"Well, I got some news for you, too," George said as the buckboard pulled to a stop next to them.

"You do?" The Sheriff couldn't imagine what he might have heard.

"Our prayers were answered, Sheriff. Marissa's come home to us."

"What?" The lawman was shocked. He looked over at the buckboard and realized who was riding in it. Marissa was seated next to Louise and a young boy, and she looked in fine health. He stared at her in complete disbelief.

"Hello, Sheriff," Marissa said with a smile.

"Well, I'll be damned—er, uh, excuse me, ladies," he said awkwardly, blushing a little at having forgotten himself. "How did you manage to get away?" He was amazed and delighted by the good news.

George motioned for Zach to come forward and introduced the two men. He told the lawman how Zach had gotten both Marissa and Joe out of the village.

"It's a pleasure to meet you, Mr. Ryder," Sheriff Spiller told him, shalling his hand. "Welcome to Dry Springs."

"Thank you, Sheriff."

"We're thrilled to be here," Marissa told him happily.

"We're thrilled to have you here," he answered, tipping his hat to her. It wasn't often that anyone got good news where the Comanche were concerned. "Enjoy your stay in town."

"We will."

They moved on and reined in before the mercantile.

"We may be a while," Louise warned George.

George just smiled, glad to have the problem of having to wait for them while they were shopping.

"We'll take care of sending the telegram. Then I imagine Zach and Joe will want to stop off at the barbershop. We'll plan on meeting you back here after we've finished our business."

Marissa and Louise went inside as the men started off toward the telegraph office.

"We need to send a wire," George told the man at the desk.

"Yes, sir. You're in the right place. Where to?"

"Sidewinder," he answered firmly.

"Who you wanting to send it to?"

"Just to the sheriff there. We're trying to contact the Carter family." He quickly explained the boy's situation.

"I'll take care of it," the telegraph operator told them, giving the boy an encouraging look. "How long will you be in town?"

"Just for the day. Otherwise, you can notify us out at the Crown."

"The minute I hear anything, I'll get word out to you right away."

"My ma and pa will be here soon, won't they, Zach?" Joe asked, looking up at him, his eyes round with excitement as they left the telegraph office.

"I hope so, Joe."

"You two ready to see the barber?" George asked, wanting to distract the boy. There was no telling how long it would be before the reunion would take—if it took place at all.

"Let's go," Zach said, ready to shed the last visible reminder of his Comanche life.

"What about you, Joe? You ready to have your ears lowered?" George teased.

The boy immediately covered his ears with his hands and looked a bit scared. "He ain't going to cut my ears off, is he?"

Zach and George both laughed.

"I was just teasing you, son," George told him, putting a calming hand on his shoulder.

Joe was openly relieved as they entered the barbershop.

"Afternoon, George. How you been doing?" Pete, the town barber, asked.

"Life is good, Pete. My niece is back, safe and sound, thanks to this gentleman here. Say hello to Zach Ryder. Zach, this is Pete Wilkins, a good friend of mine."

They shook hands.

Pete got a look at Zach's hair and frowned a bit.

"Kinda long, isn't it?" he asked cautiously.

"Yes," was all Zach answered.

"The boy needing a trim, too?"

"If you got the time," George said.

"I sure do. Who wants to go first?"

Joe quickly volunteered. He hopped eagerly into the chair. Zach and George settled in to watch. As the barber went to work on Joe, George told him about Marissa's miraculous return and how Zach had saved Joe, too.

"You're a brave man, Zach," Pete told him.

"I was glad I was able to bring them back," he answered as the barber finished the boy's hair, and he and Joe switched seats.

Pete set to work on Zach.

"You had a lot of hair," Joe said, looking down at the strands that lay on the floor when the barber finished.

"It's been a few years since I had my last haircut," Zach said.

He got out of the chair. He rubbed the back of his neck and glanced over his shoulder to catch a glimpse of himself in the mirror on the wall. He had known the change in his appearance would be dramatic, and it was. He didn't stare at himself for long, but he knew the truth: he was a white man now.

George paid the barber, and they left the shop.

"There's one other person I want you to meet before we go back to the mercantile, Zach," George said, telling him about Hawk. "Let's take a walk down to the stable."

He led the way. They reached the stable and went in.

"Hawk?" George called out to his friend.

Hawk appeared out of the back, leading a haltered horse behind him.

"George—what brings you to town? Did you get news about your niece?" Hawk asked as he came forward.

"I've got two friends here I want you to meet," George said. "Hawk Morgan, this is Zach Ryder and Joe Carter. Zach brought Marissa and Joe back, Hawk. He got them out of the Comanche village."

Hawk was astounded at the news. Such escapes were rare, almost unheard of. He looked at the stranger with even more respect as he held out his hand to him.

"I don't know how you did it, but I'm sure glad you did. We tracked that raiding party for weeks, but after the storm, we could never find the trail again. How did you get them out? Did you have enough men with you to attack the village, or did you sneak in and steal the captives away?"

"Neither," Zach answered, instinctively liking Hawk right away. "I was already in the village. I'd been raised there as a Comanche, but I knew the time had come for me to leave and take the captives with me."

Hawk nodded in understanding as he looked at Zach with even more respect. This man had sacrificed a lot to bring Marissa and the boy back to their families. He was a good man. "If you need anything while you're here in Dry Springs, just let me know, but I got a feeling George will take good care of you." He looked over at George. "And Marissa is all right?"

"She's fine—thanks to Zach."

Hawk nodded and smiled. "It's nice to hear good news every once in a while."

"That it is," George agreed.

They talked awhile longer, then left Hawk so he could get back to work.

"Now all we have to do is get you two some new clothes," George said as they made their way through town to the mercantile.

"I won't need much," Zach told him.

"Let me take care of this."

"I'll pay you back."

"Consider it a gift—a small way for me to thank you."

"Do you think that man at the telegraph office heard back from my pa yet?" Joe piped up eagerly, interrupting them.

George answered in a calming tone, "It's a little soon yet, Joe. Sometimes it takes a while for messages to get through, but I know he'll find us right away when he does hear."

Joe nodded, but his excitement didn't lessen. He was positive that he would be going home any day now, and he could hardly wait to see his ma and pa again.

Zach saw the mercantile ahead and found himself looking for Marissa.

As they drew near the store, two women came out. The women hurried past, barely taking notice of their presence as they talked to each other in hushed voices.

"Can you believe they even let her in the store?" one woman was saying in outrage.

"I shudder to think she actually was touching some of the merchandise. Why, she even tried some of the dresses on," the other woman remarked hatefully. "I don't know if I will ever shop in there again. Who would want to buy something she'd touched?"

Zach knew immediately whom they were talking about. It was what he had long feared might happen to Marissa when they returned. Crazy One had warned them how the whites might react, and he had just witnessed some of it firsthand. He glanced over at George and saw his pained expression. He had heard the women, too.

They went inside.

"That looks like it fits you perfectly," Louise was saying as Marissa stood before her in a sedate day-gown. She noticed George and smiled at him. "We're just about done, I think."

Marissa turned to greet them, and her gaze fell upon Zach. Once again, he was dramatically changed, and she could only stare at him as her heartbeat quickened. Long ago in the village, she had imagined how he would look this way. He was every bit as devastatingly handsome as she'd thought he would be.

"Don't Zach and Joe look handsome?" Louise asked happily.

"Yes, they do," Marissa answered.

"We'll be over here," George said, indicating the men's side of the store. "They need some clothes, too."

"We only have a few more things to get and we'll be ready to go," Louise assured him.

"Well, Tom, how's my credit with you? Think I can afford to keep these two women?" he joked with the owner.

"I don't know, George, they're doing a pretty good job of running up your bill," Tom warned facetiously.

"Good," he answered. "Let them have whatever they want. Same for my two friends here. They need to be outfitted, too. Think you can help them out?"

"Let's see what we can do," Tom said, hurrying to wait on them. He liked it when the rancher was in a spending mood. The man had money, and he liked to spread it around. It wasn't often the store had so many good customers at once.

An hour later they had finished their shopping.

"Louise and I have one last stop to make before we return home," George announced, giving her a knowing look. He glanced at Zach. "You want to see about packing up everything while we pay a visit to the reverend?"

"We'll take care of it," Marissa promised, delighted, for she knew they were going to the preacher to set a date for their wedding.

It didn't take George and Louise very long. Zach had just finished stowing the last of their purchases when the couple returned, and they were smiling in delight.

"Well?" Marissa asked excitedly.

"It's all set," Louise told them.

"We're going to be married next month," George said.

"Congratulations!" Marissa hugged them both.

Zach offered his good wishes, too.

There was going to be a wedding.

Zach thought of the day he'd claimed Marissa as his wife in the village, then told himself it meant nothing. It had been a Comanche marriage. He did not look her way.

Marissa did not look at Zach either. She kept her thoughts focused only on Louise's happiness.

"Let's go home," George said. He helped the women up into the buckboard while Joe climbed in the back on his own.

"Thank you for your business," Tom said, following them outside to see them off.

"We appreciate all your help," Louise said.

"Well, don't forget the big dance next Saturday night," Tom reminded them.

"We won't," Louise said.

They set out for the Crown.

Zach turned his thoughts to the weeks to come as they made the trip back. He was uncomfortable with the amount of money George had spent on him at the store. Though George had told him the clothes were a gift for helping Marissa, Zach was determined to find a way to repay him. He'd already made up his mind to do all the work he could around the ranch until Joe was taken care of.

After they'd ridden out of sight, Beatrice, Tom's wife, appeared at his side. She had not come out the entire time Louise and Marissa had been in the store. She had stayed in the back in their living quarters. Tom had been bothered by her absence. He could have used her help.

"Thank God, they're gone!" Beatrice spat out hatefully.

Tom looked at her in disbelief. "What are you talking about, woman?"

She shuddered visibly for effect as she faced him. "That—that woman! I can't believe you actually let her into the store."

"Which woman?"

"Why, Marissa Williams, that's who! Tom, she's been living with the Comanche."

"Yes, and she's home now. She's safe again."

"Well, I don't want the likes of her in my store ever again. You hear me?"

Tom grew furious with her close-minded attitude. "Shut your mouth, Beatrice! That poor young woman was a victim. She didn't ask to be taken captive. I just thank God that she's back with George."

"We're going to lose business if you wait on her!"

He gave her a smug look. "No, we won't."

"Of course we will! None of the self-respecting women in town will want to go anywhere she's been."

"Yes, they will, dear wife. They'll have no choice, since we're the only mercantile in town."

She hated his logic. "It still doesn't make it right to let her in our store."

"Marissa Williams is George Williams's niece, and she is a valued customer." He showed her the bills George had just rung up—bills that he knew would be paid in a timely manner, unlike those of some other regular customers.

"Oh, my! They spent that much today?" She was shocked.

"That's right. I don't think we have to worry about offending our other customers. They'll come around, and if they don't, that's too damned bad. George and his family will always be welcome in my place of business."

With that, Tom turned his back on his small-minded wife and went back to work.

Chapter Twenty-seven

Once they returned to the Crown, Zach made sure he kept busy. As each day passed with no news about Joe's family, the boy became more unhappy and more worried. Zach worked with George to find small chores to keep the boy active. He watched over Joe and grew even more fond of him as the days passed. He knew he would miss him greatly if the time ever came for him to be reunited with his relatives.

The day of the dance in town arrived almost too quickly.

George went to find Zach in the stables where he'd been working with the horses.

"Zach—I need to talk with you," George said.

"Is something wrong?" he asked, wondering why the rancher sounded so serious.

"No, nothing's wrong. I just wanted you to know that we'll be riding out a little after noon today. So be ready to go."

"Go? Where?"

"We're going to town for the dance tonight."

"There's no reason for me to go along," Zach said. He didn't know how to dance, and he had no interest in returning to Dry Springs.

"I don't want to hear any arguments. As hard as you've been working around here, you deserve a night off. You're going with

us, and here—" George handed him an envelope with money in it. "I don't want to hear a word out of you," he said gruffly. "You're supposed to be a guest here on the Crown, not hired help. But if you insist on acting like hired help, I'm going to pay you."

"I owe you too much already," Zach argued, trying to give the envelope back.

George wouldn't hear of it. "Go get cleaned up. I'll be expecting you to be ready to ride out when we are. I thought we'd take Joe along, too. Mark and a few of the other men are also going."

"I can stay here and watch over things for you."

"No need. Sarah and Claude will be staying behind to keep an eye on things."

Zach knew he was defeated, so he offered no further protest. He was not looking forward to going to the dance, though. It was difficult enough seeing Marissa around the ranch every day, but going into town and watching her dance with other men was going to be hard on him. He told himself he could do it—mainly because he had no choice.

"Plan on spending the night in town, too," George went on. "I always rent some rooms at the hotel so we don't have to worry about riding back to the ranch late at night. We'll attend church services in the morning before we start home."

Zach agreed and went on to finish what he was doing. When he was done, he got ready for the trip. He was resigned to the fact that he would have to be around Marissa. There could be no avoiding her company on the trip to and from town, but he hoped he could find some way to stay away from her at the dance. It wasn't going to be easy, but he would do it.

Marissa couldn't believe the week had passed so quickly. Now here they were back in Dry Springs at the hotel, getting dressed for the dance.

"I'm just about ready to go downstairs," Louise announced from where she was sitting at the dressing table, putting the finishing touches on her hair.

"So am I. If you'll just fasten the last few buttons on my dress, I'll be ready, too," Marissa said as she came to stand before her and presented her back.

Louise made short work of buttoning the gown. "Now turn around so I can see you."

Marissa did as she was told.

"It's even lovelier on you than I thought it would be," Louise said, very pleased with the way the gown had turned out.

She and Marissa had picked out the dress pattern and material at the mercantile, and Louise had worked hard all week to have the gown ready for the weekend.

"You are so talented, Louise. I have no sewing ability whatsoever," Marissa said as she looked in the mirror. "Oh, my. It does look pretty, doesn't it?"

The turquoise gown fit her perfectly. The modestly cut neckline revealed nothing untoward, but did flatter her figure, as did the fitted waistline.

Louise stood up, ready to meet George.

"You look pretty, too," Marissa said.

"I hope so. I want to look nice for your uncle," Louise replied as she smoothed her skirts.

"Uncle George will be pleased, I'm sure. Tonight should be fun," she said, remembering the dance they'd attended the last time she'd visited the ranch. For an instant, she thought about how much had changed in her life in the last year—her father's death—the raid—Zach—Then she pushed the thoughts aside. Tonight she wanted to be happy.

They left the room and made their way downstairs to find George cleaned up and waiting for them in the small lobby. He looked very handsome in his dress clothes, and Louise told him so.

It was dark outside, and as they left the hotel, they could hear music playing in the distance.

"I'm the luckiest man in Dry Springs," George said with a grin. "I've got a beautiful woman on each arm."

Marissa and Louise both laughed, delighted by his compliment.

When they reached the dance, the festivities were already in full swing. Couples were dancing on a raised platform surrounded by colorful hanging lanterns as the band played a lively melody.

They had just come to stand at the side of the dance floor when Mark appeared.

"May I have this dance, Marissa?" he asked, sounding quite the gentleman.

"Why, yes, thank you, Mark," she replied courteously, but she had really been looking for Zach in the crowd.

Mark squired her out among the other couples as George took Louise in his arms and followed.

Marissa enjoyed dancing with Mark. He was a good dancer, and twirling to the music reminded her of her last visit with her father. She had not missed one dance that night. She had been very popular with all the young men in town.

As she followed Mark's lead, Marissa wondered where Zach and Joe were. They had an ridden into town together that morning, but she had not seen either of them since earlier that afternoon.

It had been a sad day for Joe. They'd checked with the telegraph office as soon as they arrived, only to discover that there was still no response to their wire to Sidewinder. Joe's disappointment had been obvious. She thought that perhaps Zach had taken the boy off to keep him entertained so he wouldn't have time to think about what they'd learned.

When the dance ended, Mark escorted her back to join her uncle and Louise. They were standing with a group of neighboring ranchers.

"Thank you, Marissa," Mark said in a courtly manner.

"It was my pleasure," she assured him.

He excused himself from her side.

The music started up again. There were many single young men around. George noticed that several glanced in Marissa's direction every now and then, but not a one of them came over to ask her to dance. George wasn't about to let Marissa feel lonely.

"This dance is mine," George stated possessively. "Louise, if you'll excuse us?"

"Of course. You two have fun," she told them with a smile.

Marissa enjoyed every minute of their dance, but she knew why Uncle George had invited her. Crazy One had warned her that the whites would consider her a ruined woman when she returned, and apparently she'd been right. Except for Mark and her uncle, no other man had come near her.

Though for a moment the realization was painful, Marissa quickly dismissed her hurt feelings.

She had told herself when they left the village that being an outcast in the white world was infinitely better than being a slave to the Comanche. And she had meant it. Not being the belle of the ball was not going to bother her.

She was free and she was safe.

That was all that mattered.

Mark came to claim Marissa for the next dance.

"Are you having a good time tonight?" he asked.

"Oh, yes."

Mark had been watching her from across the way, and he knew no other man had danced with her except her uncle. That pleased him. He didn't want any competition for her affections. He wanted her all to himself.

It annoyed Mark a bit to think Marissa was truly ruined socially, but in the long run, it was only her inheritance that mattered to him—not her.

Money meant a lot to Mark, and Marissa had money.

Mark had resigned himself to suffering the taunts of men who would say he was taking some Comanche warrior's leftovers. He couldn't argue with them, since it was probably true. After all, he had seen her kiss Zach that night out at the ranch.

The memory of their kiss still angered him. He knew he couldn't waste any time before proposing to her. He would have to make his move soon.

He would woo her and court her tonight. In a few weeks, he'd propose.

Feeling quite confident, Mark drew Marissa a little closer as they danced. He enjoyed the feel of her body pressed against him. It wouldn't be long before he'd be able to take her any time he wanted her. The prospect pleased him.

When the music ended, Mark escorted her back to her uncle's side.

"Would you like me to get you a drink?" he asked.

"Yes, Mark. Thank you."

Marissa had an ulterior motive in accepting his offer. She wanted to get away from him for a while, and if he went to the crowded refreshment table, she'd have a moment without him.

Something about Mark was bothering Marissa. The way he'd held her so close during that last dance troubled her. Zach's touch had always excited her and sent shivers through her. Mark's touch sent a different kind of trembling through her. He made her nervous and wary and uncomfortable.

Thinking of Zach, Marissa glanced around but saw no sign of him. She told herself it was ridiculous to think he would ask her to dance. This past week, he'd stayed as far away from her as he could

without leaving the ranch completely, and she admitted to herself that she missed him.

The music started again. It was a slow melody this time. Marissa stayed where she was, expecting Mark to return with her drink. She would use the beverage as an excuse to avoid a slow dance with him.

"May I have this dance?"

Marissa went still at the sound of Zach's voice. She turned to find him coming up behind her.

Zach had been watching Marissa from afar all night long. He had seen how she'd been treated by most of the townsfolk, and he'd watched her dancing with Mark.

He had had enough of seeing her in Mark's arms. Mark had held her too close. The jealousy he'd been fighting and trying to deny could not be ignored any longer.

A thrill went through Marissa, and she answered quickly, "Yes. I'd love to dance with you."

The sight of Zach dressed in dark pants and a white shirt made her acutely conscious of what an attractive man he was. Her heartbeat quickened as she took a step toward him, more than ready to go into his arms.

Zach had been observing the other couples on the dance floor, too, and though he knew he wasn't practiced in the art, he thought he had learned enough by watching to make it through one dance with Marissa. Actually, he didn't care if they danced at all. He just wanted to take her in his arms and hold her close.

They moved out among the other couples, unmindful of anyone watching them.

Zach kept the steps simple. He concentrated only on the pleasure of having Marissa in his arms as they moved to the slow, sensuous rhythm.

He looked down at Marissa, and their gazes met.

They were lost in a haze of sensuality as they both remembered other times when their rhythm together had been at a much quicker pace. The memories sent heat through him. He swallowed tightly as he fought for control.

He wanted to hold Marissa closer. He wanted to kiss her and strip away the clothing that was a barrier between them. He wanted to be one with her, to know the beauty of loving her again.

He looked away from her and forced himself to settle for a dance.

Marissa closed her eyes and became a creature of sensation as she moved with Zach to the tempo of the music. It was heavenly being in his arms. The touch of his hands sent delight coursing through her.

She never wanted to be away from him. She wanted to hold him close and never let him go. Marissa made up her mind right then and there. She was going to tell Zach that she loved him.

She certainly had nothing to lose. The worst that could happen had already happened. At least, if she told him, she would know that she had been honest with him about her feelings. What he did after that would be his decision.

Marissa was ready. She girded herself and prepared to tell Zach the truth of her love.

And then she heard Mark say, "Excuse me." His tone was terse. "I'm cutting in."

Her eyes flew open. Mark was standing next to them, a belligerent look on his face.

Zach was surprised by the other man's intrusion. When he felt Mark's hand on his shoulder to stop their dance, he was almost ready to fight him. But he stopped. He did not want to make trouble for Marissa. Zach dropped his hands away from her as Mark boldly stepped in front of him and took over.

Marissa stiffened as Mark's hand settled possessively at her waist to guide her through the rest of the dance. She was upset, very upset, but she fought not to let it show. She managed to smile up at him.

Zach walked to the edge of the dance floor and looked back. He saw Marissa smiling at Mark as if she hadn't a care in the world.

He stalked off into the night.

He had the money George had given him and he had seen a saloon on his way to the dance earlier that evening. He was glad Joe was with Louise and George, so he could get away for a while.

Zach strode angrily toward the saloon.

Chapter Twenty-eight

*H*awk never attended the town dances. He knew he wasn't wanted. He stood at the bar in the Palace Saloon, enjoying a whiskey and minding his own business. The place was emptier than usual on this Saturday night because of the dance, and Hawk was glad.

He heard someone come into the bar behind him, but he didn't turn to look as the man settled at the end of the bar. He kept on drinking, minding his own business.

"Whiskey," the new customer ordered.

The voice sounded familiar, and Hawk looked up in the mirror behind the bar to see the other man's reflection. It surprised him to find it was Zach Ryder. Picking up his glass, he moved down to speak with him.

"Evening, Zach," Hawk said. "Good to see you in town."

"Hawk," Zach answered, nodding to him as he paid the bartender for his drink. He hadn't really wanted to talk to anyone when he'd come into the bar, but he hadn't thought he'd run into Hawk. He was the exception.

"Come on, you want to sit at a table?"

"Sure." Zach took his tumbler of whiskey and followed Hawk to the back of the saloon.

"How are you doing out at the Crown?" Hawk asked once they'd settled in.

"George is a good man. Marissa will be well taken care of. We're still waiting to hear about the boy's family. We sent the telegram to Sidewinder a week ago, but there's been no word at all," he said as he took a deep swallow.

"What's going to happen if his family's all dead?"

"I don't know. Joe's a good boy. He's suffered a lot, and I don't like to think of him being alone." Zach knew those words described himself, as well, but at least he was a man. He could make his own way in the world, unlike Joe.

"Let's hope it turns out all right."

"I know. It was hard enough on him in the village, but if he finds out his whole family is dead ..."

"Is that what happened to you?" Hawk asked perceptively.

"That was a long time ago." Zach looked up at him. "From what I can remember, there was no way any of my family could have survived the raid on our ranch. I'm hoping things will be different for Joe."

"I'm sorry about your family."

"So am I."

They both fell silent for a moment. Each took a drink.

"How did you end up in Dry Springs?" Zach asked, changing the subject. "Do you have family here?"

"No. I don't have any family. I settled here on my own a few years back."

"And I'm real glad he did," purred the bar girl known only as Red because of her flaming hair color. She came to stand beside the table. "Evening, Hawk." She smiled seductively down at him, then looked at Zach "You're new in town, aren't you?"

"Yes."

"This is Zach Ryder, Red," Hawk told her. "He's the man who brought Marissa Williams, back from the Comanche."

"I heard you were raised by the Comanche," Red said, eyeing Zach thoughtfully.

"That's right," Zach answered, expecting condemnation from her.

"Well, welcome back to civilization—if you can call Dry Springs civilized," she said with a wicked grin, not the least bit put off by his background. "Hey, Stan! These boys need another round—and make it on the house!"

She sashayed to the bar to get them two more drinks, then served them at their table.

"You enjoy yourselves tonight, and if you need anything—anything at all—you just let me know. All right, Hawk?" Her tone left no doubt as to her meaning.

"We will, Red," Hawk promised.

She winked at him and went off to wait on another customer.

Zach and Hawk had been there for quite a while when a group of men came in and went to the bar to order drinks. They were loud and raucous and intent on having a good time.

"The dance must be over," Hawk remarked as the place started to fill up.

Zach noticed that Mark was among the group at the bar. Zach wasn't at all glad to see him, but he was quietly pleased that, at least, the cowboy wasn't with Marissa. Zach shifted his chair so his back was to the bar. He wanted to ignore the other man's presence. He'd seen enough of Mark already that night.

Mark was more than satisfied with the events of the evening. Marissa had seemed quite receptive to him, and he believed it would only be a matter of a few weeks or maybe a month before he could propose. The only annoyance he'd had all night had been

when Zach danced with her. He didn't know what was going on between the two of them, but it was going to stop. He was going to have several stiff drinks to celebrate his success.

Red worked the crowd. She enjoyed flirting with the cowboys, and she wasn't averse to taking one of them upstairs to make a little extra money on the side. She lingered at the bar, laughing with the men, trying to decide which one to set her sights on.

"Hey, Mark!" one of the men called out in a slurred voice. "Why don't you take Red upstairs and have some fun?"

Mark could have used some female companionship that night, but it wasn't the saloon girl he wanted. He wanted Marissa.

"Not tonight," he answered.

The drunk wasn't about to be ignored. "But, Mark—at least Red is honest about her trade. She ain't no damned Comanche squaw like that Marissa Williams you was dancing with all night. How many of them bucks you think the Williams girl did while she was a captive? You know she was probably bedding half the tribe."

Mark laughed at the man's insults. The drunk hadn't said anything that he hadn't already thought himself. He was only speaking the truth.

Mark downed the rest of his drink and signaled the bartender to refill his glass as he responded, "Yeah, she probably did. But so what? It don't matter that she's a slut. It only matters that she's got money. I can forgive just about anything when there's money involved."

Zach had been listening to Mark and growing angrier by the minute. It had been hard enough watching him with Marissa at the dance. But to learn now that he was just using her broke his self-control.

He pushed his chair back, ready to fight.

"Zach—" Hawk saw the fury in his face and knew what he planned to do.

Zach didn't answer. He just got to his feet and walked straight up to the bar.

"Looks like you got company," one of the men said to Mark.

Mark turned to see who was coming.

Zach hit him full-force and sent him sprawling to the ground. Chaos erupted around them as everyone scrambled to get out of the way.

Though he had been caught off guard, Mark was ready to fight. He launched himself at Zach. The two men grappled in a violent confrontation. Each man landed powerful, bruising blows.

Zach's fury was intense. This man had danced with Marissa and acted like he cared about her. But it had all been a lie.

The hatred Zach felt for Mark fueled his anger. He gave a roar of rage as he threw himself bodily at his opponent and knocked him down. With savage intensity, he beat the other man into submission. His last, most powerful blow caught Mark squarely on the chin, leaving him unconscious.

When Zach realized Mark was out, he stood up in complete disgust. He looked around at the others in the saloon, ready for more trouble. When he had no takers, he relaxed a bit, spitting blood as he turned away from Mark's prone body.

Hawk was there.

"Let's get out of here," Hawk told him. He looked over at the bar girl. "See you later, Red."

Red just nodded as she watched them go. She'd seen many fights in her time, but never any as intense as this one had been. She realized the others in the bar were staring at Zach and Hawk as they walked out.

"Hey, what are you looking at?" she asked. "I guess Zach didn't like what Mark was saying about the Williams girl. The excitement's over. Let's all have another drink."

Red looked one last time in Zach and Hawk's direction. They were two tall, fine men, the likes of which weren't seen very often. She didn't show it, but deep within her she felt a bit sad. No man had ever defended her honor that way.

Hawk and Zach hadn't gotten far down the street when Zach stopped at a watering trough to wash up. He could feel his cheek swelling, and he was tasting blood.

"And I thought it was going to be a quiet night," Hawk joked.

"It was, for you," Zach countered. He tried to grin as he straightened up, but his cheek hurt too much.

"Do you love her?" he asked.

"Yes." Zach knew there was no point in lying to Hawk.

"What are you going to do about it?"

"Nothing. She's better off without me. I have nothing to offer her."

Hawk knew how pride could get a man in trouble. "Sounds like she's got all the money she needs."

"A man should be able to take care of his family."

"So get a job," Hawk said simply.

Zach growled something unintelligible at him.

"Think about what I said," Hawk told him. "You need me for anything, my house is the one out behind the stable."

Hawk walked off, hoping things would get better for Zach. He understood the difficulties the other man was having in adapting to the white world. He hoped Zach would be able to sort out what it was he really wanted before it was too late and he missed his best chance at happiness.

As Zach made his way back to the hotel, he was glad it was late so he wouldn't run into anyone on the streets. The lobby was deserted as he crossed it and went upstairs to his room. George had gotten him his own hotel room that night so he didn't have

to worry about Joe, and he was relieved. He didn't want the boy to see him this way. It was going to be awkward enough the next morning when he came face to face with Mark again.

Marissa and Louise were up bright and early the next morning. They were sharing a room, and enjoyed having the time together. They were looking forward to attending church services.

"I wonder what happened to Zach last night?" Marissa said.

Her tone was nonchalant enough, but she was worried. She had only seen him for that one dance, and then Mark had cut in and ruined everything. She'd kept hoping that Zach would return and ask her to dance again, but he hadn't. There had been no sign of him, either, when they'd returned to the hotel.

"I don't know," Louise said. "I didn't see very much of him last night, but I'm sure he'll be joining us for church this morning."

They left their room and met George and Joe in the lobby.

"Did you see Zach on your way down?" George asked.

"No. I guess he's still in his room," Louise said.

"I'll go get him and be right back."

George went upstairs and knocked on Zach's door.

"Yeah?" came Zach's muffled response to the knock.

"We're ready to go to church. Should we wait for you?"

"No, go on. I'll meet you there." Zach answered through the door.

George returned to escort the ladies and Joe to the church.

"Zach will be along," he told them, trying not to smile. Judging from the sound of his voice, he had a good idea where Zach had disappeared to last night.

Zach stifled a groan and sat up on the side of his bed. He stood and went to the washstand, ready to get cleaned up. It was then that he made the mistake of looking in the mirror. He looked just

like he felt—as if he'd been in a bad fight. He would have preferred to just ride on out to the ranch without seeing anyone that morning, but since George had stopped by to get him, he knew he had to show up at church. They would be expecting him.

Zach wondered if George had seen or spoken to Mark yet. He figured he hadn't. If he had, George would certainly have had more to say to him when he'd come by the room.

As quickly as he could, Zach finished washing and then donned his best clothes for church. He was going to be late as it was.

Chapter Twenty-nine

Marissa was sitting with Joe, trying to listen attentively to the minister's sermon. She wanted to concentrate on the good news he was sharing, but her heart was distracting her. She kept wondering where Zach was. Uncle George had said he'd promised to meet them at church, but so far he hadn't shown up.

Marissa scolded herself for caring so much about Zach, but she couldn't forget how it had felt to be in his arms the night before. They had danced only once, but it had been wonderful. She was certain Zach had to feel something for her. How else could they have moved so perfectly together? They had seemed so attuned to one another—and then Mark had cut in.

"God bless you all," Reverend Gibson said, ending his sermon.

Marissa had been so caught up in her thoughts about Zach that she was surprised to find he was finished. She stood up with Joe to follow Louise and George as they left the pew. Glancing around the crowded church, she hoped to catch sight of Zach. Her heart stirred within her when she saw him. There was no mistaking his tall, broad-shouldered form as he walked out the main doorway ahead of them into the sunshine.

Marissa was glad to know he'd kept his word, even if he hadn't come to sit with them. She realized he'd probably arrived late and had sat in a back pew. A part of her wanted to rush down the

crowded aisle and seek him out, but she couldn't. She was trapped there, and she realized it was for the best. There was no point in throwing herself at him. Zach had made it clear he didn't want anything to do with her. Bringing her wayward emotions under control, Marissa offered up one last prayer as she departed the church.

She asked God to help her find a way to win Zach's love.

"It won't be long," Louise said to George in a quiet voice as they moved down the center aisle. She gave him secret smile.

They both realized that in a few short weeks they would be getting married in that very church.

"I can hardly wait," he said, taking her hand in his.

"Me, either."

They followed Marissa and Joe from the church.

"There's Zach," George said, pointing him out.

Zach was standing off to the side, facing slightly away from them.

George thought nothing of the way Zach was standing as they drew near to speak with him.

"I'm glad Zach made it in time to hear at least a part of the service," Louise said. "Will we be going back to the ranch now?"

"Yes. It's that time. Most of the men have already started back. Not all of them stay around for services."

"I wondered where Mark was this morning."

As they drew near and got a look at Zach's face, everyone stopped dead.

"What happened to you?" George demanded. Evidently, Zach had been in a fight, a serious one judging by the look of him.

"Whoa!" Joe said, shocked as he stared up at Zach. "Who hit you?"

"Zach," Marissa gasped. "Are you all right?" She wanted to go to him, but controlled the desire with an effort. "Your face—"

"The other man looks worse," Zach told her, remembering her fight with Moon Cloud and the answers she'd given him when he'd confronted her about it.

Marissa's gaze caught and held his.

Zach stared down at her, entranced by her innocence and beauty. It was all he could do not to take her in his arms and hold her to his heart. He remembered how angry he'd gotten listening to Mark in the saloon last night. This woman deserved only the best in life. She did not deserve the fate she'd been dealt.

"But are you all right?" she repeated.

"I'm fine," he answered.

"You sure? Where did this happen?" George asked.

Zach wanted to answer George honestly, but he wanted to do it when Marissa wasn't around. What he had to say to him needed to be said in private.

"I'll tell you later," Zach answered George, glancing at the women. "Now's not the time."

George scowled, but respected his wishes. "Are you feeling well enough to make the trip to the ranch?"

"I can ride. We need to get back."

"Why don't you come with me to the stable?"

"Fine."

They left Joe with the women and arranged to meet them at the hotel. Then they went to get the buckboard and the horses.

Louise and Marissa wondered what was going on, but said nothing in front of Joe. They were sure they would find out later.

Once they'd gotten away from Louise and Marissa, George turned to Zach.

"All right. We're away from the women. What happened? Did you get drunk and end up in a fight with somebody?"

"I was at the Palace with Hawk last night when some men came in," Zach began.

"And?"

"Mark was one of them. I didn't like was he was saying, and I let him know it."

"Mark?" George was surprised. "You fought with Mark?"

Zach nodded.

"What about?" George thought for a moment, then remembered Mark cutting in when Zach and Marissa were dancing. "Did you fight over Marissa? I know Mark cares deeply about her."

It pained Zach to speak up, but he knew George deserved the truth.

"Mark cares about Marissa's money," he stated flatly.

"What?" George was shocked.

"When he was at the Palace last night, some comments were made." Zach told him all that had been said in the saloon.

George was shaking with barely controlled fury when Zach finished. "That lowlife son of a bitch!"

Zach couldn't have agreed more.

"You say he looks worse than you?" The older man's mood lightened at the thought.

"That's right."

"Good."

George was glad Mark was no longer in town. He wasn't sure he would have been able to control himself if he ran into him. He knew exactly what he was going to do once they got back to the ranch.

Hawk was working at the stable when they arrived. He helped George hitch up the buckboard while Zach went to saddle the horses.

"You were there at the bar, too, last night, weren't you?" George asked Hawk.

"I was there. You'd have been proud of Zach. He's a good man."

George nodded. "I'm just sorry I missed it. I would have enjoyed helping Zach make his point to Mark, but I'm going to have my chance to deal with Mark very shortly."

Hawk was glad George wasn't mad at him. He knew what a determined man George Williams could be. It didn't pay to be on the wrong side of him.

Zach and George returned to the hotel to pick up Joe and the women.

They rode for the Crown.

George was outwardly calm as they made the trip, but with every passing mile, his anger grew. He was looking forward to facing Mark down.

"Did you have a good trip?" Sarah asked as the party reined in before the house.

"Oh, yes," Louise answered. "The dance was very nice, and we got some more shopping done."

Claude saw the packages stowed in the back. "Let me help you with those."

"Have you seen Mark around?" George asked.

"Not so far this morning," he answered.

"I'll be back."

George wheeled his horse around and rode down to the bunkhouse. He wanted to talk to Mark, and he wanted to talk to him now.

"Where's Mark?" he bellowed as he stuck his head in the bunkhouse.

"Down at the stable last I seen him, but that's been a while."

"Well, get off your ass and go find him!" George bellowed. "Tell him I want to see him up at the house."

"Yes, boss," the hand replied, moving quickly at his order.

It wasn't often that George got in one of these moods, but all the men knew better than to mess with him when he was angry. Most of them knew better than to make him angry in the first place.

George returned to the house to await Mark. The women were still busy unloading the last of their purchases from the buckboard. He went to help and had just started up the front steps when he saw Mark coming.

"Here, Joe. Take these inside," George ordered gruffly. "You might want to stay in there for a few minutes, too."

Joe looked from George to Mark and nodded in response as he hurried indoors. Everyone was about to go back outside for another load.

"You shouldn't go out there right now," Joe warned them.

"Why not?" Louise asked.

"George just told me I had to stay inside," he answered.

Louise thought that was odd. Zach and Claude took a look out the window and saw Mark talking with George in front of the house. They hurried toward the front door. Louise, Marissa, and Sarah exchanged puzzled looks. They glanced outside and saw Mark—his face battered and one eye swollen almost shut.

"Did Zach fight Mark last night?" Louise asked Marissa.

"I don't know."

The women hurried after Zach and Claude to see what was going on.

Joe wasn't about to be left out. He was curious, too.

"What the hell do you mean, I'm fired?" Mark was shouting.

"Get your things and get off my property—*now*!" George was glad Mark looked much worse than Zach did. He hoped the man was suffering greatly.

"You can't fire me!"

"I just did."

"I've worked my ass off for you on this ranch!"

"I paid you. You could have quit at any time."

"When we were on the trail trying to track down Marissa, I was the one who didn't want to give up."

"And we all know why now, don't we?" George's tone was deadly. Hate filled him. He wanted Mark gone right now, and he never wanted to see him again.

"Hell, after she'd been with the Comanche, nobody else in town would want her!"

At his words, Louise stepped to Marissa's side and slipped a supportive arm around her.

Mark went on. "At least I planned to make an honest woman out of her! I was going to marry her!"

Joe was confused by all that was going on. He was frowning as he stepped to the edge of the porch. "I don't understand," he began. "You can't marry Marissa. She's already married. She's married to Zach."

"What?" George looked back at Zach and Marissa, shocked.

"Isn't that right, Zach?" Joe went on. "Crazy One told me so."

Zach glanced at Marissa. Neither spoke.

The truth Zach had denied to protect her had been revealed. He hadn't meant for her to be hurt. He loved her. He had married her in the Comanche world to protect her. But what had protected her there would ruin her in the white world.

Mark laughed, a harsh, cruel laugh. His plan of marrying for money was ruined, so he decided to be as vicious as he could. "So Marissa really is a squaw! She was Zach's squaw! Wait till I tell the boys in town!"

Until that moment, Zach had held himself back, but he could no longer stand by and let this man say such things about the woman he loved. He started forward, ready to fight him again.

But George held out an arm to block Zach's way. "There's no need for violence."

Zach didn't want to stop. He wanted to teach Mark a lesson once and for all. He stood there, his jaw locked, his hands clenched into fists at his sides.

Mark looked at them, feeling cocky. George might have fired him, but he'd had the last word.

George had listened to Mark's comments in disbelief. He had trusted this man. He had thought a lot of him, but now he knew the truth.

George had stopped Zach from hitting him because this was his fight. And he intended to fight it.

He swung out at the now unsuspecting Mark. His one fierce, violent blow knocked the younger man to the ground. Mark lay flat on his back, sprawled in the dirt, stunned and bleeding.

"Get off my ranch," George ordered, glaring down at him. "And don't ever come back."

Chapter Thirty

George ordered Claude to make sure Mark packed up and got off the Crown. Once Claude had escorted Mark away, George turned to Zach.

"I think we need to talk," George said.

Zach respected George, but there was one thing he had to do before he spoke with him. "I understand, but first I need to talk to Marissa."

George didn't argue the point.

Zach turned back toward the house, where Marissa stood on the porch with Louise, Sarah, and Joe.

"Is something wrong?" Joe asked, feeling the tension in the air and not understanding it.

Mark was gone. Everybody should have been happy.

Zach walked slowly to the porch. It seemed the longest distance he'd ever crossed in his life.

He had tried to let Marissa go.

He had wanted what he'd thought would be a better life for her—a life without him. But now he knew the truth. He loved her and he could not let her go.

He had told her the Comanche marriage meant nothing. He'd been wrong.

And if she would have him, he would spend the rest of his life proving it to her. It wouldn't be easy. He had no real place in the white world, but he would do what he had to do to keep her by his side.

Marissa watched Zach coming toward her, and she thought he had never looked more wonderful than he did in that moment—bruises and all. He had fought to defend her and her honor.

If Zach didn't care about her, why had he fought for her?

Hope soared within her, but she remained unmoving, more than a little frightened by the power of the emotions sweeping through her. When Zach stopped at the bottom of the porch steps, she wanted to run to him, but she feared being rejected.

And then Zach held out his hand to her.

Marissa took a step forward and put her hand in his.

Zach drew her down the steps and away from the house. He took her to the place where he'd slept out under the stars their first night at the ranch, down to the place where he would tell her he loved her and didn't want to live without her.

"Louise—what's wrong?" Joe asked, seeing the tears in her eyes.

"Nothing, Joe, dear. Nothing at all." She hugged him impulsively as George came to stand with them.

"Let's go inside," George said.

He gave Louise a soft, quick kiss, then held the door for her and Sarah and Joe to enter ahead of him.

Zach stood gazing down at Marissa.

It was time for the truth between them.

"I thought you would have a better life without me. I thought Mark was the better man for you," he began slowly. "I thought

I could let you go—but I can't. I love you, Marissa. Though a Comanche marriage may not be recognized in the white world, in my heart you are my wife."

Marissa gazed up at him, her love for him shining in her eyes. "Zach—without you, I have no life. You're the most wonderful, bravest man I've ever known. I want to be with you—to spend the rest of my life with you."

"But I have nothing to offer you," Zach said, deeply troubled. "I don't even really know who I am."

"I know who you are. You are the man I love, Zach Ryder, and your love is all I'll ever need," she said simply.

Marissa reached up and looped her arms around his neck, drawing him down to her.

"I love you," she whispered as her lips met his.

Zach crushed her to him, deepening the exchange. In that moment, they both knew there was no greater joy in the world than true love.

They would find a way to be together.

They would find a way to happiness.

With love, all things were possible.

The church was filled with well-wishers as Reverend Gibson intoned, "I now pronounce you man and wife. George, you may kiss your bride."

George drew Louise near and kissed her sweetly. He had never been this happy before, and he knew the future was only going to get better.

The reverend then turned to the other couple standing before him.

"I now pronounce *you* man and wife," he repeated with a smile. "Zach, you may kiss your bride."

Zach needed no further urging.

He gazed down at Marissa, his wife now in all ways—Comanche and white.

With utmost care, he kissed her.

"Now they're really married," Joe told his grandpa.

They were sitting together in the first pew, watching as Zach and Marissa and George and Louise started back up the aisle, the ceremony over.

"That they are, Joe," Al Carter said as he returned his grandson's smile.

"And now we can go home to Pa, right, Grandpa?" Joe asked.

"That's right. He's waiting to see you."

Al Carter had been overjoyed when he'd received the telegram in Sidewinder telling him that Joe was alive and well in Dry Springs. The only survivor of the raid on Joe's ranch had been Joe's father, Steve. Al had taken Steve in and had been nursing him back to health since the Comanche attack. When the news had come about Joe, they had been thrilled.

Al knew their homecoming would be a sorrowful, bittersweet one, but at least they had each other, and they would be together again. Joe was alive—that was all that mattered.

Al had thanked Zach a thousand times, it seemed, for saving Joe. He would be eternally grateful for the man's help.

Al smiled up at Zach and Marissa as they passed by the pew on their way out of the church. In his heart, he wished them happiness forever.

Marissa was in heaven as Zach escorted her from the church.

She had never known she could be this happy.

Zach loved her, and she loved him.

Tonight was their wedding night, and this time she would *know* that it was her wedding night.

Tonight they would make love for the first time in a real bed.

The thought made Marissa's smile even brighter.

Zach was looking down at her and saw her expression. There was a definite twinkle in her eyes. "What are you thinking about?"

"You'll see," Marissa answered, and she pulled him down for another kiss.

When the kiss ended and they moved apart, Zach thought of the chain and cross from his childhood that he carried in his pocket, and he was filled with an overwhelming sense of peace. The past had been difficult for him, but as they stepped out into the sunshine, he knew their future would be as bright as this day was—and just as full of love.

About the Author

After working as a department manager for Famous-Barr, and briefly as a clerk at a bookstore, **BOBBI SMITH** gave up on career security and began writing. She sold her first book to Zebra in 1982. Since then, Bobbi has written over twenty books and several short stories. To date, there are more than three million of her novels in print. Her books have appeared on several bestseller lists and she was awarded the prestigious *Romantic Times* Storyteller of the Year Award. When she's not working on her novels, she frequently appears as a guest speaker for Romance Writers of America conferences.

The mother of two boys, Bobbi resides in St. Charles, Missouri, with her husband.

Made in United States
North Haven, CT
26 March 2023

This title was previously published by Dorchester Publishing; this version has been reproduced from the Dorchester book archive files.

For Dr. Richard Murray. You're brilliant!
And for Sharon Moss Sutton and Bart Moss,
two great friends from my high school days!

Text copyright © 2002 by Bobbi Smith
All rights reserved.
Printed in the United States of America.

Published by Montlake Romance
P.O. Box 400818
Las Vegas, NV 89140

ISBN-13: 9781477835098
ISBN-10: 1477835091

Lone Warrior

BOBBI SMITH

Lone Warrior

Other books by Bobbi Smith:

EDEN
SWEET SILKEN BONDAGE
THE HALF-BREED (SECRET FIRES)
WESTON'S LADY
HALF-BREED'S LADY
OUTLAW'S LADY
FORBIDDEN FIRES
RAPTURE'S RAGE
THE LADY & THE TEXAN
RENEGADE'S LADY
THE LADY'S HAND
LADY DECEPTION

The *Brides of Durango* series by Bobbi Smith:

ELISE
TESSA
JENNY

Bound

"Will you bind me to you again tonight?" Marissa asked as she followed him inside.

"Yes." Wind Ryder's answer was terse.

"There is no need. I will not run away again," she said.

Wind Ryder managed to give her a cold look of distrust as he reached for the rope.

"Lie down," he directed, going to her.

Marissa lay on the blankets as he'd ordered and waited as he tied the rope securely around her leg. The night before she'd been afraid, thinking about what might happen, but tonight, the warmth of his hands upon her leg sent an unexpected thrill through her. She looked on without saying anything more as he tied the other end of the rope to his own leg and made himself comfortable.

"Did the Comanche tie you up like this when you were little to keep you from running away?" she asked quietly.

"Captives must be trained to obey," he answered without emotion.

"That must have been hard for you—as a child."

"Go to sleep," he ordered, not wanting to discuss his past with her. He was already far too aware of her....

SO-AZT-855

CONTENTS

INTRODUCTION

You, too, can join women all over America who are working intelligently and getting ahead in their careers. Management has long since realized employees with high levels of personal ambition do well for their companies and for themselves. Personal success does not preclude excellence in service to one's employer. Moreover, individuals who are motivated to upgrade their pay scale and job status make the most desirable employees. In short, they hustle.

Don't be embarrassed or apologetic if you want to get ahead. On the contrary, be embarrassed if you don't. But remember, getting ahead can't happen by wishing. What you do at work today affects your success for tomorrow. If you are engaging in questionable work habits, you're holding yourself back. Perhaps you think you deserve bad habits since something about your work displeases you. The reality you must face is negative behavior invariably makes things more displeasing, at which point you may rationalize another bad habit, and from there you keep going downhill and defeating yourself.

However, if you are making a conscientious effort toward developing productive work habits, you will experience success. A systematic effort toward training yourself in positive behaviors and attitudes at work is the key. Picture what you know about building an elegantly designed house complete with beautiful landscaping. If the house is to turn out as lovely as imagined, every step in building must be executed properly; no step may be skipped. We've all seen hundreds of unattractive houses which stand for decades with no character or charm whatsoever. Your job will probably stand the same way, but is mediocrity all you want? Think again of building a stunning house. Apply the same step-by-step building principles to your work, and you may very well find yourself with a'stunning career. You will absolutely find out about the huge difference between feeling successful and feeling stagnant at work.

The following characteristics are constants in the careers of all women who are getting ahead:

- An abundance of energy and initiative.

- A determination to do things right.

- An understanding of the way their particular work fits into the major goals of their companies.

- A level of interest that stays vibrant over the years.

- A cooperative spirit and teamwork advocacy with male and female colleagues.

Make these key concepts a regular part of your work life and you will enjoy your own brand of success. You'll be among the most quietly effective and powerful group of people in America today.

MYTHS
AND
REALITIES

(and the benefits of knowing the difference)

MYTH NUMBER ONE

Getting ahead means becoming president of a company and earning six figures.

A WOMAN AT WORK

"If I can sell clothes in a department store for ten years, I know I can sell clothes in a shop of my own."

This is what Jayne Centerfield told herself at age fifty when she started preparing to open her new shop. Was she looking to make megabucks? No, she was looking to run an outstanding shop with a style all its own. Was she trying to become a queen bee boss? No, she was interested mainly in managing herself well enough to work productively with employees as well as handle all the other aspects of running a business. With these general goals in mind, Jayne spent a year doing research, identified short and long range goals, and put together a sound business plan to acquire financing.

This preliminary work gave her a big dose of experience in self-management before the shop ever served its first customer. It wasn't easy all the time, but Jayne refused to lose heart. By the time she finally opened to the public, Jayne had already experienced a special and personal brand of success as a business woman. Somehow, she had found the self-discipline to pull together all the necessary details to open her store properly.

From day one, the shop reflected all the creative touches and stylishness Jayne had visualized in her mind. Old customer relationships built over the years in her department store job served as a beginning base of customers for the new shop, and Jayne was off to a terrific start. Ironically, she did end up in the six figure and big boss category (three stores and 46 employees later), but not because she sought those things to the exclusion of everything else. Jayne insists that she made it, and is still in the process of making it, because she always focused on her two original goals; developing above-average shops and adhering to a strict code of professionalism.

MYTH NUMBER ONE

Getting ahead means becoming president of a company and earning six figures.

REALITY

The business of getting ahead is not an all or nothing proposition. It can be more accurately described as any improvement in pay, title, responsibility, and/or working conditions. These improvements usually come in the form of small steps forward that go unnoticed by others. But take heart, for these seemingly insignificant steps can lead to major breakthroughs. Don't underestimate the importance of any move toward getting ahead. You probably have many to your credit already.

- Be proud of them.

- Be thankful for them.

- Be ever on the alert for opportunities to add to them.

BENEFITS OF DISPELLING THE MYTH

Debunking the myth that getting ahead means becoming president of a company and earning six figures reveals the following valuable truths:

- Personal success at work must be defined in terms of goals reached. Therefore, if you have no goals, you can have no success.

- Goals may be conceived in hopes and dreams, but to be of value, goals must ultimately be clearly defined and reachable.

- Success is different things to different people.

To determine your personal definition of career success, you must examine your goals. Therefore, your most important present goal should go something like this:

"I am going to have three short range goals and three long range goals formulated and written down within the next two weeks. I will accomplish this by thinking carefully about what I want from my career, by collecting information on what is available to me, and by selecting goals well within my reach in order to give myself a chance to experience success."

EXAMPLES OF SHORT RANGE GOALS

1. By next month, put together a one page resume that is formal, polished, and professional. (There are dozens of resources to help you with this. Check the library.)

2. Start a journal entitled, *Personal Work Experience and Training*. Each week for six months write cryptic notes about your work life. Include job responsibilities, involvement in training programs, progress toward reaching your goals, and personal observations on what has and has not helped you move forward. Be sure to date each entry.

3. Set a date to review and evaluate your journal notes before continuing them. Can you see how useful a journal could be in helping you organize and document your work experience? Can you also see what a valuable tool it could become as you prepare to meet long range goals?

EXAMPLES OF LONG RANGE GOALS

1. Receive a substantial raise this year. Here's where the documented information in your journal could prove invaluable as you organize reasons why you deserve a raise. You can't ask for a raise and expect to get it if you can't communicate in a positive and professional way why you deserve it. A clear and specific statement of what you've done and what you plan to do will get far more attention than whining about needing more money, or, worse than that, making edgy demands for a bigger paycheck.

2. By this time next year, seek consideration for a higher level job than you have now. The same common sense applies in this situation that applies in asking for a raise. First, a cultivation

process must be developed. The rapport you establish with your colleagues, the people who work under you, and your superiors sets the stage for them to think of you as advancement material. You can't seriously expect to be considered for upper level jobs if you skip the process of building mutual respect with people above and below you.

3. Be funded in next year's budget to take part in a work-related out of town conference or training session. Again, requests of this magnitude require setting up over a period of time. If you spot a conference you'd like to attend, make sure it's dated far enough in the future to allow for planning and budgeting on the part of your boss, and make double sure you can articulate how the information you intend to bring back is going to make your department and boss look good.

NOTE: The examples of written goals outlined above were designed to help you formulate written goals of your own. You may have many different goals than the ones mentioned. As you hammer out personal goals, make sure you have a specific time frame surrounding each one. Also keep in mind that short range goals are easier to manage. Long range goals can also be reached with great success, but they require more persistence.

EXAMPLE: Jenna decided she wanted to change jobs within two years. Her secretarial position in a printing company had provided her much experience, but she felt a job in sales would allow her to make more money and develop a wider range of skills. Jenna put her goal in writing and then set up a two pronged effort toward reaching it. First, she tried to make herself a model employee in her current job. Second, she set about establishing a professional relationship with all the sales people who called on her boss at the printing company. It took six months longer than she planned, but Jenna finally landed a sales job she found out about through one of her newly cultivated contacts. Selling office supplies became Jenna's new job responsibility, and her former employer became her first and best customer. Jenna feels no less successful that her job change took six months longer than she anticipated, but she does admit she might have pulled it off sooner had she approached it a bit more systematically. Jenna realizes, as should you and I, that although creative strategies and goals for getting ahead are limitless, we must tap into them persistently and systematically if they are to do us any good. The following quote speaks eloquently about the value of persistence. Make it a KEY POINTER in planning your career.

"Press on: Nothing in the world can take the place of persistence. Talent will not; nothing is more common than unsuccessful individuals with talent. Genius will not; unrewarded genius is almost a proverb. Education will not; the world is full of educated derelicts. Persistence and determination alone are omnipotent."

STRATEGIES FOR BROADENING YOUR CAREER HORIZON

1. Go forward with a *Personal Work Experience and Training Journal* as described on page 11. Reserve a section in the back of your journal and label it, "GOALS." Be sure to date all entries in your journal, including goals. Do not overload the goals section or you will defeat yourself. Better to check off completed goals than to struggle with unrealistic goals you can't meet. To save time, make your weekly entries thoughtful but short. If you keep a notebook of this type for six months, you will establish in your own mind that you do, indeed, intend to get ahead. You will experience the gratification of translating vague wishes and dreams into organized, written goals.

   Maintaining a journal for six months will also give you insight into yourself. You may see patterns emerge which will cue you to take a career direction that never occurred to you before. You may even find yourself doing something constructive just to have the pleasure of recording it in your journal. And you absolutely will benefit from practice in setting and meeting goals.

2. Start a campaign of getting to know people all over your company or agency (and other companies when you get a chance), and make a special effort to become pleasantly acquainted with people in jobs above your level. If you present yourself as a courteous, friendly, and well groomed person who doesn't mind introducing herself, you will be hard to resist and

even harder to forget. Throw in a carefully built reputation for working hard and producing results, and your credibility factor will soar. Remember, moves forward (and backward) occur because of decisions made by people. Obviously then, you would benefit from getting to know a great many worthwhile people in your field. You can do it; just stick out your hand and say "hello."

THOUGHT QUESTIONS TO PROBE YOUR MIND

1. Can you give two positive examples of goal-oriented behavior at work?

2. How would you describe the condition of being without goals?

3. From your observation, do you think many of the people you work with have bothered to write down specific, well thought out goals for their work lives?

4. What do the following phrases mean to you?

   "Drawing your breath and drawing your pay."
   "Marking time."
   "Living the same year over and over."

MYTH NUMBER TWO

Getting ahead means
becoming a workaholic.

A WOMAN AT WORK

"I've always worked, I've always played tennis, and I've always enjoyed my husband and children. Sure, different things take precedence at different times, but everyone has to do a certain amount of juggling whether she works or not. My secret to handling everything is in setting priorities and planning my time. I know it sounds simplistic, but it works. Granted, a wheel runs off occasionally, but that's to be expected. When it happens, I just pick it up and move on."

Marian Joyner, an energetic branch bank manager, makes her philosophy clear. Work is a big part of her life, but it isn't all there is. With such a cavalier attitude how did she work her way up to branch manager? Simple. She has well developed goals and a good sense of perspective on what is important. She practices excellent time management and depends on her ability to focus intensively on important tasks rather than wasting endless hours on things that don't matter. She is organized and efficient, but has also learned that a sense of humor can carry her through much pressure and many foul-ups. Marian doesn't see herself as very different from other women, and she is generous with encouragement to everyone who works at her branch. Although only thirty-five, her superiors already view her as an up-and-coming employee. Marian is known to be a very professional career woman, as well as a warm and loving family person, and the nicest part about her is her certainty that any woman can be known the same way.

MYTH NUMBER TWO

Getting ahead means becoming a workaholic.

REALITY

A balanced life contributes far more to your advancement than excessive hours at work. A forty hour work week provides enough time to set in motion scores of tactics designed to improve your job situation. You have to spend the time at work anyway, so you may as well make it count for your future. Think of your actual hours at work as having two purposes; working for your employer and working for yourself. Now think of your pay as having two forms; money and experience. Start looking at the time you spend at work as a paid education. Your employer will benefit from having you learn all you can about your job, and you will benefit from broadening your skill and knowledge base. Get in the habit of using your workday to sharpen your skills.

Now let's consider after work activities designed to help you with career development. There are literally hundreds of degrees, books, tapes, manuals, trade journals, lectures, and classes chock-full of information for career people who want to hone their skills. Some after work time needs to be devoted to these learning avenues, but you must be selective. The more intensely you train yourself during working hours to identify useful skills and strategies, the easier it will be to choose appropriate after work career development opportunities. Make your involvement in career training a routine part of your life, but schedule activities outside your home at reasonable intervals.

Reserve a few drawers or shelves in your home for books and other printed materials related specifically to the advancement of your career. It will be gratifying to watch your collection grow over the years. Be cautious, however, of trying to do too much too soon. It's far better to train for success at a pace you can sustain over a lifetime than to race ahead toward exhaustion and burnout.

- Do use your working hours to discover and practice skills for advancement.

- Do seek appropriate training after work.

- Do pace yourself so you can work for a lifetime toward getting ahead.

- Don't neglect your personal life by scheduling all your time for work and training.

- Do be good to yourself by spending time regularly on relaxation, play, or whatever else makes you happy.

- Do understand you are more likely to get ahead if you:

1. Approach it as a manageable system as opposed to an overwhelming impossibility.

2. Activate the process regularly over the whole span of your work life.

3. Pace yourself as you move along by scheduling your time sensibly in all areas of your life.

BENEFITS OF DISPELLING THE MYTH

Debunking the myth that getting ahead means becoming a workaholic eradicates one more excuse for not acting. You can no longer say, "There's no use in my trying to advance because I don't have the energy or time to make it happen." Many women will continue saying and believing this, but not you. You will start using the time you have instead of complaining about the time you don't have. You may not be able to quit your job and work on an advanced degree, but you can use your workday to learn everything possible about your job and the field of work in which you are involved. You may not be able to attend week-long seminar training sessions, but you can enroll in appropriate local classes. The main thing is to use your time wisely and to make the very best of whatever training programs are within your reach. Forget limitations and concentrate on opportunities. Smart women have been doing this for decades.

KEY POINTERS

- Successful people may use their time differently, but they don't have any more of it than you do.

- Successful people may go through periods of working too hard or putting in grueling hours, but they can't sustain it indefinitely any more than you can.

- Successful people have learned to strike time and energy balances in their lives. These same balances are available to you.

- Successful people really believe they deserve to be on a track of advancement, and you must believe the same thing about yourself.

- You deserve to get ahead; now start behaving as though you do.

- Don't believe in magic wishes that take you to a career fantasyland, but don't believe in hopelessness, either.

- You have control.

- Your actions and attitudes make a difference.

- You can get ahead if you want to.

STRATEGIES FOR BROADENING YOUR CAREER HORIZON

1. Think about how your twenty-four hour day breaks down. Most of us spend a third or more of each weekday at our jobs. Ask yourself if you want to let a whole third of your life slip away with no concrete plan for improvement.

2. Now think about how your workday breaks down. As you go through your schedule mentally, jot down a few self advancement opportunities you've been missing. Let the following examples help you get started:

- Reserve a large file folder at work for materials specifically related to career advancement.

- Make a list of women working in positions above your level. If you can't think of any, your employer may have an unwritten understanding about which jobs women can fill, and your career advancement may have to continue elsewhere.

- Observe closely the men and women in positions above you.

- Dress and carry yourself as well or better than they do, and do it consistently. You have to look and act the part if you expect to get the part.

- Establish yourself as a serious and hard working employee, and then ask your direct superior for advice on how to advance. Only a real brute would discourage you.

- Speak positively every chance you get about your department or work setting. Your boss will be grateful, and you will be viewed as someone who is in an excellent job situation instead of as someone who is downtrodden and miserable.

- Monitor your speech carefully because what you say at work greatly influences how you're viewed at work.

THOUGHT QUESTIONS TO PROBE YOUR MIND

1. Do you really acknowledge the fact that a significant portion of your time and energy is spent in a formal work setting? If you spent the same amount of time playing tennis or golf, do you think you could advance in skill? Are you now open to the idea of applying this line of reasoning to your career life?

2. Have you thought much about the value of time? You wouldn't squander $800.00 a day, or even $8.00 a day. Why then would you squander eight hours a day at work by drifting along instead of plotting your advancement?

MYTH NUMBER THREE

Men have it easy.

A WOMAN AT WORK

"When I started moving through the ranks of college administrative positions, I acquired a different perspective on the accomplishments of men. The work required is just as demanding for men as it is for women. I no longer assume men receive more amenities in the working world just because they are male, nor do I still think women receive less just because they are female. Before passing judgment on the fairness of a person's career situation, I want to know two things: the difficulty of the work, and what the individual, male or female, has done to help himself or herself.

The intense responsibility connected with my own job has caused me to develop a new respect for individuals who held the position before me, and it just so happens all those individuals were men. I think a lot of women at my level are realizing the guys have been working a lot harder all these years than we may have first thought."

Anna Parker spoke another language a decade ago when she was in graduate school. At that time she was very vocal about her belief that men had all the power simply because they were men. She was always on the band-

29

wagon of showing up her male classmates, which she
did quite well by being an honor graduate and the re-
cipient of several awards. Her competitive spirit and
willingness to work hard ultimately lifted her to the
high level college administrative job she now holds. The
curious thing is that along the way she was forced to
overcome many of the same obstacles men have been
overcoming for years. She has also felt the pressure of
several jobs that were previously for men only. Were
these jobs easy? Anna's five word answer sums up her
new awareness succinctly. "No, and they *never were*."

MYTH NUMBER THREE

Men have it easy.

REALITY

Nothing could be further from the truth. Men have been slugging it out in the world of work for centuries, and it was never easy. Men have been so busy working they have not had time to raise an outcry against unfair obstacles in the way of their career development. Whether confronting a World War, a Great Depression, or a simple office conflict, men have pressed on stoically in their efforts to make a living. They have not railed against the unjust system that decided their fate. In fact, they have totally embraced society's measure of what it means to be a man. They believe all worthwhile men:

- Work and work hard.

- Compete with other men for the job and the dollar.

- Compete with ever increasing numbers of working women for the same job and dollar.

- Ask no questions as to what they might do with their lives other than work.

- Labor for decades to put food on the table and a degree of financial security in the bank.

- Stand aghast when flatly informed that what men have really been doing all these years is self actualizing and engaging in personal growth and development at the expense of their wives and other women. ("Self actualizing?" echo the fellows. "And all this time we thought we were just trying to make a living.")

- Press on in spite of their newest and most confusing competitors, women.

BENEFITS OF DISPELLING THE MYTH

Debunking the myth that men have it easy can trigger attitude changes which make you ripe for learning and applying techniques needed to get ahead at work. Like it or not, fair or not, men have seniority in the work arena. They've earned it. Now it's your turn to earn it the same way. Watch and learn from successful men (and women, too, of course). Read voraciously about the ones you don't know personally. Observe the ones you do know and notice the smallest details of how they operate. Ask them questions about how they started. You'll find most of them came from humble beginnings in their careers and had to work up through many menial jobs. You'll also learn volumes about their tenacity, perseverance, and strong beliefs in themselves.

Was it easy for them to become successful? A resounding no.

Has it become easier as their successes built up over the years? Perhaps a bit, but it certainly was never the snap you might have expected or wished it to be.

Was it worth the effort? A resounding yes.

KEY POINTER

You have the privilege and opportunity to choose your male and female work models. Select those of the highest caliber and think consciously about their work styles. Emulate as many of their finer work habits and attitudes as you can, and you will see unmistakable evidence of progress in your work life. The wisdom of this strategy is very useful, but it's entirely up to you to claim it.

STRATEGIES FOR BROADENING YOUR CAREER HORIZON

1. Think broadly about work. There is a context within which we all operate which can be described as follows: Men and women as groups are at different levels developmentally in the world of work. Don't think of this in terms of bad or good; think of it in terms of what is real. You will make better decisions if you make them based on reality.

2. Cooperate with men at work; don't fight them. They control plenty and have the power to help or hinder you.

3. Approach people as individuals and be sensitive to their perspectives. For example, if an older man calls you Honey or Sweetheart in a business setting, don't be offended and don't make an issue of it. Understand that he probably means no disrespect and may very well be trying to express approval.

4. Help people save face. If you do things to help associates feel good about themselves, you make business friends. The simple courtesy of remembering a person's name is a good example. People find it hard to forget an individual who makes them feel good.

5. Keep your guard up. Be on the alert for hidden agenda and learn to read people and situations on deeper than surface levels. The beast called ''office politics'' thrives on what is going on beneath the surface, but he isn't deadly if you stay alert to the fact that people very often have hidden motives. Moreover, as you practice being perceptive about the intricacies of relationships, you'll find you can learn as much from subtleties of behaviors and attitudes as you can from what people say and do at surface levels.

6. Never underestimate people. You don't have the market cornered on figuring things out. People may not say it to your face, but they know if you try to use, manipulate, or undermine them. They also see through bragging, shallow attempts at acting superior, and name dropping. If you can see positives and negatives in others, be assured they can see them in you.

7. Concentrate on your individual effort toward getting ahead rather than depending on women as a group to help you. If you make breakthroughs for yourself, you'll pave the way for other women to do the same. Remember, any successful group is made up of individuals who realize they must help themselves before they can help others. Approach your advancement as an individual, not as a crusader for a cause. Women who excel individually lend a degree of credibility to all women. Be that kind of woman and you will enjoy the power and satisfaction of being able to help others.

THOUGHT QUESTIONS TO PROBE YOUR MIND

1. There are hundreds of positives for being a woman in today's work force. Can you name three?

2. Admit to yourself at least two ways you've taken advantage of being a woman on the job. (Come on now. We're all guilty of this one.)

3. Have you ever criticized men as a group for the way they treat women at work? If so, have you stopped to think about your grievances in an historical context or from the male point of view? Do you really, sincerely, honestly believe that men are the enemy?

MYTH NUMBER FOUR

Successful men and women
are smarter than you.

A WOMAN AT WORK

"I made better grades in college and law school than many of my male classmates, but that doesn't mean I can compete with them in the real world. They know so much more than I do about inspiring confidence in clients. Sometimes I think they were just born with that ability. I know for certain that making clients feel secure is what it takes to build a thriving practice, but I'm not sure I can pull it off."

Amelia Canfield testifies by word and deed that she believes her male colleagues are brighter. The sad thing is the men haven't tried to intimidate her at all. They don't need to because Amelia intimidates herself. The job she holds as attorney for a private women's college has become a hiding place, almost a prison. Amelia has outgrown her job, but she's afraid to break out and do what she originally planned which was to start a law practice of her own. She is terrified of failing, so she won't allow herself to pursue her dream. It's interesting to hear Amelia relate story after story of the ups and downs experienced by her friends in private practice.

Some of the downs she describes are fairly rugged, but she always maintains that her friends can handle them. Why can't she give herself the same credit?

MYTH NUMBER FOUR

Successful men and women are smarter than you.

REALITY

You are just as intelligent and capable as your fellow human beings. They are not smarter than you. In point of fact, the process of learning and applying strategies for getting ahead doesn't require a superhuman intellect anyway. Be advised now and forevermore that you have ample brain power to think up hundreds of creative ideas to help yourself get ahead. The suggestions and encouragement offered on these pages are meant to help you in tangible and specific ways, but they are also designed to make you aware of your own responsibility. You must not only practice applying these suggestions, you must also get in the habit of continually devising new ones. If you're uncertain about whether or not you're able to help yourself get ahead, consider what you've already accomplished. Mustering the self discipline to get up and go to work at any job every day for even six months is significant. You've done that and much more, so stop selling yourself short and take hold of the notion that you can get ahead because of your own initiative.

BENEFITS OF DISPELLING THE MYTH

Debunking the myth that successful men and women are smarter than you is of paramount importance. It breaks down a tremendous barrier between you and advancement. It also allows you to confidently explore the following thought processes:

- Facing the fact that there is no mystique or magic about getting ahead.

- Forsaking any secret wish you may be harboring that there are short cuts, easy routes, or simplistic formulas for advancement.

- Giving up the idea that lightning will strike and catapult you ahead.

KEY POINTER

You have a perfectly adequate brain. Trust it as your very best resource in developing personal strategies for advancing in your career.

STRATEGIES FOR BROADENING YOUR CAREER HORIZON

1. Practice thinking of yourself as a very smart and capable individual. I once saw a bank president lock his keys inside his car. After twenty minutes of struggling, he managed to open the car door with a coat hanger, but not without shredding the rubber window insulation. Two hours later the same man locked the same keys in his trunk. This time he had to call a locksmith to pick the lock for a fee of $25. Clearly, this bank president isn't smarter than you. He may be older, more experienced, or more intimidating, but he is not smarter. Remember this story the next time you come across people you think are successful and brainy. Your head is just as good as theirs.

2. Abide by the following LAWS to insure that others perceive you as the intelligent person you are:

   L ook sharp.
   A ct sharp.
   W rite sharp.
   S peak sharp.

3. Align yourself with the most responsible and serious minded people you can find in your work setting. You know precisely which ones are respected and which ones are viewed as lazy and incompetent. Cultivate the former; keep your distance from the latter.

4. Be so smart that you know when to be ignorant. The ability to keep your mouth shut about sensitive issues is practically considered a spir-

itual virtue by employers. After all, is it really necessary to talk about the argument you overheard your boss having with her spouse on the phone? When pumped for sensitive information by others, resist the temptation to be "in the know." It is very valuable to be considered an information resource, but restrict the information you give out to professional matters.

5. Have the wisdom to recognize situations that can work to your advantage. The psychological balancing act in work relationships can often tip the scales in your favor. For instance, if you have a scheduled appointment with someone and they forget about it or show up late, you will have a psychological advantage the next time you see that person. You may even discover a willingness on their part to do something extra for you to even the score. Be ready to guide this person toward a favor you want. Men have been cashing in chips with each other for years, but you can "cash in" as well as they can. If you really want things like raises and promotions, keep track of your psychological "chips," but do it gracefully, subtly, and fairly.

6. Become smarter by reading about your area of work on a regular basis. Since most people don't bother to read very much or think very deeply, this one strategy has the potential to lift you head and shoulders above your colleagues. READ!

THOUGHT QUESTIONS TO PROBE YOUR MIND

1. Have you ever played the "if only" game? It goes like this: If only I were smarter or richer or better looking or better educated, I might be able to get further ahead at work. If only I were as bright as the people I see sailing through their careers, maybe I could do better for myself. Will you be able to recognize yourself or others playing the "if only" game the next time you come across it? How do you intend to cure yourself of indulging in these kinds of self defeating activities?

2. Do you treat yourself gently or harshly when you make mistakes? It's normal to be cautious for a while after a botch-up, but do you become immobilized? Have you figured out that most people are too busy with their own lives to concern themselves with your shortcomings? Do you really believe the old axiom, "You learn more from failure than from success?" Can you remember to be kind to yourself the next twelve times you miss the mark? If you can, you'll be joining a prestigious group of people who manage to go forward in spite of, as well as because of, their hundreds of mistakes and failures.

3. Are you open to new ideas and change, or are you more comfortable following the same patterns year after year? Fear of change can raise many emotion-packed questions in your psyche:

   • Will I have to work longer hours?

   • Will I have to learn something new?

- Am I capable of learning something new?

- Will I have to give up anything?

- Am I losing ground or gaining ground?

- Will it be too much work?

- Why can't I just do what I'm accustomed to?

4. Which of the above questions creeps into your mind? Can you see that if you rigidly hang onto status quo and refuse to flow with change, you will become hopelessly outdated? Can you describe what it means to be a living anachronism?

MYTH NUMBER FIVE

Assertiveness yields power. It is responsible for a new thrust of progress among women striving to advance at work.

A WOMAN AT WORK

"I never said anything that wasn't perfectly true or fair. In fact, my willingness to articulate what is right is the main reason I was hired in the first place. Too bad it had to be my undoing, too."

Barbara Marshall still hasn't figured out why she was fired from her job as lobbyist for a well known professional association. Even as she tells her story, it's clear from her tone and choice of words that she believes fairness has been totally violated. Barbara is convinced a co-worker filtered information to her boss that Barbara was losing effectiveness on behalf of the association due to repeated incidents of abrasiveness in committee meetings. Barbara, however, believes she did nothing more than stand up for what was right. It has been only recently that she began to suspect her style may have been too strong, aggressive, and perhaps even too argumentative. She now concedes her efforts were unsuccessful because she alienated more people than she befriended. Barbara is learning the confusing lesson that being right isn't always enough in the working world. You not only have to be right, you have to be tactfully right.

MYTH NUMBER FIVE

Assertiveness yields power. It is responsible for a new thrust of progress among women striving to advance at work.

REALITY

"Assertiveness" has become a fashionable word, a buzz word, a word which holds out false hope to women by suggesting that if only they can become "assertive," they can gain enough power to get ahead. By one definition *assert* means, "to state positively; affirm; aver." It also means, "to maintain as a right or claim, by words or by force." Some women have used a shrill tone in documenting the "rights and claims" of women. Basically, they've issued two lists: *Things We Should Not Tolerate*, and *Things We Should Demand*. It is time to compile a third list labeled, *Things We Should Learn About: Professionalism, Cooperation, Getting Along, and Contribution*. Successful people have always focused on the positive and minimized the negative, and so must you if you want to move ahead.

BENEFITS OF DISPELLING THE MYTH

Debunking the myth that assertiveness yields power will
help you think more clearly about good and bad advice
on career advancement. No issue is cut and dried, and
that includes the question of assertiveness. Evaluating
assertiveness training in terms of the following guidelines will also help you appraise other career related
advice as it applies to you personally:

Point—Beware assertiveness if it becomes a veiled excuse for:

- Abrasiveness
- Aggression
- Complaining
- Rudeness
- Clamoring to be understood
- Airing resentments
- Putting down others

Point—Embrace assertiveness if it means finding the
courage to affirm the following positives:

- Sharpening your technical capabilities.
- Learning and practicing people skills.
- Improving your attitude.
- Setting and achieving realistic goals.
- Being on the lookout for all opportunities to en-
  hance your value to your employer.

- Declaring confidently to yourself and others that you are working to get ahead and are trying to learn and activate all positive and reasonable strategies to that end.

KEY POINTERS

Assertiveness in the form of bemoaning unfairness, making demands, and attempting to negotiate on trivial matters will not endear you to your employer. Whether or not this is fair is beside the point; we are addressing what is real, not what is fair.

Assertiveness in the form of steadiness, poise, and a positive attitude is a valued and rare trait. Couple this positive form of assertiveness with a willingness to do your official job plus a little more, and you will set yourself apart. You will have an edge. You will, indeed, have power. It may mean training yourself to wait a week before expressing what you think about someone or something that has made you angry. It may mean withstanding subtle, and not so subtle, pressure from fellow employees who would rather see you remain on their level of mediocrity. It may mean being clever enough to maintain positive relationships with your peers, subordinates, and bosses, at the same time you're actively advancing your own cause. You will not succeed in every situation, but don't worry about that. Instead, dwell on the large and small successes that spring from consistent effort. Say to yourself every day:

"I am steady and poised."
"I have a positive attitude."

"I am known to be a hard worker which helps my em-
   ployer as much as it helps me."
"I am recognized as being serious about my work."
"My co-workers know I enjoy my work."

If you repeat the suggested phrases and act them out,
things will start falling into place. When you get dis-
couraged, pick up this book and review the basics. Then
encourage yourself to go forward positively. You deserve to get ahead. You are able to get ahead. You will
get ahead if you train your mind to expect it. Practice
the positive kind of assertiveness that will help you hang
onto your desire, and you will be giving yourself something no one else can give you. Yes, there's room for
being assertive in your quest for career advancement,
but only in exceedingly positive manifestations.

STRATEGIES TO BROADEN YOUR CAREER HORIZON

1. Listen with a third ear to trendy words and
   phrases such as assertiveness, productivity, networking, stress management, time management,
   management by objectives, and "1" minute
   anything. These are just a few terms suffering
   from overkill. The ideas behind them contain
   gems of wisdom, but the words themselves are
   bandied about by many people who are often
   guilty of talking the talk without walking the
   walk. Keep yourself out of that category.

2. Learn the meanings of these words:

   Discern—". . . to distinguish mentally; rec-
        ognize as distinct or different."

> Discriminate—". . . to note or observe a
> difference; distinguish accu-
> rately."

EXAMPLE: A life insurance plan featuring very low
premiums was presented to a group of employees.
It was an excellent offering made possible because
the insurance company also handled the group's
health insurance. The employees were winning in
two ways; health insurance premiums were being
paid by the employer, and inexpensive life insurance policies were being made available as options for group members. It was a genuinely good
deal, but only four of fifty-five employees signed
up for the life insurance program. The other fifty-
four were suffering from jaded notions about deals
having to do with money. They thought like this:
Since most money deals work out poorly, I should
reject all money deals. The four employees who
bought the insurance were much more discerning
and discriminating thinkers. They applied the following logic: If I categorically reject all money
deals, I will miss the good ones along with the
bad.

Go back and review the meanings of discern and
discriminate. Now you can begin looking for opportunities at work to activate your own discerning and discriminating mind.

3. Develop a mental junk detector for ideas. As
   you filter information through your "detector," trash will be discarded and valuables will
   be saved. Just be sure you put good information to use when you find it. For instance, it
   doesn't do you any good to know how to build

a business correspondence network if you refuse to discipline yourself to find time for letter
writing.

EXAMPLE: You conceive the notion of starting an an-
notated index card file of pertinent people you
meet during the course of each workday.

- Possible Outcome Number One: You start the
  file and maintain it for a month or two before
  letting it go by the wayside.

- Possible Outcome Number Two: You start the
  file, maintain it for a year, and make an effort to stay in touch with the people in it by
  sending them Christmas cards, personal
  notes, and interesting clippings and articles.
  Then you decide to open your own secretarial service across town, or look for a better
  job, or market an original newsletter. Your
  card file could easily provide a base of clients which would propel you on your way to
  success.

Now do you see the importance of not letting
valuable ideas slip away with worthless information? A recent study by Burke Marketing Research, Incorporated, yielded some very useful
information for employees who want to be viewed
positively. As you review the article which describes the study, try to put yourself in your boss's
shoes in order to analyze how your work habits
and behaviors are perceived. Empathy for others
and a bit of introspection can help you monitor
your behavior, make better decisions, and establish improved work habits.

RESULTS OF STUDY REPORTED

Liars, goof-offs, egomaniacs, laggards, rebels, whiners, airheads and sloths—these are the eight banes of a boss's existence, according to a new survey, and each is advised to repent or risk unemployment.

Burke Marketing Research, Inc. asked executives in 100 of the nation's 1,000 largest companies, "What employee behaviors disturb you most?"

The result was a "hit parade of things that stick in the boss's craw—the kind of behavior that hits a nerve," said Marc Silbert whose temporary personnel agency commissioned the survey. "They can blind employers to employees' good qualities. They become beyond redemption."

1. Dishonesty and lying topped the list. "If a company believes that an employee lacks integrity, all positive qualities—ranging from skill and experience to productivity and intelligence—become meaningless," said Silbert, vice president of Accountemps.

"This isn't just the guy who steals money from petty cash," he explained. "It includes intellectual dishonesty. We had one employer complain about an employee who took on a job with a Nov. 16 deadline even though he knew he'd be on vacation that week."

The seven other deadly sins, in order of irritation:

2. Irresponsibility, goofing-off, and doing personal business on company time. "We found some people literally conducting their own ongoing businesses on company time," Silbert said. "It's not just a guy getting a phone call from his wife to pick up eggs on the way home. This is someone running a T-shirt busi-

ness out of the office. It's entrepreneurial behavior gone wild in a very real way.''

3. Arrogance, ego problems, and excessive aggressiveness. ''Employees who spend more time boasting about their accomplishments than on actually getting the job done . . . who think that being loud or boisterous will have a positive effect bother their bosses,'' Silbert said. ''If you have this kind of person in a supervisory role, you don't have one problem, you have twenty. You have little range wars breaking out all over the office.''

4. Absenteeism and lateness. ''One employer said, 'It doesn't make any difference when we start, 9 a.m. or 10 a.m., some people will be 15 minutes late,' '' Silbert reported.

5. Not following instructions or ignoring company policies. ''Such behavior is more serious in larger, more conservative companies,'' Silbert said, citing, ''a guy working for a dark-suit-and-school-tie kind of company who wears an I'm-from-Florida tie.''

6. Whining and complaining. ''There's one in every office. They always have a problem: 'Do we have to do it by Thursday?' 'This project is so boring,' '' Silbert whined in imitation.

7. Absence of commitment, concern, or dedication. ''This often is grounds for absence of raises and promotions,'' Silbert said.

8. Laziness and lack of motivation. ''Both demonstrate that these people don't care about the company, so why should the company care about them,'' Silbert pointed out.

Among the also-rans: lack of character, inability to get along with others, disrespect, displays of anger or pettiness, making ill-informed decisions and judgments, and taking credit for the work of others.

After studying the preceding article, try to put yourself in your boss's shoes in order to analyze how your own habits and behaviors are perceived. Empathy for others and a bit of introspection can help you monitor your behavior, make better decisions, and establish improved work habits.

THOUGHT QUESTIONS TO PROBE YOUR MIND

1. Have you considered the notion that a back to basics approach to work habits does not have to be in conflict with learning and using new ideas and techniques? Have you identified a personal set of fundamental work habits?

2. Why do you think it is valid to make a case that new work related ideas are not worth much if they ignore or deny the basics?

3. Name one woman you view as having what it takes to get ahead. In your opinion is she attentive to the basics? Does she keep abreast of new ideas? How well does she integrate the two?

4. How do you think your boss and colleagues would describe you in terms of question number three?

MYTH NUMBER SIX

Men must develop their careers;
women still have a choice.

A WOMAN AT WORK

"I have come to the conclusion that it isn't fair for me to expect a man to give me the kind of security I want. Oh yes, I'm married, but my husband and I are both developing careers of our own. He expresses a great deal of gratitude for my desire to make significant financial contributions to our family, but the truth is he doesn't have to. I'm doing it for myself as much as for him and the children. He also tells me sad stories about his male friends who suffer terrible guilt over the fact that their wives are forced to work to make ends meet for their families. My question is what would these long suffering women do if they had no man to pick up the major portion of the tab? How can they be so insensitive as to play the role of martyr with their husbands and ignore the millions of single women who have no choice but to make their own way? My theory is that every woman ought to make her own way, and I intend to do just that."

Meg Connelly has no qualms about injecting an element of reality into any conversation about women and careers. Moreover, she presents an excellent model in that she has worked successfully in two fields while managing family life, too. Meg taught school several years and then moved into a bottom rung editor's job in a medium sized publishing company. After several years of experience and interim promotions, she has reached the position of senior editor in charge of manuscript acquisition. One of her ongoing concerns is for women who are just entering the work force. Meg takes every opportunity to encourage them and build up their confidence. "I'm a fan of any working woman," she states emphatically, "no matter what her creed, color, or age, and no matter what her job."

MYTH NUMBER SIX

Men must develop their careers; women still have a choice.

REALITY

Women absolutely need to develop their careers if they aspire to enjoy real security and fulfillment. Now that we have faced the economic reality of having to work, we must go to the next step of advancing as far as we can. Smart women are accepting the challenge. They are finding creative ways to get beyond phase one. They are taking the responsibility of helping themselves and are no longer waiting for husbands, employers, or the women's movement to save them.

BENEFITS OF DISPELLING THE MYTH

Debunking the myth that men must develop their careers and women still have a choice can make you aware of an irreversible trend. There is a great awakening among thinking women on what getting ahead really means. These women find the notion of controlling their own advancement refreshing, and they find the long list of benefits resulting from the effort inspiring.

BENEFITS OF MAKING THE EFFORT

- Being in the mainstream with forward thinking people.

- Realizing that getting ahead results from hundreds of small accomplishments over the years.

- Learning to value every success no matter how small.

- Learning how to take care of yourself and knowing that if you do, you are better able to help others.

- Becoming more valuable to yourself and others.

- Enjoying the fact that you are building your own security.

- Finding the kind of fulfillment which frees you from living vicariously through others.

- Eliminating from your future many of the problems unprepared women will face. For you there will be no:

  1. Empty nest syndrome. (You will be too busy developing your career.)

  2. Financially disastrous widowhood. (Widowhood is never easy emotionally, but at least

you will have the comfort of knowing you
can provide for yourself.)

3. Financially disastrous divorce. (You will be
able to recover faster with the backup of a
serious career.)

KEY POINTERS

The first step in getting ahead in your career is realizing
you owe it to yourself to try. Other women are not only
trying, they are making respectable headway. You, too,
must go forward or risk being left behind to be controlled by others. We have put away one set of debilitating laments. Let's check them off one by one and
leave them behind forever.

✓• No one told me I was going to have to work
indefinitely for a living.

✓• My family and society didn't prepare me for
a lifetime of work.

✓• I resent having to work when I planned to stay
at home and be a proper wife and mother.

Now it's time to put away another set of laments. Let's
check them off, too.

✓• I know I have to work for a living, but I don't
have to spend more than the minimal amount
of time and energy on my job, and I certainly
don't have to like it.

√• My job is not my real life. I just work to get
to the end of the day and the beginning of the
next paycheck.

√• I believe most working women are ill equipped
to advance in their careers because they are
oppressed by men, not taken seriously, and
too overworked at home to even consider trying to get ahead in a career.

It is imperative to expose the above excuses and negative thought patterns if you want to make something
special of your career. Many women will continue to
hang onto useless and self destructive thought patterns,
but not you. You will adhere to the philosophy that work
is a grand opportunity, not a distasteful necessity. This
positive philosophical stance, plus the belief that you
have much personal control over your own progress,
will result in work becoming a great source of satisfaction in your life.

STRATEGIES FOR BROADENING YOUR CAREER HORIZON

1. Assume work will be a lifetime proposition,
not a temporary inconvenience. Assume you
will most likely need to work no matter what
else happens in your life.

2. Listen for verbal cues from others that reveal
the kind of distorted views listed below:

Distorted Thinking	*Clear Thinking*
"I'm just working here until something better comes along."	"Working here is good experience. I'm trying to soak up everything I can."
"When I get married and have children, I'll probably stop working."	"My work life is something I don't plan to give up. The personal security and fulfillment it provides are too precious to sacrifice."
"When my children finish college, I can finally quit working."	"When my children finish college, I plan to go to more conventions, trade shows, and association meetings. It will be great to have the money to fund more of these growth experiences."
"I'm only working to help my husband."	"I'm really working for myself, but my family benefits a great deal from it, too."
"I had to find a job to get us through a money crisis, but it's strictly temporary."	"Nothing and nobody forces me to work. I do it because it gives me control over my own fate. Delusions are for others. Getting ahead in my career is for me."
"It doesn't matter so much if my pay is lower than my husband's. After all, it's only a second income."	"My career is just as important to me as a man's career is to him. Besides, women are not immune to being cast in the role of chief breadwinner. I'll never minimize the importance of my career."
"I hate this job, but from what I hear, everybody else hates theirs, too. I guess working is a necessary evil."	"I'm too selfish to give up a third of my life to a job I hate, but I also realize it's my responsibility to either adjust my attitude or move on. Nobody is going to fix things for me. I have to fix things for myself."

Distorted Thinking	*Clear Thinking*
"If I had known I was going to be working this long, I would have trained for a better paying job."	"I want to be like the exciting men and women I see who are having a great time developing their skills. They always seem to be learning and training and doing exciting things. That's what I want to do, too."

3. Practice telling yourself good things about what you can accomplish and enjoy at work. Repeated affirmations, whether they are positive or negative, make their way into your subconscious mind. This is the part of your brain which can't differentiate between what is vividly imagined and what is real. If you affirm an idea to yourself on a regular basis, your subconscious not only accepts it as fact, it causes you to behave in ways that will make the idea actually become fact. Creating and repeating positive affirmations can be very helpful to you, but it may take a little effort to wade through the negatives your mind has already internalized. If you remember three simple rules, positive affirmations will be of tremendous help to you:

1. Use present tense.

2. Say the words with great intensity and emotion.

3. Speak and act as if the affirmation already exists.

EXAMPLES OF POSITIVE AFFIRMATIONS OF A GENERAL NATURE

- "I'm lucky to be alive at a time when opportunities are plentiful for working women."

- "I'm proud to see other women making bold efforts to learn and advance."

- "I'm glad my personal efforts to do well in my career are opening up more and more opportunities for other women."

NOTE: Positive affirmations like the ones listed above can help you, but specific ones are even more useful.

EXAMPLES OF POSITIVE AFFIRMATIONS OF A SPECIFIC NATURE

- "I am capable of speaking successfully to a large group."

- "I am able to run my boss's job."

- "I make an excellent impression when being interviewed."

With the listed examples in mind, you can begin creating your own positive affirmations. Just be sure to isolate the affirmations that really mean something to you and say them daily as if they are already fact.

THOUGHT QUESTIONS TO PROBE YOUR MIND

1. Can you recall three negative affirmations you have fallen into the habit of repeating? Bring them to the front of your mind and think seriously about how they are hurting you.

2. Have you heard others affirm negatively about their own work lives?

3. Do you ever think of your mind as a computer capable of being programmed? If you could choose programs for your brain, what kind would you select? How much responsibility are you willing to take for the information that goes into your mind? Are you willing to let others program you, or do you want to program yourself?

MYTH NUMBER SEVEN

Women encounter too many blocks
and problems at work to gain real
momentum in getting ahead.

A WOMAN AT WORK

"I should have quit a dozen times, but, thank goodness, I didn't know it."

Linda Nelson can joke now about the first three years of her jewelry business, but in 1975, things weren't so funny. She started making jewelry seriously after her homemade earrings became the most popular item at her Women's Club Spring Festival. Her booth was out of stock in an hour, but Linda had the foresight to keep back a few samples and take orders the rest of the day. The next problem was filling the orders and figuring out how to get more. Friends and family encouraged her, but Linda insists no one really thought a housewife could get much further than a garage studio and a few orders from the community. Linda's tone makes it obvious that she had as much fun proving she was able to build a business as she had in actually doing it. Her husband got interested in the effort, and together they traveled to endless and exhausting craft and trade shows to set up Linda's booth and take orders. During these first years of traveling, their file of customers grew into a substantial mailing list. Linda's creative energy surged during this period, and her designs became more and more popular. Next, she put together a small mailing catalog to serve the customers she had met while selling in different cities, and that's how she broke into mail order. It was a short step to display ads in magazines and purchased mailing lists. The nicest breakthrough, though, was in capturing the interest of retail stores. Linda's biggest business problem these days is distributing her jewelry. Employees handle it very well, but Linda says she retains worrying rights. Her most important current functions in the business are the two things she does best, designing and selling. What happened to her family along the way? They're all working in a $3,000,000.00 jewelry business started in a garage storage room by a simple (don't you believe it) housewife.

MYTH NUMBER SEVEN

Women encounter too many blocks and problems at work to gain real momentum in getting ahead.

REALITY

Solutions to work related problems are bound up in the application of two kinds of skills; people skills and technical skills. You must concentrate on developing both if you plan to advance. As you attempt to work through technical and people problems, keep the points below in mind. They will help you avoid becoming immobilized:

- It's never too early or too late in your career to seek creative solutions to problems.

- Don't be mentally and emotionally undone by blocks and problems. Everyone experiences them and everyone has to figure out how to cope. When you feel like you're drowning in problems, remember you are not alone.

- Dreaming up workable strategies to solve career problems is not a knack or an art form. It is a learnable skill that improves with practice.

- Any strategy you use must be implemented with
  sensitivity to timing, personalities involved, formal company rules and regulations, and informal company rules and regulations. Remember,
  your actions are not without context.

BENEFITS OF DISPELLING THE MYTH

Debunking the myth that problems at work prevent
women from gaining momentum helps you realize that
this is only true when women don't recognize the need
for developing competence in problem solving. In trying to work out a personal style for dealing with blocks
and problems, you need to consider the following:

- Problems are inevitable. You cannot escape them.

- Every job has a unique set of problems. Therefore, whether you're on your first job or whether
  you've changed jobs ten times, you can always
  expect problems to appear.

- Developing the ability to handle problems
  smoothly is a valuable skill in the working world.
  Anyone can manage regular tasks and schedules,
  but it takes a special person to keep people and
  work under control when things go wrong. With
  a little practice, you can be that kind of person.

- A crisis has the potential to make you look like a
  genius or an idiot, depending on how you choose
  to work through it. Did you notice the word, choose,
  in the previous sentence? It was used to emphasize
  the point that you really do have a choice of behaving sensibly or foolishly during a crisis. If you pretend otherwise, you are only deceiving yourself.

KEY POINTERS

Approach problems as opportunities instead of disasters and you'll put yourself in an entirely different category from most of your co-workers. Remember, it's not the problems, it's how you handle them that counts. Cool heads prevail, so let the coolest head be yours.

STRATEGIES FOR BROADENING YOUR CAREER HORIZON

Dealing with career blocks and problems calls for the use of many options. Consider the following examples of ways to unblock conditions which impede progress. The strategies suggested will stimulate you to think creatively about formulating your own strategic options.

BLOCK

- Can't get a job at all or can't get the job you want.

STRATEGIC OPTIONS

- New graduates often run into trouble in this area, but seasoned workers sometimes suffer from it, too. What can you do about it? First, stop whining and complaining. Recently, a college graduate stated angrily on a nationally televised talk show that she had been to 52 interviews over 18 months and still had no job. This is not the kind of language that motivates contacts to recommend you or employers to hire you. If you can't find a job, take it as your responsibility to analyze and correct your approach

to employers. Don't think employers ought to tailor
their requirements to meet your personal needs. It
won't happen, so don't expect it.

BLOCK

- Don't know how to find out what's available.

STRATEGIC OPTIONS

- Responding to want ads and registering with
  employment agencies can be productive, but
  more and better jobs are found through personal
  contacts. Make a job contact list of friends, relatives, people you know from other jobs you've
  held, contacts in professional organizations,
  friends you've made in seminar and training sessions, and anyone else who might be in the position of hearing about a good job. Start asking
  your contacts for help. It's an accepted job hunting practice, but be sure you ask in a positive
  and professional manner. You can't honestly expect anyone to refer you if they aren't sure you
  will reflect well on them. Try to have your contacts perceive you in the best light possible.

- As you work your contacts, think about the
  young woman who went to 52 fruitless interviews. This means she now knows 52 people
  whose job responsibilities include hiring others.
  There is no doubt that an analysis of these interviews would reveal their value goes far beyond consideration for the job at hand. Ask
  yourself the following questions to determine the
  real worth of a specific interview:

1. In developing your list of contacts, did you include people who have interviewed you for jobs you didn't get?

2. Are you aware of the levels of evaluation going on in interviews? For example, interviewers will most likely be in the position of knowing about different jobs as they come open in their companies. If you project a professional attitude in your interview, you will be remembered and you may be considered for a job other than the one for which you applied.

- Do you think contacts are worth keeping warm even when you're not in the market for a job? Here is where networking is most abused. People too often use contacts, get what they're after, and then immediately drop the people who helped them. Those who are guilty of this never realize for themselves or others the full benefit of networking.

- Do you understand there is no disgrace in taking a job for which you're over qualified just to get your foot in the door, meet people, and establish yourself as a hard worker?

BLOCK

- Don't know how to apply or interview for jobs.

STRATEGIC OPTIONS

- You need to learn how to package yourself properly. Resumes, cover letters, thank you notes, and all other correspondence with potential employers must express a high level of professionalism. Concise and courteous written communications are appreciated. Use them, but also use personal visits and the telephone to further your job hunting cause. Think of your efforts as having two purposes; first getting appointments and then getting a job. An appointment doesn't necessarily have to be focused on a specific job. It may be exploratory in nature, at the same time giving you an excellent opportunity to put your best foot forward. People who hire keep files on good job candidates, and make no mistake about it, they will evaluate you closely even if they are not interviewing you for a specific job. Do your best to make a good impression. Use the following checklist as you prepare for interviews or for appointments with people who can help you with leads.

1. Good use of professional looking written communications.

2. Pleasant and professional telephone usage.

   - Give your name immediately when you make business calls. It's also helpful to relate why you're calling.

   - Answer the phone with a greeting and your name.

   - Be careful about asking people to return calls. They often can't or won't, and then you're in the position of waiting for a phone call that never comes. Try asking when it would be convenient for you to call back.

3. Good anticipation of questions.

   - Make a written list of the questions you might be asked.

- Write your answers and work in points you want to make about your experience, training, and aspirations. Keep your answers short and to the point. Avoid rambling. If you don't know the answer to a question, say, "I don't know, but I will try to find out if you'd like."

Example of a Typical Interview Question and a Good Response

Q. You've been working as a receptionist for two years which gives you no experience in managing other people. What makes you think you could make the transition to office manager?

A. Yes, I have been a receptionist for two years, but my duties covered much more than answering the phone. I was responsible for the appointment book, billing clients, and paying office bills. We had a high rate of absenteeism and turnover the first year I had the job, and I often found myself filling in as secretary to one or more of the four lawyers in our office. We also had a lot of temporary help coming in as a result of the absenteeism, and it always fell to me to train them. During my second year, my boss and I worked out an arrangement so the secretaries could have some scheduled time off instead of having to call in sick all the time. We also hired a part-time person to do relief work so we wouldn't have so many temporaries in and out of the office. My boss was very satisfied with my work on these innovations, and I'm certain I could do just as well in handling the responsibilities of office manager.

4. Make out your own list of questions that apply to whatever appointment or interview for which you are preparing. You can take this list with you and jot down answers in the meeting. Any sort of written agenda or list of questions, plus note taking, gives you a more organized and serious look.

EXAMPLES OF GOOD QUESTIONS TO ASK IN AN INTERVIEW

- To whom would I be reporting directly?

- Will there be any training opportunities to help me do a better job?

- What training would you recommend for me to complete on my own to better prepare myself for this job or other jobs in your firm?

BLOCK

- Can't compete with other applicants because of lack of experience or training.

STRATEGIC OPTIONS

If you truly don't have adequate skills to land the job you want, go after a lower echelon job and immediately get yourself into some kind of skill building program designed to prepare you for the working world. Watch the newspaper for available classes, look in the yellow pages under education and instruction, and call colleges and technical schools to find out what they offer in the area of career planning and development. You have to look and ask for help before you can expect to get help.

BLOCK

- Unable to present characteristics which counter balance other inadequacies.

STRATEGIC OPTIONS

- Perhaps you don't have very much work experience, but you were reared by parents who always worked hard, made their own way, and who encouraged you to do the same. Find a way to mention these values in an interview.

- Perhaps you have not actually worked in management, but you have taken night courses and seminars in this area over the past two years. In an interview, point to your student based competency and assert your intention to keep training. Your persistence will pay off.

- Always lead with strength. In areas where you are strong, be very strong. In areas where you are weak, be able to articulate how you intend to improve.

SUMMING UP

The blocks and strategic options outlined above relate generally to the ultimate problem of getting a job in the first place, and to the need for maintaining mobility in the work place once you break in. It was appropriate to make this limitation since virtually every other section of this guide offers creative strategies for dealing with problems that crop up after you are already on the job. Fortunately, we have all matured enough to wax philosophical when problems occur at work. We have realized that women experience special problems, but so do men, minorities, and other groups. Yes, women have had to do well on their jobs, and, at the same time, continually prove they are serious about career and advancement. This has been a very real and sometimes emotionally draining situation, but I maintain we would do well to simply acknowledge it as a part of the real world of work. If we approach it as just another problem to work through, we will have a better chance of overcoming it.

THOUGHT QUESTIONS TO PROBE YOUR MIND

1. How do you think the concept known as the transferral of ideas would relate to solving career problems?

2. How would you interpret the following quote? "It doesn't matter whether they occur at work or at home, problems are all the same."

3. Think of a specific work related problem you have right now and pretend it belongs to someone else. Name at least three ways to approach the problem and decide which one should be tried first.

4. If you make more money than your spouse, what are a few strategies that could be used to keep this from becoming a problem? Do you think there are people, male or female, who actually enjoy having a problem develop in this area? Why?

MYTH NUMBER EIGHT

Gaining visibility with people who make
decisions is almost impossible for
women at work.

A WOMAN AT WORK

"I didn't have anyone to teach me how to get raises and promotions, so I learned by imitating my boss and other company executives. Nobody told me to do that, but I'm glad I did because it worked very well."

Carol Woodruff assumed the role of chief breadwinner in her family when she had to take a job to put her husband through college. Her position as secretary in a large recreational vehicle company headquarters didn't pay too well, so she immediately started looking for ways to improve her salary. She learned quickly that the best way to stand out and gain visibility was to become a clever mimic. She patterned her own image by those of her superiors, which meant she had to concentrate on many details that were ignored by her equals: offering new ideas, being on time with assignments, dressing like management, volunteering for push jobs, and executing them successfully. These were but a few angles Carol employed to make herself known. By the time her husband got his degree, Carol was being called on regularly by company execs to help with special assignments, in addition to serving as office manager for the secretarial pool. Her title, which she dreamed up herself and requested along with her last sizable raise, is Special Project Coordinator. That's not bad for a woman who started working just to help her husband. Do you think she quit her job when he graduated? *No way.*

MYTH NUMBER EIGHT

Gaining visibility with people who make decisions is almost impossible for women at work.

REALITY

Gaining visibility at work is becoming less and less
elusive for women. Smart women are not only succeeding at being noticed and remembered, they are often
doing it better than their male counterparts. Men are
expected to try hard and excel in their jobs. Therefore,
it doesn't seem unusual when they do. But women who
excel are still in the fortunate position of creating a stir.
A hard working male executive is just another hard
working guy, but a hard working female executive is
viewed as exceptional. And a hard working black female executive is considered practically superhuman. If
you approach work as men do, you will be considered
a real go getter. If you go just a little further and activate a carefully orchestrated, systematic process toward
significant advancement in your career, you will be
considered brilliant. It's like being the only girl on the

baseball team. Who do you think gets written up in the
newspaper? The value of positive visibility is great
enough to attract much competition for its benefits.
Companies don't pay $500,000 a minute for prime TV
advertising time because visibility isn't important. It is
very important, and if you haven't figured out how to
capture it yet, now is the time to learn.

BENEFITS OF DISPELLING THE MYTH

Debunking the myth that gaining visibility is impossible for women opens the door to literally hundreds of
opportunities. In taking advantage of these opportunities, you would be wise to keep in mind the following
sensitivities:

- Visibility without credibility is worthless. If you
  aren't willing to deliver the goods in substantive
  work, don't shoot your mouth off around people
  who are in a position to evaluate and make decisions about employees.

- You are not the only one seeking visibility.
  Competition is stiff. Also, don't think people
  won't realize what you're after.

- Many times helping your boss, co-workers, and
  your company gain recognition can be the perfect avenue to being recognized yourself.

- Characteristics like sincerity, integrity, and a
  willingness to help others will enhance your efforts to be noticed. Phoniness, excessive selfish-
  ness, or an inflated ego may help you succeed

in being remembered, but not in the way you'd like.

STRATEGIES TO BROADEN YOUR CAREER HORIZON

1. To become more visible, observe your superiors' schedules and look for chances to see them "accidentally." Sometimes arriving at work a few minutes early or staying a few minutes late will provide informal time for you to chat casually with superiors. This will also set you apart as one who doesn't mind giving extra time and preparation to work.

2. Try arriving early for meetings. You may get a chance to get to know individuals in charge of the sessions.

3. Volunteer to serve on committees with groups that include management in the membership. For example, if your company has a committee organized to encourage communications between line and staff employees, volunteer to serve on the committee as a representative from your department.

4. Learn to use memos and reports to communicate with your boss and subordinates. Keep messages concise, to the point, dated, and extremely courteous in tone. Having all your colleagues know you keep a neat and orderly file of documented communications is a very polite and effective way of keeping everyone honest about whose ideas are whose.

5. Send written communications to superiors when appropriate: congratulations, interesting articles or clippings, thank you notes, positive comments on their recent speeches, meetings, and new plans for the company. Be sincere, specific, and brief.

6. Take a class or seminar related to your department's key concerns. Let your boss know what you're studying and ask if she would like you to conduct a mini-workshop on the new information you've learned in your course.

7. Watch for areas of responsibility you might take over for your boss, or better yet, initiate a new program designed to increase sales or efficiency.

8. Understand that being used and abused is one thing, but being willing to do menial tasks to get the job done is another. Grasping the difference in these two things takes real sensitivity and can make or break you in your work setting. Here is where observing the habits and attitudes of someone you respect can help you. I've seen company presidents shove chairs and tables around to make a room more comfortable for a meeting. If they can do menial tasks, so can you.

9. Be an attentive listener and ask good questions. Whether talking with an individual or participating in a group meeting, well thought out questions can upgrade your chances of being remembered. Beware of pointless, argumentative, or ax grinding comments and

questions designed simply to draw attention to yourself, and don't try to steal the show or keep the floor. Do exercise good judgment in timing, phrasing, and articulating thoughtful questions so you come off looking helpful and interested instead of egotistical or adversative.

10. Always project a professional image at work. Your appearance, attitudes, communication skills, and work habits speak volumes. You must attend to these meticulously. However, they can only be of partial benefit if you aren't willing to show them off. You don't have to be a glory hog to acquire the kind of attention getting ahead requires, but you can't be a wallflower, either. Think creatively about how to become a known entity, especially to people who make decisions. They don't automatically know or remember how great you are, so you have to remind them regularly and tastefully.

11. Every time you express an idea or suggest a change, remember to include an implementation plan. It sets you apart from idea junkies who talk great ideas but can't put them into positive action.

KEY POINTERS

Properly packaged women who try to achieve career visibility by using planned, systematic processes can expect to see excellent results. What does properly packaged mean? In simple terms, it means tailoring your appearance, skills, contacts, papers (credentials, functional resumes, business cards, brochures, portfolios of projects, recommendations, photos, etc.), speech, writing, and experience to the career area in which you want to advance.

THOUGHT QUESTIONS TO PROBE YOUR MIND

1. Your friend complains to you that she and a co-worker were in line for the same promotion, but the co-worker got it "just because she throws herself in the boss's path every chance she gets." What would you say to your friend about going after her own visibility? Name three specific tactics you would advise her to employ.

2. Aside from the information in the course itself, what would be the value of taking a course or seminar for people in levels of work above yours?

3. How might you attend a meeting and show off your preparedness without having to speak excessively?

MYTH NUMBER NINE

There is a clear-cut path to advancement and success.

A WOMAN AT WORK

"My only problem has been coordinating my skills with my ambition. There really wasn't a track for me to follow, so I had to forge my own path."

Marjorie Sanders is proud of the twists and turns in her career development. They attest to her steadfast confidence in her own good judgment. Marjorie started out in the military where she received extensive training as a public information specialist. Her experience in this area helped her land a civilian job with a public relations firm when she finished her last tour of duty. However, Marjorie wanted to do something more daring than simply changing employers. That's why she spent so much time away from her job trying to get other firms to hire her as a public relations consultant. She was fired for this forthwith, and efforts toward marketing herself as a consultant had to be stepped up considerably. At the same time, she started her executive services business which offers typing, business addresses and mail boxes, plus an answering service. Marjorie's efforts have paid off steadily in securing consulting clients and in marketing her executive services business, and she insists that finding the courage to conquer her fear of changing work venues and environments has been the key to her success.

MYTH NUMBER NINE

There is a clear-cut path to advancement and success.

REALITY

Advancing at work results from managing many different processes all of which must be adapted to individual situations and styles. These processes don't always yield quick and easy gratification, but don't let that fool you. Keep at it and the rewards will come. You cannot do A, B, C, and instantly experience X, Y, Z. Your efforts must have time to develop, so don't abandon them. Scurrying about from activity to activity and then complaining that nothing works insures many of your efforts will end in frustration. You can avoid this by sticking with productive behaviors once you've started them. If they've worked for others, they can work for you. Be patient and tenacious enough to see them to fruition.

BENEFITS OF DISPELLING THE MYTH

Debunking the myth that there is a clear-cut path to
advancement allays gnawing fears. These fears can lead
to an inability to make the decisions necessary to move
forward, but you can overcome this by taking action.
Since anxiety, uncertainty, and fear are relieved when
you do something about them, use three simple tactics
to calm your mind: (a) confront fears, (b) put them in
perspective, and (c) realize you are not alone in experiencing anxiety and fears.

The following analyses of a few common fears will help
you deal with your own troublesome apprehensions:

- You no longer have to be afraid you are the only
  one who doesn't know exactly what to do to get
  ahead. Women have suffered from this fear for
  decades because their traditional responsibilities
  at work seldom required skills in decision making. We have always done what we were told,
  assuming all the while that the people doing the
  telling knew what they were talking about. Admittedly, it's a bit disconcerting to find out
  bosses don't always know if they are right or
  wrong, but understanding this fact can help you
  get over your own fear of making decisions. It
  also frees you from thinking there are absolute
  right and wrong decisions, and introduces you
  to thinking in terms of a long continuum of reasonable choices. In actuality, sound decisions
  are usually somewhere between totally right and
  totally wrong, and you have more than enough
  brain power to think through all the gray areas

and arrive at your own perfectly acceptable decisions.

• You no longer have to be unduly scared of failure. Again, our inexperience in the working world has led us to believe we are always supposed to get things right. Why should women set up such unrealistic expectations? The important thing is to give ourselves plenty of chances to learn from mistakes and to try again.

• You should not worry that you can't handle career and family responsibilities at the same time. Your family life is not going to be perfect if you stay at home all the time, and it's not going to be perfect if you work. What it can be is reasonable, workable, manageable, and even enjoyable, but never, never perfect. The only solution to this dilemma is to set priorities, do what you can to accomplish them, be flexible, and *let the rest go*.

KEY POINTERS

• Certain basics exist which you must comprehend.

1. Searching for the easy path to success is futile. It's much better to expect success via a series of planned and then continually modified activities.

2. Important career and business decisions are never without some risk and chance for failure. If a planned action doesn't get the result

you want, change your course and keep going.

- As you grow in the world of work, you will
benefit from resisting the tendency to try to put
everything and everyone into rigid formulas and
categories.

- The ability to live with ambiguity, cope with
ambiguity, and deal effectively with ambiguity
is a mark of real maturity.

STRATEGIES FOR BROADENING YOUR CAREER HORIZON

- Search out or organize a small group of women
like yourself who listen, talk, encourage, suggest, support, nurture, and love, but who never
evaluate or judge. Of course, building a base of
male and female business contacts (networking)
is vital, but it fills a different need than an intimate group who really try to help each other
integrate their insides with their images.

- Seek mentors above your level who are willing
to offer guidance and counseling based on their
experience.

- As much as you possibly can, stay away from
critics, doom and gloom predictors, and nay
sayers. Avoiding this kind of person is a healthy
strategy for you, so don't feel guilty about it.

- Do the hardest things first to keep from wasting
time and energy fearing or worrying about them.

- Don't over analyze. If you face a delicate situation, such as speaking before a group, ap-

proach it mechanically. Preparing and
organizing beats worrying in two ways: (1) It
takes away the anxiety of feeling unprepared,
and (2) it keeps you too busy to worry.

• Other than planning for basic contingencies, focus your energy on going forward instead of
fretting over what might happen. Simply, contingency planning means lining up reasonable
backup options. For example, it makes sense to
prepare for questions from your audience when
you speak publicly, but it isn't feasible to try
and think of every possible question. Again, go
forward or you will end up suffering paralysis
from analysis.

THOUGHT QUESTIONS TO PROBE YOUR MIND

1. Where would you go for help if you encountered what seemed to be an insurmountable
   problem at work?

2. If you found yourself assigned to a project in
   some unclear capacity, what are some alternatives for dealing with not knowing exactly
   what's expected of you?

3. What is your working definition of contingency
   planning?

MYTH NUMBER TEN

Big corporations offer the
best opportunities.

TWO WOMEN AT WORK

"Sometimes I have to laugh at the differences in Laura and me. I work so hard to maintain my corporate image, and she goes to work at her daycare center in sweat pants and a knit shirt. I'm sure she nets more money than I do, but that's all right because I could never have handled the risks she has taken. I really do admire Laura's spunk."

Ruth Metcalf doesn't realize her friend, Laura Mitchell, expresses the same sentiments about her. Laura feels Ruth displayed the superior courage by competing successfully in a big corporation. The truth is both women have much to be proud of even though their careers are going in very different directions.

Ruth graduated from college with a business degree and took a job with a large computer firm. She felt very secure within the structured environment and literally plodded her way to executive status by way of a pre-set track.

Laura dropped out of college after her first year because she couldn't get in step with all the rules and guidelines that go along with academic endeavors. She went to work at a daycare center as the lowest paid attendant and didn't go much further for over two years. What she did do, though, was learn every detail of the business from her boss who became her mentor. Over a period of years, most of the responsibilities of managing the business were turned over to Laura, and she also helped her boss expand the operation to two additional sites. When the boss wanted to retire, who went to the bank and secured financing to buy her out? None other than our college dropout, Laura Mitchell.

MYTH NUMBER TEN

Big corporations offer the best opportunities.

REALITY

Some do . . . some don't. But let's not forget the real business of corporations is business, not mapping out career paths for employees. The profit motive has had a wonderful side effect of serving the nation's economy and providing jobs. However, this fit would never have occurred, and certainly won't last, if the basic needs of the corporation are choked off by demands of employees. It is a symbiotic relationship that must be understood by individuals who aspire to get ahead in the corporate structure. Smart women have carefully analyzed their places in the big picture of corporate life. Their astute examination and analysis have helped them decide if they are going in the right direction. You have to do the same analyzing and deciding for yourself. No one is going to do it for you. Others can advise, encourage, and help you, but ultimately, you must make and live with your own decisions based on your own well thought out conclusions. Things are improving for women who elect to join large corporations, but there are some realities that can't be ignored. For instance, the woman who goes back to school in her late thirties and earns a business degree by age forty will be competing with twenty-two year old graduates for entry level jobs in big business. She can't really expect to start at the same level as men and women who have already been working twenty years just because she is the same age. This reality, plus a range of others, contributes to career problems for women whose skills, experience, age, and ambition are incompatible with the needs of large corporations. If you fall in this category, for whatever reason, your career energy might best be spent in a framework other than a large company.

BENEFITS OF DISPELLING THE MYTH

Debunking the myth that big corporations offer the best opportunities paves the way to success for women who are not bound for the boardroom. It also reinforces the idea that tried and true strategies for getting ahead are useful across career lines. In other words, precepts and principles for advancement remain the same wherever you are working.

Another benefit of debunking the myth that big corporations offer the only route to success is a new awareness of basic differences in working for large or small businesses. Understanding these differences is a necessary prerequisite to deciding which setting is right for you. Consider the following advantages and disadvantages of working in three kinds of organizational structures: large corporations or agencies, small businesses, and entrepreneurial enterprises. Perhaps you will gain insight as to which structure complements your particular strengths and weaknesses.

I. LARGE CORPORATIONS AND AGENCIES

Advantages	*Disadvantages*
Job security	Large numbers of people competing for a relatively small number of advancement opportunities.
Necessary steps to advancement are easy to plot because they are generally known.	Criteria regarding age, years in the field, experience, and training are strictly adhered to in making advancement decisions.
Benefits such as health insurance, retirement programs, sick leave, and vacations are part of the job package.	Jobs are highly categorized and usually offer a set range of responsibilities at each level. Also, salaries, benefits, and schedules are not readily negotiable.

II. SMALL BUSINESSES

Advantages	*Disadvantages*
Since there is a small number of jobs, each one covers several areas of responsibility. This provides for a wide range of experience over a short period of time.	Small businesses are not as stable as large corporations or agencies. Therefore, job security is lessened.
Salaries, schedules, and responsibilities are more negotiable because decision makers are not bound by rigid rules and policies.	Job settings can be too close for comfort, causing personalities to clash and work problems to intensify.

Requirements for employment are more flexible. Therefore, people who don't fit absolute standards can still expect reasonable consideration for jobs.

Incompetent employees are hard to phase out when the company you work for is supposed to be a small, happy family.

III. ENTREPRENEURIAL ENTERPRISES

Advantages	*Disadvantages*
Set your own hours. Be your own boss. Enjoy fewer age, sex, experience, and training limitations.	Requires an enormous amount of energy and discipline to make the work effort consistent and productive.
Opportunity to earn more money.	Overhead is increased and benefits (health insurance, retirement, etc.) have to be paid out of pocket.
Opportunity to build a business of your own and provide employment for others.	Great risks are involved. Entrepreneurial activities are not for the fainthearted.

KEY POINTERS

We live in an age when doors are opening wide for women who want to move up the corporate ladder, but some of us don't fit into corporate life no matter what creative strategies we devise. If you find yourself in this position, don't despair. Other avenues exist for you, avenues that have just as much and maybe more potential as moving through the ranks of a big bureaucracy.

STRATEGIES FOR BROADENING YOUR CAREER HORIZON

- Take stock of your values, training, career aspirations, and commitment in terms of varied work settings. Be brutally honest about what you want, what you have to offer, and what you think you can return. On the other hand, don't discount things you haven't tried before. Stretching your abilities provides more growth than clinging to a worn out skill base, so include in your self assessment an intangible known as the willingness to grow and learn. Keep in mind that if you can't articulate to yourself or on paper what it is you have to offer, you're not going to be able to convince others of your value. Self assess. It will crystallize in your mind exactly what you are all about, and that is the first step in persuading others to have confidence in you.

- Ask people who know you well where they think you'd do best. Describe the three broad areas you're researching; large corporations, small businesses, and entrepreneurial enterprises, and solicit opinions on which area seems to be the natural place for you. Someone may come up with a good suggestion. Keep your mind open to the creative thoughts of other people as they will often encourage you to do things they'd like to do themselves. Many times people won't follow their own advice because they don't have the courage, not because they think their suggestions are unsound. Courage comes from confidence, and confidence comes from preparedness. Do your homework in the area of self evaluation, and you'll have an edge on the preparation necessary to make courageous decisions about your career.

- Do research. Interview people who work in differing environments. Think about which of these people you relate to best. Check your assumptions and theories against their firsthand experiences. Look for discrepancies and consider how you would handle them if you had to.

- Determine which career related articles and books interest you most. You may have a pattern that you haven't identified yet. Monitor your reading habits to decide which areas spark your imagination.

- Attend meetings and conferences that draw participants from alternative organizations. Identify which of the attendees you get along with best and which of their work settings intrigue you most.

- Write or call a few key executives from different sized businesses and ask them how they evaluate prospective employees. Consider your own congruence with what you find out.

- In the process of collecting information, be totally frank with yourself about the advantages and disadvantages of each work setting you examine. Your candor will support the correctness of personal career decisions.

- Illusions and realities exist in every job. Thus, you need to be aware of falling victim to selective curiosity. You need to know the good and the bad, so make it a definite part of your search to identify the illusions which may initially capture your imagination. It's a long way down when a dazzling job confronts you with some miserable realities. If you can fine tune your expectations to fit what is real, you'll be happier with your decisions and choices. This is not to say you should expect little or nothing from your career. Women have already done that too long. It's a matter of aligning what you want with what you can actually get, and then maximizing your chances for achieving it.

- Remember, no career is totally devoid of tedium, difficulties, and problems. Whether just beginning or whether contemplating a change, you can count on putting up with a certain level of pure aggravation. Knowing this to start with may help you avoid being blindsided with problems you didn't expect. You'll be able to deal with them more effectively.

- When you finally select a work environment suited to your stage of development, prepare a portfolio which summarizes what you've learned in your explorations. You'll be better prepared to tell people who make decisions regarding jobs why you want to work in the environment you've chosen. From the comparative data you've gathered about workplaces, include a problem or two in your portfolio which you believe you could help solve. Don't go overboard, but using qualified language express how you would at least assist with a solution. Cap your discussion with well conceived questions and your stock will go up with interviewers and decision makers.

THOUGHT QUESTIONS TO PROBE YOUR MIND

1. What is your fit in the big picture of your work environment? Can you identify another environment where you'd rather work?

2. As you assess your values, interests, and skills,
   what type of organizational structure do you
   think is best for you?

3. Why do you think you can grow and advance
   to your fullest in the setting you selected in
   question two?

MYTH NUMBER ELEVEN

Changing jobs or career fields is
extremely difficult, fraught with pain,
and viewed as unprofessional.

A WOMAN AT WORK

"What child wants a stale old burnout for a school teacher? I knew that's what I had become, but it took me quite a while to figure out what to do about it. Then one Sunday I spent the whole day clipping want ads from three different newspapers. That was the beginning of a year long job search, but it was worth the effort. Yes, ten years and two promotions later, I can definitely say it was worth it."

Dianne Harris has benefited from all the excitement and growth that comes with changing jobs, and she has done it without abandoning her chosen field of education. She hired a professional resume writer to help her prepare cover letters and resumes for each individual job she applied for. That way she could feature the skills most applicable to the job in question. Dianne is convinced this tactic, plus improving her performance in interviews, landed her a position as ancillary staff trainer in the inservice education program of a major hospital. At first her pay was lower than her teaching salary, but that was remedied in less than a year when she took over the position of assistant director. Her next major promotion occurred in four years when Dianne was asked to serve as director for the hospital's education program. A healthy raise, travel opportunities, and several other perks came with her new title and job, which explains very well why she is glad she had the courage ten years ago to make a sensible change.

MYTH NUMBER ELEVEN

Changing jobs or career fields is extremely difficult, fraught with pain, and viewed as unprofessional.

REALITY

There are times when change is the best alternative. It may be needed to stimulate new growth or to relieve deep seated discontent and frustration. Dealing with problems at work is something we all have to do, but real suffering isn't necessary. The key is to find a balance between the positives and the negatives. Women, in particular, put up with all manner of situations they should either change or leave. Fortunately, our career self concepts have now improved enough to allow us to seek better conditions.

If you're working in a setting that is making you miserable most of the time, start the processes necessary to make a change. Be sure however, that it really is your work that is the problem. Many people blame everything and everybody for problems they create for themselves. Make sure you're honest about what is really at the base of your dissatisfaction. If you want to advance, you can't dissipate energy on severe problems you are powerless to solve. It's better to face facts and move on than to spin your wheels trying to fix the unfixable. A healthy way to think about career or job change is to focus on the potential for excitement, fresh experiences, a different environment, meeting new people, and the opportunity for growth. After all, you don't want to change directions simply to get rid of things you don't like. It would be better to make changes based on forward, positive thinking. There's nothing wrong with trying to escape a bad situation, but make significant career changes based on what you're going toward, not what you're leaving behind.

BENEFITS OF DISPELLING THE MYTH

Debunking the myth that changing jobs or careers is too difficult routs the fears surrounding it. Competent women are finding the courage to analyze their career situations and make sensible changes. They no longer accept being stereotyped, nor do they allow themselves to be locked into inflexible career tracks. Smart, competent women understand the concepts of process, interrelationships, and the give and take of problem solving. They have become experts at the application of this knowledge, and they know when and how to use it in advancing themselves in their current work. More importantly, they know how to use it in making successful career or job changes. Fear is no longer their jailer, and limitations are no longer their focus. They have learned how to (a) anticipate events and peoples' reactions, (b) recognize what is and isn't working, (c) make decisions to change directions and cut losses, and (d) implement change in ways that are profitable to themselves.

STRATEGIES FOR BROADENING YOUR CAREER HORIZON

Some legitimate reasons for seeking job changes are listed below. You're going to run into some of them in every job, but struggling with too many at a time will definitely inhibit your progress. As you read through the list, evaluate your own environment as to conduciveness to growth and advancement. If you find your situation skewed toward hopeless or serious problems, plan to make a change. Do it professionally and tactfully, but do it.

REASONS AND SITUATIONS WHICH INDICATE A CHANGE IS NEEDED

- Poor staffing. (There's nothing wrong with working for a while in an area that doesn't match your skills and strengths, but if you find yourself doing it too long, you need to take action.)

- Poorly organized environment. (You can use this to your advantage if your contributions toward better organization are noticed by decision makers. Keep written records of your improvements and projects. Then, if you can't get recognition for what you've learned and implemented in your present job, use your knowledge to create a better resume and improve your interviews when you go after the next job.)

• Poor supervision. (This one can be a killer if you aren't accustomed to figuring out a course and then following it on your own. Not knowing what you're supposed to do can create great anxiety. However, if you manage to do a few things right by yourself, you may end up looking better than if you had been required to follow a set formula. Whether or not poor supervision is a serious problem also depends on whether it equates to little supervision, confusing supervision, or harsh supervision. Only you can make the final analysis about your particular situation, and only you can decide if it's intolerable. Trust your own judgment.)

• Unclear reward systems and obscure routes to advancement. (This situation might be a problem to some people and an advantage to others. Carving out your own territory can be stimulating if you are able to persuade your superiors to support and reward you for your ideas and for your success in executing them. You may even have to dream up and request your own rewards. The rub comes when superiors aren't open to having subordinates initiate change or make requests. I've always gone forward on the assumption that intelligent people are open to new ideas well presented. However, very often the inability to get people to consider new ideas is connected either to the quality of the ideas themselves or the way in which they are presented. Evaluate your ability in this area before you complain too loudly about unclear reward systems and obscure routes to advancement. Maybe you can think of better ways to work around the ambiguity. If you're sure you cannot, don't waste your time complaining. Get busy and find a place to work where you can.)

- Individuals and cliques who create conflict and who purposely upset interpersonal relationships. (There are two areas of study which offer help in easing people problems. One is conflict management and the other is group dynamics. Let's take a look at managing conflict first. The ability to defuse anger, hostility, and sensitive situations is a golden skill. To acquire it, however, you must first learn to control yourself. Emotions are much affected by rest, diet, and exercise, so don't shortchange yourself in these very important areas. Another way to avoid sensitive situations is to guard against being baited by others. Allowing yourself to be lured into arguments is a classic example of being controlled by others. When you sense trouble brewing, concentrate very hard on speaking slowly, quietly, and in an even tone. Breathe in and out slowly and avoid gesticulating. It's also important that you learn some key counseling phrases to counter verbal attacks in a positive way. Practice starting your responses with the following phrases:

"A lot of people have probably felt as you do, but perhaps . . ."

"Have you ever considered . . ."

"I can see you feel badly about this. Why don't we . . ."

"I could certainly use your help in working through this problem because I'm at a loss as to how to make it right. What do you think . . ."

Now let's consider how the study of group dynamics can help. Group dynamics teaches us that many times work settings spawn rivalries between individuals or groups who try to instigate conflict surreptitiously. Motives stem from jealousy, competition, basic incompetence, lack of integrity, problems with the opposite sex, and difficulties with the work itself. You may even occasionally fall victim to one or two of these frailties yourself, but do your best to keep it to a minimum. Try to stay clear of problems and the people who cause them by focusing on your work and avoiding excessive groupiness. Make it a point to be genuinely friendly toward everyone in your workplace, but make sure you maintain a serious and professional identity of your own. Never forget how you want to be viewed, and always behave accordingly. However, if individuals and cliques are continually destroying your efforts, move on. You will certainly encounter interpersonal problems wherever you work, but it's your responsibility to find a setting where they aren't intense enough to hold you back. You also need to continually improve your deftness at handling interpersonals.)

- Inadequate or unfair evaluation systems. (Evaluation systems fall into two categories, formal and informal. The real purpose behind them is to foster improvement, but many times they backfire and cause nothing but ill will. Improving the situation may not be possible, but it's worth a try before making the decision to leave because of it. Does your employer use a checklist and a one on one meeting to let you know which areas of your work are satisfactory and which areas need improvement? If so, ask if you might attach an addendum, agreed to by the two of you, of course, to the evaluation document. Then produce a few short paragraphs describing positive things you've accomplished that are not covered by the checklist. In an evaluation conference, always ask where you need to improve and later make a few specific written comments about what you intend to do during the next evaluation period to enhance your value to the company. Give a copy to your boss for placement in your personnel file. This will give you something to point to in your next meeting if you discipline yourself to follow through on what you wrote. Sooner or later you'll have to decide whether the evaluation process where you work is helping or hindering you. If you honestly feel the evaluation process is holding you back, marshal your forces and make a change.)

- Limited or no teamwork. (Careers don't get built in a vacuum. Therefore, teamwork must be employed. You can and should foster it no matter what your level of responsibility, but the cold fact is you are still subject to the philosophies of management. Employees have to be encouraged and taught to function as a team, and if your company hasn't caught onto this yet, it may not be the company to stay with for the long haul.)

- Poorly trained superiors and subordinates. (Money is usually at the root of this problem. Poorly trained employees come cheaper than skilled people. The trouble is that their lack of productivity matches their low price tags. Companies which habitually hire poorly trained people, and then make little effort to help them improve, often manifest other debilitating characteristics. Low creativity, unclear goals, lack of motivation, little effort to improve, no planning, negative disposition toward change, and poor hiring systems are but an unfortunate few. You should extricate yourself immediately from this kind of environment. Don't equivocate; just get out.)

THOUGHT QUESTIONS TO PROBE YOUR MIND

1. What is the basic difference between a hot-headed approach and a process approach to change?

2. How would you explain the phrase, "burning bridges behind you"? How does it relate to job or career changes?

3. Think about the women you know who have made significant and successful work changes. Were many of their skills transferrable? Which of your skills would fit into other career areas?

4. Are you intrigued by the notion of a career change? Try to articulate why you answered the way you did.

MYTH NUMBER TWELVE

A fine education is the ticket to success.

A WOMAN AT WORK

"The friends I made in medical school were all like me, very goal oriented. My problem was that I got caught up in the goals of the group instead of really analyzing my own needs. Graduating was the only thing I focused on, forgetting entirely that there is, indeed, life after med school. It wasn't until after I finished that it struck me to change directions. It was painful, but I finally faced the fact that a career in medicine was not going to make me happy."

Cynthia Hollins never had any trouble actualizing goals. Her problem lay in distinguishing between goals she thought she ought to have and goals which were really in her own best interest. It took a lot of courage to walk into a career counseling office at a major university and admit to being a recent honor graduate from medical school who didn't want to be a doctor. These days Cynthia is working happily as a journalist. It took a lot of experimenting for her to settle into this field, but who knows? Maybe she'll make another career change next year.

MYTH NUMBER TWELVE

A fine education is the ticket to success.

REALITY

First of all, a good education does not necessarily begin and end within the confines of schools and colleges. Classroom training can be an excellent beginning, but the depth and quality of a really fine education can only result from a lifelong process of learning and application.

One of the most progressive, and now time honored, innovations on the career scene is the use of internships and cooperative education programs. Learning through the merger of classroom work and hands on experience has proven to be of exceptional value. The apprenticeship is also an old but useful educational device. Since experts agree that learning by doing is as important today as it ever was, perhaps you would do well to evaluate your own training opportunities in that context.

The trick is to make sure your education does not take place in a vacuum. Therefore, choose your training experiences carefully because they are only useful if you can apply them in the real world. I will concede that many skills don't have to be restricted to one career area to be useful, but I stand on the premise that if you can't or won't apply the skills you learn, they will not do you much good.

BENEFITS OF DISPELLING THE MYTH

Debunking the myth that a fine education is the ticket to success will offer you a new perspective on selection of training and choice of career. With appropriate alternative training and work experience in your background, a full blown college education is not an absolute prerequisite to being successful. There is no question about it being a door opener (many employers won't consider hiring anyone without a college degree), but once you're hired, you have to prove your worth despite the quality of your credentials. But what should the job prove to you? Assuming you've sought training in a field which interests you in the first place, you still have no guarantee that your interests and values won't change. I would recommend that you always retain the psychological luxury of entertaining thoughts about varied career directions. It's healthy. Education is wonderful and I recommend it wholeheartedly, but sampling real work experience is far more enlightening. This is where you effectively test the following subtle and not so subtle dimensions of what you really want in a career:

- the integrity of what you assumed were your real interests and values.

- the sharpness of your skills.

- your vigor, energy, and ambition.

- the importance of specific personal needs such as money, security, prestige, leadership position, and work style.

- your innermost feelings about other career areas which may offer you more personal satisfaction.

STRATEGIES FOR BROADENING YOUR CAREER HORIZON

- Start by understanding the fact that there is no substitute for work experience as you develop marketable skills.

- Look at life broadly as a series of experiences all of which, when dissected, can teach you something applicable to your career.

- Do something, anything, to gain experience.

- Do it again.

- Carefully observe people who are doing well in various jobs. Interview them. Mimic them. Ask someone in a supposedly preferred career if you can tag along with him/her for half a day. Treat your own work and career research as a proving ground. Think seriously and realistically about which areas of work suit you best. Be candid about how successful you really think you could be in the various jobs you evaluate.

- Recognize that when you elect to try out different jobs, you will have to take risks and make mistakes, but you'll also do plenty right. Imagine yourself as being on a shake-down mission. You'll get the bugs out of your career system and be much the wiser for it. Go to libraries and study what professional associations are saying to their members in newsletters and periodicals. Find out what workers in the respective professions are concerned with or fighting about. Get a reading of frustrations workers confront in varying fields. Figure out the positives, too, but do it against the benchmark of reality. This kind of study is the next best thing to actually working in a particular field.

KEY POINTERS

- You must properly integrate experience with education if education itself is going to have real meaning to your career.

- Don't make an absolute career decision before you get a fair amount of work experience. Make only tentative decisions and go forward on a contingency basis.

- Break down the basic question of formal education versus experience by asking these two fundamental questions:

  1. After counseling, testing, and soul searching, what have I determined my skills, interests, and values to be?

  2. What will serve my skills, interests, and values best in terms of training and real work?

(Perhaps some blend of the two would be a good choice.)

You probably find yourself unable to come up with absolute answers to the questions above. As you work through them, consider the wisdom that more complete answers may not emerge until you actually involve yourself in a bona fide educational program, and, at the same time or later on, some real work experience. A smart woman knows that experience is a great teacher. She is always connecting the learning from experience to her career goals. For example: If experience suggests that a particular job will never yield promotions or financial advancement, she will have no problem looking elsewhere. If experience suggests that only additional training will foster a successful job change or promotion, she will actively pursue the necessary training to upgrade herself.

- No linkage between experience and career goals can take place without action. Decisiveness is called for after you make the experience-goal connection, so make some ambitious decisions for yourself and follow up to make them work.

THOUGHT QUESTIONS TO PROBE YOUR MIND

1. Review the two questions in the preceding section. You must come to grips honestly with your true skills, interests, values, and priorities. Can you find any discrepancies in what you think they ought to be and what they really are?

2. Select a hypothetical career area you think may be right for you. Now try to identify several educational and work oriented experiences which would help you achieve success in this field. Where would you begin looking for the educational experience you've identified? Where would you seek the appropriate work experience?

3. Financially, what do you think would hurt more, a lack of education or a lack of experience?

4. Is promotion contingent upon education, experience, or both? Back up your answer with reasons.

5. Name several careers that require endless continuing education. Do you think all desirable careers have that characteristic?

SUCCESS FOR WORKING WOMEN
and
TWELVE SECRETS
TO INSURE IT

SUCCESS FOR WORKING WOMEN

I am convinced there has never been a better time than now to be a working woman. It gives me pause to consider the great strides made by career women in recent decades, and I acknowledge with pride and gratitude that our new and unfolding opportunities stem directly from the hard work and commitment of courageous women who have gone before us. It is also gratifying to live in a time when men and women have learned to honor the full and varied potential of both sexes instead of relegating each other to stereotyped roles. Thus, we are all on the threshold, men and women alike, of enjoying a new spirit of cooperation and contribution.

Statistics prove women as a group are moving forward slowly but steadily in their careers. I believe this is largely the result of a new and voracious hunger to learn and use strategies that work for the future as well as for the present. This willingness to learn, to change, grow, and develop makes a strong statement about our permanence in the world of work. We intend to persevere, to keep improving, and to pass on these closely held values to our children. We point with pride to new trends. U.S. corporations are actively recruiting up-and-coming female executives to their boards of directors. Heidrick and Struggles, a major executive search firm, recently reported in a study called, "The Changing Board," that in 1984, 49.6 percent of the Fortune 1,000 firms that were surveyed had at least one female director. This shows a great improvement from 43 percent in 1983, and 41.3 percent in 1982.

Interestingly, a current *Wall Street Journal* Gallup Survey notes that women who have made it to senior executive levels in their companies do not report racing to the top. On the contrary, these women say emphatically that their career climbs were slow and methodical. One fifty year old bank vice president relates that she started as a teller, then progressed to head teller, customer service rep., manager, and vice president. She maintains her personal ambition at work emerged late, and that many of her successes came through trial and error. Most of the other senior female executives described the same kind of unplanned development in their careers. Sixty-three percent of them were already working when they became interested in significant advancement, and many present female execs worked their way up from secretarial positions. I can only wonder what these outstanding women would have accomplished had they set out from the beginning to do something special with their careers.

Younger working women are planning earlier and better than their older colleagues. However, they have learned that no amount of planning, education, or strategizing can take the place of time and experience on the job, hard work, and dedication. They have also learned that competition is stiffening because it is becoming not only acceptable, but expected for women to pay as much attention to career development as men do. This is a healthy sign although somewhat scary in that it calls for regular updating of attitudes and behaviors. How fortunate that women already know how to be adaptable. As we make our marks in the world of work, we will use this trait to our benefit. How convenient that we have had so much practice in task oriented activities, detail work, making do, and picking up the slack. We will use this experience to lay unshakable foundations for our careers. As we go forward, let's be encouraged to use these attributes in every possible, conceivable way. We also need to continue our long tradition of gathering together all the positives and making the very best out of whatever situation is at hand. Finally, let's all be thankful that the new reality of career life for women has developed into such a wide range of achievable and desirable opportunities.

I have tried very hard to help you make your range of opportunities even broader. I have also tried to communicate on a personal level and to make room for a two way conversation between you and me on the pages of this book. Those of us who want to do well in our careers have so many things to talk over as we refine our efforts toward advancement. We have much to gain and much to offer by opening lines of communication and exchanging information. I'm extremely interested in your personal concerns about progress in your career. Please write to me and let me know how things are going for you. Again, I am interested.

Now I'd like to give you twelve secrets that have worked for me and for other women who are trying to make career progress. Use them and share them to help yourself and others achieve fulfillment and prosperity. Here's wishing you the best of luck in your quest.

TWELVE SECRETS

1. Successful career women make a habit of doing work related things unsuccessful women do not like to do.

   • You must get your hands dirty to get ahead. Don't avoid the distasteful tasks. Your boss probably didn't.

2. Being successful requires believing in yourself and in your company or organization.

   • You must feel you are choosing the right job for yourself and for those you serve to achieve true success.

3. An intelligent career woman will not divorce herself from sales and marketing roles.

   • Every aspect of sales and marketing should be understood, implemented, and/or accepted by an upward bound career woman. Sales and marketing make the economy work. You can't avoid it.

4. Your work habits will, in the final analysis, be the ingredient which will make or break your career.

   • People in management have known the positive or negative value of habits for years. Your habits are noticed. Make yours perfect.

5. Listening, writing, and speaking are skill areas in which you must excel.

   • The real world judges you mercilessly in these three areas. Your communication skills are critical to getting ahead. Don't assume you're skillful here. Get professional training in communications.

6. Become famous for your excellent questions.

   • People in the world of work respect astute, non-ax-grinding questions. Good questions help you make correct decisions.

7. Getting ahead career wise will mean change. Make any major change as simple as possible for yourself.

   • Studies of change in human behavior show that change is more easily accommodated the simpler it is. As you encounter career change, promotion, added responsibilities, and more complex assignments, don't over-

load your circuits by endless analysis or
forecasting. Keep things simple and pro-
ceed step by step.

8. As you advance into management, leave your
   old job behind.

   • A critical mistake women make, as they go
   up the career ladder into management, involves the failure to understand that management means supervision. Too many
   women new in management cling to the old
   role and don't accept the new one. Doing
   your old job in your new management position will curtail further advancement.

9. When you start a new job, you have exceptional opportunities to lay the foundation for
   rapid advancement. Don't let these chances
   get away.

   • When beginning a new job, three often
   overlooked opportunities await you:

   1. You have a wide open field to learn more
      about the organization than anyone else.
      Your questions will be expected and
      welcomed. Formal interviews will be
      appropriate as well. Knowing more
      about the organization than anyone else
      should be your goal. You can use your
      information in hundreds of ways later on
      to help you look good.

   2. Your organizational contacts, made in
      the course of orientation and training,
      will be free from political bias because

you are new. Therefore, this is a full and ripe time to learn your job well. Do your homework, execute your new tasks better because of your study, and soar to the top. Enjoy the distance you will have from office politics and maintain it as long as you can. You'll be respected for it.

3. Your interview landed you the job, so your superiors in the organization obviously think highly of you. This honeymoon period can last on and on if you carry over the tone of your entry into the first weeks and months of your new position. Don't get slack. Don't miss this golden opportunity.

10. Successful career women have an unfailing sense of humor.

   • Humor relieves stress, helps resolve conflict, motivates, energizes, and creates healthy chemical reactions in the body. Keep your humorous perspective.

11. You must believe absolutely in the benefits that customers, clients, patients, and others get from your product or service.

   • For you to apply fully your skills and energies—and accordingly advance your career—you have to know in your heart and head that you're providing something worthwhile. Your success is linked to your belief.

12. Passionately love yourself and your work.

- Real productivity is rooted in love. When you love yourself and your work, you'll find it easy to love other people, too. And love will come back to you automatically.

ABOUT THE AUTHOR

Speaker, consultant, and professional trainer, Terry Ward is the director of her own career development training company. The author lives in Winter Park, Florida.